Internetworking with TCP/IP

Internetworking with TCP/IP

Volume III: Client-Server Programming and Applications

Windows Sockets Version

DOUGLAS E. COMER
and
DAVID L. STEVENS

Department of Computer Sciences
Purdue University
West Lafayette, IN 47907

Prentice-Hall, Inc.
Upper Saddle River, New Jersey 07458

Library of Congress Cataloging-in-Publication Data

Comer, Douglas E.
   Internetworking with TCP/IP Volume III: Client-Server Programming
   and Applications Windows Sockets Version/Douglas E. Comer and David L. Stevens
     p. cm.
   Includes bibliographical references and index.
   ISBN 0-13-848714-6
   CIP Data Available

Publisher: Alan Apt
Development Editor: Sondra Chavez
Production Editor: Sharyn Vitrano
Managing Editor: Bayani Mendoza DeLeon
Editor-in-Chief: Marcia Horton
Director of Production and Manufacturing: David W. Riccardi
Art Director: Heather Scott
Cover Illustrator in part: Tamara Newnam Cavallo
Manufacturing Buyer: Donna Sullivan
Editorial Assistant: Toni Holm

This book was typeset by the author and sent across the Internet in digital form to a publishing company, where it was converted to photographic form for printing.

TRADEMARKS

Yahoo is a trademark of Yahoo! Corporation.
AltaVista is a trademark of Digital Corporation.
Lycos is a trademark of Carnegie Mellon University.
UNIX is a registered trademark of UNIX System Laboratories, Incorporated.
SUN is a trademark of of Sun Microsystems, Incorporated.
DECNET is a trademark of Digital Equipment Corporation.
MS DOS, Windows, Windows 95, and Windows NT are trademarks of Microsoft Corporation.
Solaris is a registered trademark of Sun Microsystems, Incorporated.
SNA is a trademark of International Business Machines Corporation.

ISBN 0-13-848714-6

Printed in the United States of America

10 9 8 7 6 5 4 3

Prentice-Hall International (UK) Limited, *London*
Prentice-Hall of Australia Pty. Limited, *Sydney*
Prentice-Hall Canada Inc., *Toronto*
Prentice-Hall Hispanoamericana, S.A., *Mexico*
Prentice-Hall of India Private Limited, *New Delhi*
Prentice-Hall of Japan, Inc., *Tokyo*
Pearson Education Asia Pte. Ltd., *Singapore*
Editora Prentice-Hall do Brasil, Ltda., *Rio de Janeiro*

to windows and those who can see through them

Contents

Chapter 5   The Socket API   **47**

Chapter 6   Algorithms And Issues In Client Software Design   **61**

Chapter 7   Example Client Software   79

Chapter 8   Algorithms And Issues In Server Software Design   99

Chapter 9   Iterative, Connectionless Servers (UDP)   119

Chapter 10   Iterative, Connection-Oriented Servers (TCP)   127

Chapter 15   Uniform, Efficient Management Of Server Concurrency   177

Chapter 16   Concurrency In Clients   189

Chapter 17   Tunneling At The Transport And Application Levels   203

Chapter 18   Application Level Gateways   213

Chapter 19   External Data Representation (XDR)   231

Chapter 20   Remote Procedure Call Concept (RPC)   243

Chapter 23   Network File System Concepts (NFS)   313

Chapter 24   Network File System Protocol (NFS, Mount)   343

Chapter 25   A TELNET Client (Program Structure)   **361**

Chapter 26   A TELNET Client (Implementation Details)   399

Chapter 27   Porting Servers From UNIX To Windows   429

Foreword

It is indeed a pleasure to introduce the reader to the Windows Sockets edition of Dr. Douglas E. Comer's remarkable series: Internetworking with TCP/IP. This series, which began so innocently back in 1987, is now the premiere source for learning about the suite of protocols that have made vendor-independent computer-communications possible - the Internet suite of protocols.

To my mind, this seminal work is our best hope against the "dumbing down of the Internet." Whilst the media and entrepreneurs fill the popular imagination with visions of "Internet mysticism," it is Dr. Comer who clearly explains the technical reality of the technology that makes the Internet possible.

This edition, which Doug has authored with David L. Stevens, is particularly important given the increasing popularity of the Windows platform in the Internet. Volume 3, Client-Server Programming and Applications, teaches us how to architect and build client-server applications, and – more importantly – how to understand what trade-offs are involved with each design decision. This is a crucial skillset for the myriad of Windows programmers who are now discovering the power of open systems and the Internet!

So, I invite you to undertake a memorable journey into "how's and why's" of the theory, design, and realization of internetworking technology.

Marshall T. Rose
Theorist, Implementor, and Agent Provocateur
Del Mar, California

Preface

We are pleased to add a Windows Sockets version of the third book in the Internet-working series. Broadly speaking, Volume *1* explores the question, "What is a TCP/IP Internet?" Volume *2* examines the question, "How does TCP/IP software work?" This volume answers the question, "How does application software use TCP/IP to communicate over an Internet?" It focuses on the client-server paradigm, and examines algorithms for both the client and server components of a distributed program. The text shows an implementation that illustrates each design, and discusses techniques including application-level gateways and tunneling. In addition, it reviews several standard application protocols, and uses them to illustrate the algorithms and implementation techniques. A chapter on deadlock and livelock discusses the ways client-server systems fail, and examines causes of the problems as well as techniques for preventing them.

We wrote this text to meet the demand from programmers who are building software for personal computers. The software of choice for PCs comes from Microsoft. There are two popular systems: Windows 95 and Windows NT. Both systems support the Win32 programming interface, and can use the Windows Sockets API discussed in the text.

The text describes abstractions available in both Windows 95 and Windows NT. For example, the discussion of concurrency reviews the Windows thread abstraction, which is central to later discussions of concurrent servers. More important, the example code throughout the text has been tested on both Windows 95 and Windows NT. The code is available on-line. To access a copy via the Web, look for this text in the list of networking books at location:

http://www.cs.purdue.edu/homes/comer/books.html

or look for file names beginning *TCPIP-vol3* in the FTP directory:

ftp://ftp.cs.purdue.edu/pub/comer

The text is organized for easy reading. Beginning chapters introduce the client-server paradigm and the socket interface that application programs use for network communication. They also describe concurrent threads and the operating system functions used to create them. Chapters that follow the introductory material discuss client and server designs. The text explains that the myriad of possible designs are not random. Instead, they follow a pattern that can be understood by considering the choice of concurrency and transport. For example, one chapter discusses a nonconcurrent server design that uses connection-oriented transport (e.g., TCP), while another discusses a similar design that uses connectionless transport (e.g., UDP).

We describe how each design fits into the space of possible implementations, but do not try to develop an abstract "theory" of client-server interactions. Instead, we emphasize practical design principles and techniques that are important to programmers. Each technique has advantages in some circumstances, and each has been used in working software. We believe that understanding the conceptual ties among the designs will help the reader appreciate the strengths and weaknesses of each approach, and will make it easier to choose among them.

The text contains example programs that show how each design operates in practice. Most of the examples implement standard Internet application protocols. In each case, we tried to select an application protocol that would convey a single design idea without being too complex to understand. Thus, while few of the example programs are exciting, they each illustrate one important concept.

Later chapters discuss the remote procedure call concept and describe how it can be used to construct distributed programs. They relate the remote procedure call technique to the client-server model, and show how software can be used to generate client and server programs from a remote procedure call description. The chapters on TEL-NET show how small details dominate a production program and how complex the code can become for even a simple, character-oriented protocol.

Much of the text concentrates on concurrent processing. Many of the concepts described may seem familiar to students who have written concurrent programs because they apply to all concurrent programs, not only network applications. Students who have not written concurrent programs may find the concepts difficult.

The text is suitable for a single semester introductory networking course at the senior or graduate level. Because the text concentrates on how to use an internet rather than on how it works, students need little background in networking to understand the material. No particular concept is too difficult for lower level courses as long as the instructor proceeds at a suitable pace. A basic course in operating systems concepts or experience with concurrent programming may provide the best background.

Students will not appreciate the material until they use it first hand. Thus, any course should have programming exercises that force the students to apply the ideas to practical programs. Undergraduates can learn the basics by repeating the designs on other application protocols. Graduate students should build more complex distributed programs that emphasize some of the subtle techniques (e.g., the concurrency management techniques in Chapter *15* and the interconnection techniques in Chapter *17*).

Many people deserve credit for their help. Members of the Internet Research Group at Purdue contributed technical information and suggestions to the original text. Vince Russo provided technical assistance, and John Lin proofread the text. Christine Comer edited the revision and improved both wording and consistency.

Douglas E. Comer
David L. Stevens

1

Introduction And Overview

1.1 Use Of TCP/IP

In 1986, the TCP/IP Internet included a few thousand computers at sites concentrated primarily in North America. By 1997, over *16,000,000* computer systems attach to the Internet in over *85* countries spread across *7* continents; its size continues to double every ten months. Many of the over *80,000* networks that comprise the Internet are located outside the US.

In addition, most large corporations have chosen TCP/IP protocols for their private corporate internets, many of which are now as large as the connected Internet was twelve years ago. TCP/IP accounts for a significant fraction of networking throughout the world. Its use is growing rapidly in Europe, India, South America, and countries on the Pacific rim.

Besides quantitative growth, the past decade has witnessed an important change in the way sites use TCP/IP. Early use focused on a few basic services like electronic mail, file transfer, and remote login. More recently, browsing information on the World Wide Web has replaced file transfer as the most popular global service; Uniform Resource Locators used with Web browsers appear on billboards and television shows. In addition, many companies are designing application protocols and building private application software. In fact, over one fifth of all traffic on the connected Internet arises from applications other than well-known services. New applications rely on TCP/IP to provide basic transport services. They add rich functionality that has enhanced the Internet environment and has enabled new groups of users to benefit from connectivity.

The variety of applications using TCP/IP is staggering: it includes hotel reservation systems, applications that monitor and control offshore oil platforms, warehouse inventory control systems, applications that permit geographically distributed machines to

1

share file access and display graphics, applications that transfer images and manage printing presses, as well as teleconferencing and multimedia systems. In addition, new applications are emerging constantly.

As corporate intranets mature, emphasis shifts from building networks to using them. As a result, more programmers need to know the fundamental principles and techniques used to design and implement distributed applications.

1.2 Designing Applications For A Distributed Environment

Programmers who build applications for a distributed computing environment follow a simple guideline: they try to make each distributed application behave as much as possible like the nondistributed version of the program. In essence, the goal of distributed computing is to provide an environment that hides the geographic location of computers and services and makes them appear to be local.

For example, a conventional database system stores information on the same machine as the application programs that access it. A distributed version of such a database system permits users to access data from computers other than the one on which the data resides. If the distributed database applications have been designed well, a user will not know whether the data being accessed is local or remote.

1.3 Standard And Nonstandard Application Protocols

The TCP/IP protocol suite includes many application protocols, and new application protocols appear daily. In fact, whenever a programmer devises a distributed program that uses TCP/IP to communicate, the programmer has invented a new application protocol. Of course, some application protocols have been documented in RFCs and adopted as part of the official TCP/IP protocol suite. We refer to such protocols as *standard application protocols*. Other protocols, invented by application programmers for private use, are referred to as *nonstandard application protocols*.

Most network managers choose to use standard application protocols whenever possible; one does not invent a new application protocol when an existing protocol suffices. For example, the TCP/IP suite contains standard application protocols for services like *file transfer*, *remote login*, and *electronic mail*. Thus, a programmer would use a standard protocol for such services.

1.4 An Example Of Standard Application Protocol Use

Remote login ranks among the most popular TCP/IP applications. Although a given remote login session only generates data at the speed a human can type and only receives data at the speed a human can read, remote login is the fourth highest source of packets on the connected Internet, exceeded by Web browsing, file transfer, and network news. Many users rely on remote login as part of their working environment; they do not have a direct connection to the machines that they use for most computation.

The TCP/IP suite includes a standard application protocol for remote login known as *TELNET*. The TELNET protocol defines the format of data that an application program must send to a remote machine to log onto that system and the format of messages the remote machine sends back. It specifies how character data should be encoded for transmission and how one sends special messages to control the session or abort a remote operation.

For most users, the internal details of how the TELNET protocol encodes data are irrelevant; a user can invoke software that accesses a remote machine without knowing or caring about the implementation. In fact, using a remote service is usually as easy as using a local one. For example, computer systems that run TCP/IP protocols usually include a command that users invoke to run TELNET software. On Windows 95 systems, the command is named *telnet*. To invoke it, a user can type:

```
telnet machine
```

in an MS-DOS shell, where the argument *machine* denotes the domain name of the machine to which remote login access is desired. Thus, to form a TELNET connection to machine *nic.ddn.mil* a user types:

```
telnet nic.ddn.mil
```

From the user's point of view, running *telnet* creates a window on the user's machine that connects directly to the remote system. Once the connection has been established, the *telnet* application sends each character the user types to the remote machine, and displays each character the remote machine emits on the user's screen.

After a user invokes *telnet* and connects to a remote system, the remote system displays a prompt that requests the user to type a login identifier and a password. The prompt a machine presents to a remote user is identical to the prompt it presents to users who login on local terminals. Thus, TELNET provides each remote user with the illusion of being on a directly-connected terminal.

1.5 An Example Connection

As an example, consider what happens when a user invokes *telnet* and connects to machine *cnri.reston.va.us*:

```
SunOS UNIX (CNRI)

login:
```

telnet creates a new window for the login session. As soon as the connection has been established, *telnet* prints the lines above, telling the user that the connection attempt has succeeded.

The lines of output come from the remote machine. They identify the operating system as *SunOS*, and provide a standard login prompt. The cursor stops after the *login:* message, waiting for the user to type a valid login identifier. The user must have an account on the remote machine for the TELNET session to continue. After the user types a valid login identifier, the remote machine prompts for a password, and only permits access if the login identifier and password are valid.

1.6 Using TELNET To Access An Alternative Service

TCP/IP uses protocol port numbers to identify application services on a given machine. Software that implements a given service waits for requests at a predetermined (well-known) protocol port. For example, the remote login service accessed with the TELNET application protocol has been assigned port number *23*. Thus, when a user invokes the *telnet* program, the program connects to port *23* on the specified machine.

Interestingly, the TELNET protocol can be used to access services other than the standard remote login service. To do so, a user must specify the protocol port number of the desired service. The Windows *telnet* command uses an optional second argument to allow the user to specify an alternative protocol port. If the user does not supply a second argument, *telnet* uses port *23*. However, if the user supplies a port number, *telnet* connects to that port number. For example, if a user types:

```
telnet cnri.reston.va.us 185
```

the *telnet* program will form a connection to protocol port number *185* at machine *cnri.reston.va.us*. The machine is owned by the *Corporation For National Research Initiatives (CNRI)*.

Port *185* on the machine at *CNRI* does not supply remote login service. Instead, it prints information about a recent change in the service offered, and then closes the connection.

```
******NOTICE******
The KIS client program has been moved from this machine
to info.cnri.reston.va.us (132.151.1.15) on port 185.
******************
```

Contacting port *185* on machine *info.cnri.reston.va.us* allows one to access the Knowbot Information Service. After a connection succeeds, the user receives information about the service followed by a prompt for Knowbot commands:

```
                    Knowbot Information Service
        KIS Client (V2.0).  Copyright CNRI 1990.  All Rights Reserved.

        KIS searches various Internet directory services to find
        someone's street address, email address and phone number.

        Type 'man' at the prompt for a complete reference with
        examples.  Type 'help' for a quick reference to commands.
        Type 'news' for information about recent changes.
        Backspace characters are '^H' or DEL

        Please enter your email address in our guest book...
        (Your email address?) >
```

The output lines differ, and clearly show that the service available on port *185* is not a remote login service. The greater-than symbol on the last line serves as the prompt for Knowbot commands.

The Knowbot service searches well-known white pages directories to help a user find information about another user. For example, suppose one wanted to know the e-mail address for David Clark, a researcher at MIT. Typing *clark* in response to the Knowbot prompt retrieves over *675* entries that each contain the name *Clark*. Most of the entries correspond to individuals with a first or last name of *Clark*, but some correspond to individuals with *Clark* in their affiliation (e.g., *Clark College*). Searching through the retrieved information reveals only one entry for a David Clark at MIT:

```
        Clark, David D. (DDC1)    ddc@LCS.MIT.EDU   (617) 253-6003
```

1.7 Application Protocols And Software Flexibility

The example above shows how a single piece of software, in this instance the *telnet* program, can be used to access more than one service. The design of the TELNET protocol and its use to access the Knowbot service illustrate two important points. First, the goal of all protocol design is to find fundamental abstractions that can be reused in multiple applications. In practice, TELNET suffices for a wide variety of services because it provides a basic interactive communication facility. Conceptually, the protocol used to access a service remains separate from the service itself. Second, when architects specify application services, they use standard application protocols whenever possible. The Knowbot service described above can be accessed easily because it uses the standard TELNET protocol for communication. Furthermore, because most TCP/IP software includes an application program that users can invoke to run TELNET, no additional client software is needed to access the Knowbot service. Designers who invent new interactive applications can reuse software if they choose TELNET for their access protocol. The point can be summarized:

> *The TELNET protocol provides incredible flexibility because it only*
> *defines interactive communication and not the details of the service*
> *accessed. TELNET can be used as the communication mechanism for*
> *many interactive services besides remote login.*

1.8 Viewing Services From The Provider's Perspective

The examples of application services given above show how a service appears
from an individual user's point of view. The user runs a program that accesses a remote service, and expects to receive a reply with little or no delay.

From the perspective of a computer that supplies a service, the situation appears
quite different. Users at multiple sites may choose to access a given service at the same
time. When they do, each user expects to receive a response without delay.

To provide quick responses and handle many requests, a computer system that supplies an application service must use *concurrent processing*. That is, the provider cannot keep a new user waiting while it handles requests for the previous user. Instead, the
software must process more than one request at a time.

Because application programmers do not often write concurrent programs, concurrent processing can seem like magic. A single application program must manage
multiple activities at the same time. In the case of TELNET, the program that provides
remote login service must allow multiple users to login to a given machine and must
manage multiple active login sessions. Communication for one login session must
proceed without interference from others.

The need for concurrency complicates network software design, implementation,
and maintenance. It mandates new algorithms and new programming techniques.
Furthermore, because concurrency complicates debugging, programmers must be especially careful to document their designs and to follow good programming practices. Finally, programmers must choose a level of concurrency and consider whether their
software will exhibit higher throughput if they increase or decrease the level of concurrency.

This text helps application programmers understand the design, construction, and
optimization of network application software that uses concurrent processing. It
describes the fundamental algorithms for both sequential and concurrent implementations of application protocols and provides an example of each. It considers the trade-
offs and advantages of each design. Later chapters discuss the subtleties of concurrency
management and review techniques that permit a programmer to optimize throughput
automatically. To summarize:

> *Providing concurrent access to application services is important and*
> *difficult; many chapters of this text explain and discuss concurrent im-*
> *plementations of application protocol software.*

1.9 The Remainder Of The Text

This text describes how to design and build distributed applications. Although it uses TCP/IP transport protocols to provide concrete examples, the discussion focuses on principles, algorithms, and general purpose techniques that apply to most network protocols. Early chapters introduce the client-server model and socket interface. Later chapters present specific algorithms and implementation techniques used in client and server software as well as interesting combinations of algorithms and techniques for managing concurrency.

In addition to its description of algorithms for client and server software, the text presents general techniques like tunneling, application-level gateways, and remote procedure calls. Finally, it examines a few standard application protocols like NFS and TELNET.

Most chapters contain example software that helps illustrate the principles discussed. The software should be considered part of the text. It shows clearly how all the details fit together and how the concepts appear in working programs.

1.10 Summary

Many programmers are building distributed applications that use TCP/IP as a transport mechanism. Before programmers can design and implement a distributed application, they need to understand the client-server model of computing, the operating system interface an application program uses to access protocol software, the fundamental algorithms used to implement client and server software, and alternatives to standard client-server interaction including the use of application gateways.

Most network services permit multiple users to access the service simultaneously. The technique of concurrent processing makes it possible to build an application program that can handle multiple requests at the same time. Much of this text focuses on techniques for the concurrent implementation of application protocols and on the problem of managing concurrency.

FOR FURTHER STUDY

The manuals that vendors supply with their operating systems contain information on how to invoke commands that access services like *TELNET*. Many organizations also purchase third-party software to augment the standard applications. Check with your site administrator to find out about software available on your system.

EXERCISES

1.1   Use TELNET from your local machine to login to another machine. How much delay, if any, do you experience when the second machine connects to the same local area network? How much delay do you notice when connected to a remote machine?

1.2   Read the vendor's manual to find out whether your local version of the TELNET software permits connection to a port on the remote machine other than the standard port used for remote login.

1.3   Determine the set of TCP/IP services available on your local computer.

1.4   Use an FTP program to retrieve a file from a remote site. If the software does not provide statistics, estimate the transfer rate for a large file. Is the rate higher or lower than you expected?

2

The Client Server Model
And Software Design

2.1 Introduction

From the viewpoint of an application, TCP/IP, like most computer communication protocols, merely provides basic mechanisms used to transfer data. In particular, TCP/IP allows a programmer to establish communication between two application programs and to pass data back and forth. Thus, we say that TCP/IP provides *peer-to-peer* communication. The peer applications can execute on the same machine or on different machines.

Although TCP/IP specifies the details of how data passes between a pair of communicating applications, it does not dictate when or why peer applications interact, nor does it specify how programmers should organize such application programs in a distributed environment. In practice, one organizational method dominates the use of TCP/IP to such an extent that almost all applications use it. The method is known as the *client-server paradigm*. In fact, client-server interaction has become so fundamental in peer-to-peer networking systems that it forms the basis for most computer communication.

This text uses the client-server paradigm to describe all application programming. It considers the motivations behind the client-server model, describes the functions of the client and server components, and shows how to construct both client and server software.

Before considering how to construct software, it is important to define client-server concepts and terminology. The next sections define terminology that is used throughout the text.

2.2 Motivation

The fundamental motivation for the client-server paradigm arises from the problem of rendezvous. To understand the problem, imagine a human trying to start two programs on separate machines and have them communicate. Also remember that computers operate many orders of magnitude faster than humans. After the human initiates the first program, the program begins execution and sends a message to its peer. Within a few milliseconds, it determines that the peer does not yet exist, so it emits an error message and exits. Meanwhile, the human initiates the second program. Unfortunately, when the second program starts execution, it finds that the peer has already ceased execution. Even if the two programs retry to communicate continually, they can each execute so quickly that the probability of them sending messages to one another simultaneously is low.

The client-server model solves the rendezvous problem by asserting that in any pair of communicating applications, one side must start execution and wait (indefinitely) for the other side to contact it. The solution is important because TCP/IP does not respond to incoming communication requests on its own.

> *Because TCP/IP does not provide any mechanisms that automatically create running programs when a message arrives, a program must be waiting to accept communication before any requests arrive.*

Thus, to ensure that computers are ready to communicate, most system administrators arrange to have communication programs start automatically whenever the operating system boots. Each program runs forever, waiting for the next request to arrive for the service it offers.

2.3 Terminology And Concepts

The client-server paradigm divides communicating applications into two broad categories, depending on whether the application waits for communication or initiates it. This section provides a concise, comprehensive definition of the two categories, and relies on later chapters to illustrate them and explain many of the subtleties.

2.3.1 Clients And Servers

The client-server paradigm uses the direction of initiation to categorize whether a program is a client or server. In general, an application that initiates peer-to-peer communication is called a *client*. End users usually invoke client software when they use a network service. Most client software consists of conventional application programs. Each time a client application executes, it contacts a server, sends a request, and awaits a response. When the response arrives, the client continues processing. Clients are often easier to build than servers, and usually require no special system privileges to operate.

By comparison, a *server* is any program† that waits for incoming communication requests from a client. The server receives a client's request, performs the necessary computation, and returns the result to the client.

2.3.2 Privilege And Complexity

Because servers often need to access data, computations, or protocol ports that the operating system protects, server software usually requires special system privileges. Because a server executes with special system privilege, care must be taken to ensure that it does not inadvertently pass privileges on to the clients that use it. For example, a file server that operates as a privileged program must contain code to check whether a given file can be accessed by a given client. The server cannot rely on the usual operating system checks because its privileged status overrides them.

Servers must contain code that handles the issues of:

- *Authentication* – verifying the identity of the client
- *Authorization* – determining whether a given client is permitted to access the service the server supplies
- *Data security* – guaranteeing that data is not unintentionally revealed or compromised
- *Privacy* – keeping information about an individual from unauthorized access
- *Protection* – guaranteeing that network applications cannot abuse system resources.

As we will see in later chapters, servers that perform intense computation or handle large volumes of data operate more efficiently if they handle requests concurrently. The combination of special privileges and concurrent operation usually makes servers more difficult to design and implement than clients. Later chapters provide many examples that illustrate the differences between clients and servers.

2.3.3 Standard Vs. Nonstandard Client Software

Chapter *1* describes two broad classes of client application programs: those that invoke standard TCP/IP services (e.g., electronic mail) and those that invoke services defined by the site (e.g., an institution's private database system). *Standard application services* consist of those services defined by TCP/IP and assigned well-known, universally recognized protocol port identifiers; we consider all others to be *locally-defined application services* or *nonstandard application services.*

The distinction between standard services and others is only important when communicating outside the local environment. Within a given environment, system administrators usually arrange to define service names in such a way that users cannot distinguish between local and standard services. Programmers who build network applications that will be used at other sites must understand the distinction, however, and must be careful to avoid depending on services that are only available locally.

---

†Technically, a *server* is a program and not a piece of hardware. However, computer users frequently (mis)apply the term to the computer responsible for running a particular server program. For example, they might say, ''That computer is our file server,'' when they mean, ''That computer runs our file server program.''

Although TCP/IP defines many standard application protocols, most commercial computer vendors supply only a handful of standard application client programs with their TCP/IP software. For example, TCP/IP software usually includes a *remote terminal client* that uses the standard TELNET protocol for remote login, an *electronic mail client* that uses the standard SMTP protocol to transfer electronic mail to a remote system, a *file transfer client* that uses the standard FTP protocol to transfer files between two machines, and a *Web browser* that uses the standard HTTP protocol to access Web documents†.

Of course, many organizations build customized applications that use TCP/IP to communicate. Customized, nonstandard applications range from simple to complex, and include such diverse services as image transmission and video teleconferencing, voice transmission, remote real-time data collection, hotel and other on-line reservation systems, distributed database access, weather data distribution, and remote control of ocean-based drilling platforms.

2.3.4 Parameterization Of Clients

Some client software provides more generality than others. In particular, some client software allows the user to specify both the remote machine on which a server operates and the protocol port number at which the server is listening. For example, Chapter *1* shows how standard application client software can use the *TELNET* protocol to access services other than the conventional TELNET remote terminal service, as long as the program allows the user to specify a destination protocol port as well as a remote machine.

Conceptually, software that allows a user to specify a protocol port number has more input parameters than other software, so we use the term *fully parameterized client* to describe it. Many TELNET client implementations interpret an optional second argument as a port number. To specify only a remote machine, the user supplies the name of the remote machine:

telnet machine-name

Given only a machine name, the *telnet* program uses the well-known port for the TELNET service. To specify both a remote machine and a port on that machine, the user specifies both the machine name and the port number:

telnet machine-name port

Not all vendors provide full parameterization for their client application software. Therefore, on some systems, it may be difficult or impossible to use any port other than the official TELNET port. In fact, it may be necessary to modify the vendor's TELNET client software or to write new TELNET client software that accepts a port argument and uses that port. Of course, when building client software, full parameterization is recommended.

---

†SMTP is the Simple Mail Transfer Protocol, FTP is the File Transfer Protocol, and HTTP is the Hyper-Text Transfer Protocol.

When designing client application software, include parameters that
allow the user to fully specify the destination machine and destination
protocol port number.

Full parameterization is especially useful when testing a new client or server because it allows testing to proceed independent of the existing software already in use.
For example, a programmer can build a TELNET client and server pair, invoke them
using nonstandard protocol ports, and proceed to test the software without disturbing
standard services. Other users can continue to access the old TELNET service without
interference during the testing.

2.3.5 Connectionless Vs. Connection-Oriented Servers

When programmers design client-server software, they must choose between two
types of interaction: a *connectionless style* or a *connection-oriented style*. The two
styles of interaction correspond directly to the two major transport protocols that the
TCP/IP protocol suite supplies. If the client and server communicate using UDP, the
interaction is connectionless; if they use TCP, the interaction is connection-oriented.

From the application programmer's point of view, the distinction between connectionless and connection-oriented interactions is critical because it determines the level of
reliability that the underlying system provides. TCP provides all the reliability needed
to communicate across an internet. It verifies that data arrives, and automatically retransmits segments that do not. It computes a checksum over the data to guarantee that
it is not corrupted during transmission. It uses sequence numbers to ensure that the data
arrives in order, and automatically eliminates duplicate packets. It provides flow control to ensure that the sender does not transmit data faster than the receiver can consume
it. Finally, TCP informs both the client and server if the underlying network becomes
inoperable for any reason.

By contrast, clients and servers that use UDP do not have any guarantees about reliable delivery. When a client sends requests, the requests may be lost, duplicated, delayed, or delivered out of order. Similarly, responses the server sends back to a client
may be lost, duplicated, delayed, or delivered out of order. The client and/or server application programs must take appropriate actions to detect and correct such errors.

UDP can be deceiving because it provides *best effort delivery*. UDP does not introduce errors – it merely depends on the underlying IP internet to deliver packets. IP,
in turn, depends on the underlying hardware networks and intermediate gateways. From
a programmer's point of view, the consequence of using UDP is that it works well if the
underlying internet works well. For example, UDP works well in a local environment
because local area networks seldom lose, duplicate, or reorder packets. Errors usually
arise only when communication spans a wide area internet.

Programmers sometimes make the mistake of choosing connectionless transport
(i.e., UDP), building an application that uses it, and then testing the application software
only on a local area network. Because a local area network seldom or never delays

packets, drops them, or delivers them out of order, the application software appears to work well. However, if the same software is used across a wide area internet, it may fail or produce incorrect results.

Beginners, as well as most experienced professionals, prefer to use the connection-oriented style of interaction. A connection-oriented protocol makes programming simpler, and relieves the programmer of the responsibility to detect and correct errors. In fact, adding reliability to a connectionless internet message protocol like UDP is a nontrivial undertaking that usually requires considerable experience with protocol design.

Usually, application programs only use UDP if: (1) the application protocol specifies that UDP must be used (presumably, the application protocol has been designed to handle errors that cause packets to be lost, duplicated, or reordered), (2) the application protocol relies on hardware broadcast or multicast, or (3) the application cannot tolerate the computational overhead or delay required to establish a TCP connection. We can summarize:

> *When designing client-server applications, beginners are strongly advised to use TCP because it provides reliable, connection-oriented communication. Programs only use UDP if the application protocol handles reliability, the application requires hardware broadcast or multicast, or the application cannot tolerate virtual circuit overhead.*

2.3.6 Stateless Vs. Stateful Servers

Information that a server maintains about the status of ongoing interactions with clients is called *state information*. Servers that do not keep any state information are called *stateless servers*; others are called *stateful servers*.

The desire for efficiency motivates designers to keep state information in servers. Keeping a small amount of information in a server can reduce the size of messages that the client and server exchange, and can allow the server to respond to requests quickly. Essentially, state information allows a server to remember what the client requested previously and to compute an incremental response as each new request arrives. By contrast, the motivation for statelessness lies in protocol reliability: state information in a server can become incorrect if messages are lost, duplicated, or delivered out of order, or if the client computer crashes and reboots. If the server uses incorrect state information when computing a response, it may respond incorrectly.

2.3.7 A Stateful File Server Example

An example will help explain the distinction between stateless and stateful servers. Consider a file server that allows clients to remotely access information kept in the files on a local disk. The server operates as an application program. It waits for a client to contact it over the network. The client sends one of two request types. It either sends a request to extract data from a specified file or a request to store data in a specified file. The server performs the requested operation and replies to the client.

On one hand, if the file server is stateless, it maintains no information about the transactions. Each message from a client that requests the server to extract data from a file must specify the complete file name (the name could be quite lengthy), a position in the file from which the data should be extracted, and the number of bytes to extract. Similarly, each message that requests the server to store data in a file must specify the complete file name, a position in the file at which the data should be stored, and the data to store.

On the other hand, if the file server maintains state information for its clients, it can eliminate the need to pass file names in each message. The server maintains a table that holds state information about the file currently being accessed. Figure 2.1 shows one possible arrangement of the state information.

Handle	File Name	Current Position
1	test_program.cpp	0
2	tcp_book.doc	456
3	dept_budget.txt	38
4	tetris.exe	128

Figure 2.1 Example table of state information for a stateful file server. To keep messages short, the server assigns a handle to each file. The handle appears in messages instead of a file name.

When a client first opens a file, the server adds an entry to its state table that contains the name of the file, a *handle* (a small integer used to identify the file), and a current position in the file (initially zero). The server then sends the handle back to the client for use in subsequent requests. Whenever the client wants to extract additional data from the file, it sends a small message that includes the handle. The server uses the handle to look up the file name and current file position in its state table. The server increments the file position in the state table, so the next request from the client will extract new data. Thus, the client can send repeated requests to move through the entire file. When the client finishes using a file, it sends a message informing the server that the file will no longer be needed. In response, the server removes the stored state information. As long as all messages travel reliably between the client and server, a stateful design makes the interaction more efficient. The point is:

> In an ideal world, where networks deliver all messages reliably and computers never crash, having a server maintain a small amount of state information for each ongoing interaction can make messages smaller and processing simpler.

Although state information can improve efficiency, it can also be difficult or impossible to maintain correctly if the underlying network duplicates, delays, or delivers messages out of order (e.g., if the client and server use UDP to communicate). Consider what happens to our file server example if the network duplicates a *read* request. Recall that the server maintains a notion of file position in its state information. Assume that the server updates its notion of file position each time a client extracts data from a file. If the network duplicates a *read* request, the server will receive two copies. When the first copy arrives, the server extracts data from the file, updates the file position in its state information, and returns the result to the client. When the second copy arrives, the server extracts additional data, updates the file position again, and returns the new data to the client. The client may view the second response as a duplicate and discard it, or it may report an error because it received two different responses to a single request. In either case, the state information at the server can become incorrect because it disagrees with the client's notion of the true state.

When computers reboot, state information can also become incorrect. If a client crashes after performing an operation that creates additional state information, the server may never receive messages that allow it to discard the information. Eventually, the accumulated state information exhausts the server's memory. In our file server example, if a client opens *100* files and then crashes, the server will maintain *100* useless entries in its state table forever.

A stateful server may also become confused (or respond incorrectly) if a new client begins operation after a reboot using the same protocol port numbers as the previous client that was operating when the system crashed. It may seem that this problem can be overcome easily by having the server erase previous information from a client whenever a new request for interaction arrives. Remember, however, that the underlying internet may duplicate and delay messages, so any solution to the problem of new clients reusing protocol ports after a reboot must also handle the case where a client starts normally, but its first message to a server becomes duplicated and one copy is delayed.

In general, the problems of maintaining correct state can only be solved with complex protocols that accommodate the problems of unreliable delivery and computer system restart. To summarize:

> In a real internet, where machines crash and reboot, and messages
> can be lost, delayed, duplicated, or delivered out of order, stateful
> designs lead to complex application protocols that are difficult to
> design, understand, and program correctly.

2.3.8 Statelessness Is A Protocol Issue

Although we have discussed statelessness in the context of servers, the question of whether a server is stateless or stateful centers on the application protocol more than the implementation. If the application protocol specifies that the meaning of a particular message depends in some way on previous messages, it may be impossible to provide a stateless interaction.

In essence, the issue of statelessness focuses on whether the application protocol assumes the responsibility for reliable delivery. To avoid problems and make the interaction reliable, an application protocol designer must ensure that each message is completely unambiguous. That is, a message cannot depend on being delivered in ord-

er, nor can it depend on previous messages having been delivered. In essence, the protocol designer must build the interaction so the server gives the same response no
matter when or how many times a request arrives. Mathematicians use the term *idempotent* to refer to a mathematical operation that always produces the same result. We
use the term to refer to protocols that arrange for a server to give the same response to a
given message no matter how many times it arrives.

> *In an internet where the underlying network can duplicate, delay or*
> *deliver messages out of order or where computers running client ap-*
> *plications can crash unexpectedly, the server should be stateless. The*
> *server can only be stateless if the application protocol is designed to*
> *make operations idempotent.*

2.3.9 Servers As Clients

Programs do not always fit exactly into the definition of client or server. A server
program may need to access network services that require it to act as a client. For example, suppose our file server program needs to obtain the time of day so it can stamp
files with the time of access. Also suppose that the system on which it operates does
not have a time-of-day clock. To obtain the time, the server acts as a client by sending
a request to a time-of-day server as Figure 2.2 shows.

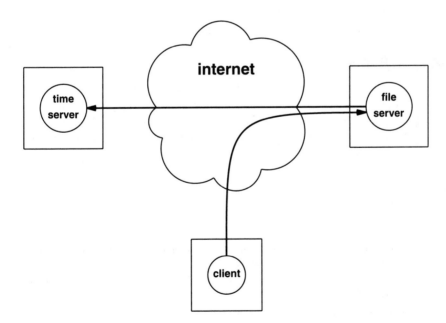

Figure 2.2 A file server program acting as a client to a time server. When
the time server replies, the file server will finish its computation
and return the result to the original client.

In a network environment that has many available servers, it is not unusual to find a server for one application acting as a client for another. Of course, designers must be careful to avoid circular dependencies among servers.

2.4 Summary

The client-server paradigm classifies a communicating application program as either a client or a server depending on whether it initiates communication. In addition to client and server software for standard applications, many TCP/IP users build client and server software for nonstandard applications that they define locally.

Beginners and most experienced programmers use TCP to transport messages between the client and server because it provides the reliability needed in an internet environment. Programmers only resort to UDP if TCP cannot solve the problem.

Keeping state information in the server can improve efficiency. However, if clients crash unexpectedly or the underlying transport system allows duplication, delay, or packet loss, state information can consume resources or become incorrect. Thus, most application protocol designers try to minimize state information. A stateless implementation may not be possible if the application protocol fails to make operations idempotent.

Programs cannot be divided easily into client and server categories because many programs perform both functions. A program that acts as a server for one service can act as a client to access other services.

FOR FURTHER STUDY

Stevens [1990] briefly describes the client-server model and gives UNIX examples. Berson [1993] describes client-server architectures, and Sinha [1992] reviews the technology. Other examples can be found by consulting applications that accompany various vendors' operating systems.

EXERCISES

2.1   Which of your local implementations of standard application clients are fully parameterized? Why is full parameterization needed?

2.2   Are standard application protocols like TELNET, FTP, SMTP, and NFS (Network File System) connectionless or connection-oriented?

2.3   What does TCP/IP specify should happen if no server exists when a client request arrives? (Hint: look at ICMP.) What happens on your local system?

2.4 Write down the data structures and message formats needed for a stateless file server. What happens if two or more clients access the same file? What happens if a client crashes before closing a file?

2.5 Write down the data structures and message formats needed for a stateful file server. Use the operations *open*, *read*, *write*, and *close* to access files. Arrange for *open* to return an integer used to access the file in *read* and *write* operations. How do you distinguish duplicate *open* requests from a client that sends an *open*, crashes, reboots, and sends an *open* again?

2.6 In the previous exercise, what happens in your design if two or more clients access the same file? What happens if a client crashes before closing a file?

2.7 Examine the NFS remote file access protocol carefully to identify which operations are idempotent. What errors can result if messages are lost, duplicated, or delayed?

3

Concurrent Processing In Client-Server Software

3.1 Introduction

The previous chapter defines the client-server paradigm. This chapter extends the notion of client-server interaction by discussing concurrency, a concept that provides much of the power behind client-server interactions but also makes the software difficult to design and build. The notion of concurrency also pervades later chapters, which explain in detail how servers provide concurrent access.

In addition to discussing the general concept of concurrency, this chapter also reviews the facilities that an operating system supplies to support concurrent execution. It is important to understand the functions described in this chapter because they appear in many of the server implementations in later chapters.

Because an operating system supplies the fundamental facilities needed for concurrent execution, the details of techniques used to make clients and servers concurrent depend on the operating system being used. After describing the general concept of concurrency, the chapter explains the facilities available to an application running under Windows 95 or Windows NT. A later section contrasts the mechanisms with those available under UNIX. Although an understanding of UNIX is not essential for building concurrent applications under Windows, it is important for anyone who is porting software from a UNIX system.

3.2 Concurrency In Networks

The term *concurrency* refers to real or apparent simultaneous computing. For example, a multi-user computer system can achieve concurrency by *time-sharing*, a design that arranges to switch a single processor among multiple computations quickly enough to give the appearance of simultaneous progress; or by *multiprocessing*, a design in which multiple processors perform multiple computations simultaneously.

Concurrent processing is fundamental to distributed computing and occurs in many forms. Among machines on a single network, many pairs of application programs can communicate concurrently, sharing the network that interconnects them. For example, application *A* on one machine may communicate with application *B* on another machine, while application *C* on a third machine communicates with application *D* on a fourth. Although they all share a single network, the applications appear to proceed as if they operate independently. The network hardware enforces access rules that allow each pair of communicating machines to exchange messages. The access rules prevent a given pair of applications from excluding others by consuming all the network bandwidth.

Concurrency can also occur within a given computer system. For example, multiple users on a timesharing system can each invoke a client application that communicates with an application on another machine. One user can transfer a file, while another user conducts a remote login session. From a user's point of view, it appears that all client programs proceed simultaneously.

In addition to concurrency among clients on a single machine, the set of all clients on a set of machines can execute concurrently. Figure 3.1 illustrates concurrency among client programs running on several machines.

Client software does not usually require any special attention or effort on the part of the programmer to make it usable concurrently. The application programmer designs and constructs each client program without regard to concurrent execution; concurrency among multiple client programs occurs automatically because the operating system allows multiple users to each invoke a client concurrently. Thus, the individual clients operate much like any conventional program. To summarize:

> *Most client software achieves concurrent operation because the underlying operating system allows users to execute client programs concurrently or because users on many machines each execute client software simultaneously. An individual client program operates like any conventional program; it does not manage concurrency explicitly.*

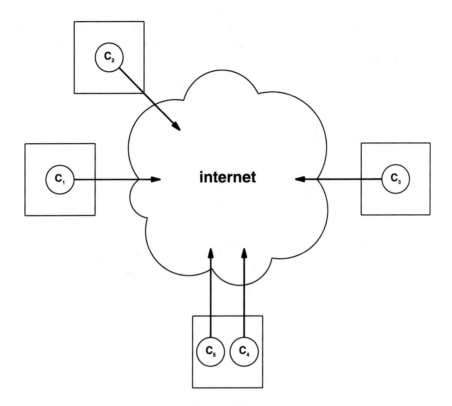

Figure 3.1 Concurrency among client programs occurs when users execute
them on multiple machines simultaneously or when a multitasking
operating system allows multiple copies to execute concurrently
on a single computer.

3.3 Concurrency In Servers

In contrast to concurrent client software, concurrency within a server requires considerable effort. As Figure 3.2 shows, a single server program must handle incoming requests concurrently.

To understand why concurrency is important, consider server operations that require substantial computation or communication. For example, think of a remote login server. If it operates with no concurrency, it can handle only one remote login at a time. Once a client contacts the server, the server must ignore or refuse subsequent requests until the first user finishes. Clearly, such a design limits the utility of the server, and prevents multiple remote users from accessing a given machine at the same time.

Chapter *8* discusses algorithms and design issues for concurrent servers, showing how they operate in principle. Chapters *9* through *13* each illustrate one of the algorithms, describing the design in more detail and showing code for a working server. The remainder of this chapter concentrates on terminology and basic concepts used throughout the text.

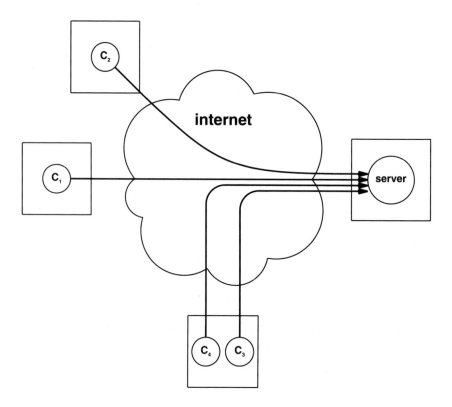

Figure 3.2 Server software must be explicitly programmed to handle concurrent requests because multiple clients contact a server using its single, well-known protocol port.

3.4 Terminology And Concepts

Because few application programmers have experience with the design of concurrent programs, understanding concurrency in servers can be challenging. This section explains the basic concept of concurrent processing and shows how an operating system supplies it. It gives examples that illustrate concurrency, and defines terminology used in later chapters.

3.4.1 The Process Concept

In some concurrent processing systems, the *process* abstraction defines the fundamental unit of computation†. The most essential information associated with a process is an *instruction pointer* that specifies the address at which the process is executing. Other information associated with a process includes the identity of the user that owns it, the compiled program that it is executing, and the memory locations of the process' program text and data areas.

A process differs from a program because the process concept includes only the active execution of a computation, not the code. After the code has been loaded into a computer, the operating system allows one or more processes to execute it. In particular, a concurrent processing system allows multiple processes to execute the same piece of code ''at the same time.'' This means that multiple processes may each be executing at some point in the code. Each process proceeds at its own rate, and each may begin or finish at an arbitrary time. Because each has a separate instruction pointer that specifies which instruction it will execute next and its own copy of variables, there is never any confusion.

Of course, on a uniprocessor architecture, the single CPU can only execute one process at any instant in time. The operating system makes the computer appear to perform more than one computation at a time by switching the CPU among all executing processes rapidly. From a human observer's point of view, many processes appear to proceed simultaneously. In fact, one process proceeds for a short time, then another process proceeds for a short time, and so on. We use the term *concurrent execution* to capture the idea. It means ''apparently simultaneous execution.'' On a uniprocessor, the operating system handles concurrency, while on a multiprocessor, each CPU can execute a process simultaneously with other CPUs.

The important concept is:

> *Application programmers build programs for a concurrent environment without knowing whether the underlying hardware consists of a uniprocessor or a multiprocessor.*

3.4.2 Threads

Some operating systems, including Windows 95 and Windows NT, provide a second form of concurrent execution known as *threads of execution‡*. Similar to the process concept described above, a thread has its own instruction pointer and copy of local variables, and it executes independently of other threads. A thread mechanism differs from a process mechanism, however, because each thread must be associated with a single process. Although each thread in a process has its own copy of local variables, all threads in a process share access to a single copy of global variables. More important, all threads in a process share resources that the operating system allocates to the process, including the descriptors used for network communication. Thus, in a multithreaded program, if one thread opens a file and obtains a descriptor, other threads can

---

†Some systems use the terms *task* or *job* instead of *process*.

‡The term is often abbreviated *threads*, which are sometimes called *lightweight processes* because they incur less system overhead than conventional processes.

use the descriptor to access the file. Similarly, if one thread closes a descriptor, none of the other threads can continue to use it. We will see that shared descriptors are especially important when a multithreaded program interacts over a network.

A concurrent program can be written either to create separate processes or to create multiple threads within a single process. Each has advantages and disadvantages; the optimal design may depend on the details of the operating system being used. One of the potential disadvantages of a multithreaded design is interference – a thread that malfunctions can interfere with other threads by releasing resources or changing the contents of global variables. Interference can be difficult to debug because it may not be obvious which thread has caused the problem. Thus, programmers who write multithreaded code must be especially careful when creating the program.

3.4.3 Programs vs. Threads

In a concurrent processing system, a conventional application program is merely a special case: it consists of a piece of code that is executed by exactly one thread at a time. The notion of *thread* differs from the conventional notion of *program* in other ways. For example, most application programmers think of the set of variables defined in the program as being associated with the code. However, if more than one thread executes the code concurrently, it is essential that each thread has its own copy of the local variables. To understand why, consider the following segment of C code that prints the integers from *1* to *10*:

```
for ( i=1 ; i <= 10 ; i++)
        printf("%d\n", i);
```

The iteration uses an index variable, i, usually declared to be a local variable. In a conventional program, the programmer thinks of storage for variable i as being allocated with the code. However, if two or more threads execute the code segment concurrently, one of them may be on the sixth iteration when the other starts the first iteration. Each must have a different value for i. Thus, each thread must have its own copy of variable i or confusion will result. To summarize:

> *When multiple threads execute a piece of code concurrently, each thread has its own, independent copy of the local variables associated with the code.*

3.4.4 Procedure Calls

In a procedure-oriented language, like Pascal or C, executed code can contain calls to subprograms (procedures or functions). Subprograms accept arguments, compute a result, and then return just after the point of the call. If multiple threads execute code concurrently, they can each be at a different point in the sequence of procedure calls. One thread, *A*, can begin execution, call a procedure, and then call a second-level procedure before another thread, *B*, begins. Thread *B* may return from a first-level procedure call just as thread *A* returns from a second-level call.

The run-time system for procedure-oriented programming languages uses a stack mechanism to handle procedure calls. The run-time system pushes a *procedure activation record* on the stack whenever it makes a procedure call. Among other things, the activation record stores information about the location in the code at which the procedure call occurs. When the procedure finishes execution, the run-time system pops the activation record from the top of the stack and returns to the procedure from which the call occurred. Analogous to the rule for variables, concurrent programming systems provide separation among procedure calls in executing threads:

> *When multiple threads execute a piece of code concurrently, each has its own run-time stack of procedure activation records.*

3.5 An Example Of Concurrent Thread Creation

3.5.1 A Sequential C Example

The following example illustrates concurrent processing. As with most computational concepts, the programming language syntax is trivial; it occupies only a few lines of code. For example, the following code is a conventional C program that prints the integers from *1* to *5* along with their sum:

```c
/* sum.cpp - A conventional C program that sums integers 1 to 5     */
#include <stdlib.h>
#include <stdio.h>
#include <process.h>

int     addem(int);

int
main(int argc, char *argv[])
{
        addem(5);
        return 0;
}

int
addem(int count)
{
        int i, sum;                         /* these are local variables*/

        sum = 0;
        for (i=1 ; i<=count ; i++) {    /* iterate i from 1 to count */
                printf("The value of i is %d\n", i);
```

```
        fflush(stdout);              /* flush the buffer        */
        sum += i;
    }
    printf("The sum is %d\n", sum);
    fflush(stdout);
    return 0;                        /* terminate the program   */
}
```

When executed, the program emits six lines of output:

```
                The value of i is 1
                The value of i is 2
                The value of i is 3
                The value of i is 4
                The value of i is 5
                The sum is 15
```

3.5.2 A Concurrent Version

To create a new thread in Windows, a program calls the operating system function _beginthread. To a programmer, the call to _beginthread looks like an ordinary function call in C. However, instead of calling a conventional function, _beginthread passes control to the operating system, which creates a new thread and allows both threads to continue executing. We use the term *parent* to refer to the original thread, and *child* to refer to the newly created thread. The parent continues executing after the call to _beginthread (i.e., exactly as if the function call returned). The child begins executing at whichever function was passed as an argument to _beginthread. For example, the following modified version of the example above calls _beginthread to create a new thread. Note that although the introduction of concurrency changes the functionality of the program completely, the call to _beginthread occupies only a single line of code:

```
/* consum.cpp - A concurrent C program that sums integers 1 to 5     */
#include <stdlib.h>
#include <stdio.h>
#include <process.h>

int     addem(int);

int
main(int argc, char *argv[])
{
        _beginthread((void (*)(void ())addem, 0, (void *)5);
        addem(5);
        return 0;
}
```

```
int
addem(int count)
{
        int i, sum;                         /* these are local variables*/

        sum = 0;
        for (i=1 ; i<=count ; i++) {    /* iterate i from 1 to count */
                printf("The value of i is %d\n", i);
                fflush(stdout);             /* flush the buffer        */
                sum += i;
        }
        printf("The sum is %d\n", sum);
        fflush(stdout);
        return 0;                           /* terminate the program   */
}
```

When a user executes the concurrent version of the program, the application begins execution with a single thread executing the code. When execution reaches the call to _beginthread, the system allocates a run-time stack for the newly created thread, and allows both the original thread and the new thread to execute. In fact, the easiest way to envision what happens in this example is to imagine that the system creates a second application program, and initializes the second program to start running procedure *addem*. Then imagine that both applications run simultaneously (just as if two users had both simultaneously executed the program). To summarize:

> *To understand thread execution, imagine that* _beginthread *causes the operating system to start another application program executing at a specified procedure and allows both to run at the same time.*

On one particular uniprocessor system, the execution of our example concurrent program produced the following twelve lines of output:

```
                The value of i is 1
                The value of i is 2
                The value of i is 1
                The value of i is 3
                The value of i is 4
                The value of i is 2
                The value of i is 3
                The value of i is 4
                The value of i is 5
                The sum is 15
                The value of i is 5
                The sum is 15
```

The program ran quickly; the entire execution, including the creation of a second thread, completed in less than a second. Furthermore, the operating system overhead incurred in switching between threads and handling system calls, including the call to _beginthread_ and the calls required to write the output, accounted for less than *20%* of the total time.

3.5.3 Timeslicing

The output from the example above shows an interesting pattern: instead of all output from one thread being followed by all output from the other, output from the two threads are intermixed. In general, the mixture occurs because the two threads compete for the processor, with the operating system allocating the available CPU power to each thread for a short time before moving on to the next. We use the term *timeslicing* to describe systems that share available CPU among several threads concurrently. For example, if a timeslicing system has only one CPU and a program divides into two threads, one of the threads will execute for a while, then the second will execute for a while, then the first will execute again, and so on.

A timeslicing mechanism attempts to allocate the available processing equally among all available threads. If only two threads are eligible to execute and the computer has a single processor, each receives approximately 50% of the CPU. If more than two threads are ready to run, the system will run each thread for a short time before running any of them again. Thus, if *N* threads are eligible on a computer with a single processor, each receives approximately 1/*N* of the CPU. From a human's perspective, all threads appear to proceed at an equal rate, no matter how many threads execute. With many threads executing, the rate is low; with few, the rate is high.

The effects of timeslicing can be seen by comparing how a concurrent program performs on different timesharing computer systems. For example, the program above can be modified to iterate 10,000 times instead of *5* times:

```
/* consum.cpp - A concurrent C program that sums integers 1 to 10000 */
#include <stdlib.h>
#include <stdio.h>
#include <process.h>

int     addem(int);

int
main(int argc, char *argv[])
{
        _beginthread((void (*)(void ())addem, 0, (void *)10000);
        addem(10000);
        return 0;
}
```

```
int
addem(int count)
{
        int i, sum;                          /* these are local variables*/

        sum = 0;
        for (i=1 ; i<=count ; i++) {   /* iterate i from 1 to count */
                printf("The value of i is %d\n", i);
                fflush(stdout);              /* flush the buffer         */
                sum += i;
        }
        printf("The sum is %d\n", sum);
        fflush(stdout);
        return 0;                            /* terminate the program    */
}
```

When the resulting concurrent program is executed, it always emits 20,002 lines of output. However, the order depends on the operating system. On one system, the first thread iterated *74* times before the second thread executed at all. Then the second thread iterated *63* times before the system switched back to the first thread. On subsequent timeslices, the threads each received enough CPU service to iterate between *60* and *90* times. Of course, the two threads compete with all other threads executing on the same computer, so the apparent rate of execution varies slightly depending on the mix of programs running.

3.6 Diverging Threads

In the examples above, both the parent and child threads execute the same procedure: *addem*. In practice, multiple threads in a concurrent program seldom execute a single procedure. Instead, they usually diverge, with each thread executing its own procedure.

How can threads diverge? The answer is that the second argument to *_beginthread* specifies a procedure for the newly created thread to execute. Meanwhile, the parent continues execution at the point following the call to *_beginthread*. Thus, divergence is straightforward. For example, consider the two lines of code:

```
_beginthread((void (*)(void ())addem, 0, (void *)5);
proc2();
```

The parent thread first calls *_beginthread* and then calls *proc2*. The child thread begins executing *addem* with an argument of *5*. That is, the child thread is created to call

```
addem(5);
```

If the call to *addem* returns, the thread ceases execution.

3.7 Context Switching And Protocol Software Design

Although the concurrent processing facilities that operating systems provide make programs more powerful and easier to understand, they do have computational cost. We said that to ensure that all threads proceed concurrently, the operating system uses timeslicing, switching the CPU (or CPUs) among threads so fast that it appears to a human that the threads execute simultaneously.

When the operating system temporarily stops executing one thread and switches to another, a *context switch* has occurred. Switching context requires use of the CPU, and while the CPU is busy switching, none of the application threads receives any service. Thus, we view context switching as the overhead needed to support concurrent processing†.

To avoid unnecessary overhead, protocol software should be designed to minimize context switching. In particular, programmers must always be careful to ensure that the benefits of introducing concurrency into a server outweigh the cost of switching context among the concurrent threads. Later chapters discuss the use of concurrency in server software, present nonconcurrent designs as well as concurrent ones, and describe circumstances that justify the use of each.

3.8 Concurrency And Asynchronous I/O

In addition to providing support for concurrent use of the CPU, some operating systems allow a single application program to initiate and control concurrent input and output operations. In Windows, the *select* socket function provides a fundamental operation that programmers use to manage concurrent I/O. In principle, *select* is easy to understand: it allows a program to ask the operating system which source of I/O is ready for use.

As an example, imagine an application program that needs to provide network communication between two remote users. Assume the program runs on computer *A* and the users are on computers *B* and *C*. Further assume that either user can enter keystrokes, which are sent across the network to the program for transmission to the other user.

The program cannot know which user will touch their keyboard first; they might both type at the same time, or one might choose to sit idle for a long period. Unfortunately, conventional network I/O operations are *blocking*‡ in the sense that when an application attempts to receive data from a network, the system blocks the application until data arrives. On one hand, if the program attempts to receive data from the connection leading to *B*, the program will block until the user on *B* types. On the other hand, if the program attempts to receive data from the connection leading to *A*, the program will block until the user on *A* types. The problem is that the application cannot know whether input will arrive first from the connection with *A* or from the connection with *B*. To solve the dilemma, a Windows program calls *select*. In doing so, it asks the operating system to let it know which source of input becomes available first. The call

---

†Because switching context between threads incurs less overhead than switching context between processes, threads are often called *lightweight processes*.

‡Blocking I/O is also called *synchronous* I/O.

returns as soon as a source is ready, and the program reads from that source. For now, it is only important to understand the idea behind *select*; later chapters present the details and illustrate its use.

3.9 Concurrency Under UNIX

We said that each operating system offers a function that a program can call to start concurrent execution. Although the examples in this text use the thread mechanism available in Windows, other systems offer slightly different mechanisms. This section examines the concurrency mechanism in the UNIX timesharing system. Understanding UNIX concurrency is helpful in two ways. First, because the source code for many UNIX network applications is available publicly, Windows programmers often use UNIX code as an example. Second, because professional programmers are often asked to develop a version of an application that runs on many systems, knowledge of UNIX can help programmers to accommodate both styles.

Instead of the thread mechanism available in Windows, UNIX offers a *process* abstraction. When an application program begins running, UNIX creates a single process to run the program. To become concurrent, a UNIX application calls the system function *fork*.

Like *_beginthread* in Windows, *fork* is part of the operating system. Unlike the *_beginthread* function, however, *fork* does not take any arguments. When invoked, *fork* creates another process executing at exactly the same location as the original. In fact, the new child process begins with a complete copy of the parent's run-time stack, including all the procedure calls and variables (both local and global). In each process, execution continues after the call to *fork*.

Creating a truly identical copy of a running program is neither interesting nor useful because it means that both copies perform exactly the same computation. In practice, a new process is not absolutely identical to the original. The processes differ in one small detail: the value that the *fork* function returns. In the newly created process, the *fork* returns zero; in the original process, *fork* returns a small positive integer that identifies the newly created process. Technically, the value returned is called a *process identifier* or *process id*†.

Concurrent programs running under UNIX use the value returned by the *fork* function to decide how to proceed. In the most common case, the code contains a conditional statement that tests to see if the value returned is nonzero‡:

```
#include <stdlib.h>
#include <stdio.h>
int     sum;

main(int argc, char *argv[]) {
        int pid;
```

---

†Many programmers abbreviate *process id* as *pid*.

‡Production code also checks to see if *fork* returns a value less than zero, which indicates that an error occurred.

```
sum = 0;
pid = fork();
if (pid != 0) {              /* original process      */

    printf("The original process prints this.\n");

} else {                     /* newly created process */

    printf("The new process prints this.\n");

}
exit(0);
}
```

In the example code, variable *pid* records the value returned by the call to *fork*. Remember that each process has its own copy of all variables, and that *fork* will either return zero (in the newly created process) or nonzero (in the original process). Following the call to *fork*, the *if* statement checks variable *pid* to see whether the original or the newly created process is executing. The two processes each print an identifying message and exit. When the program runs, two messages appear: one from the original process and one from the newly created process. To summarize:

> *The value returned by the UNIX* fork *function differs in the original and newly created processes; concurrent programs use the difference to allow the new process to execute different code than the original process.*

3.10 Executing A Separately Compiled Program

In addition to *fork*, both Windows and UNIX provide a mechanism that allows any process to stop executing one application and begin executing an independent program that has been compiled separately and stored on disk. The mechanism consists of a family of operating system functions named *exec*†. Arguments to *exec* specify the name of a disk file that contains an executable program, a list of arguments to pass to the program, and a specification of *environment* variables the program will inherit.

Exec replaces the currently executing process completely. The code and all variables are replaced by the code and variables from the program on disk; the run-time stack is replaced by a newly created run-time stack for the new program. Under UNIX, a process must call both *fork* and *exec* to create a new process that executes the object code from a file. Under Windows, a single function, *CreateProcess*, handles both tasks.

Servers that handle many services can use *exec* to simplify the server program and allow services to change independently. The code for each service is placed in a separate program. For example, when a UNIX server needs to handle a particular ser-

---

†There are several variants of *exec* that differ in small details such as the exact format of arguments.

vice, it calls *fork* and *exec* to create a process that runs the appropriate program. The chief advantage of using a separate program for the service lies in ease of maintenance: the program for a particular service can be modified and recompiled without recompiling the main server. In fact, the central server can continue to execute while the program for an individual service is changed and installed.

3.11 Summary

Concurrency is fundamental to TCP/IP applications because it allows users to access services without waiting for one another. Concurrency in clients arises easily because multiple users can execute client application software at the same time. Concurrency in servers is much more difficult to achieve because server software must be programmed explicitly to handle requests concurrently.

In Windows, the primary mechanism used for concurrency is a *thread of execution*. A conventional application consists of a program executed by a single thread. At any time, an executing program can call the function *_beginthread* to create an additional thread of execution. Arguments to *_beginthread* specify a procedure at which the new thread should begin execution, and a list of arguments to be passed to that procedure.

After a call to *_beginthread*, both threads appear to execute simultaneously. In fact, only one thread can be executing at any time on a computer that has a single CPU. To achieve apparent concurrency, the operating system switches the CPU rapidly among the threads, executing one for a short time before moving on to the next. To a human, switching among threads occurs so rapidly that they all appear to execute.

Concurrency is not free. When an operating system switches context from one thread to another, the system uses the CPU. Programmers who introduce concurrency into server designs must ensure that the benefits of a concurrent design outweigh the additional overhead introduced by context switching.

The *select* call permits a single thread to manage concurrent network I/O. A thread calls *select* to wait for a set of network I/O sources; *select* informs the thread as soon as any of the sources becomes ready.

FOR FURTHER STUDY

Many texts on operating systems describe concurrent processing. Beveridge and Weiner [1997] describes threads in Windows. Peterson and Silberschatz [1985] covers the general topic. Comer [1984] discusses the implementation of processes, message passing, and process coordination mechanisms.

EXERCISES

3.1 Run the example programs on your local computer system. Approximately how many iterations of the output loop can a thread make in a single timeslice?

3.2 Write a concurrent program that starts five threads. Arrange for each thread to print a few lines of output and then halt. Is output from the threads intermixed? Explain.

3.3 Find out about the mechanisms that systems other than Windows use to create concurrent programs.

3.4 Read more about the UNIX *fork* function. What information does the newly created process share with the original process?

3.5 Write a program that uses *select* to read text from two network connections, and displays each line of text on a screen with a label that identifies the source.

3.6 Rewrite the program in the previous exercise so it does not use *select*. Which version is easier to understand? more efficient? easier to terminate cleanly?

4

Program Interface To Protocols

4.1 Introduction

Previous chapters describe the client-server model of interaction for communicating programs and discuss the relationship between concurrency and communication. This chapter considers general properties of the interface an application program uses to communicate in the client-server model. The following chapter illustrates these properties by giving details of a specific interface.

4.2 Loosely Specified Protocol Software Interface

In most implementations, TCP/IP protocol software is part of the computer's system software. Thus, whenever an application program uses TCP/IP to communicate, it must interact with the system software to request service. From a programmer's point of view, the set of facilities that the system supplies defines an *Application Program Interface* or *API*.

TCP/IP was designed to operate in a multi-vendor environment. To remain compatible with a wide variety of machines, TCP/IP designers carefully avoided choosing any vendor's internal data representation. In addition, the TCP/IP standards carefully avoid specifying an API that uses features available only on a single vendor's computer system. Thus, the interface between TCP/IP and applications that use it has been *loosely specified*. In other words:

The TCP/IP standards do not specify the details of how application software interfaces with TCP/IP protocol software; they only suggest the required functionality, and allow system designers to choose the details when creating an API.

4.2.1 Advantages And Disadvantages

Using a loose specification for the protocol interface has advantages and disadvantages. On the positive side, it provides flexibility and tolerance. It allows designers to implement TCP/IP using operating systems that range from the simplest systems available on personal computers to the sophisticated systems used on supercomputers. More important, it means designers can use either a procedural or message-passing interface style of API (whichever style the system software supports).

On the negative side, a loose specification means that designers can make the interface details different for each operating system. As vendors add new interfaces that differ from existing interfaces, application programming becomes more difficult and applications become less portable across machines. Thus, while system designers favor a loose specification, application programmers desire a restricted specification because it means applications can be compiled for new machines without change.

In practice, only a few APIs have been developed for use with TCP/IP. The University of California at Berkeley defined an API for the Berkeley UNIX operating system that has become known as the *socket interface*, or *sockets*. AT&T defined an interface for System V UNIX known by the acronym *TLI*†. Others adapted the socket interface for use with Microsoft's systems software; the result is known as the *Windows Sockets Interface*, and is often abbreviated *WINSOCK*. A few other interfaces have been defined, but it seems unlikely that they will gain wide acceptance.

4.3 Interface Functionality

Although TCP/IP does not define details of an API, the standards do suggest the functionality needed. An interface must support the following conceptual operations:

- Allocate local resources for communication
- Specify local and remote communication endpoints
- Initiate a connection (client side)
- Wait for an incoming connection (server side)
- Send or receive data
- Determine when data arrives
- Generate urgent data
- Handle incoming urgent data
- Terminate a connection gracefully
- Handle connection termination from the remote site
- Abort communication

---

†TLI stands for *Transport Layer Interface*.

- Handle error conditions or a connection abort
- Release local resources when communication finishes

4.4 Conceptual Interface Specification

The TCP/IP standards do not leave implementors without any guidance. They specify a *conceptual interface* for TCP/IP that serves as an illustrative example. Because most operating systems use a procedural mechanism to transfer control from an application program into the system, the standard defines the conceptual interface as a set of procedures and functions. The standard suggests the parameters that each procedure or function requires as well as the semantics of the operation it performs. For example, the TCP standard discusses a *SEND* procedure, and lists the arguments an application needs to supply to send data on an existing TCP connection.

The point of defining conceptual operations is simple:

> *The conceptual interface defined by the TCP/IP standards does not specify data representations or programming details; it merely provides an example of one possible interface that an operating system can offer to application programs that use TCP/IP.*

Thus, the conceptual interface loosely illustrates how applications interact with TCP. Because it does not prescribe exact details, operating system designers are free to choose alternative procedure names or parameters as long as they offer equivalent functionality.

4.5 Implementation Of An API

All implementations of a particular API appear the same to programmers: the API merely consists of a set of procedures (or functions) that an application program can call to establish communication or to send and receive data. In practice, however, the implementation of the API depends on the underlying system. For example, early software systems designed for personal computers did not include an operating system in the conventional sense. On such systems, procedures in the API were handled like any other library procedures – a copy of API procedures that an application called were linked into the application program along with the TCP/IP code that was needed. Such a scheme makes sense on a computer that can only run one application at a given time because all the code that the application needs is loaded into memory along with the application.

More sophisticated computer systems can load more than one application into memory simultaneously. On such systems, linking a separate copy of networking code into each application does not make sense. Instead, a single copy of the code is placed in memory, where it is shared by all applications. The exact implementation of sharing depends on the computer's software system. The code might reside in the computer's operating system, or it might reside in a region of memory devoted to *shared libraries*.

For example, Windows 95 uses a shared library scheme known as a *Dynamic Linked Library* (*DLL*). The socket API procedures are located in one DLL, while the TCP/IP code is placed in another. None of the networking code is loaded into memory until an application uses the network. At that time, a copy of the DLL is loaded. If another application uses the network, it shares the copy of the DLL already in memory. Figure 4.1 illustrates the relationship among multiple applications and a single copy of a DLL.

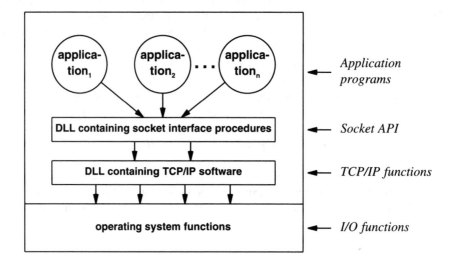

Figure 4.1 The organization of the socket API and TCP/IP code in a Dynamic Linked Library under Windows 95. One copy of a DLL is loaded into memory when needed; all applications share the copy.

In contrast to the implementation used in Windows 95, Windows NT uses a hybrid scheme that includes both a DLL and resident code. The code to implement TCP/IP is linked into the operating system. Thus, TCP/IP code is loaded into memory when the operating system first begins, and remains resident until the operating system terminates. However, procedures in the socket API are not part of the operating system. Instead, such procedures reside in a DLL. A copy of the socket DLL is loaded when an application uses the network, the copy is shared by all applications, and the DLL is removed when no application needs access. Figure 4.2 illustrates the implementation.

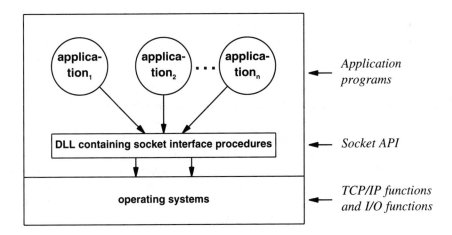

Figure 4.2 The organization of the socket API and TCP/IP code under Windows NT. Although code for TCP/IP is part of the operating system, procedures for the socket API are part of a DLL.

Other implementations are possible. In particular, some computer systems do not support dynamic libraries. On others, a program does not have sufficient privilege to perform input or output operations unless the program uses an operating system function. In such systems, all the procedures in the API are part of the operating system.

From a programmer's point of view, the exact implementation of an API does not matter:

> *A programmer can create an application program that uses the socket API without knowing how the API is implemented. The programmer makes procedure calls, which may invoke procedures that are linked into the application, procedures in a dynamic linked library, or procedures in the operating system.*

4.6 Two Basic Approaches To Network Communication

Designers must choose the exact set of procedures used to access TCP/IP protocols when they create an API. Implementations follow one of two approaches:

- The designer invents entirely new procedure calls that applications use to access TCP/IP.
- The designer attempts to use conventional I/O calls to access TCP/IP.

In the first approach, the designer makes a list of all conceptual operations, invents names and parameters for each, and implements each as a system function. Windows uses this approach. In the second approach, the designer uses conventional I/O primitives but overloads them so they work with network protocols as well as conventional I/O devices. Of course, some designers choose a hybrid approach that uses basic I/O functions whenever possible, but adds additional functions for those operations that cannot be expressed conveniently.

4.7 The Basic I/O Functions Available In ANSI C

Although the Windows Sockets API does not allow a programmer to use basic I/O functions for network I/O, the original socket API does. The distinction is especially important for programmers who need to port application programs from the UNIX socket API to the Windows socket API. To understand how to port socket applications from UNIX to Windows, consider the six functions ANSI C uses for input/output. The table in Figure 4.3 lists the operations and their conventional meanings.

Operation	Meaning
open	Prepare a device or a file for input or output operations
close	Terminate use of a previously opened device or file
read	Obtain data from an input device or file, and place it in the application program's memory
write	Transmit data from the application program's memory to an output device or file
lseek	Move to a specific position in a file or device (this operation only applies to files or devices like disks)
ioctl†	Control a device or the software used to access it (e.g., specify the size of a buffer or change the character set mapping)

Figure 4.3 The basic I/O operations available in ANSI C. The information is
important for programmers who need to port applications from
the UNIX socket API to the Windows Sockets API.

When an application program calls *open* to initiate input or output, the system returns a small integer called a *file descriptor* that the application uses in further I/O operations. The call to *open* takes three arguments: the name of a file or device to open, a set of bit flags that controls special cases such as whether to create the file if it does not exist, and an access mode that specifies read/write protections for newly created files. For example, the code segment:

---

†*ioctl* stands for Input Output ConTroL.

```
int     desc;

desc = open("filename", O_RDWR, 0)
```

opens an existing file, *filename*, with a mode that allows both reading and writing. After obtaining the integer descriptor, *desc*, the application uses it in further I/O operations on the file. For example, the statement:

```
read(desc, buffer, 128);
```

reads *128* bytes of data from the file into array *buffer*.

Finally, when an application finishes using a file, it calls *close* to deallocate the descriptor and release associated resources (e.g., internal buffers):

```
close(desc);
```

4.8 History Of The UNIX Socket API

When designers added TCP/IP protocols to UNIX and created the socket API, they extended the conventional I/O facilities. First, they extended the set of file descriptors and made it possible for applications to create descriptors used for network communication. Second, they extended the *read* and *write* functions so they worked with the new network descriptors as well as with conventional file descriptors. Thus, when a UNIX application needs to send data across a TCP connection, it creates the appropriate descriptor, and then uses *write* to transfer data.

However, not all network communication fits easily into UNIX's *open-read-write-close* paradigm. An application must specify the local and remote protocol ports and the remote IP address it will use, whether it will use TCP or UDP, and whether it will initiate transfer or wait for an incoming connection (i.e., whether it wants to behave as a client or server). If it is a server, it must specify how many incoming connection requests the operating system should enqueue before rejecting them. Furthermore, if an application chooses to use UDP, it must be able to transfer UDP datagrams, not merely a stream of bytes. The designers of Berkeley UNIX added new procedures to the UNIX API to accommodate these special cases. In addition, the designers included procedures that make it unnecessary to use conventional I/O primitives; the Windows Sockets API uses the new procedures and does not generally use conventional I/O functions. The next chapter describes the Windows Sockets API in detail.

4.9 Summary

Because TCP/IP is designed for a multi-vendor environment, the protocol standards loosely specify the interface that application programs use, allowing operating system designers freedom in choosing how to implement it. The standards do discuss a conceptual interface, but it is intended only as an illustrative example. Although the standards present the conceptual interface as a set of procedures, designers are free to choose different procedures or to use an entirely different style of interaction (e.g., message passing).

The set of procedures available to an application defines an Application Program Interface (API). The API used to access TCP/IP protocol software is known as the socket API. The socket API was originally defined as part of the Berkeley UNIX operating system. The version defined for use with Windows operating systems is known as the Windows Sockets interface or WINSOCK.

The original socket API used with UNIX and the socket API used with Windows operating systems differ in an important way: the UNIX version allows an application to mix conventional I/O functions with socket functions. Thus, a programmer who ports a socket application from UNIX to Windows needs to understand the semantics of I/O functions such as *read*, *write*, and *close*.

A variety of API implementations are possible. Under older microcomputer systems, both the socket functions and TCP/IP code are linked into each application. Under Windows 95, both the socket API and TCP/IP reside in shared libraries known as DLLs; under Windows NT, TCP/IP resides in the operating system kernel, while the socket API resides in a DLL. On some UNIX systems, both the socket functions and TCP/IP code are part of the operating system. From a programmer's point of view, the implementation details are irrelevant – applications call procedures in the API without knowing how the API is implemented.

FOR FURTHER STUDY

Hall et. al. [1993] contains the original standard for Windows Sockets. It describes each of the socket functions, related database functions, and extensions that must be present in a sockets implementation to make it compliant with the standard. For each function, the document describes the semantics, lists the types of the arguments and return value, and lists the error codes that the function can return. Hall et. al. [1996] describes version 2.

EXERCISES

4.1 Examine a message-passing operating system. How would you extend the application program interface to accommodate network communication?

4.2 Compare the *Windows Sockets Interface* with the *Transport Layer Interface* (*TLI*) from AT&T. What are the major differences? How are the two similar? What reasons could designers have for choosing one design over the other?

4.3 On some computers, the hardware architecture limits the number of functions built into the operating system to a small number (e.g., 64 or 128). It can be difficult to add socket functions to such systems. How many functions are allowed in your local operating system?

4.4 Think about the hardware limit on operating system functions discussed in the previous exercise. How can an operating system designer add additional functions without changing the hardware?

4.5 Find out how the Korn shell uses */dev/tcp* to allow UNIX shell scripts to communicate with TCP. Is the same functionality needed in Windows systems? Why or why not?

4.6 Investigate the interpretive language *Perl*. How many socket functions are available to a Perl script? Which are not?

4.7 Find out when Windows 95 loads a DLL into memory. Does the operation occur when the application starts or when the application first calls one of the procedures in the DLL?

4.8 Read about DLLs in the vendor's manual. Can a DLL be unloaded once it has been loaded? Explain.

5

The Socket API

5.1 Introduction

The previous chapter describes the mechanisms used to provide communication between an application program and TCP/IP software. The chapter describes how an application invokes library routines, which then interact with TCP/IP protocols.

This chapter describes the details of the specific set of functions in the Windows Sockets API and explains how an application uses the functions to communicate. It covers concepts in general, and gives the intended use of each call. Later chapters show how clients and servers use these functions, and provide examples that illustrate many of the details.

5.2 The History Of Sockets

In the early 1980s, the Advanced Research Projects Agency (ARPA) funded a group at the University of California at Berkeley to transport TCP/IP software to the UNIX operating system and to make the resulting software available to other sites. As part of the project, the designers created an interface that applications use for network communication. When necessary, they extended the UNIX operating system by adding new procedures to allow applications to access TCP/IP protocols. Because the operating system was known as *Berkeley UNIX* or *BSD UNIX*, and the interface used an abstraction known as a *socket*, the API became known as the *Berkeley socket interface*†, or simply the *socket API*.

Because many computer vendors, especially workstation manufacturers like Sun Microsystems Incorporated, Tektronix Incorporated, and Digital Equipment Corporation, adopted the Berkeley UNIX operating system, the socket interface became avail-

---

†The socket interface is sometimes called the *Berkeley socket interface*.

47

able on many machines. Subsequently, Microsoft chose the socket interface as the primary network API for its operating systems. Thus, the socket interface has become a *de facto* standard throughout the computer industry.

5.3 Specifying A Protocol Interface

When designers consider how to add functions to an operating system that provide application programs access to TCP/IP protocol software, they must choose names for the functions and must specify the parameters that each function accepts. In so doing, they decide the scope of services that the functions supply and the style in which applications use them. Designers must also consider whether to make the interface specific to the TCP/IP protocols or whether to plan for additional protocols. Thus, the designers must choose one of two broad approaches:

- Define functions specifically to support TCP/IP communication.
- Define functions that support network communication in general, and use parameters to make TCP/IP communication a special case.

Differences between the two approaches are easiest to understand by their impact on the names of system functions and the parameters that the functions require. For example, in the first approach, a designer might choose to have a system function named *maketcpconnection*, while in the second, a designer might choose to create a general function *makeconnection* and use a parameter to specify the TCP protocol.

Because the designers at Berkeley wanted to accommodate multiple sets of communication protocols, they used the second approach. In fact, throughout the design, they provided for generality far beyond TCP/IP. They allowed for multiple *families* of protocols, with all TCP/IP protocols represented as a single family (family *PF_INET*). They also decided to have applications specify operations using a *type of service* required instead of specifying the protocol name. Thus, instead of specifying that it wants a TCP connection, an application requests the *stream transfer* type of service using the Internet family of protocols. We can summarize:

> *The socket interface provides generalized functions that support network communication using many possible protocols. Socket functions refer to all TCP/IP protocols as a single protocol family. The functions allow the programmer to specify the type of service required rather than the name of a specific protocol.*

The overall design of the socket API and the generality it provides have been debated since its inception. Some computer scientists argue that generality is unnecessary and merely makes application programs difficult to read. Others argue that having programmers specify the type of service instead of the specific protocol makes it easier to program because it frees the programmer from understanding the details of each protocol family. Finally, some commercial vendors of TCP/IP software have argued in favor of alternative interfaces because adding the socket API to a computer can require changes to the operating system, which usually requires a special license agreement and source code.

5.4 The Socket Abstraction

5.4.1 Socket Descriptors

In most operating systems, an application that needs to perform I/O asks the operating system to open a file. The system responds by creating a *file descriptor* that the application uses to access the file. From an application's point of view, a file descriptor is an integer that the application uses when reading or writing the file. Figure 5.1 illustrates how an operating system can implement file descriptors as an array of pointers to internal data structures.

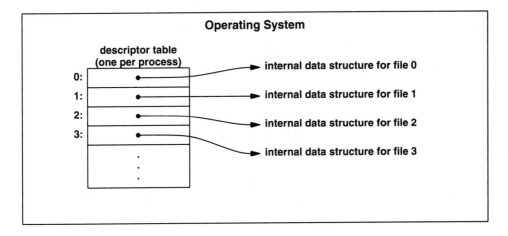

Figure 5.1 The per-process file descriptor table in UNIX. The operating system uses a process' descriptor table to store pointers to internal data structures for files that the process has opened. The process (application) uses the descriptor when referring to the file.

The operating system has a separate table for each program. To be precise, the system maintains one file descriptor table for each running process. When a process opens a file, the system places a pointer to the internal data structures for that file in the process' file descriptor table and returns the table index to the caller. The application program only needs to remember the descriptor and to use it in subsequent calls that request operations on the file. The operating system uses the descriptor as an index into the process' descriptor table, and follows the pointer to the data structures that hold all information about the file.

The socket interface adds a new abstraction for network communication, the *socket*. Like files, each active socket is identified by an integer called its *socket descriptor*. The Windows operating system keeps a separate table of socket descriptors for each process. Thus, an application can have both a file descriptor and a socket descriptor with the same value.

The socket API contains a function, *socket*, that an application calls to create a socket. The general idea underlying sockets is that a single system call is sufficient to create any socket because a socket is quite general. Once the socket has been created, an application must make additional calls to specify the details of its exact use. The paradigm will become clear after we examine the data structures the system maintains.

5.4.2 System Data Structures For Sockets

The easiest way to understand the socket abstraction is to envision the data structures in the operating system. When an application calls *socket*, the operating system allocates a new data structure to hold the information needed for communication, and fills in a new entry in the process' socket descriptor table with a pointer to the data structure. For example, Figure 5.2 illustrates a process' socket descriptor table after a call to *socket*†. In the example, arguments to the socket call have specified protocol family *PF_INET* and type of service *SOCK_STREAM*.

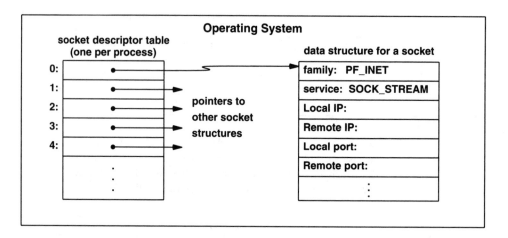

Figure 5.2 Conceptual operating system data structures after five calls to *socket*. The system keeps a separate socket descriptor table for each process; threads in the process share the table.

---

†Actual data structures are more complex than shown in Figure 5.2; the diagram illustrates the concept, not the details.

Although the internal data structure for a socket contains many fields, the system leaves most of them unfilled when it creates the socket. As we will see, the application that creates the socket must make additional procedure calls to fill in information in the socket data structure before the socket can be used.

5.4.3 Using Sockets

Once a socket has been created, it can be used to wait for an incoming connection or to initiate a connection. A socket used by a server to wait for an incoming connection is called a *passive socket*, while a socket used by a client to initiate a connection is called an *active socket*. The only difference between active and passive sockets lies in how applications use them; the sockets are created the same way initially.

5.5 Specifying An Endpoint Address

When a socket is created, it does not contain detailed information about how it will be used. In particular, the socket does not contain information about the addresses of either the local machine or the remote machine. Before an application uses a socket, it must specify one or both of these addresses.

TCP/IP protocols define a *communication endpoint* to consist of an IP address and a protocol port number. Other protocol families define their endpoint addresses in other ways. Because the socket abstraction accommodates multiple families of protocols, it does not specify how to define endpoint addresses nor does it define a particular protocol address format. Instead, it allows each protocol family to specify endpoints however it likes.

To allow protocol families the freedom to choose representations for their addresses the socket abstraction defines an *address family* for each type of address. A protocol family can use one or more address families to define address representations. The TCP/IP protocols all use a single address representation, with the address family denoted by the symbolic constant *AF_INET*.

In practice, much confusion arises between the TCP/IP protocol family, denoted *PF_INET*, and the address family it uses, denoted *AF_INET*. The chief problem is that both symbolic constants have the same numeric value (*2*), so programs that inadvertently use one in place of the other operate correctly. Even the original Berkeley UNIX source code contains examples of misuse. Programmers should observe the distinction, however, because it helps clarify the meaning of variables and makes programs more portable.

5.6 A Generic Address Structure

Application programs may need to manipulate protocol addresses without knowing the details of how every protocol family defines its address representation. For example, it may be necessary to write a procedure that accepts an arbitrary protocol endpoint specification as an argument and chooses one of several possible actions depending on the address type. To accommodate such programs, the socket system defines a generalized format that all endpoint addresses use. The generalized format consists of a pair:

(address family, endpoint address in that family)

where the address family field contains a constant that denotes one of the preassigned address types, and the endpoint address field contains an endpoint address using the standard representation for the specified address type.

In practice, the socket API provides declarations of predefined data types for address endpoints. Application programs use the predefined data types when they need to declare variables that store endpoint addresses or when they need to use an overlay to locate fields in a structure. The most general structure is known as a *sockaddr structure*. It contains a 2-byte address family identifier and a 14-byte array to hold an address†:

```
struct  sockaddr {          /* struct to hold an address */
     u_short sa_family;     /* type of address           */
     char    sa_data[14];   /* value of address          */
};
```

Unfortunately, not all address families define endpoints that fit into the *sockaddr* structure. For example, the Berkeley UNIX operating system also defines an *AF_UNIX* address family to specify what UNIX programmers think of as a named *pipe*. Endpoint addresses in the *AF_UNIX* family consist of UNIX path names that can be much longer than 14 bytes. Therefore, application programs should not use *sockaddr* in variable declarations because a variable declared to be of type *sockaddr* is not large enough to hold all possible endpoint addresses.

Confusion often arises in practice because the *sockaddr* structure accommodates addresses in the *AF_INET* family. Thus, TCP/IP software works correctly even if the programmer declares variables to be of type *sockaddr*. However, to keep programs portable and maintainable, TCP/IP code should not use the *sockaddr* structure in declarations. Instead, *sockaddr* should be used only as an overlay, and code should reference only the *sa_family* field in it.

Each protocol family that uses sockets defines the exact representation of its endpoint addresses, and the socket software provides corresponding structure declarations. Each TCP/IP endpoint address consists of a 2-byte field that identifies the address type (it must contain *AF_INET*), a 2-byte port number field, a 4-byte IP address field, and an 8-byte field that remains unused. Predefined structure *sockaddr_in* specifies the format:

---

†This text describes the structure as defined in the Windows Sockets API; more recent versions of the *sockaddr* structure include an 8-bit *sa_len* field that contains the total length.

```
struct   sockaddr_in {            /* struct to hold an address        */
        u_short sin_family;       /* type of address(always AF_INET)  */
        u_short sin_port;         /* protocol port number             */
        struct  in_addr sin_addr; /* IP address (declared to be       */
                                  /*  u_long on some systems)         */
        char    sin_zero[8];      /* unused (set to zero)             */
};
```

An application that uses TCP/IP protocols exclusively can use structure *sockaddr_in* exclusively; it never needs to use the *sockaddr* structure†. Thus,

> *When representing a TCP/IP communication endpoint, an application program uses structure* sockaddr_in, *which contains both an IP address and a protocol port number. Programmers must be careful when writing programs that use a mixture of protocols because some non-TCP/IP endpoint addresses require a larger structure.*

5.7 Functions In The Socket API

Socket calls can be separated into two groups: primary socket functions that provide access to the underlying functionality and other library routines that help the programmer. This section describes the procedures that provide the primary functionality needed by client and server applications.

The details of socket system calls, their parameters, and their semantics can seem overwhelming. Much of the complexity arises because sockets have parameters that allow programs to use them in many ways. A socket can be used by a client or by a server, for stream transfer (e.g., TCP) or datagram (e.g., UDP) communication, with a specific remote endpoint address (usually needed by a client) or with an unspecified remote endpoint address (usually needed by a server).

To help understand sockets, we will begin by examining the primary socket calls and describing how a straightforward client and server use them to communicate with TCP. Later chapters each discuss one way to use sockets, and illustrate many of the details and subtleties not covered here.

5.7.1 The WSAStartup Function

Programs using Windows Sockets must call *WSAStartup* before using sockets. The call requires two arguments. The program uses the first to specify the version of Windows Sockets that is requested; the operating system uses the second to return information about the version of Windows Sockets actually used. The first argument is an integer that gives the version number in hexadecimal (e.g., the hex constant *0x102* specifies version *2.1*). The second argument points to a *WSADATA* structure into which the operating system writes version information.

---

†Structure *sockaddr* is used to cast (i.e., change the type of) pointers or the results of system functions to make programs pass strict type checking.

WSAStartup is needed with the Windows operating systems because the system uses dynamically linked libraries (*DLLs*). Thus, instead of hardwiring code into the operating system, such systems bind to a version of the code at run-time. When a program calls *WSAStartup*, the system searches for an appropriate library and binds to it.

5.7.2 The WSACleanup Function

Once an application finishes using and closing sockets, the application calls *WSA-Cleanup* to deallocate all data structures and socket bindings. A program usually calls *WSACleanup* only when it is completely finished and ready to exit.

5.7.3 The Socket Function

An application calls *socket* to create a new socket that can be used for network communication. The call returns a descriptor for the newly created socket. Arguments to the call specify the protocol family that the application will use (e.g., *PF_INET* for TCP/IP) and the protocol or type of service it needs (i.e., stream or datagram). For a socket that uses the Internet protocol family, the protocol or type of service argument determines whether the socket will use TCP or UDP.

5.7.4 The Connect Function

After creating a socket, a client calls *connect* to establish an active connection to a remote server. An argument to *connect* allows the client to specify the remote endpoint, which includes the remote machine's IP address and protocol port number. Once a connection has been made, a client can transfer data across it.

5.7.5 The Send Function

Both clients and servers use *send* to send data across a TCP connection. Clients usually use *send* to transmit requests, while servers use it to transmit replies. A call to *send* requires four arguments. The application passes the descriptor of a socket to which the data should be sent, the address of the data to be sent, the length of the data, and bits that control transmission. Usually, *send* copies outgoing data into buffers in the operating system kernel, and allows the application to continue execution while it transmits the data across the network. If the system buffers become full, the call to *send* may block temporarily until TCP can send data across the network and make space in the buffer for new data.

5.7.6 The Recv Function

Both clients and servers use *recv* to receive data from a TCP connection. Usually, after a connection has been established, the server uses *recv* to receive a request that the client sends by calling *send*. After sending its request, the client uses *recv* to receive a reply.

To receive data from a connection, an application calls *recv* with four arguments. The first specifies the socket descriptor to use, the second specifies the address of a buffer, the third specifies the length of the buffer, and the fourth contains bits that control reception. *Recv* extracts data bytes that have arrived at the specified socket, and copies them to the user's buffer area. If no data has arrived, the call to *recv* blocks until it does. If more data has arrived than fits into the buffer, *recv* only extracts enough to fill the buffer. If less data has arrived than fits into the buffer, *recv* extracts all the data and returns the number of bytes it found.

Clients and servers can also use *recv* to receive messages from sockets that use UDP. As with the connection-oriented case, the caller supplies four arguments that identify a socket descriptor, the address of a buffer into which the data should be placed, the size of the buffer, and control bits. Each call to *recv* extracts one incoming UDP message (i.e., one user datagram). If the buffer cannot hold the entire message, *recv* fills the buffer, discards the remainder of the message, and returns an error code.

5.7.7 The Closesocket Function

Once a client or server finishes using a socket, it calls *closesocket* to deallocate it. If only one process is using the socket, *closesocket* immediately terminates the connection and deallocates the socket†. If several processes share a socket, *closesocket* decrements a reference count and deallocates the socket when the reference count reaches zero.

5.7.8 The Bind Function

When a socket is first created, it has no endpoint addresses (neither the local nor remote addresses are assigned). An application calls *bind* to specify the local endpoint address for a socket. The call takes arguments that specify a socket descriptor and an endpoint address. For TCP/IP protocols, the endpoint address uses the *sockaddr_in* structure, which includes both an IP address and a protocol port number. Primarily, servers use *bind* to specify the well-known port at which they will await connections.

5.7.9 The Listen Function

When a socket is created, the socket is neither *active* (i.e., ready for use by a client) nor *passive* (i.e., ready for use by a server) until the application takes further action. Connection-oriented servers call *listen* to place a socket in *passive mode* and make it ready to accept incoming connections.

---

†There is no socket reference count for the threads within a process; if one thread in a process closes a socket, the descriptor is deallocated for all threads in the process.

Most servers consist of an infinite loop that accepts the next incoming connection, handles it, and then returns to accept the next connection. Even if handling a given connection takes only a few milliseconds, it may happen that a new connection request arrives during the time the server is busy handling an existing request. To ensure that no connection request is lost, a server must pass *listen* two arguments that tell the operating system to enqueue connection requests for a socket. One argument to the *listen* call specifies a socket to be placed in passive mode, and the other specifies the size of the queue to be used for that socket.

5.7.10 The Accept Function

For TCP sockets, after a server calls *socket* to create a socket, *bind* to specify a local endpoint address, and *listen* to place it in passive mode, the server calls *accept* to extract the next incoming connection request. An argument to *accept* specifies the socket from which a connection should be accepted.

Accept creates a new socket for each new connection request, and returns the descriptor of the new socket to its caller. The server uses the new socket only for the new connection; it uses the original socket to accept additional connection requests. Once it has accepted a connection, the server can use the new socket to transfer data. After it finishes using the new socket, the server closes it.

5.7.11 Summary Of Socket Calls Used With TCP

The table in Figure 5.3 provides a brief summary of the functions in the Windows Sockets API.

5.8 Utility Routines For Integer Conversion

TCP/IP specifies a standard representation for binary integers used in protocol headers. The representation, known as *network byte order*, represents integers with the most significant byte first.

Although the protocol software hides most values used in headers from application programs, a programmer must be aware of the standard because some socket routines require arguments to be stored in network byte order. For example, the protocol port field of a *sockaddr_in* structure uses network byte order.

The socket routines include several functions that convert between network byte order and the local host's byte order. Programs should always call the conversion routines even if the local machine's byte order is the same as the network byte order because doing so makes the source code portable to an arbitrary architecture.

The conversion routines are divided into *short* and *long* sets to operate on 16-bit integers and 32-bit integers. Functions *htons* (*host to network short*) and *ntohs* (*network to host short*) convert a short integer from the host's native byte order to the network

byte order, and vice versa. Similarly, *htonl* and *ntohl* convert long integers from the host's native byte order to network byte order and vice versa. To summarize:

> *Software that uses TCP/IP calls functions* htons, ntohs, htonl *and* ntohl *to convert binary integers between the host's native byte order and network standard byte order. Doing so makes the source code portable to any machine, regardless of its native byte order.*

Function Name	Meaning
WSAStartup	Initialize the socket library (Windows only)
WSACleanup	Terminate use of socket library (Windows only)
socket	Create a descriptor for use in network communication
connect	Connect to a remote peer (client)
closesocket	Terminate communication and deallocate a descriptor
bind	Bind a local IP address and protocol port to a socket
listen	Place the socket in passive mode and set the number of incoming TCP connections the system will enqueue (server)
accept	Accept the next incoming connection (server)
recv	Acquire incoming data from a stream connection or the next incoming message
recvfrom	Receive the next incoming datagram and record its source endpoint address
select	Wait until the first of a specified set of sockets becomes ready for I/O
send	Send outgoing data or a message
sendto	Send an outgoing datagram to a specified endpoint address
shutdown	Terminate a TCP connection in one or both directions
getpeername	After a connection arrives, obtain the remote machine's endpoint address from a socket
getsockopt	Obtain the current options for a socket
setsockopt	Change the options for a socket

Figure 5.3 A summary of functions in the Windows Sockets API and the meaning of each.

5.9 Using Socket Calls In A Program

Figure 5.4 illustrates a sequence of calls made by a client and a server using TCP.

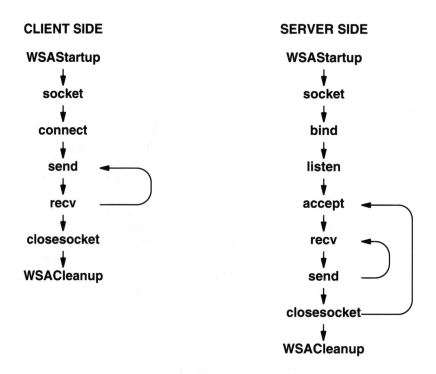

Figure 5.4 An example sequence of socket system calls made by a client and server using TCP. The server runs forever. It waits for a new connection on the well-known port, accepts the connection, interacts with the client, and then closes the connection.

The client creates a socket, calls *connect* to connect to the server, and then interacts using *send* to send requests and *recv* to receive replies. When it finishes using the connection, it calls *closesocket*. A server uses *bind* to specify the local (well-known) protocol port it will use, calls *listen* to set the length of the connection queue, and then enters a loop. Inside the loop, the server calls *accept* to wait until the next connection request arrives, uses *recv* and *send* to interact with the client, and finally uses *closesocket* to terminate the connection. The server then returns to the *accept* call, where it waits for the next connection.

5.10 Symbolic Constants For Socket Call Parameters

In addition to the system functions that implement sockets, most implementations of the socket API provide a set of predefined symbolic constants and data structure declarations that applications use to declare data and to specify arguments. For example, when specifying whether to use datagram service or stream service, an application program uses symbolic constants *SOCK_DGRAM* or *SOCK_STREAM*. To do so, the program must incorporate the appropriate definitions into each program. For example, in the C programming language, one uses the C preprocessor *include* statement. Usually, *include* statements appear at the beginning of a source file; they must appear before any use of the constants they define. The *include* statement needed for sockets under Windows has the form:

```
#include <winsock.h>
```

We will assume throughout the remainder of this text that applications always begin with the necessary include statement, even if it is not shown explicitly in the examples. To summarize:

> *Most implementations of the socket API supply predefined symbolic constants and data structure declarations used with the socket functions. C programs that use predefined constants must begin with preprocessor* include *statements that reference the files in which the definitions appear.*

5.11 Summary

The socket abstraction was introduced by the BSD UNIX operating system as a mechanism that allows application programs to interface with protocol software. Because many vendors have adopted sockets, they have become a *de facto* standard.

A program calls *socket* to create a socket and obtain a descriptor for it. Arguments to the *socket* call specify the protocol family to be used and the type of service required. All TCP/IP protocols are part of the Internet family, specified with symbolic constant *PF_INET*. The system creates an internal data structure for the socket, fills in the protocol family, and uses the type of service argument to select a specific protocol (usually either UDP or TCP).

Additional system calls allow the application to specify a local endpoint address (*bind*), to force the socket into passive mode for use by a server (*listen*), or to force the socket into active mode for use by a client (*connect*). Servers can make further calls to obtain incoming connection requests (*accept*), and both clients and servers can send or receive information (*recv* and *send*). Finally, both clients and servers can deallocate a socket once they have finished using it (*closesocket*).

The socket structure allows each protocol family to define one or more address representations. All TCP/IP protocols use the Internet address family, *AF_INET*, which specifies that an endpoint address contains both an IP address and a protocol port number. When an application specifies a communication endpoint to a socket function, it uses predefined structure *sockaddr_in*. If a client specifies that it needs an arbitrary, unused local protocol port, the TCP/IP software will select one.

Before an application program written in C can use the predefined structures and symbolic constants associated with sockets, it must include a file that defines them. In particular, we assume that all C programs begin with a statement that includes file *<winsock.h>*.

FOR FURTHER STUDY

Hall et. al. [1993] specifies each of the functions available with the Windows Sockets standard, including an exact description of arguments and return codes. Hall et. al. [1996] contains the same descriptions for version 2. Appendix 1 summarizes the information for the major functions used with sockets.

Leffler et. al. [1989] describes the *Berkeley Software Distribution (BSD)* socket system from which Windows Sockets was derived. Presotto and Ritchie [June 1990] describes an alternative to sockets that uses a file system namespace.

EXERCISES

5.1   Look at the *include* file for sockets (i.e., the file *<winsock.h>*). What socket types are allowed? Does the file specify any socket types that do not makes sense for TCP/IP protocols?

5.2   If your system has a clock with at least microsecond accuracy, measure how long it takes to execute each of the socket system calls. Why do some calls require orders of magnitude more time than others?

5.3   Read the manual pages for *connect* carefully. What network traffic is generated if one calls *connect* on a socket of type *SOCK_DGRAM*?

5.4   Arrange to monitor your local network while an application executes *connect* for the first time on a socket of type *SOCK_STREAM*. How many packets do you see?

6

Algorithms And Issues In Client Software Design

6.1 Introduction

Previous chapters consider the socket abstraction that applications use to interface with TCP/IP software, and review the basic functions in the Windows Sockets API. This chapter discusses the basic algorithms underlying client software. It shows how applications become clients by initiating communication, how they use TCP or UDP protocols to contact a server, and how they use socket calls to interact with those protocols. The next chapter continues the discussion, and shows complete client programs that implement the ideas discussed here.

6.2 Learning Algorithms Instead Of Details

Because TCP/IP provides rich functionality that allows programs to communicate in a variety of ways, an application that uses TCP/IP must specify many details about the desired communication. For example, the application must specify whether it wishes to act as a client or a server, the endpoint address (or addresses) it will use, whether it will communicate with a connectionless or connection-oriented protocol, how it will enforce authorization and protection rules, and details such as the size of the buffers it will need.

So far, we have examined the set of operations available to an application without discussing how applications should use them. Unfortunately, knowing the low-level details of all possible socket functions and their exact parameters does not provide programmers with an understanding of how to build well-designed, distributed programs. In fact, while a general understanding of the functions used for network communication is important, few programmers remember all the details. Instead, they learn and remember the possible ways in which programs can interact across a network, and they understand the trade-offs of each possible design. In essence, programmers know enough about the algorithms underlying distributed computing to make design decisions and to choose among alternative algorithms quickly. They then consult a programming manual to find the details needed to write a program that implements a particular algorithm on a particular system. The point is that if the programmer knows *what* a program should do, finding out *how* to do it is straightforward.

> *Although programmers need to understand the conceptual capabilities of the protocol interface, they should concentrate on learning about ways to structure communicating programs instead of memorizing the details of a particular interface.*

6.3 Client Architecture

Applications that act as clients are conceptually simpler than applications that act as servers for several reasons. First, most client software does not explicitly handle concurrent interactions with multiple servers. Second, most client software executes as a conventional application program. Unlike server software, client software does not usually require special privilege because it does not usually access privileged protocol ports. Third, most client software does not need to enforce protections. Instead, client programs can rely on the operating system to enforce protections automatically. In fact, designing and implementing client software is so straightforward that experienced application programmers can learn to write basic client applications quickly. The next sections discuss client software in general; later sections will focus on the differences between clients that use TCP and those that use UDP.

6.4 Identifying The Location Of A Server

Client software can use one of several methods to find a server's IP address and protocol port number. A client can:

- have the server's domain name or IP address specified as a constant when the program is compiled,
- require the user to identify the server when invoking the program,
- obtain information about the server from stable storage (e.g., from a file on a local disk), or
- use a separate protocol to find a server (e.g., multicast or broadcast a message to which all servers respond).

Specifying the server's address as a constant makes the client software faster and less dependent on a particular local computing environment. However, it also means that the client must be recompiled if the server is moved. More important, it means that the client cannot be used with an alternative server, even temporarily for testing. As a compromise, some clients fix a machine name instead of an IP address. Fixing the name instead of an address delays the binding until run-time. It allows a site to choose a generic name for the server and add an alias to the domain name system for that name. Using aliases permits a site manager to change the location of a server without changing client software. To move the server, the manager needs to change only the alias. For example, it is possible to add an alias for *mailhost* in the local domain and to arrange for all clients to look up the string "mailhost" instead of a specific machine. Because all clients reference the generic name instead of a specific machine, the system manager can change the location of the mail host without recompiling client software.

Storing the server's address in a file makes the client more flexible, but it means that the client program cannot execute unless the file is available. Thus, the client software cannot be transported to another machine easily.

While using a broadcast protocol to find servers works in a small, local environment, it does not scale well to large internets. Furthermore, use of a dynamic search mechanism introduces additional complexity for both clients and servers, and adds additional broadcast traffic to the network.

To avoid unnecessary complexity and dependence on the computing environment, most clients solve the problem of server specification in a simple manner: they require the user to supply an argument that identifies the server when invoking the client program. Building client software to accept the server address as an argument makes the client software general and eliminates dependency on the computing environment.

> *Allowing the user to specify a server address when invoking client software makes the client program more general and makes it possible to change server locations.*

An important point to note is that using an argument to specify the server's address results in the most flexibility. A program that accepts an address argument can be combined with other programs that extract the server address from disk, find the address using a remote nameserver, or search for it with a broadcast protocol. Thus,

> *Building client software that accepts a server address as an argument makes it easy to build extended versions of the software that use other ways to find the server address (e.g., read the address from a file on disk).*

Some services require an explicit server, while others can use any available server. For example, when a user invokes a remote login client, the user has a specific target machine in mind; logging into another machine usually does not make sense. However, if the user merely wants to find the current time of day, the user does not care which server responds. To accommodate such services, the designer can modify any of the server look-up methods discussed above so they supply a set of server names instead of a single name. Clients must also be changed so they try each server in a set until they find one that responds.

6.5 Parsing An Address Argument

On computer systems that use a textual interface, a user specifies arguments on the command line when invoking a client program. On computer systems that use a graphical user interface, the system presents a window that asks a user to fill in arguments. In most cases the arguments are stored in character strings; the client program uses an argument's syntax to interpret its meaning. For example, most client software requires the user to enter the domain name of the machine on which the server operates:

merlin.cs.purdue.edu

or an IP address in dotted decimal notation:

128.10.2.3

To determine whether the user has specified a name or an address, the client scans the argument. If it contains alphabetic characters, the client interprets the argument as a name. If it contains only digits and decimal points, the client assumes the argument is a dotted decimal address and parses it accordingly.

Of course, client programs sometimes need additional information beyond the server's machine name or IP address. In particular, fully parameterized client software allows a user to specify a protocol port as well as a machine. It is possible to use an additional argument or to encode such information in a single string. For example, to specify the protocol port associated with the *smtp* service on machine with name *merlin.cs.purdue.edu*, the client could accept two arguments:

merlin.cs.purdue.edu smtp

or could combine both the machine name and protocol port into a single argument:

merlin.cs.purdue.edu:smtp

Although each client can choose the details of its argument syntax independently, having many clients with their own syntax can be confusing. From the user's point of view, consistency is always important. Thus, programmers are advised to follow whatever conventions their local system uses for client software. For example, if most applications require a user to specify the server's machine and protocol port separately, new client software should use two arguments instead of one.

6.6 Looking Up A Domain Name

A client must specify the address of a server using structure *sockaddr_in*. Doing so means converting an address in dotted decimal notation (or a domain name in text form) into a 32-bit IP address represented in binary. Converting from dotted decimal notation to binary is trivial. Converting from a domain name, however, requires considerably more effort. The socket interface includes functions, *inet_addr* and *gethostbyname*, that perform the conversions. *Inet_addr* takes an ASCII string that contains a dotted decimal address and returns the equivalent IP address in binary. *Gethostbyname* takes an ASCII string that contains the domain name for a machine. It returns the address of a *hostent* structure that contains, among other things, the host's IP address in binary. The *hostent* structure is declared in include file *winsock.h*:

```
struct hostent {
        char FAR*       h_name;      /* official host name  */
        char FAR* FAR*  h_aliases;   /* other aliases       */
        short           h_addrtype;  /* address type        */
        short           h_length;    /* address length      */
        char FAR* FAR*  h_addr_list; /* list of addresses   */
};
#define  h_addr  h_addr_list[0]
```

Fields that contain names and addresses must be lists because hosts that have multiple interfaces also have multiple names and addresses. For compatibility with earlier versions, the file also defines the identifier *h_addr* to refer to the first location in the host address list. Thus, a program can use *h_addr* as if it were a field of the structure.

Consider a simple example of name conversion. Suppose a client has been passed the domain name *merlin.cs.purdue.edu* in string form and needs to obtain the IP address. The client can call *gethostbyname* as in:

```
struct  hostent *hptr;
char    *examplenam = "merlin.cs.purdue.edu";

if ( hptr = gethostbyname( examplenam ) ) {
        /* IP address is now in  hptr->h_addr */
} else {
        /* error in name - handle it */
}
```

If the call is successful, *gethostbyname* returns a pointer to a valid *hostent* structure. If the name cannot be mapped into an IP address, the call returns a *NULL* pointer. Thus, the client examines the value that *gethostbyname* returns to determine if an error occurred.

6.7 Looking Up A Well-Known Port By Name

Most client programs must look up the protocol port for the specific service they wish to invoke. For example, a client of an SMTP mail server needs to look up the well-known port assigned to SMTP. To do so, the client invokes library function *getservbyname*, which takes two arguments: a string that specifies the desired service and a string that specifies the protocol being used. It returns a pointer to a structure of type *servent*, also defined in include file *winsock.h*:

```
struct   servent {
            char FAR*          s_name;     /* official service name */
            char FAR* FAR* s_aliases;      /* other aliases         */
            short              s_port;     /* port for this service */
            char FAR*          s_proto;    /* protocol to use       */
};
```

If a TCP client needs to look up the official protocol port number for SMTP, it calls *getservbyname*, as in the following example:

```
struct   servent *sptr;

if (sptr = getservbyname( "smtp", "tcp" )) {
        /* port number is now in sptr->s_port */
} else {
        /* error occurred - handle it */
}
```

6.8 Port Numbers And Network Byte Order

Function *getservbyname* returns the protocol port for the service in network byte order. Chapter 5 explains the concept of network byte order, and describes library routines that convert from network byte order to the byte order used on the local machine. It is sufficient to understand that *getservbyname* returns the port value in exactly the form needed for use in the *sockaddr_in* structure, but the representation may not agree with the local machine's usual representation. Thus, if a program prints out the value that *getservbyname* returns without converting to local byte order, it may appear to be incorrect.

6.9 Looking Up A Protocol By Name

The socket interface provides a mechanism that allows a client or server to map a protocol name to the integer constant assigned to that protocol. Library function *getprotobyname* performs the look-up. A call passes the protocol name in a string argument, and *getprotobyname* returns the address of a structure of type *protoent*. If *getprotobyname* cannot access the database or if the specified name does not exist, it returns a *NULL* pointer. The database of protocol names allows a site to define aliases for each name. The *protoent* structure has a field for the official protocol name as well as a field that points to the list of aliases. The C include file *winsock.h* contains the structure declaration:

```
struct  protoent {
        char FAR*      p_name;    /* official protocol name   */
        char FAR* FAR* p_aliases; /* list of aliases allowed  */
        short          p_proto;   /* official protocol number */
};
```

If a client needs to look up the official protocol number for UDP, it calls *getprotobyname*, as in the following example:

```
struct  protoent *pptr;

if (pptr = getprotobyname( "udp" )) {
        /* official protocol number is now in pptr->p_proto */
} else {
        /* error occurred - handle it */
}
```

6.10 The TCP Client Algorithm

Building client software is usually easier than building server software. Because TCP handles all reliability and flow control problems, building a client that uses TCP is the most straightforward of all network programming tasks. A TCP client follows Algorithm 6.1 to form a connection to a server and communicate with it. The sections following the algorithm discuss each of its steps in more detail.

Algorithm 6.1

1. Find the IP address and protocol port number of the server with which communication is desired.
2. Allocate a socket.
3. Specify that the connection needs an arbitrary, unused protocol port on the local machine, and allow TCP to choose one.
4. Connect the socket to the server.
5. Communicate with the server using the application-level protocol (this usually involves sending requests and awaiting replies).
6. Close the connection.

Algorithm 6.1 A connection-oriented client. The client application allocates a socket and connects it to a server. It then sends requests across the connection and receives replies back.

6.11 Allocating A Socket

Previous sections have already discussed the methods used to find the server's IP address and the *socket* function used to allocate a communication socket. Clients that use TCP must specify protocol family *PF_INET* and service *SOCK_STREAM*. A program begins with an *include* statement that references a file that contains the definitions of symbolic constants used in the call and a declaration of the variable used to hold the socket descriptor. If more than one protocol in the family, specified by the first argument, offers the service requested by the second argument, the third argument to the *socket* call identifies a particular protocol. In the case of the Internet protocol family, only TCP offers the *SOCK_STREAM* service. Thus, the third argument is irrelevant; zero should be used.

```
#include <winsock.h>

SOCKET    s;

s = socket(PF_INET, SOCK_STREAM, 0);
```

6.12 Choosing A Local Protocol Port Number

An application needs to specify remote and local endpoint addresses for a socket before it can be used in communication. A server operates at a well-known protocol port address, which all clients must know. However, a TCP client does not operate on a preassigned port. Instead, it must select a local protocol port to use for its endpoint address. In general, the client does not care which port it uses as long as: (1) the port does not conflict with the ports that other applications on the machine are already using and (2) the port has not been assigned to a well-known service.

Of course, when a client needs a local protocol port, it could choose an arbitrary port at random until it finds one that meets the criteria given above. However, the socket interface makes choosing a client port much simpler because it provides a way that the client can allow TCP to choose a local port automatically. The choice of a local port that meets the criteria listed above happens as a side-effect of the *connect* call.

6.13 A Fundamental Problem In Choosing A Local IP Address

When forming a connection endpoint, a client must choose a local IP address as well as a local protocol port number. For a host that attaches to one network, the choice of a local IP address is trivial. However, because gateways (routers) or multi-homed hosts have multiple IP addresses, making the choice can be difficult.

In general, the difficulty in choosing an IP address arises because the correct choice depends on routing and applications seldom have access to routing information. To understand why, imagine a computer with multiple network interfaces and, therefore, multiple IP addresses. Before an application can use TCP, it must have an endpoint address for the connection. When TCP communicates with a foreign destination, it encapsulates each TCP segment in an IP datagram and passes the datagram to the IP software. IP uses the remote destination address and its routing table to select a next-hop address and a network interface that it can use to reach the next hop.

Herein lies the problem: the IP source address in an outgoing datagram should match the IP address of the network interface over which IP routes the datagram. However, if an application chooses one of the machine's IP addresses at random, it might select an address that does not match that of the interface over which IP routes the traffic.

In practice, a client may appear to work even if the programmer chooses an incorrect address because packets may travel back to the client by a different route than they travel to the server. However, using an incorrect address violates the specification, makes network management difficult and confusing, and makes the program less reliable.

To solve the problem, the socket functions make it possible for an application to leave the local IP address field unfilled and to allow TCP/IP software to choose a local IP address automatically at the time the client connects to a server.

*Because choosing the correct local IP address requires the applica-
tion to interact with IP routing software, TCP client software usually
leaves the local endpoint address unfilled, and allows TCP/IP
software to select the correct local IP address and an unused local
protocol port number automatically.*

6.14 Connecting A TCP Socket To A Server

The *connect* function allows a TCP client to initiate a connection. In terms of the
underlying protocol, *connect* forces the initial TCP 3-way handshake. The call to *connect* does not return until a TCP connection has been established or TCP reaches a
timeout threshold and gives up. The call returns *0* if the connection attempt succeeds or
SOCKET_ERROR if it fails. *Connect* takes three arguments:

```
retcode = connect(s, remaddr, remaddrlen)
```

where *s* is the descriptor for a socket, *remaddr* is the address of a structure of type
sockaddr_in that specifies the remote endpoint to which a connection is desired, and
remaddrlen is the length (in bytes) of the second argument.

Connect performs four tasks. First, it tests to ensure that the specified socket is
valid and that it has not already been connected. Second, it fills in the remote endpoint
address in the socket from the second argument. Third, it chooses a local endpoint address for the connection (IP address and protocol port number) if the socket does not
have one. Fourth, it initiates a TCP connection, and returns a value to tell the caller
whether the connection succeeded.

6.15 Communicating With The Server Using TCP

Assuming the *connect* call succeeds in establishing a connection, the client can use
the connection to communicate with the server. Usually, the application protocol specifies a *request-response interaction* in which the client sends a sequence of *requests* and
waits for a *response* to each.

Usually, a client calls *send* to transmit each request and *recv* to await a response.
For the simplest application protocols, the client sends only a single request and receives only a single response. More complicated application protocols require the client
to iterate, sending a request and waiting for a response before sending the next request.
The following code illustrates the request-response interaction by showing how a program writes a simple request over a TCP connection and reads a response:

```
/* Example code segment */

#define BLEN 120      /* buffer length to use */
char    *req = "request of some sort";
char    buf[BLEN];    /* buffer for answer     */
char    *bptr;        /* pointer to buffer     */
int     n;            /* number of bytes read */
int     buflen;       /* space left in buffer */

bptr = buf;
buflen = BLEN;


/* send request */

send(s, req, strlen(req), 0);

/* read response (may come in many pieces) */

n = recv(s, bptr, buflen, 0);
while (n != SOCKET_ERROR && n != 0) {
        bptr += n;
        buflen -= n;
        n = recv(s, bptr, buflen, 0);
}
```

6.16 Reading A Response From A TCP Connection

The code in the previous example shows a client that sends a small message to a server and expects a small response (less than *120* bytes). The code contains a single call to *send*, but makes repeated calls to *recv*. As long as the call to *recv* returns data, the code decrements the count of space available in the buffer and moves the buffer pointer forward past the data read. Iteration is necessary on input, even if the application at the other end of the connection sends only a small amount of data because TCP is not a block-oriented protocol. Instead, TCP is stream-oriented: it guarantees to deliver the sequence of bytes that the sender writes, but it does not guarantee to deliver them in the same grouping as they were written. TCP may choose to break a block of data into pieces and transmit each piece in a separate segment (e.g., it may choose to divide the data such that each piece fills the maximum sized segment, or it may need to send a small piece if the receiver does not have sufficient buffer space for a large one). Alternatively, TCP may choose to accumulate many bytes in its output buffer before sending a segment (e.g., to fill a datagram). As a result, the receiving application may receive data in small chunks, even if the sending application passes it to TCP in a single call to *send*. Or, the receiving application may receive data in a large chunk, even if the sending application passes it to TCP in a series of calls to *send*. The idea is fundamental to programming with TCP:

> *Because TCP does not preserve record boundaries, any program that reads from a TCP connection must be prepared to accept data a few bytes at a time. This rule holds even if the sending application writes data in large blocks.*

6.17 Closing A TCP Connection

6.17.1 The Need For Partial Close

When an application finishes using a connection completely, it can call *closesocket* to terminate the connection gracefully and deallocate the socket. However, closing a connection is seldom simple because TCP allows two-way communication. Thus, closing a connection usually requires coordination among the client and server.

To understand the problem, consider a client and server that use the request-response interaction described above. The client software repeatedly issues requests to which the server responds. On one hand, the server cannot terminate the connection because it cannot know whether the client will send additional requests. On the other hand, while the client knows when it has no more requests to send, it may not know whether all data has arrived from the server. The latter is especially important for application protocols that transfer arbitrary amounts of data in response to a request (e.g., the response to a database query).

6.17.2 A Partial Close Operation

To resolve the connection shutdown problem, most implementations of the socket interface include an additional primitive that permits applications to shut down a TCP connection in one direction. The *shutdown* function takes two arguments, a socket descriptor and a direction specification, and shuts down the socket in the specified direction:

```
errcode = shutdown(s, direction);
```

The *direction* argument is an integer. If it contains *0*, no further input is allowed. If it contains *1*, no further output is allowed. Finally, if the value is *2*, the connection is shutdown in both directions.

The advantage of a partial close should now be clear: when a client finishes sending requests, it can use *shutdown* to specify that it has no further data to send without deallocating the socket. The underlying protocol reports the shutdown to the remote machine, where the server application program receives an *end-of-file* signal. Once the server detects an end-of-file, it knows no more requests will arrive. After sending its last response, the server can close the connection. To summarize:

> *The partial close mechanism removes ambiguity for application proto-*
> *cols that transmit arbitrary amounts of information in response to a*
> *request. In such cases, the client issues a partial close after its last*
> *request; the server then closes the connection after its last response.*

6.18 Programming A UDP Client

At first glance, programming a UDP client seems like an easy task. Algorithm 6.2 shows that the basic UDP client algorithm is similar to the client algorithm for TCP (Algorithm 6.1).

Algorithm 6.2

1. Find the IP address and protocol port number of the server with which communication is desired.
2. Allocate a socket.
3. Specify that the communication needs an arbitrary, unused protocol port on the local machine, and allow UDP to choose one.
4. Specify the server to which messages must be sent.
5. Communicate with the server using the application-level protocol (this usually involves sending requests and awaiting replies).
6. Close the socket.

Algorithm 6.2 A connectionless client. The sending program creates a connected socket and uses it to send one or more requests iteratively. This algorithm ignores the issue of reliability.

The first few steps of the UDP client algorithm are much like the corresponding steps of the TCP client algorithm. A UDP client obtains the server address and protocol port number, and then allocates a socket for communication.

6.19 Connected And Unconnected UDP Sockets

Client applications can use UDP in one of two basic modes: *connected* and *uncon-*
nected. In connected mode, the client uses the *connect* call to specify a remote endpoint address (i.e., the server's IP address and protocol port number). Once it has specified the remote endpoint, the client can send and receive messages much like a TCP client does. In unconnected mode, the client does not connect the socket to a specific remote

endpoint. Instead, it specifies the remote destination each time it sends a message. The chief advantage of connected UDP sockets lies in their convenience for conventional client software that interacts with only one server at a time: the application only needs to specify the server once no matter how many datagrams it sends. The chief advantage of unconnected sockets lies in their flexibility; the client can wait to decide which server to contact until it has a request to send. Furthermore, the client can easily send each request to a different server.

> *UDP sockets can be* connected, *making it convenient to interact with a specific server, or they can be* unconnected, *making it necessary for the application to specify the server's address each time it sends a message.*

6.20 Using Connect With UDP

Although a client can connect a socket of type *SOCK_DGRAM*, the *connect* call does not initiate any packet exchange, nor does it test the validity of the remote endpoint address. Instead, it merely records the remote endpoint information in the socket data structure for later use. Thus, when applied to *SOCK_DGRAM* sockets, *connect* only stores an address. Even if the *connect* call succeeds, it does not mean that the remote endpoint address is valid or that the server is reachable.

6.21 Communicating With A Server Using UDP

After a UDP client calls *connect*, it can use *send* to send a message or *recv* to receive a response. Unlike TCP, UDP provides message transfer. Each time the client calls *send*, UDP sends a single message to the server. The message contains all the data passed to *send*. Similarly, each call to *recv* returns one complete message. Assuming the client has specified a sufficiently large buffer, the *recv* call returns all the data from the next message. Therefore, a UDP client does not need to make repeated calls to *recv* to obtain a single message.

6.22 Closing A Socket That Uses UDP

A UDP client calls *closesocket* to close a socket and release the resources associated with it. Once a socket has been closed, the UDP software will reject further messages that arrive addressed to the protocol port that the socket had allocated. However, the machine on which the *closesocket* occurs does not inform the remote endpoint that the socket is closed. Therefore, an application that uses connectionless transport must be designed so the remote side knows how long to retain a socket before closing it.

6.23 Partial Close For UDP

Shutdown can be used with a connected UDP socket to stop further transmission in a given direction. Unfortunately, unlike the partial close on a TCP connection, when applied to a UDP socket, *shutdown* does not send any messages to the other side. Instead, it merely marks the local socket as unwilling to transfer data in the direction(s) specified. Thus, if a client shuts down further output on its socket, the server will not receive any indication that the communication has ceased.

6.24 A Warning About UDP Unreliability

Our simplistic UDP client algorithm ignores a fundamental aspect of UDP: namely, that it provides unreliable datagram delivery. While a simplistic UDP client can work well on local networks that exhibit low loss, low delay, and no packet reordering, clients that follow our algorithm will not work across a complex internet. To work in an internet environment, a client must implement reliability through timeout and retransmission. It must also handle the problems of duplicate or out-of-order packets. Adding reliability can be difficult, and requires expertise in protocol design.

> *Client software that uses UDP must implement reliability with techniques like packet sequencing, acknowledgements, timeouts, and retransmission. Designing protocols that are correct, reliable, and efficient for an internet environment requires considerable expertise.*

6.25 Summary

Client programs are among the most simple network programs. The client must obtain the server's IP address and protocol port number before it can communicate; to increase flexibility, client programs often require the user to identify the server when invoking the client. The client then converts the server's address from dotted decimal notation into binary, or uses the domain name system to convert from a textual machine name into an IP address.

The TCP client algorithm is straightforward: a TCP client allocates a socket and connects it to a server. The client uses *send* to send requests to the server and *recv* to receive replies. Once it finishes using a connection, either the client or server invokes *closesocket* to terminate it.

Although a client must explicitly specify the endpoint address of the server with which it wishes to communicate, it can allow TCP/IP software to choose an unused protocol port number and to fill in the correct local IP address. Doing so avoids the problem that can arise on a gateway (router) or multi-homed host when a client inadvertently chooses an IP address that differs from the IP address of the interface over which IP routes the traffic.

The client uses *connect* to specify a remote endpoint address for a socket. When used with TCP, *connect* initiates a 3-way handshake and ensures that communication is possible. When used with UDP, *connect* merely records the server's endpoint address for later use.

Connection shutdown can be difficult if neither the client nor the server know exactly when communication has ended. To solve the problem, the socket interface supplies the *shutdown* primitive that causes a partial close and lets the other side know that no more data will arrive. A client uses *shutdown* to close the path leading to the server; the server receives an end-of-file signal on the connection that indicates the client has finished. After the server finishes sending its last response, it uses *closesocket* to terminate the connection.

FOR FURTHER STUDY

Many RFCs that define protocols also suggest algorithms or implementation techniques for client code. Umar [1997b] discusses object-oriented client-server architectures.

EXERCISES

6.1 Read about the *sendto* and *recvfrom* socket calls. Do they work with sockets using TCP or sockets using UDP?

6.2 When the domain name system resolves a machine name, it returns a set of one or more IP addresses. Why?

6.3 Build client software that uses *gethostbyname* to look up machine names at your site and print all information returned. Which official names, if any, surprised you? Do you tend to use official machine names or aliases? Describe the circumstances, if any, when aliases may not work correctly.

6.4 Measure the time required to look up a machine name (*gethostbyname*). Repeat the test for both valid and invalid names. Does a look-up for an invalid name take substantially longer than for a valid one? Explain any differences you observe.

6.5 Use a network monitor to watch the network traffic your computer generates when you look up an IP address name using *gethostbyname*. Run the experiment more than one time for each machine name you resolve. Explain the differences in network traffic between look-ups.

6.6 To test whether your machine's local byte order is the same as the network byte order, write a program that uses *getservbyname* to look up the *ECHO* service for UDP and then prints the resulting protocol port value. If the local byte order and network byte order agree, the value will be *7*.

6.7 Write a program that allocates a local protocol port, closes the socket, delays a few seconds, and allocates another local port. Run the program on an idle machine and on a busy timesharing system. Which port values did your program receive on each system? If they are not the same, explain.

6.8 Under what circumstances can a client program use *closesocket* instead of *shutdown*?

6.9 Should a client use the same protocol port number each time it begins? Why or why not?

6.10 If a client program contains multiple threads, can each use the same protocol port number to form connections to different servers? The same server? Explain.

7

Example Client Software

7.1 Introduction

The previous chapter discusses the basic algorithms underlying client applications as well as specific techniques used to implement those algorithms. This chapter gives examples of complete, working client programs that illustrate the concepts in more detail. The examples use UDP as well as TCP. Most important, the chapter shows how a programmer can build a library of procedures that hide the details of socket calls and make it easier to construct client software that is portable and maintainable.

7.2 The Importance Of Small Examples

TCP/IP defines a myriad of services and the standard application protocols for accessing them. The services range in complexity from the trivial (e.g., a character generator service used only for testing protocol software) to the complex (e.g., a file transfer service that provides authentication and protection). The examples in this chapter and the next few chapters concentrate on implementations of client-server software for simple services. Later chapters review client-server applications for several of the complex services.

While it may seem that the protocols used in the examples do not offer interesting or useful services, studying them is important. First, because the services themselves require little code, the client and server software that implements them is easy to understand. More important, the small program size highlights fundamental algorithms and illustrates clearly how client and server programs use system functions. Second, studying simple services provides the reader with an intuition about the relative size of services and the number of services available. Having an intuitive understanding of small services will be especially important for the chapters that discuss the need for multiprotocol and multiservice designs.

7.3 Hiding Details

Most programmers understand the advantage of dividing large, complex programs into a set of procedures: a modular program becomes easier to understand, debug, and modify than an equivalent monolithic program. If programmers design procedures carefully, they can reuse them in other programs. Finally, choosing procedures carefully can also make a program easier to port to new computer systems.

Conceptually, procedures raise the level of the language that programmers use by hiding details. Programmers working with the low-level facilities available in most programming languages find programming tedious and prone to error. They also find themselves repeating basic segments of code in each program they write. Using procedures helps avoid repetition by providing higher-level operations. Once a particular algorithm has been encoded in a procedure, the programmer can use it in many programs without having to consider the implementation details again.

A careful use of procedures is especially important when building client and server programs. First, because network software includes declarations for items like endpoint addresses, building programs that use network services involves a myriad of tedious details not found in conventional programs. Using procedures to hide those details reduces the chance for error. Second, much of the code needed to allocate a socket, bind addresses, and form a network connection is repeated in each client; placing it in procedures allows programmers to reuse the code instead of replicating it. Third, because TCP/IP was designed to interconnect heterogeneous machines, network applications often operate on many different machine architectures. Programmers can use procedures to isolate operating system dependencies, making it easier to port code to a new machine.

7.4 An Example Procedure Library For Client Programs

To understand how procedures can make the programming task easier, consider the problem of building client programs. To establish connectivity with a server, a client must choose a protocol (e.g., TCP or UDP), look up the server's machine name, look up and map the desired service into a protocol port number, allocate a socket, and connect it. Writing the code for each of these steps from scratch for each application wastes time. Furthermore, if programmers ever need to change any of the details, they have to modify each application. To minimize programming time, a programmer can write the code once, place it in a procedure, and simply call the procedure from each client program.

The first step of designing a procedure library is abstraction: a programmer must imagine high-level operations that would make writing programs simpler. For example, an application programmer might imagine two procedures that handle the work of allocating and connecting a socket:

$$socket = connectTCP(\text{\textit{machine, service}});$$

and

$$socket = connectUDP(\text{\textit{machine, service}});$$

It is important to understand that this is not a prescription for the ''right'' set of abstractions, it merely gives one possible way to form such a set. The important idea is:

> *The procedural abstraction allows programmers to define high-level operations, share code among applications, and reduce the chances of making mistakes with small details. Our example procedures used throughout this text merely illustrate one possible approach; programmers should feel free to choose their own abstractions.*

7.5 Implementation Of ConTCP

Because both of the proposed procedures, *connectTCP* and *connectUDP*, need to allocate a socket and fill in basic information, we chose to place all the low-level code in a third procedure, *connectsock*, and to implement both higher-level operations as simple calls. File *conTCP.cpp* illustrates the concept:

```
/* conTCP.cpp - connectTCP */

#include <winsock.h>

SOCKET  connectsock(const char *, const char *, const char *);

/*------------------------------------------------------------------------
 * connectTCP - connect to a specified TCP service on a specified host
 *------------------------------------------------------------------------
 */
SOCKET
connectTCP(const char *host, const char *service )
{
        return connectsock( host, service, "tcp");
}
```

7.6 Implementation Of ConUDP

File *conUDP.cpp* shows how *connectsock* can be used to establish a connected socket that uses UDP.

```
/* conUDP.cpp - connectUDP */

#include <winsock.h>

SOCKET  connectsock(const char *, const char *, const char *);

/*------------------------------------------------------------------------
 * connectUDP - connect to a specified UDP service on a specified host
 *------------------------------------------------------------------------
 */
SOCKET
connectUDP(const char *host, const char *service )
{
        return connectsock(host, service, "udp");
}
```

7.7 A Procedure That Forms Connections

Procedure *connectsock* contains all the code needed to allocate a socket and connect it. The caller specifies whether to create a UDP socket or a TCP socket.

```
/* consock.cpp - connectsock */

#include <stdlib.h>
#include <stdio.h>
#include <string.h>
#include <winsock.h>

#ifndef INADDR_NONE
#define INADDR_NONE     0xffffffff
#endif  /* INADDR_NONE */

void    errexit(const char *, ...);

/*------------------------------------------------------------------------
 * connectsock - allocate & connect a socket using TCP or UDP
 *------------------------------------------------------------------------
```

```
 */
SOCKET
connectsock(const char *host, const char *service, const char *transport )
{
        struct hostent  *phe;    /* pointer to host information entry    */
        struct servent  *pse;    /* pointer to service information entry */
        struct protoent *ppe;    /* pointer to protocol information entry*/
        struct sockaddr_in sin;  /* an Internet endpoint address         */
        int     s, type;         /* socket descriptor and socket type    */


        memset(&sin, 0, sizeof(sin));
        sin.sin_family = AF_INET;

    /* Map service name to port number */
        if ( pse = getservbyname(service, transport) )
                sin.sin_port = pse->s_port;
        else if ( (sin.sin_port = htons((u_short)atoi(service))) == 0 )
                errexit("can't get \"%s\" service entry\n", service);

    /* Map host name to IP address, allowing for dotted decimal */
        if ( phe = gethostbyname(host) )
                memcpy(&sin.sin_addr, phe->h_addr, phe->h_length);
        else if ( (sin.sin_addr.s_addr = inet_addr(host)) == INADDR_NONE)
                errexit("can't get \"%s\" host entry\n", host);

    /* Map protocol name to protocol number */
        if ( (ppe = getprotobyname(transport)) == 0)
                errexit("can't get \"%s\" protocol entry\n", transport);
    /* Use protocol to choose a socket type */
        if (strcmp(transport, "udp") == 0)
                type = SOCK_DGRAM;
        else
                type = SOCK_STREAM;

    /* Allocate a socket */
        s = socket(PF_INET, type, ppe->p_proto);
        if (s == INVALID_SOCKET)
                errexit("can't create socket: %d\n", GetLastError());

    /* Connect the socket */
        if (connect(s, (struct sockaddr *)&sin, sizeof(sin)) ==
            SOCKET_ERROR)
                errexit("can't connect to %s.%s: %d\n", host, service,
```

```
                        GetLastError());
        return s;
}
```

Although most steps are straightforward, a few details make the code seem complicated. First, the C language permits complex expressions. As a result, the expressions
in many of the condition statements contain a function call, an assignment, and a comparison, all on one line. For example, the call to *getprotobyname* appears in an expression that assigns the result to variable *ppe*, and then compares the result to *0*. If the
value returned is zero (i.e., an error occurred), the *if* statement executes a call to *errexit*.
Otherwise, the procedure continues execution. Second, the code uses two library procedures defined by ANSI C, *memset* and *memcpy*. Procedure *memset* places bytes of a
given value in a block of memory; it is the fastest way to zero a large structure or array.
Procedure *memcpy* copies a block of bytes from one memory location to another, regardless of the contents†. *Connectsock* uses *memset* to fill the entire *sockaddr_in* structure with zeroes, and then uses *memcpy* to copy the bytes of the server's IP address into
field *sin_addr*. Finally, *connectsock* calls procedure *connect* to connect the socket. If
an error occurs, it calls *errexit*.

```
/* errexit.cpp - errexit */

#include <stdarg.h>
#include <stdio.h>
#include <stdlib.h>
#include <winsock.h>


/*------------------------------------------------------------------------
 * errexit - print an error message and exit
 *------------------------------------------------------------------------
 */
/*VARARGS1*/
void
errexit(const char *format, ...)
{
        va_list args;

        va_start(args, format);
        vfprintf(stderr, format, args);
        va_end(args);
        WSACleanup();
        exit(1);
}
```

---

†Function *strcpy* cannot be used to copy an IP address because IP addresses can contain zero bytes which
strcpy interprets as *end of string*.

Errexit takes a variable number of arguments, which it passes on to *vfprintf* for output. *Errexit* follows the *printf* conventions for formatted output. The first argument specifies how the output should be formatted; remaining arguments specify values to be printed according to the given format. Finally, *errexit* calls function *WSACleanup* to release system socket resources before exiting.

7.8 Using The Example Library

Once programmers have selected abstractions and built a library of procedures, they can construct client applications. If the abstractions have been selected well, they make application programming simple and hide many of the details. To illustrate how our example library works, we will use it to construct example client applications. Because the clients each access one of the standard TCP/IP services, they also serve to illustrate several of the simpler application protocols.

7.9 The DAYTIME Service

The TCP/IP standards define an application protocol that allows a user to obtain the date and time of day in a format fit for human consumption. The service is officially named the *DAYTIME service*.

To access the DAYTIME service, the user invokes a client application. The client contacts a server to obtain the information, and then prints it. Although the standard does not specify the exact syntax, it suggests several possible formats. For example, DAYTIME could supply a date in the form:

weekday, month day, year time-timezone

like

Thursday, February 22, 1997 17:37:43-EST

The standard specifies that DAYTIME is available for both TCP and UDP. In both cases, it operates at protocol port *13*.

The TCP version of DAYTIME uses the presence of a TCP connection to trigger output: as soon as a new connection arrives, the server forms a text string that contains the current date and time, sends the string, and then closes the connection. Thus, the client need not send any request at all. In fact, the standard specifies that the server must discard any data sent by the client.

The UDP version of DAYTIME requires the client to send a request. A request consists of an arbitrary UDP datagram. Whenever a server receives a datagram, it formats the current date and time, places the resulting string in an outgoing datagram, and sends it back to the client. Once it has sent a reply, the server discards the datagram that triggered the response.

7.10 Implementation Of A TCP Client For DAYTIME

File *TCPdtc.cpp* contains code for a TCP client that accesses the DAYTIME service.

```
/* TCPdtc.cpp - main, TCPdaytime */

#include <stdlib.h>
#include <stdio.h>
#include <winsock.h>

void    TCPdaytime(const char *, const char *);
void    errexit(const char *, ...);
SOCKET  connectTCP(const char *, const char *);

#define LINELEN            128
#define WSVERS             MAKEWORD(2, 0)

/*------------------------------------------------------------------------
 * main - TCP client for DAYTIME service
 *------------------------------------------------------------------------
 */
int
main(int argc, char *argv[])
{
        char    *host = "localhost";   /* host to use if none supplied */
        char    *service = "daytime";  /* default service port        */
        WSADATA wsadata;

        switch (argc) {
        case 1:
                host = "localhost";
                break;
        case 3:
                service = argv[2];
                /* FALL THROUGH */
        case 2:
                host = argv[1];
                break;
        default:
                fprintf(stderr, "usage: TCPdaytime [host [port]]\n");
                exit(1);
        }
```

```
        if (WSAStartup(WSVERS, &wsadata) != 0)
                errexit("WSAStartup failed\n");
        TCPdaytime(host, service);
        WSACleanup();
        return 0;        /* exit */
}


/*------------------------------------------------------------------------
 * TCPdaytime - invoke Daytime on specified host and print results
 *------------------------------------------------------------------------
 */
void
TCPdaytime(const char *host, const char *service)
{
        char    buf[LINELEN+1];         /* buffer for one line of text  */
        SOCKET  s;                      /* socket descriptor            */
        int     cc;                     /* recv character count         */

        s = connectTCP(host, service);

        cc = recv(s, buf, LINELEN, 0);
        while( cc != SOCKET_ERROR && cc > 0) {
                buf[cc] = '\0';         /* ensure null-termination      */
                (void) fputs(buf, stdout);
                cc = recv(s, buf, LINELEN, 0);
        }
        closesocket(s);
}
```

Notice how using *connectTCP* simplifies the code. Once a connection has been established, DAYTIME merely reads input from the connection and prints it, iterating until it detects an end of file condition.

7.11 Reading From A TCP Connection

The DAYTIME example illustrates an important idea: TCP offers a stream service
that does not guarantee to preserve record boundaries. In practice, the stream paradigm
means that TCP decouples the sending and receiving applications. For example, suppose the sending application transfers *64* bytes of data in a single call to *send*, followed
by *64* bytes in a second call. The receiving application may receive all *128* bytes in a
single call to *recv*, or it may receive *10* bytes in the first call, *100* bytes in the second
call, and *18* bytes in the third call. The number of bytes returned in a call depends on

the size of datagrams in the underlying internet, the buffer space available, and the delays encountered when crossing the internet.

> *Because the TCP stream service does not guarantee to deliver data in the same blocks that it was written, an application receiving data from a TCP connection cannot depend on all data being delivered in a single transfer; it must repeatedly call* recv *until all data has been obtained.*

7.12 The TIME Service

TCP/IP defines a service that allows one machine to obtain the current date and time of day from another. Officially named *TIME*, the service is quite simple: a client program executing on one machine sends a request to a server executing on another. Whenever the server receives a request, it obtains the current date and time of day from the local operating system, encodes the information in a standard format, and sends it back to the client in a response.

To avoid the problems that occur if the client and server reside in different timezones, the TIME protocol specifies that all time and date information must be represented in *Universal Coordinated Time*†, abbreviated *UCT* or *UT*. Thus, a server converts from its local time to universal time before sending a reply, and a client converts from universal time to its local time when the reply arrives.

Unlike the DAYTIME service, which is intended for human users, the TIME service is intended for use by programs that store or manipulate times. The TIME protocol always specifies time in a 32-bit integer, representing the number of seconds since an *epoch date*. The TIME protocol uses midnight, January 1, 1900, as its epoch.

Using an integer representation allows computers to transfer time from one machine to another quickly, without waiting to convert it into a text string and back into an integer. Thus, the TIME service makes it possible for one computer to set its time-of-day clock from the clock on another system.

7.13 Accessing The TIME Service

Clients can use either TCP or UDP to access the TIME service at protocol port *37* (technically, the standards define two separate services, one for UDP and one for TCP). A TIME server built for TCP uses the presence of a connection to trigger output, much like the DAYTIME service discussed above. The client forms a TCP connection to a TIME server and waits to read output. When the server detects a new connection, it sends the current time encoded as an integer, and then closes the connection. The client does not send any data because the server never reads from the connection.

---

†Universal Coordinated Time was formerly known as *Greenwich Mean Time*.

Clients can also access a TIME service with UDP. To do so, a client sends a request, which consists of a single datagram. The server does not process the incoming datagram, except to extract the sender's address and protocol port number for use in a reply. The server encodes the current time as an integer, places it in a datagram, and sends the datagram back to the client.

7.14 Accurate Times And Network Delays

Although the TIME service accommodates differences in timezones, it does not handle the problem of network latency. If it takes *3* seconds for a message to travel from the server to the client, the client will receive a time that is *3* seconds behind that of the server. Other, more complex protocols handle clock synchronization. However, the TIME service remains popular for three reasons. First, TIME is extremely simple compared to clock synchronization protocols. Second, most clients contact servers on a local area network, where network latency accounts for only a few milliseconds. Third, except when using programs that use timestamps to control processing, humans do not care if the clocks on their computers differ by small amounts.

In cases where more accuracy is required, it is possible to improve TIME or use an alternative protocol. The easiest way to improve the accuracy of TIME is to compute an approximation of network delay between the server and client, and then add that approximation to the time value that the server reports. For example, one way to approximate latency requires the client to compute the time that elapses during the round trip from client to server and back. The client assumes equal delay in both directions, and obtains an approximation for the trip back by dividing the round trip time in half. It adds the delay approximation to the time of day that the server returns.

7.15 A UDP Client For The TIME Service

File *UDPtime.cpp* contains code that implements a UDP client for the TIME service.

```cpp
/* UDPtime.cpp - main */

#include <stdlib.h>
#include <stdio.h>
#include <time.h>
#include <winsock.h>

#define BUFSIZE          64
#define WSVERS           MAKEWORD(2, 0)

#define WINEPOCH         2208988800      /* Windows epoch, in UCT secs  */
#define MSG              "what time is it?\n"

SOCKET  connectUDP(const char *, const char *);
void    errexit(const char *, ...);

/*------------------------------------------------------------------------
 * main - UDP client for TIME service that prints the resulting time
 *------------------------------------------------------------------------
 */
int
main(int argc, char *argv[])
{
        char    *host = "localhost";    /* host to use if none supplied */
        char    *service = "time";      /* default service name         */
        time_t  now;                    /* 32-bit integer to hold time  */
        SOCKET  s;                      /* socket descriptor            */
        int     n;                      /* recv count                   */
        WSADATA wsadata;

        switch (argc) {
        case 1:
                host = "localhost";
                break;
        case 3:
                service = argv[2];
                /* FALL THROUGH */
        case 2:
                host = argv[1];
                break;
        default:
                fprintf(stderr, "usage: UDPtime [host [port]]\n");
                exit(1);
        }
```

```
if (WSAStartup(WSVERS, &wsadata))
        errexit("WSAStartup failed\n");

s = connectUDP(host, service);

(void) send(s, MSG, strlen(MSG), 0);

/* Read the time */

n = recv(s, (char *)&now, sizeof(now), 0);
if (n == SOCKET_ERROR)
        errexit("recv failed: recv() error %d\n", GetLastError());
WSACleanup();
now = ntohl((u_long)now);        /* put in host byte order      */
now -= WINEPOCH;                 /* convert UCT to Windows epoch */
printf("%s", ctime(&now));
return 0;        /* exit */
}
```

The example code contacts the TIME service by sending a datagram. It then calls *recv* to wait for a reply and extract the time value from it. Once *UDPtime* has obtained the time, it must convert the time into a form suitable for the local machine. First, it uses *ntohl* to convert the 32-bit value (a *long* in C) from network standard byte order into the local host byte order. Second, *UDPtime* must convert to the machine's local representation. The example code is designed for Windows. Like the Internet protocols, Windows represents time in a 32-bit integer and interprets the integer to be a count of seconds. Unlike the Internet, however, Windows assumes an epoch date of January 1, 1970. Thus, to convert from the TIME protocol epoch to the Windows epoch, the client must subtract the number of seconds between January 1, 1900 and January 1, 1970. The example code uses the conversion value *2208988800*. Once the time has been converted to a representation compatible with that of the local machine, *UDPtime* can invoke the library procedure *ctime†*, which converts the value into a human readable form for output.

7.16 The ECHO Service

TCP/IP standards specify an *ECHO service* for both UDP and TCP protocols. At first glance, ECHO services seem almost useless because an ECHO server merely returns all the data it receives from a client. Despite their simplicity, ECHO services are important tools that network managers use to test reachability, debug protocol software, and identify routing problems.

---

†Under Windows, *ctime* will not compute the correct local time unless the MS-DOS environment variable *TZ* is set to the correct timezone.

The TCP ECHO service specifies that a server must accept incoming connection requests, read data from the connection, and write the data back over the connection until the client terminates the transfer. Meanwhile, the client sends input and then reads it back.

7.17 A TCP Client For The ECHO Service

File *TCPecho.cpp* contains a simple client for the ECHO service.

```
/* TCPecho.cpp - main, TCPecho */

#include <stdlib.h>
#include <stdio.h>
#include <string.h>
#include <winsock.h>

void    TCPecho(const char *, const char *);
void    errexit(const char *, ...);
SOCKET  connectTCP(const char *, const char *);

#define LINELEN         128
#define WSVERS          MAKEWORD(2, 0)


/*------------------------------------------------------------------------
 * main - TCP client for ECHO service
 *------------------------------------------------------------------------
 */
void
main(int argc, char *argv[])
{
        char    *host = "localhost";    /* host to use if none supplied */
        char    *service = "echo";      /* default service name         */
        WSADATA wsadata;

        switch (argc) {
        case 1:
                host = "localhost";
                break;
        case 3:
                service = argv[2];
                /* FALL THROUGH */
        case 2:
                host = argv[1];
```

```
                break;
        default:
                fprintf(stderr, "usage: TCPecho [host [port]]\n");
                exit(1);
        }
        if (WSAStartup(WSVERS, &wsadata) != 0)
                errexit("WSAStartup failed\n");
        TCPecho(host, service);
        WSACleanup();
        exit(0);
}


/*------------------------------------------------------------------------
 * TCPecho - send input to ECHO service on specified host and print reply
 *------------------------------------------------------------------------
 */
void
TCPecho(const char *host, const char *service)
{
        char    buf[LINELEN+1];          /* buffer for one line of text  */
        SOCKET  s;                       /* socket descriptor            */
        int     cc, outchars, inchars;  /* characters counts            */

        s = connectTCP(host, service);

        while (fgets(buf, sizeof(buf), stdin)) {
                buf[LINELEN] = '\0';    /* ensure line null-termination */
                outchars = strlen(buf);
                (void) send(s, buf, outchars, 0);

                /* read it back */
                for (inchars = 0; inchars < outchars; inchars += cc) {
                        cc = recv(s, &buf[inchars], outchars-inchars, 0);
                        if (cc == SOCKET_ERROR)
                                errexit("socket recv failed: %d\n",
                                        GetLastError());
                }
                fputs(buf, stdout);
        }
        closesocket(s);
}
```

After opening a connection, *TCPecho* enters a loop that repeatedly reads one line of input, sends the line across the TCP connection to the ECHO server, reads it back again, and prints it. After all input lines have been sent to the server, received back, and printed successfully, the client exits.

7.18 A UDP Client For The ECHO Service

File *UDPecho.cpp* shows how a client uses UDP to access an ECHO service.

```
/* UDPecho.cpp - main, UDPecho */

#include <stdlib.h>
#include <stdio.h>
#include <string.h>
#include <winsock.h>

void    UDPecho(const char *, const char *);
void    errexit(const char *, ...);
SOCKET  connectUDP(const char *, const char *);

#define LINELEN         128
#define WSVERS          MAKEWORD(2, 0)

/*------------------------------------------------------------------------
 * main - UDP client for ECHO service
 *------------------------------------------------------------------------
 */
void
main(int argc, char *argv[])
{
        char    *host = "localhost";
        char    *service = "echo";
        WSADATA wsadata;

        switch (argc) {
        case 1:
                host = "localhost";
                break;
        case 3:
                service = argv[2];
                /* FALL THROUGH */
        case 2:
                host = argv[1];
```

```
                break;
        default:
                fprintf(stderr, "usage: UDPecho [host [port]]\n");
                exit(1);
        }
        if (WSAStartup(WSVERS, &wsadata))
                errexit("WSAStartup failed\n");
        UDPecho(host, service);
        WSACleanup();
        exit(0);
}


/*------------------------------------------------------------------------
 * UDPecho - send input to ECHO service on specified host and print reply
 *------------------------------------------------------------------------
 */
void
UDPecho(const char *host, const char *service)
{
        char    buf[LINELEN+1];         /* buffer for one line of text  */
        SOCKET  s;                      /* socket descriptor */
        int     nchars;                 /* read count*/

        s = connectUDP(host, service);

        while (fgets(buf, sizeof(buf), stdin)) {
                buf[LINELEN] = '\0';    /* ensure null-terminated */
                nchars = strlen(buf);
                (void) send(s, buf, nchars, 0);

                if (recv(s, buf, nchars, 0) < 0)
                        errexit("recv failed: error %d\n",
                                        GetLastError());
                fputs(buf, stdout);
        }
}
```

The example UDP ECHO client follows the same general algorithm as the TCP version. It repeatedly reads a line of input, sends it to the server, reads it back from the server, and prints it. The biggest difference between the UDP and TCP versions lies in how they treat data received from the server. Because UDP is datagram-oriented, the client treats an input line as a unit and places each in a single datagram. Similarly, the ECHO server receives and returns complete datagrams. Thus, while the TCP client reads incoming data as a stream of bytes, the UDP client either receives an entire line back from the server or receives none of it; each call to *recv* returns the entire line unless an error has occurred.

7.19 Summary

Programmers use the procedural abstraction to keep programs flexible and easy to maintain, to hide details, and to make it easy to port programs to new computers. Once a programmer writes and debugs a procedure, he or she places it in a library where it can be reused in many programs easily. A library of procedures is especially important for programs that use TCP/IP because they often operate on multiple computers.

This chapter presents an example library of procedures used to create client software. The primary procedures in our library, *connectTCP* and *connectUDP*, make it easy to allocate and connect a socket to a specified service on a specified host.

The chapter presents examples of a few client applications. Each example contains the code for a complete C program that implements a standard application protocol: DAYTIME (used to obtain and print the time of day in a human-readable format), TIME (used to obtain the time in 32-bit integer form), and ECHO (used to test network connectivity). The example code shows how a library of procedures hides many of the details associated with socket allocation and makes it easier to write client software.

FOR FURTHER STUDY

The application protocols described here are each part of the TCP/IP standard. Postel [RFC 867] contains the standard for the DAYTIME protocol, Postel and Harrenstien [RFC 868] contains the standard for the TIME protocol, and Postel [RFC 862] contains the standard for the ECHO protocol. Mills [RFC 1305] specifies version 3 of the Network Time Protocol, NTP.

EXERCISES

7.1   Use program *TCPdtc* to contact servers on several machines. How does each format the time and date?

7.2   The Internet standard represents time in a 32-bit integer that gives seconds past the epoch, midnight January 1, 1900. Some systems represent time in a 32-bit integer that measures seconds, but use January 1, 1970 as the epoch. What is the maximum date and time that can be represented in each scheme?

7.3   Improve the TIME client so it checks the date received to verify that it is greater than January 1, 1997 (or some other date you know to be in the recent past).

7.4 Modify the TIME client so it computes E, the time that elapses between when it sends the request and when it receives a response. Add one-half E to the time the server sends.

7.5 Build a TIME client that contacts two TIME servers, and reports the differences between the times they return.

7.6 Explain how deadlock can occur if a programmer changes the line size in the TCP ECHO client to be arbitrarily large (e.g., 20,000).

7.7 The ECHO clients presented in this chapter do not verify that the text they receive back from the server matches the text they sent. Modify them to verify the data received.

7.8 The ECHO clients presented in this chapter do not count the characters sent or received. What happens if a server incorrectly sends one additional character back that the client did not send?

7.9 The example ECHO clients in this chapter do not use *shutdown*. Explain how the use of *shutdown* can improve client performance.

7.10 Rewrite the code in *UDPecho.cpp* so it tests reachability by generating a message, sending it, and timing the reply. If the reply does not arrive in *5* seconds, declare the destination host to be unreachable. Be sure to retransmit the request at least once in case the Internet happens to lose a datagram.

7.11 Rewrite the code in *UDPecho.cpp* so it creates and sends a new message once per second, checks replies to be sure they match transmissions, and reports only the round trip time for each reply without printing the contents of the message itself.

7.12 Explain what happens to *UDPecho* when the underlying network: duplicates a request sent from the client to the server, duplicates a response sent from the server to the client, loses a request sent from the client to the server, or loses a response sent from the server to the client. Modify the code to handle each of these problems.

8

Algorithms And Issues In Server Software Design

8.1 Introduction

This chapter considers the design of server software. It discusses fundamental issues, including: connectionless vs. connection-oriented server access, stateless vs. stateful applications, and iterative vs. concurrent server implementations. It describes the advantages of each approach, and gives examples of situations in which the approach is valid. Later chapters illustrate the concepts by showing complete server programs that each implement one of the basic design ideas.

8.2 The Conceptual Server Algorithm

Conceptually, each server follows a simple algorithm: it creates a socket and binds the socket to the well-known port at which it desires to receive requests. It then enters an infinite loop in which it accepts the next request that arrives from a client, processes the request, formulates a reply, and sends the reply back to the client.

Unfortunately, this unsophisticated, conceptual algorithm suffices only for the most trivial services. To understand why, consider a service like file transfer that requires substantial time to handle each request. Suppose the first client to contact the server requests the transfer of a giant file (e.g., 200 megabytes), while the second client to contact the server requests the transfer of a trivially small file (e.g., 20 bytes). If the server waits until the first transfer completes before starting the second transfer, the second client may wait an unreasonable amount of time for a small transfer. The second user would expect a small request to be handled immediately. Most practical servers do handle small requests quickly, because they handle more than one request at a time.

8.3 Concurrent Vs. Iterative Servers

We use the term *iterative server* to describe a server implementation that processes one request at a time, and the term *concurrent server* to describe a server that handles multiple requests at one time. Although most concurrent servers achieve apparent concurrency, we will see that a concurrent implementation may not be required – it depends on the application protocol. In particular, if a server performs small amounts of processing relative to the amount of I/O it performs, it may be possible to implement the server as a single thread that uses asynchronous I/O to allow simultaneous use of multiple communication channels. From a client's perspective, the server appears to communicate with multiple clients concurrently. The point is:

> The term concurrent server *refers to whether the server handles multiple requests concurrently, not to whether the underlying implementation uses multiple concurrent processes or threads.*

In general, concurrent servers are more difficult to design and build, and the resulting code is more complex and difficult to modify. Most programmers choose concurrent server implementations, however, because iterative servers cause unnecessary delays in distributed applications and can become a performance bottleneck that affects many client applications. We can summarize:

> *Iterative server implementations, which are easier to build and understand, may result in poor performance because they make clients wait for service. In contrast, concurrent server implementations, which are more difficult to design and build, yield better performance.*

8.4 Connection-Oriented Vs. Connectionless Access

The issue of connectivity centers around the transport protocol that a client uses to access a server. In the TCP/IP protocol suite, TCP provides a *connection-oriented* transport service, while UDP provides a *connectionless* service. Thus, servers that use TCP are, by definition, *connection-oriented servers*, while those that use UDP are *connectionless servers*†.

Although we apply the terminology to servers, it would be more accurate if we restricted it to application protocols, because the choice between connectionless and connection-oriented implementations depends on the application protocol. An application protocol designed to use a connection-oriented transport service may perform incorrectly or inefficiently when using a connectionless transport protocol. To summarize:

---

†The socket interface does permit an application to *connect* a UDP socket to a remote endpoint, but practical servers do not do so, and UDP is not a connection-oriented protocol.

When considering the advantages and disadvantages of various server implementation strategies, the designer must remember that the application protocol used may restrict some or all of the choices.

8.5 Connection-Oriented Servers

The chief advantage of a connection-oriented approach lies in ease of programming. In particular, because the transport protocol handles packet loss and out-of-order delivery problems automatically, the server need not worry about them. Instead, a connection-oriented server manages and uses *connections*. It accepts an incoming connection from a client, and then sends all communication across the connection. It receives requests from the client and sends replies. Finally, the server closes the connection after it completes the interaction.

While a connection remains open, TCP provides all the needed reliability. It retransmits lost data, verifies that data arrives without transmission errors, and reorders incoming packets as necessary. When a client sends a request, TCP either delivers it reliably or informs the client that the connection has been broken. Similarly, the server can depend on TCP to deliver responses or inform it that the connection has broken.

Connection-oriented servers also have disadvantages. Connection-oriented designs require a separate socket for each connection, while connectionless designs permit communication with multiple hosts from a single socket. Socket allocation and the resulting connection management can be especially important in a server that must run forever without exhausting resources. For trivial applications, the overhead of the 3-way handshake used to establish and terminate a connection makes TCP expensive compared to UDP. The most important disadvantage arises because TCP does not send any packets across an idle connection. Suppose a client establishes a connection to a server, exchanges a request and a response, and then crashes. Because the client has crashed, it will never send further requests. However, because the server has already responded to all requests received so far, it will never send more data to the client. The problem with such a situation lies in resource use: the server has data structures (including buffer space) allocated for the connection and these resources cannot be reclaimed. Remember that a server must be designed to run forever. If clients crash repeatedly, the server will run out of resources (e.g., sockets, buffer space, TCP connections) and cease to operate.

8.6 Connectionless Servers

Connectionless servers also have advantages and disadvantages. While connectionless servers do not suffer from the problem of resource depletion, they cannot depend on the underlying transport for reliable delivery. One side or the other must take responsibility for reliable delivery. Usually, clients take responsibility for retransmitting requests if no response arrives. If the server needs to divide its response into multiple data packets, it may need to implement a retransmission mechanism as well.

Achieving reliability through timeout and retransmission can be extremely difficult. In fact, it requires considerable expertise in protocol design. Because TCP/IP operates in an internet environment where end-to-end delays change quickly, using fixed values for timeout does not work. Many programmers learn this lesson the hard way when they move their applications from local area networks (which have small delays with little variation) to wider area internets (which have large delays with greater variation). To accommodate an internet environment, the retransmission strategy must be adaptive. Thus, applications must implement a retransmission scheme as complex as the one used in TCP. As a result, novice programmers are encouraged to use connection-oriented transport.

> *Because UDP does not supply reliable delivery, connectionless tran-sport requires the application protocol to provide reliability, if need-ed, through a complex, sophisticated technique known as adaptive re-transmission. Adding adaptive retransmission to an existing applica-tion is difficult and requires considerable expertise.*

Another consideration in choosing connectionless vs. connection-oriented design focuses on whether the service requires broadcast or multicast communication. Because TCP offers point-to-point communication, it cannot supply broadcast or multicast com-munication; such services require UDP. Thus, any server that accepts or responds to multicast communication must be connectionless. In practice, most sites try to avoid broadcasting whenever possible; none of the standard TCP/IP application protocols currently require multicast. However, future applications (especially those that deliver audio or video to a large set of users) may depend more on multicast.

8.7 Failure, Reliability, And Statelessness

As Chapter 2 states, information that a server maintains about the status of ongoing interactions with clients is called *state information*. Servers that do not keep any state information are called *stateless servers*, while those that maintain state information are called *stateful servers*.

The issue of statelessness arises from a need to ensure reliability, especially when using connectionless transport. Remember that in an internet, messages can be duplicat-ed, delayed, lost, or delivered out of order. If the transport protocol does not guarantee reliable delivery, and UDP does not, the application protocol must be designed to en-sure it. Furthermore, the server implementation must be done carefully so it does not introduce state dependencies (and inefficiencies) unintentionally.

8.8 Optimizing Stateless Servers

To understand the subtleties involved in optimization, consider a connectionless server that allows clients to read information from files stored on the server's computer. To keep the protocol stateless, the designer requires each client request to specify a file name, a position in the file, and the number of bytes to read. The most straightforward server implementation handles each request independently: it opens the specified file, seeks to the specified position, reads the specified number of bytes, sends the information back to the client, and then closes the file.

A clever programmer assigned to write a server observes that: (1) the overhead of opening and closing files is high, (2) the clients using this server may read only a dozen bytes in each request, and (3) clients tend to read files sequentially. Furthermore, the programmer knows from experience that the server can extract data from a buffer in memory several orders of magnitude faster than it can read data from a disk. So, to optimize server performance, the programmer decides to maintain a small table of file information as Figure 8.1 shows.

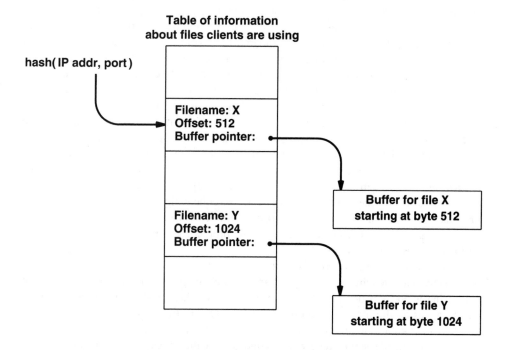

Figure 8.1 A table of information kept to improve server performance. The server uses the client's IP address and protocol port number to find an entry. This optimization introduces state information.

The programmer uses the client's IP address and protocol port number as an index into the table, and arranges for each table entry to contain a pointer to a large buffer of data from the file being read. When a client issues its first request, the server searches the table and finds that it has no record of the client. It allocates a large buffer to hold data from the file, allocates a new table entry to point to the buffer, opens the specified file, and reads data into the buffer. It then copies information out of the buffer when forming a reply. The next time a request arrives from the same client, the server finds the matching entry in the table, follows the pointer to the buffer, and extracts data from it without opening the file. If a client reads an entire file, the server deallocates the buffer and the table entry, making the resources available for use by another client.

Of course, our clever programmer builds the software carefully so that it checks the offset specified in a request to ensure that the requested data resides in the buffer. If the data is not available, the program must read data from the file into the buffer. The server also compares the file specified in a request with the file name in the table entry to verify that the client is still using the same file as the previous request.

If the clients follow the assumptions listed above and the programmer is careful, adding large file buffers and a simple table to the server can improve its performance dramatically. Furthermore, under the assumptions given, the optimized version of the server will perform at least as fast as the original version because the server spends little time maintaining the data structures compared to the time required to read from a disk. Thus, the optimization seems to improve performance without any penalty.

Adding the proposed table changes the server in a subtle way, however, because it introduces state information. Of course, state information chosen carelessly could introduce errors in the way the server responds. For example, if the server used the client's IP address and protocol port number to find the buffer without checking the file name or file offset in the request, duplicate or out-of-order requests could cause the server to return incorrect data. But remember we said that the programmer who designed the optimized version was clever and programmed the server to check the file name and offset in each request, just in case the network duplicates or drops a request or the client decides to read from a new file instead of reading sequentially from the old file. Thus, it may seem that the addition of state information does not change the way the server replies. In fact, if the programmer is careful, the protocol will remain correct. If so, what harm can the state information do?

Unfortunately, even a small amount of state information can cause a server to perform badly when machines, client programs, or networks fail. To understand why, consider what happens if one of the client programs fails (i.e., crashes) and must be restarted. Chances are high that the client will ask for an arbitrary protocol port number and UDP will assign a new protocol port number different from the one assigned for earlier requests. When the server receives a request from the client, it cannot know that the client has crashed and restarted, so it allocates a new buffer for the file and a new slot in the table. Consequently, it cannot know that the old table entry the client was using should be removed. If the server does not remove old entries, it will eventually run out of table slots.

It may seem that leaving an idle table entry around does not cause any problem as long as the server chooses an entry to delete when it needs a new one. For example, the server might choose to delete the *least recently used* (LRU) entry, much like the LRU page replacement strategy used in many virtual memory systems. However, in a network where multiple clients access a single server, frequent crashes can cause one client to dominate the table by filling it with entries that will never be reused. In the worst case, each request that arrives causes the server to delete an entry and reuse it. If one client crashes and reboots frequently enough, it can cause the server to remove entries for legitimate clients. Thus, the server expends more effort managing the table and buffers than it does answering requests†.

The important point here is that:

> *A programmer must be extremely careful when optimizing a stateless server because managing small amounts of state information can consume resources if clients crash and reboot frequently or if the underlying network duplicates or delays messages.*

8.9 Four Basic Types Of Servers

Servers can be iterative or concurrent, and can use connection-oriented transport or connectionless transport. Figure 8.2 shows that these properties group servers into four general categories.

iterative connectionless	**iterative connection-oriented**
concurrent connectionless	**concurrent connection-oriented**

Figure 8.2 The four general server categories defined by whether they offer concurrency and whether they use connection-oriented transport.

---

†Virtual memory systems describe this phenomenon as *thrashing*.

8.10 Request Processing Time

In general, iterative servers suffice only for the most trivial application protocols because they make each client wait in turn. The test of whether an iterative implementation will suffice focuses on the response time needed, which can be measured locally or globally.

We define the server's *request processing time* to be the total time the server takes to handle a single isolated request, and we define the client's *observed response time* as the total delay between the time it sends a request and the time the server responds. Obviously, the response time observed by a client can never be less than the server's request processing time. However, if the server has a queue of requests to handle, the observed response time can be much greater than the request processing time.

Iterative servers handle one request at a time. If another request arrives while the server is busy handling an existing request, the system enqueues the new request. Once the server finishes processing a request, it looks at the queue to see if it has a new request to handle. If N denotes the average length of the request queue, the observed response time for an arriving request will be approximately $N/2 + 1$ times the server's request processing time. Because the observed response time increases in proportion to N, most implementations restrict N to a small value (e.g., 5) and expect programmers to use concurrent servers in cases where a small queue does not suffice.

Another way of looking at the question of whether an iterative server suffices focuses on the overall load the server must handle. A server designed to handle K clients, each sending R requests per second must have a request processing time of less than $1/KR$ seconds per request. If the server cannot handle requests at the required rate, its queue of waiting requests will eventually overflow. To avoid overflow in servers that may have large request processing times, a designer should consider concurrent implementations.

8.11 Iterative Server Algorithms

An iterative server is the easiest to design, program, debug, and modify. Thus, most programmers choose an iterative design whenever iterative execution provides sufficiently fast response for the expected load. Usually, iterative servers work best with simple services accessed by a connectionless access protocol. As the next sections show, however, it is possible to use iterative implementations with both connectionless and connection-oriented transport.

8.12 An Iterative, Connection-Oriented Server Algorithm

Algorithm 8.1 presents the algorithm for an iterative server accessed via the TCP connection-oriented transport. The sections following the algorithm describe each of the steps in more detail.

Algorithm 8.1

1. Create a socket and bind to the well-known address for the service being offered.
2. Place the socket in passive mode, making it ready for use by a server.
3. Accept the next connection request from the socket, and obtain a new socket for the connection.
4. Repeatedly receive a request from the client, formulate a response, and send a reply back to the client according to the application protocol.
5. When finished with a particular client, close the connection and return to step *3* to accept a new connection.

Algorithm 8.1 An iterative, connection-oriented server. A single thread handles connections from clients one at a time.

8.13 Binding To A Well-Known Address Using INADDR_ANY

A server needs to create a socket and bind it to the well-known port for the service it offers. Like clients, servers use procedure *getservbyname* to map a service name into the corresponding well-known port number. For example, TCP/IP defines an *ECHO* service. A server that implements ECHO uses *getservbyname* to map the string "echo" to the assigned port, *7*.

Remember that when *bind* specifies a connection endpoint for a socket, it uses structure *sockaddr_in*, which contains both an IP address and a protocol port number. Thus, *bind* cannot specify a protocol port number for a socket without also specifying an IP address. Unfortunately, selecting a specific IP address at which a server will accept connections can cause difficulty. For hosts that have a single network connection, the choice is obvious because the host has only one IP address. However, gateways (routers) and multi-homed hosts have multiple IP addresses. If the server specifies one particular IP address when binding a socket to a protocol port number, the socket will not accept communications that clients send to the machine's other IP addresses.

To solve the problem, the socket interface defines a special constant, *INADDR_ANY*, that can be used in place of an IP address. *INADDR_ANY* specifies a *wildcard address* that matches any of the host's IP addresses. Using *INADDR_ANY* makes it possible to have a single server on a multihomed host accept incoming communication addressed to any of the host's IP addresses. To summarize:

> When specifying a local endpoint for a socket, servers use INADDR_ANY, *instead of a specific IP address, to allow the socket to receive datagrams sent to any of the machine's IP addresses.*

8.14 Placing The Socket In Passive Mode

A TCP server calls *listen* to place a socket in passive mode. *Listen* also takes an argument that specifies the length of an internal request queue for the socket. The request queue holds the set of incoming TCP connection requests from clients that have each requested a connection with the server.

8.15 Accepting Connections And Using Them

A TCP server calls *accept* to obtain the next incoming connection request (i.e., extract it from the request queue). The call returns the descriptor of a socket to be used for the new connection. Once it has accepted a new connection, the server uses *recv* to obtain application protocol requests from the client, and *send* to send replies back. Finally, once the server finishes with the connection, it calls *closesocket* to release the socket.

8.16 An Iterative, Connectionless Server Algorithm

Recall that iterative servers work best for services that have a low request processing time. Because connection-oriented transport protocols like TCP have higher overhead than connectionless transport protocols like UDP, most iterative servers use connectionless transport. Algorithm 8.2 gives the general algorithm for an iterative server that uses UDP.

Creation of a socket for an iterative, connectionless server proceeds in the same way as for a connection-oriented server. The server's socket remains unconnected and can accept incoming datagrams from any client.

Algorithm 8.2

1. Create a socket and bind to the well-known address for the service being offered.
2. Repeatedly receive the next request from a client, formulate a response, and send a reply back to the client according to the application protocol.

Algorithm 8.2 An iterative, connectionless server. A single thread handles requests (datagrams) from clients one at a time.

8.17 Forming A Reply Address In A Connectionless Server

The socket interface provides two ways of specifying a remote endpoint. Chapters 6 and 7 discuss how clients use *connect* to specify a server's address. After a client calls *connect*, it can use *send* to send data because the internal socket data structure contains the remote endpoint address as well as the local endpoint address. A connectionless server cannot use *connect*, however, because doing so restricts the socket to communication with one specific remote host and port; the server cannot use the socket again to receive datagrams from arbitrary clients. Thus, a connectionless server uses an unconnected socket. It generates reply addresses explicitly, and uses the *sendto* socket call to specify both a datagram to be sent and an address to which it should go. *Sendto* has the form:

```
retcode = sendto(s, message, len, flags, toaddr, toaddrlen);
```

where *s* is an unconnected socket, *message* is the address of a buffer that contains the data to be sent, *len* specifies the number of bytes in the buffer, *flags* specifies debugging or control options, *toaddr* is a pointer to a *sockaddr_in* structure that contains the endpoint address to which the message should be sent, and *toaddrlen* is an integer that specifies the length of the address structure.

The socket functions provide an easy way for connectionless servers to obtain the address of a client: the server obtains the address for a reply from the source address found in the request. In fact, the socket interface provides a call that servers can use to receive the sender's address along with the next datagram that arrives. The call, *recvfrom*, takes two arguments that specify two buffers. The system places the arriving datagram in one buffer and the sender's address in the second buffer. A call to *recvfrom* has the form:

```
retcode = recvfrom(s, buf, len, flags, from, fromlen);
```

where argument *s* specifies a socket to use, *buf* specifies the address of a buffer into which the system will place the next datagram, *len* specifies the space available in the buffer, *from* specifies a second buffer into which the system will place the source address, and *fromlen* specifies the address of an integer. Initially, *fromlen* specifies the length of the *from* buffer. When the call returns, *fromlen* will contain the length of the source address the system placed in the buffer. To generate a reply, the server uses the address that *recvfrom* stored in the *from* buffer when the request arrived.

8.18 Concurrent Server Algorithms

The primary reason for introducing concurrency into a server arises from a need to provide faster response times to multiple clients. Concurrency improves response time if:

- forming a response requires significant I/O,
- the processing time required varies dramatically among requests, or
- the server executes on a computer with multiple processors.

In the first case, allowing the server to compute responses concurrently means that it can overlap use of the processor and peripheral devices, even if the machine has only one CPU. While the processor works to compute one response, the I/O devices can be transferring data into memory that will be needed for other responses. In the second case, timeslicing permits a single processor to handle requests that only require small amounts of processing without waiting for requests that take longer. In the third case, concurrent execution on a computer with multiple processors allows one processor to compute a response to one request while another processor computes a response to another. In fact, most concurrent servers adapt to the underlying hardware automatically – given more hardware resources (e.g., more processors), they perform better.

> *Concurrent servers achieve high performance by overlapping processing and I/O. They are usually designed so performance improves automatically if the server is run on hardware that offers more resources.*

8.19 Master And Slave Threads

Although it is possible for a server to achieve some concurrency using a single thread, most concurrent servers use multiple processes or multiple threads. Threads can be divided into two types: a single *master server thread* begins execution initially. The master thread opens a socket at the well-known port, waits for the next request, and creates a *slave server thread* to handle each request. The master server never communicates directly with a client – it passes that responsibility to a slave. Each slave thread handles communication with one client. After the slave forms a response and sends it to the client, it exits. The next sections will explain the concept of master and slave in more detail, and will show how it applies to both connectionless and connection-oriented concurrent servers.

8.20 A Concurrent, Connectionless Server Algorithm

The most straightforward version of a concurrent, connectionless server follows Algorithm 8.3.

Algorithm 8.3

Master 1. Create a socket and bind to the well-known address for the service being offered. Leave the socket unconnected.

Master 2. Repeatedly call *recvfrom* to receive the next request from a client, and create a new slave thread to handle the response.

Slave 1. Receive a specific request upon creation as well as access to the socket.

Slave 2. Form a reply according to the application protocol and send it back to the client using *sendto*.

Slave 3. Exit (i.e., a slave thread terminates after handling one request).

Algorithm 8.3 A concurrent, connectionless server. The master server thread accepts incoming requests (datagrams) and creates a slave thread to handle each.

Programmers should remember that although the exact cost of creating a process or thread depends on the operating system and underlying architecture, the operation can be expensive. In the case of a connectionless protocol, one must consider carefully whether the cost of concurrency will be greater than the gain in speed. In fact:

Because thread or process creation is expensive, few connectionless servers have concurrent implementations.

8.21 A Concurrent, Connection-Oriented Server Algorithm

Connection-oriented application protocols use a connection as the basic paradigm for communication. They allow a client to establish a connection to a server, communicate over that connection, and then discard it. In most cases, the connection between client and server handles more than a single request: the protocol allows a client to repeatedly send requests and receive responses without terminating the connection or creating a new one. Thus,

Connection-oriented servers implement concurrency among connections rather than among individual requests.

Algorithm 8.4 specifies the steps that a concurrent server uses for a connection-oriented protocol.

Algorithm 8.4

Master 1. Create a socket and bind to the well-known address for the service being offered. Leave the socket unconnected.

Master 2. Place the socket in passive mode, making it ready for use by a server.

Master 3. Repeatedly call *accept* to receive the next request from a client, and create a new slave thread to handle the response.

Slave 1. Receive a connection request (i.e., socket for the connection) upon creation.

Slave 2. Interact with the client using the connection: receive request(s) and send back response(s).

Slave 3. Close the connection and exit. The slave thread exits after handling all requests from one client.

Algorithm 8.4 A concurrent, connection-oriented server. The master server thread accepts incoming connections and creates a slave thread to handle each. Once the slave finishes, it closes the connection.

As in the connectionless case, the master server thread never communicates with the client directly. As soon as a new connection arrives, the master creates a slave to handle that connection. While the slave interacts with the client, the master waits for other connections.

8.22 Using Separate Programs As Slaves

Algorithm 8.4 shows how a concurrent server creates a new thread for each connection. In Windows, the master server does so by calling the *_beginthread* system call. For simple application protocols, a single server program can contain all the code needed for both the master and slave threads. After the call to *_beginthread*, the original thread loops back to accept the next incoming connection, while the new thread becomes the slave and handles the connection. In some cases, however, it may be more convenient to create a separate slave process and have it execute code from a program that has been written and compiled independently. Windows can handle such cases easily because it allows the slave process to call *CreateProcess*. The general idea is:

> *For many services, a single program can contain code for both the master and server threads. In cases where an independent program makes a slave process easier to program or understand, the master program contains a call to* CreateProcess.

8.23 Apparent Concurrency Using A Single Thread

Previous sections discuss concurrent servers implemented with concurrent threads or processes. In some cases, however, it makes sense to use a single thread to handle client requests concurrently. In particular, some operating systems make thread creation so expensive that a server cannot afford to create a new thread for each request or each connection. In other systems that only have support for processes, a single process is required for any server that shares information among all connections.

To understand the motivation for a server that provides *apparent concurrency* with a single thread, consider the X window system. X allows multiple clients to paint text and graphics in windows that appear on a bit-mapped display. Each client controls one window, sending requests that update the contents. Each client operates independently, and may wait many hours before changing the display or may update the display frequently. For example, an application that displays the time by drawing a picture of a clock might update its display every minute. Meanwhile, an application that displays the status of a user's electronic mail waits until new mail arrives before it changes the display.

A server for the X window system integrates information it obtains from clients into a single, contiguous section of memory called the *display buffer*. Because data arriving from all clients contributes to a single, shared data structure and because systems that do not support threads do not allow independent processes to share memory, the server cannot execute as separate processes. Thus, a conflict arises between a desire for concurrency among processes that share memory and a lack of support for such concurrency.

Although it may be inefficient or impossible to achieve the *real concurrency* desired, it may be possible to achieve *apparent concurrency* if the total load of requests presented to the server does not exceed its capacity to handle them. To do so, the server operates as a single thread, but uses a function like *select* to provide asynchronous I/O. Algorithm 8.5 describes the steps a singly-threaded server takes to handle multiple connections.

Algorithm 8.5

1. Create a socket and bind to the well-known port for the service. Add socket to the list of those on which I/O is possible.
2. Use *select* to wait for I/O on existing sockets.
3. If original socket is ready, use *accept* to obtain the next connection, and add the new socket to the list of those on which I/O is possible.
4. If some socket other than the original is ready, use *recv* to obtain the next request, form a response, and use *send* to send the response back to the client.
5. Continue processing with step 2 above.

Algorithm 8.5 A concurrent, connection-oriented server implemented by a single thread. The server thread waits for the next descriptor that is ready, which could mean a new connection has arrived or that a client has sent a request on an existing connection.

8.24 When To Use Each Server Type

Iterative vs. Concurrent: Iterative servers are easier to design, implement, and maintain, but concurrent servers can provide quicker response to requests. Use an iterative implementation if request processing time is short and an iterative solution produces response times that are sufficiently fast for the application.

Real vs. Apparent Concurrency: A singly-threaded server must manage multiple connections and use asynchronous I/O; a multithreaded server allows the operating system to provide concurrency automatically. Use a singly-threaded solution if thread creation is expensive or not available. Use a multithreaded solution if the server must share or exchange data among connections. Use a multiprocess solution if each slave should operate in isolation or to achieve maximal concurrency (e.g., on a multiprocessor).

Connection-Oriented vs. Connectionless: Because connection-oriented access means using TCP, it implies reliable delivery. Because connectionless transport means using UDP, it implies unreliable delivery. Only use connectionless transport if the application protocol handles reliability (almost none do) or each client accesses its server on a local area network that exhibits extremely low loss and no packet reordering. Use connection-oriented transport whenever a wide area network separates the client and server. Never move a connectionless client and server to a wide area environment without checking to see if the application protocol handles the reliability problems.

8.25 A Summary of Server Types

Iterative, Connectionless Server

The most common form of connectionless server, used especially for services that require a trivial amount of processing for each request. Iterative servers are often stateless, making them easier to understand and less susceptible to failures.

Iterative, Connection-Oriented Server

A less common server type used for services that require a trivial amount of processing for each request, but for which reliable transport is necessary. Because the overhead associated with establishing and terminating connections can be high, the average response time can be non-trivial.

Concurrent, Connectionless Server

An uncommon type in which the server creates a new thread to handle each request. On many systems, the added cost of thread creation dominates the added efficiency gained from concurrency. To justify concurrency, either the time required to create a new thread must be significantly less than the time required to compute a response or concurrent requests must be able to use many I/O devices simultaneously.

Concurrent, Connection-Oriented Server

The most general type of server because it offers reliable transport (i.e., it can be used across a wide area internet) as well as the ability to handle multiple requests concurrently. Two basic implementations exist: the most common implementation uses concurrent threads or processes to handle connections; a far less common implementation relies on a single thread and asynchronous I/O to handle multiple connections.

In a concurrent process implementation, the master server process creates a slave process to handle each connection. Each process has its own address space and cannot share data among slave processes. Using multiple processes makes it easy to execute a separately compiled program for each connection instead of writing all the code in a single, large server program.

In a concurrent thread implementation, the master thread creates slave threads within the same process to handle each connection. All of the threads share the same global address space and can share data.

In the singly-threaded implementation, the server thread manages multiple connections. It achieves apparent concurrency by using asynchronous I/O. The thread repeatedly waits for I/O on any of the connections it has open and handles that request. Because a single thread handles all connections, it can share data among them, as in a design that uses multiple threads within a process. However, because the server has only one thread, it cannot handle requests faster than an iterative server, even on a computer that has multiple processors. The application must have a short processing time for each request to justify this server implementation.

8.26 The Important Problem Of Server Deadlock

Many server implementations share an important flaw: namely, the server can be subject to deadlock†. To understand how deadlock can happen, consider an iterative, connection-oriented server. Suppose some client application, C, misbehaves. In the simplest case, assume C makes a connection to a server, but never sends a request. The server will accept the new connection, and call *recv* to extract the next request. The server thread blocks in the call to *recv* waiting for a request that will never arrive.

Server deadlock can arise in a much more subtle way if clients misbehave by not consuming responses. For example, assume that a client C makes a connection to a server, sends it a sequence of requests, but never reads the responses. The server keeps accepting requests, generating responses, and sending them back to the client. At the server, TCP protocol software transmits the first few bytes over the connection to the client. Eventually, TCP will fill the client's receive window and will stop transmitting data. If the server application program continues to generate responses, the local buffer TCP uses to store outgoing data for the connection will become full and the server will block.

Deadlock arises because a thread blocks when the operating system cannot satisfy a request. In particular, a call to *send* will block the calling thread if TCP has no local buffer space for the data being sent; a call to *recv* will block the calling thread until TCP receives data. For concurrent servers, only the single slave thread associated with a particular client blocks if the client fails to send requests or read responses. For a singly-threaded implementation, however, the server blocks and cannot handle other connections. The important point is that any server using only one thread can be subject to deadlock.

> *A misbehaving client can cause deadlock in a singly-threaded server if the server uses system functions that can block when communicating with the client. Deadlock is a serious liability in servers because it means the behavior of one client can prevent the server from handling other clients.*

8.27 Alternative Implementations

Chapters *9* through *12* provide examples of the server algorithms described in this chapter. Chapters *13* and *14* extend the ideas by discussing two important practical implementation techniques not described here: multiprotocol and multiservice servers. While both techniques provide interesting advantages for some applications, they have not been included here because they are best understood as simple generalizations of the singly-threaded server algorithm illustrated in Chapter *12*.

†The term *deadlock* refers to a condition in which a program or set of programs cannot proceed because they are blocked waiting for an event that will never happen. In the case of servers, deadlock means that the server ceases to answer requests.

8.28 Summary

Conceptually, a server consists of a simple algorithm that iterates forever, waiting for the next request from a client, handling the request, and sending a reply. In practice, however, servers use a variety of implementations to achieve reliability, flexibility, and efficiency.

Iterative implementations work well for services that require little computation. When using a connection-oriented transport, an iterative server handles one connection at a time; for connectionless transport, an iterative server handles one request at a time.

To achieve efficiency, servers often provide concurrent service by handling multiple requests at the same time. A connection-oriented server provides for concurrency among connections by creating a thread or process to handle each new connection. A connectionless server provides concurrency by creating a new thread or process to handle each new request.

Any server implemented with a single thread that uses synchronous system functions like *recv* or *send* can be subject to deadlock. Deadlock can arise in iterative servers as well as in concurrent servers that use a singly-threaded implementation. Server deadlock is especially serious because it means a single misbehaving client can prevent the server from handling requests for other clients.

FOR FURTHER STUDY

Stevens [1990] describes some of the server algorithms covered in this chapter and shows implementation details.

EXERCISES

8.1 Calculate how long an iterative server takes to transfer a 200 megabyte file if the Internet has a throughput of 2.3 Kbytes per second.

8.2 If 20 clients each send 2 requests per second to an iterative server, what is the maximum time that the server can spend on each request?

8.3 How long does it take a concurrent, connection-oriented server to accept a new connection and create a new thread to handle it on the computers to which you have access? Compare this with the time it takes to create new processes instead of new threads.

8.4 Write an algorithm for a concurrent, connectionless server that creates one new thread for each request.

8.5 Modify the algorithm in the previous problem so the server creates one new thread per client instead of one new thread per request. How does your algorithm handle thread termination?

8.6   Connection-oriented servers provide concurrency among connections. Does it make sense for a concurrent, connection-oriented server to increase concurrency even further by having the slaves create additional threads for each request? Explain.

8.7   Can clients cause deadlock or disrupt service in concurrent servers? Why or why not?

8.8   Look carefully at the *select* function. How can a singly-threaded server use *select* to avoid deadlock?

8.9   The *select* call takes an argument that specifies how many I/O descriptors it should check. Explain how the argument makes a singly-threaded server portable across many systems.

8.10 In Windows, the *select* call can only be used with socket descriptors. Explain what problems this causes for singly-threaded implementations. Hint: consider a singly-threaded TCP echo client that concurrently handles input from the keyboard, input from a TCP connection and output to a TCP connection.

9

Iterative, Connectionless Servers (UDP)

9.1 Introduction

The previous chapter discusses many possible server designs, comparing the advantages and disadvantages of each. This chapter gives an example of an iterative server implementation that uses connectionless transport. The example server follows Algorithm 8.2†. Later chapters continue the discussion by providing example implementations of other server algorithms.

9.2 Creating A Passive Socket

The steps required to create a passive socket are similar to those required to create an active socket. They involve many details, and require the program to look up a service name and to obtain a well-known protocol port number.

To help simplify server code, programmers should use procedures to hide the details of socket allocation. As in the client examples, our example implementations use two high-level procedures, *passiveUDP* and *passiveTCP*, that allocate a passive socket and bind it to the server's well-known port. Each server invokes one of these procedures, with the choice dependent on whether the server uses connectionless or connection-oriented transport. This chapter considers *passiveUDP*; the next chapter shows the code for *passiveTCP*. Because the two procedures have many details in common, they both call the low-level procedure, *passivesock* to perform the work.

---

†See page 109 for a description of Algorithm 8.2.

A connectionless server calls function *passiveUDP* to create a socket for the service that it offers. An arbitrary application program can use *passiveUDP* to create a socket for services. *PassiveUDP* calls *passivesock* to create a connectionless socket, and then returns the socket descriptor to its caller.

To make it easy to test client and server software, *passivesock* relocates all port values by adding the contents of global integer *portbase*. The importance of using *portbase* will become clearer in later chapters. However, the basic idea is fairly easy to understand:

> *If a new version of a client-server application uses the same protocol port numbers as an existing, production version, the new software cannot be tested while the production version continues to execute.*

Using *portbase* allows a programmer to compile a modified version of a server, and then to have the server look up the standard protocol port and compute a final port number as a function of the standard port and the value of *portbase*. If the programmer selects a unique value of *portbase* for each particular version of a client-server pair, the ports used by the new version will not conflict with the ports used by the production version. In fact, using *portbase* makes it possible to test multiple versions of a client-server pair at the same time without interference because each pair communicates independently of other pairs.

```
/* passUDP.cpp - passiveUDP */

#include <winsock.h>

SOCKET  passivesock(const char *, const char *, int);

/*------------------------------------------------------------------------
 * passiveUDP - create a passive socket for use in a UDP server
 *------------------------------------------------------------------------
 */
SOCKET
passiveUDP(const char *service)
{
        return passivesock(service, "udp", 0);
}
```

Procedure *passivesock* contains the socket allocation details, including the use of *portbase*. It takes three arguments. The first argument specifies the name of a service, the second specifies the name of the protocol, and the third (used only for TCP sockets) specifies the desired length of the connection request queue. *Passivesock* allocates either a datagram or stream socket, binds the socket to the well-known port for the service, and returns the socket descriptor to its caller.

Recall that when a server binds a socket to a well-known port, it must specify the address using structure *sockaddr_in*, which includes an IP address as well as a protocol port number. *Passivesock* uses the constant *INADDR_ANY* instead of a specific local IP address, enabling it to work either on hosts that have a single IP address or on gateways (routers) and multi-homed hosts that have multiple IP addresses. Using *INADDR_ANY* means that the server will receive communication addressed to its well-known port at any of the machine's IP addresses.

```
/* passsock.cpp - passivesock */

#include <stdlib.h>
#include <string.h>
#include <winsock.h>

void    errexit(const char *, ...);

u_short portbase = 0;            /* port base, for test servers         */

/*------------------------------------------------------------------------
 * passivesock - allocate & bind a server socket using TCP or UDP
 *------------------------------------------------------------------------
 */
SOCKET
passivesock(const char *service, const char *transport, int qlen)
{
        struct servent  *pse;   /* pointer to service information entry */
        struct protoent *ppe;   /* pointer to protocol information entry*/
        struct sockaddr_in sin; /* an Internet endpoint address         */
        SOCKET          s;      /* socket descriptor                    */
        int             type;   /* socket type (SOCK_STREAM, SOCK_DGRAM)*/

        memset(&sin, 0, sizeof(sin));
        sin.sin_family = AF_INET;
        sin.sin_addr.s_addr = INADDR_ANY;

    /* Map service name to port number */
        if ( pse = getservbyname(service, transport) )
                sin.sin_port = htons(ntohs((u_short)pse->s_port)
                        + portbase);
        else if ( (sin.sin_port = htons((u_short)atoi(service))) == 0 )
                errexit("can't get \"%s\" service entry\n", service);
```

```
/* Map protocol name to protocol number */
    if ( (ppe = getprotobyname(transport)) == 0)
            errexit("can't get \"%s\" protocol entry\n", transport);

/* Use protocol to choose a socket type */
    if (strcmp(transport, "udp") == 0)
            type = SOCK_DGRAM;
    else
            type = SOCK_STREAM;

/* Allocate a socket */
    s = socket(PF_INET, type, ppe->p_proto);
    if (s == INVALID_SOCKET)
            errexit("can't create socket: %d\n", GetLastError());

/* Bind the socket */
    if (bind(s, (struct sockaddr *)&sin, sizeof(sin)) == SOCKET_ERROR)
            errexit("can't bind to %s port: %d\n", service,
                    GetLastError());
    if (type == SOCK_STREAM && listen(s, qlen) == SOCKET_ERROR)
            errexit("can't listen on %s port: %d\n", service,
                    GetLastError());
    return s;
}
```

9.3 Thread Structure

Figure 9.1 illustrates the simple thread structure used for an iterative, connection-less server.

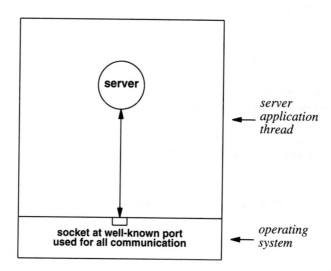

Figure 9.1 The thread structure for an iterative, connectionless server. A
singly-threadeded server communicates with many clients using
one socket.

The singly-threaded server executes forever. It uses a single passive socket that
has been bound to the well-known protocol port for the service it offers. The server obtains a request from the socket, computes a response, and sends a reply back to the
client using the same socket. The server uses the source address in the request as the
destination address in the reply.

9.4 An Example TIME Server

An example will illustrate how a connectionless server uses the socket allocation
procedures described above. Recall from Chapter 7 that clients use the TIME service to
obtain the current time of day from a server on another system. Because TIME requires
little computation, an iterative server implementation works well. File *UDPtimed.cpp*
contains the code for an iterative, connectionless TIME server.

```
/* UDPtimed.cpp - main */

#include <time.h>
#include <winsock.h>

SOCKET  passiveUDP(const char *);
void    errexit(const char *, ...);

#define WINEPOCH        2208988800      /* Windows epoch, in UCT secs  */
#define WSVERS                  MAKEWORD(2, 0)

/*------------------------------------------------------------------------
 * main - Iterative UDP server for TIME service
 *------------------------------------------------------------------------
 */
int
main(int argc, char *argv[])
{
        struct sockaddr_in fsin;        /* the from address of a client */
        char    *service = "time";      /* service name or port number  */
        char    buf[2048];      /* "input" buffer; any size > 1 packet  */
        SOCKET  sock;                   /* server socket                */
        time_t  now;                    /* current time                 */
        int     alen;                   /* from-address length          */
        WSADATA wsadata;

        switch (argc) {
        case    1:
                break;
        case    2:
                service = argv[1];
                break;
        default:
                errexit("usage: UDPtimed [port]\n");
        }

        if (WSAStartup(WSVERS, &wsadata))
                errexit("WSAStartup failed\n");
        sock = passiveUDP(service);

        while (1) {
                alen = sizeof(fsin);
                if (recvfrom(sock, buf, sizeof(buf), 0,
                    (struct sockaddr *)&fsin, &alen) == SOCKET_ERROR)
```

```
                           errexit("recvfrom: error %d\n", GetLastError());
                (void) time(&now);
                now = htonl((u_long)(now + WINEPOCH));
                (void) sendto(sock, (char *)&now, sizeof(now), 0,
                              (struct sockaddr *)&fsin, sizeof(fsin));
        }
        return 1;          /* not reached */
}
```

Like any server, the *UDPtimed* thread must execute forever. Thus, the main body of code consists of an infinite loop that accepts a request, computes the current time, and sends a reply back to the client that sent the request.

The code contains several details. After parsing its arguments, *UDPtimed* calls *passiveUDP* to create a passive socket for the TIME service. It then enters the infinite loop. The TIME protocol specifies that a client can send an arbitrary datagram to trigger a reply. The datagram can be of any length and can contain any values because the server does not interpret its contents. The example implementation uses *recvfrom* to read the next datagram. *Recvfrom* places the incoming datagram in buffer *buf*, and places the endpoint address of the client that sent the datagram in structure *fsin*.

UDPtimed uses the Windows function *time* to obtain the current time. Recall from Chapter *7* that Windows uses a 32-bit integer to represent time, measuring from the epoch of midnight, January 1, 1970. After obtaining the time from Windows, *UDP-timed* must convert it to a value measured from the Internet epoch and place the result in network byte order. To perform the conversion, it adds constant *WINEPOCH*, which is defined to have the value *2208988800*, the difference in seconds between the Internet epoch and the Windows epoch. It then calls function *htonl* to convert the result to network byte order. Finally, *UDPtimed* calls *sendto* to transmit the result back to the client. *Sendto* uses the endpoint address in structure *fsin* as the destination address (i.e., it uses the address of the client that sent the datagram).

9.5 Summary

For simple services, where a server does little computation for each request, an iterative implementation works well. This chapter presented an example of an iterative server for the TIME service that uses UDP for connectionless access. The example illustrates how procedures hide the details of socket allocation and make the server code simpler and easier to understand.

FOR FURTHER STUDY

Harrenstien [RFC 738] specifies the TIME protocol. Mills [RFC 1305] describes the Network Time Protocol (NTP); Mills [September 1991] summarizes issues related to using NTP in practical networks, and Mills [RFC 1361] discusses the use of NTP for clock synchronization. Marzullo and Owicki [July 1985] also discusses how to maintain clocks in a distributed environment.

EXERCISES

9.1 Instrument *UDPtimed* to determine how much time it expends processing each request. If you have access to a network analyzer, also measure the time that elapses between the request and response packets.

9.2 Suppose *UDPtimed* inadvertently clobbered the client's address between the time it received a request and sent a response (i.e., the server accidentally assigned *fsin* a random value before using it in the call to *sendto*). What would happen? Why?

9.3 Conduct an experiment to determine what happens if N clients all send requests to *UDPtimed* simultaneously. Vary both N, the number of senders, and S, the size of the datagrams they send. Explain why the server fails to respond to all requests.

9.4 The example code in *UDPtimed.cpp* specifies a buffer size of *2048* when it calls *recvfrom*. What happens if it specifies a buffer size of *1*?

9.5 Compute the difference between the Windows time epoch and the Internet time epoch. Remember to account for leap years. Does the value you compute agree with the constant *WINEPOCH* defined in *UDPtimed*? If not, explain. (Hint: read about leap seconds.)

9.6 As a security check, the system manager asks you to modify *UDPtimed* so it keeps a written log of all clients who access the service. Modify the code to print a line on the console whenever a request arrives. Explain how logging can affect the service.

9.7 If you have access to a pair of machines connected by a wide-area internet, use the *UDPtime* client in Chapter *7* and the *UDPtimed* server in this chapter to see if your internet drops or duplicates packets.

10

Iterative, Connection-Oriented Servers (TCP)

10.1 Introduction

The previous chapter provides an example of an iterative server that uses UDP for connectionless transport. This chapter shows how an iterative server can use TCP for connection-oriented transport. The example server follows Algorithm 8.1†.

10.2 Allocating A Passive TCP Socket

Chapter 9 mentions that a connection-oriented server uses function *passiveTCP* to allocate a stream socket and bind it to the well-known port for the service being offered. *PassiveTCP* takes two arguments. The first argument, a character string, specifies the name or number of a service, and the second specifies the desired length of the incoming connection request queue. If the first argument contains a name, it must match one of the entries in the service database accessed by library function *getservbyname*. If the first argument specifies a port number, it must represent the number as a text string (e.g., "79").

---

†See page 107 for a description of Algorithm 8.1.

```
/* passTCP.cpp - passiveTCP */

#include <winsock.h>

SOCKET  passivesock(const char *, const char *, int);

/*------------------------------------------------------------------------
 * passiveTCP - create a passive socket for use in a TCP server
 *------------------------------------------------------------------------
 */
SOCKET
passiveTCP(const char *service, int qlen)
{
        return passivesock(service, "tcp", qlen);
}
```

10.3 A Server For The DAYTIME Service

Recall from Chapter 7 that the DAYTIME service allows a user on one machine to obtain the current date and time of day from another machine. Because the DAYTIME service is intended for humans, it specifies that the server must format the date in an easily readable string of ASCII text when it sends a reply. Thus, the client can display the response for a user exactly as it is received.

Chapter 7 shows how a client uses TCP to contact a DAYTIME server and to display the text that the server sends back. Because obtaining and formatting a date requires little processing and one expects little demand for the service, a DAYTIME server need not be optimized for speed. If additional clients attempt to make connection requests while the server is busy handling a request, the protocol software enqueues the additional requests. Thus, an iterative implementation suffices.

10.4 Thread Structure

As Figure 10.1 shows, an iterative, connection-oriented server uses a single thread. The thread iterates forever, using one socket to handle incoming requests and a second, temporary socket to handle communication with a client.

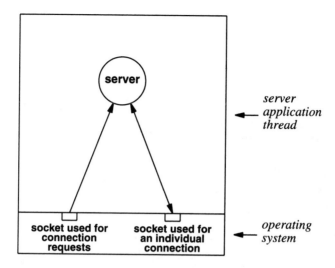

Figure 10.1 The thread structure of an iterative, connection-oriented server. The server waits at the well-known port for a connection, and then communicates with the client over that connection.

A server that uses connection-oriented transport iterates on connections: it waits at the well-known port for the next connection to arrive from a client, accepts the connection, handles it, closes the connection, and then waits again. The DAYTIME service makes the implementation especially simple because the server does not need to receive an explicit request from the client – it uses the presence of an incoming connection to trigger a response. Because the client does not send an explicit request, the server does not receive data from the connection.

10.5 An Example DAYTIME Server

File *TCPdtd.cpp* contains example code for an iterative, connection-oriented DAYTIME server.

```
/* TCPdtd.cpp - main, TCPdaytimed */

#include <stdlib.h>
#include <winsock.h>
#include <time.h>

void    errexit(const char *, ...);
void    TCPdaytimed(SOCKET);
SOCKET  passiveTCP(const char *, int);

#define QLEN        5
#define WSVERS  MAKEWORD(2, 0)

/*------------------------------------------------------------------------
 * main - Iterative TCP server for DAYTIME service
 *------------------------------------------------------------------------
 */
void
main(int argc, char *argv[])
{
        struct  sockaddr_in fsin;       /* the from address of a client */
        char    *service = "daytime";   /* service name or port number  */
        SOCKET  msock, ssock;           /* master & slave sockets       */
        int     alen;                   /* from-address length          */
        WSADATA wsadata;

        switch (argc) {
        case    1:
                break;
        case    2:
                service = argv[1];
                break;
        default:
                errexit("usage: TCPdaytimed [port]\n");
        }

        if (WSAStartup(WSVERS, &wsadata) != 0)
                errexit("WSAStartup failed\n");

        msock = passiveTCP(service, QLEN);

        while (1) {
                alen = sizeof(struct sockaddr);
                ssock = accept(msock, (struct sockaddr *)&fsin, &alen);
```

```
                if (ssock == INVALID_SOCKET)
                        errexit("accept failed: error number %d\n",
                                GetLastError());
                TCPdaytimed(ssock);
                (void) closesocket(ssock);
        }
}


/*------------------------------------------------------------------------
 * TCPdaytimed - do TCP DAYTIME protocol
 *------------------------------------------------------------------------
 */
void
TCPdaytimed(SOCKET fd)
{
        char    *pts;                   /* pointer to time string      */
        time_t  now;                    /* current time                */

        (void) time(&now);
        pts = ctime(&now);
        (void) send(fd, pts, strlen(pts), 0);
}
```

Like the iterative, connectionless server described in the previous chapter, an iterative, connection-oriented server must run forever. After creating a socket that listens at
the well-known port, the server enters an infinite loop in which it accepts and handles
connections.

The code for the server is fairly short because the call to *passiveTCP* hides the details of socket allocation and binding. The call to *passiveTCP* creates a master socket
associated with the well-known port for the DAYTIME service. The second argument
specifies that the master socket will have a request queue length of *QLEN*, allowing the
system to enqueue connection requests that arrive from *QLEN* additional clients while
the server is busy replying to a request from a given client.

After creating the master socket, the server's main program enters an infinite loop.
During each iteration of the loop, the server calls *accept* to obtain the next connection
request from the master socket. To prevent the server from consuming resources while
waiting for a connection from a client, the call to *accept* blocks the server until a connection arrives. When a connection request arrives, the TCP protocol software engages
in a 3-way handshake to establish a connection. Once the handshake completes and the
system allocates a new socket for the incoming connection, the call to *accept* returns the
descriptor of the new socket, allowing the server to continue execution. If no connection arrives, the server thread remains blocked forever in the *accept* call.

Each time a new connection arrives, the server calls procedure *TCPdaytimed* to handle it. The code in *TCPdaytimed* centers around calls to the Windows functions *time* and *ctime*. Procedure *time* returns a 32-bit integer that gives the current time in seconds since the Windows epoch. The C library function *ctime* takes an integer argument that specifies a time in seconds since the Windows epoch, and returns the address of an ASCII string that contains the time and date formatted so a human can understand it. Once the server obtains the time and date in an ASCII string, it calls *send* to send the string back to the client over the TCP connection.

Once the call to *TCPdaytimed* returns, the main program continues executing the loop, and encounters the *accept* call again. The *accept* call blocks the server until another request arrives.

10.6 Closing Connections

After it has written the response, the call to procedure *TCPdaytimed* returns. Once the call returns, the main program explicitly closes the socket on which the connection arrived.

Calling *closesocket* requests a graceful shutdown. In particular, TCP guarantees that all data will be reliably delivered to the client and acknowledged before it terminates the connection. Thus, when calling *closesocket*, a programmer does not need to worry about data being lost.

Of course, TCP's definition of graceful shutdown means that the call to *closesocket* may not return instantly – the call will block until TCP on the server receives a reply from TCP on the client. Once the client acknowledges both the receipt of all data and the request to terminate the connection, the *closesocket* call returns.

10.7 Connection Termination And Server Vulnerability

The application protocol determines how a server manages TCP connections. In particular, the application protocol usually dictates the choice of the termination strategy. For example, arranging for the server to close connections works well for the DAYTIME protocol because the server knows when it has finished sending data. Applications that have more complex client-server interactions cannot choose to have the server close a connection immediately after processing one request because they must wait to see if the client chooses to send additional request messages. For example, consider an ECHO server. The client controls server processing because it determines the amount of data to be echoed. Because the server must process arbitrary amounts of data, it cannot close the connection after receiving and sending data once. Thus, the client must signal completion so the server knows when to terminate the connection.

Allowing a client to control connection duration can be dangerous because it allows clients to control resource use. In particular, misbehaving clients can cause the server to consume resources like sockets and TCP connections. It may seem that our example server will never run out of resources because it explicitly closes connections. Even our simple connection termination strategy can be vulnerable to misbehaving clients. To understand why, recall that TCP defines a connection timeout period of *2* times the maximum segment lifetime (2*MSL) after a connection closes. During the timeout, TCP keeps a record of the connection so it can correctly reject any old packets that may have been delayed. Thus, if clients make repeated requests rapidly, they can use up resources at the server. Although a programmer may have little control over the protocol, they should understand how protocols can make distributed software vulnerable to network failures and try to avoid such vulnerabilities when designing servers.

10.8 Summary

An iterative, connection-oriented server iterates once per connection. Until a connection request arrives from a client, the server remains blocked in a call to *accept*. Once the underlying protocol software establishes the new connection and creates a new socket, the call to *accept* returns the socket descriptor and allows the server to continue execution.

Recall from Chapter 7 that the DAYTIME protocol uses the presence of a connection to trigger a response from the server. The client does not need to send a request because the server responds as soon as it detects a new connection. To form a response, the server obtains the current time from the operating system, formats the information into a string suitable for humans to read, and then sends the response back to the client. The example server closes the socket that corresponds to an individual connection after sending a response. The strategy of closing the connection immediately works because the DAYTIME service only allows one response per connection. Servers that allow multiple requests to arrive over a single connection must wait for the client to close the connection.

FOR FURTHER STUDY

Postel [RFC 867] describes the DAYTIME protocol used in this chapter.

EXERCISES

10.1   Is special privilege needed to run a DAYTIME server on your local system? Is special privilege needed to run a DAYTIME client? Explain.

10.2   What is the chief advantage of using the presence of a connection to trigger a response from a server? The chief disadvantage?

10.3   Some DAYTIME servers terminate the line of text by a combination of two characters: *carriage return* (*CR*) and *linefeed* (*LF*). Modify the example server to send *CR-LF* at the end of the line instead of sending only *LF*. How does the standard specify lines should be terminated?

10.4   TCP software usually allocates a fixed-size queue for additional connection requests that arrive while a server is busy, and allows the server to change the queue size using *listen*. How large is the queue that your local TCP software provides? How large can the server make the queue with *listen*?

10.5   Modify the example server code in *TCPdtd.cpp* so it does not explicitly close the connection after writing a response. Does it still work correctly? Why or why not?

10.6   Compare a connection-oriented server that explicitly closes each connection after sending a response to one that allows the client to hold a connection arbitrarily long before closing the connection. What are the advantages and disadvantages of each approach?

10.7   Assume that TCP uses a connection timeout of *4* minutes (i.e., keeps information for *4* minutes after a connection closes). If a DAYTIME server runs on a system that has 100 slots for TCP connection information, what is the maximum rate at which the server can handle requests without running out of slots?

11

Concurrent, Connection-Oriented Servers (TCP)

11.1 Introduction

The previous chapter illustrates how an iterative server uses a connection-oriented transport protocol. This chapter gives an example of a concurrent server that uses a connection-oriented transport. The example server follows Algorithm 8.4†, the design that programmers use most often when they build concurrent TCP servers. The server relies on the operating system's support for concurrent processing to achieve concurrency when computing responses. The system manager arranges to have the master server thread start automatically when the system boots. The master server runs forever waiting for new connection requests to arrive from clients. The master creates a new slave thread to handle each new connection, and allows each slave to handle all communication with its client.

Later chapters consider alternative implementations of concurrent servers, and show how to extend the basic ideas presented here.

11.2 Concurrent ECHO

Consider the ECHO service described in Chapter 7. A client opens a connection to a server, and then repeatedly sends data across the connection and receives the "echo" the server returns. The ECHO server responds to each client. It accepts a connection, receives data from the connection, and then sends back the same data.

---

†See page 112 for a description of Algorithm 8.4.

To allow a client to send arbitrary amounts of data, the server does not receive the entire input before it sends a response. Instead, it alternates between receiving and sending. When a new connection arrives, the server enters a loop. On each iteration of the loop, the server first receives data from the connection and then sends the data back. The server continues iterating until it encounters an end-of-file condition, at which time it closes the connection.

11.3 Iterative Vs. Concurrent Implementations

An iterative implementation of an ECHO server can perform poorly because it requires a given client to wait while it handles all prior connection requests. If a client chooses to send large amounts of data (e.g., many megabytes), an iterative server will delay all other clients until it can satisfy the request.

A concurrent implementation of an ECHO server avoids long delays because it does not allow a single client to hold all resources. Instead, a concurrent server allows communication with many clients to proceed simultaneously. Thus, from a client's point of view, a concurrent server offers better observed response time than an iterative server.

11.4 Thread Structure

Figure 11.1 illustrates the thread structure of a concurrent, connection-oriented server. As the figure shows, the master server thread does not communicate with clients directly. Instead, it merely waits at the well-known port for the next connection request. Once a request has arrived, the system returns the socket descriptor of the new socket to use for that connection. The master server thread creates a slave thread to handle the connection, and allows the slave to operate concurrently. At any time, the server consists of one master thread and zero or more slave threads.

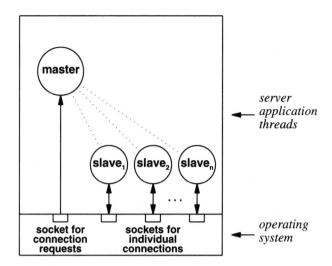

Figure 11.1 The thread structure of a concurrent, connection-oriented server.
A master server thread accepts each incoming connection, and
creates a slave thread to handle it.

To avoid using CPU resources while it waits for connections, the master thread
uses a blocking call of *accept* to obtain the next connection from the well-known port.
Thus, like the iterative server in Chapter *10*, the master server thread in a concurrent
server spends most of its time blocked in a call to *accept*. When a connection request
arrives, the call to *accept* returns, allowing the master thread to execute. The master
creates a slave thread to handle the request, and reissues the call to *accept*. The call
blocks the master thread again until another connection request arrives.

11.5 An Example Concurrent ECHO Server

File *TCPechod.cpp* contains the code for an ECHO server that uses concurrent
threads to provide concurrent service to multiple clients.

```
/* TCPechod.cpp - main, TCPechod */

#include <stdio.h>
#include <winsock.h>
#include <process.h>

#define QLEN                 5     /* maximum connection queue length    */
#define STKSIZE        16536
#define BUFSIZE        4096
#define WSVERS         MAKEWORD(2, 0)

SOCKET  msock, ssock;                /* master & slave server sockets      */

int     TCPechod(SOCKET);
void    errexit(const char *, ...);
SOCKET  passiveTCP(const char *, int);

/*------------------------------------------------------------------------
 * main - Concurrent TCP server for ECHO service
 *------------------------------------------------------------------------
 */
int
main(int argc, char *argv[])
{
        char    *service = "echo";        /* service name or port number */
        struct  sockaddr_in fsin;         /* the address of a client     */
        int     alen;                     /* length of client's address  */
        WSADATA wsadata;

        switch (argc) {
        case    1:
                break;
        case    2:
                service = argv[1];
                break;
        default:
                errexit("usage: TCPechod [port]\n");
        }

        if (WSAStartup(WSVERS, &wsadata) != 0)
                errexit("WSAStartup failed\n");
        msock = passiveTCP(service, QLEN);

        while (1) {
```

```
                  alen = sizeof(fsin);
                  ssock = accept(msock, (struct sockaddr *)&fsin, &alen);
                  if (ssock == INVALID_SOCKET)
                          errexit("accept: error number\n", GetLastError());
                  if (_beginthread((void (*)(void *))TCPechod, STKSIZE,
                      (void *)ssock) < 0) {
                          errexit("_beginthread: %s\n", strerror(errno));
                  }
          }
          return 1;          /* not reached */
}


/*------------------------------------------------------------------------
 * TCPechod - echo data until end of file
 *------------------------------------------------------------------------
 */
int
TCPechod(SOCKET fd)
{
          char    buf[BUFSIZE];
          int     cc;

          cc = recv(fd, buf, sizeof buf, 0);
          while (cc != SOCKET_ERROR && cc > 0) {
                  if (send(fd, buf, cc, 0) == SOCKET_ERROR) {
                          fprintf(stderr, "echo send error: %d\n",
                              GetLastError());
                          break;
                  }
                  cc = recv(fd, buf, sizeof buf, 0);
          }
          if (cc == SOCKET_ERROR)
                  fprintf(stderr, "echo recv error: %d\n", GetLastError());
          closesocket(fd);
          return 0;
}
```

As the example shows, the calls that control concurrency occupy only a small portion of the code. A master thread begins executing at *main*. After it checks its arguments, the master thread calls *passiveTCP* to create a passive socket for the well-known protocol port. It then enters an infinite loop.

During each iteration of the loop, the master thread calls *accept* to wait for a connection request from a client. As in the iterative server, the call blocks until a request arrives. After the underlying TCP protocol software receives a connection request, the system creates a socket for the new connection, and the call to *accept* returns the socket descriptor.

After *accept* returns, the master thread creates a slave thread to handle the connection. To do so, the master calls *_beginthread* to run procedure *TCPechod* as a separate thread. The newly created slave thread begins execution in procedure *TCPechod* and handles the connection. The master thread continues executing the infinite loop. The next iteration of the loop will wait at the *accept* call for another new connection to arrive. Note that both the original and new threads have access to the same open sockets after the call to *_beginthread*, and that either one closing a socket deallocates that socket for both of them. Thus, when the slave thread calls *closesocket* for the new connection, the socket for that connection disappears from the master thread.

The slave runs procedure *TCPechod*, which provides the ECHO service for one connection. Procedure *TCPechod* consists of a loop that repeatedly calls *recv* to obtain data from the connection and then calls *send* to send the same data back over the connection. Normally, *recv* returns the count of bytes read. It returns the value *SOCKET_ERROR* if an error occurs (e.g., the network connection between the client and server breaks) or zero if it encounters an *end-of-file* condition (i.e., no more data can be extracted from the socket). Similarly, *send* normally returns the count of characters written, but returns the value *SOCKET_ERROR* if an error occurs. The slave checks the return code, and prints an error message if an error occurs.

After performing the ECHO service or if an error occurs, the slave closes the socket it was using and returns. When a thread returns from its initial procedure, the thread ceases execution and the system releases the memory that the thread was using. Thus, after the slave returns, the memory it was using becomes available for another thread.

11.6 Summary

Connection-oriented servers achieve concurrency by allowing multiple clients to communicate with the server. The straightforward implementation in this chapter uses the *_beginthread* function to create a new slave thread each time a connection arrives. The master thread never interacts with any clients; it merely accepts connections and creates a slave to handle each of them.

Each slave thread begins execution in the *TCPechod* procedure immediately following the call to *_beginthread*. A connection to a client terminates when the slave closes the connection's socket.

FOR FURTHER STUDY

Postel [RFC 862] defines the ECHO protocol used in the example TCP server.

EXERCISES

11.1   Instrument the server so it keeps a log of the time at which it creates each slave thread and the time at which the slave terminates. How many clients must you start before you can find any overlap between the slave threads?

11.2   How many clients can access the example concurrent server simultaneously before any client must be denied service? How many can access the iterative server in Chapter *10* before any is denied service?

11.3   Build an iterative implementation of an ECHO server. Conduct an experiment to determine if a human can sense the difference in response time between the concurrent and iterative versions.

the operating system's timeslicing mechanism to share the CPU among the threads, and hence, among the connections.

In practice, however, an ECHO server seldom depends on timeslicing. If one were able to watch the execution of a concurrent ECHO server closely, one would find that the arrival of data often controls processing. The reason relates to data flow across an internet. Data arrives at the server in bursts, not in a steady stream, because the underlying internet delivers data in discrete packets. Clients add to the bursty behavior if they choose to send blocks of data so that the resulting TCP segments each fit into a single IP datagram. At the server, each slave thread spends most of its time blocked in a call to *recv* waiting for the next burst to arrive. Once the data arrives, the *recv* call returns and the slave thread executes. The slave calls *send* to send the data back to the client, and then calls *recv* again to wait for more data. A CPU that can handle the load of many clients without slowing down must execute sufficiently fast to complete the cycle of receiving and sending before data arrives for another slave.

Of course, if the load becomes so great that the CPU cannot process one request before another arrives, timesharing takes over. The operating system switches the processor among all slaves that have data to process. For simple services that require little processing for each request, chances are high that execution will be driven by the arrival of data. To summarize:

> *Concurrent servers that require little processing time per request often behave in a sequential manner where the arrival of data triggers execution. Timesharing only takes over if the load becomes so high that the CPU cannot handle it sequentially.*

12.3 Data-Driven Processing With A Single Thread

Understanding the sequential nature of a concurrent server's behavior allows us to understand how a single thread can perform the same task. Imagine a single server thread that has TCP connections open to many clients. The thread blocks waiting for data to arrive. As soon as data arrives on any connection, the thread awakens, handles the request, and sends a reply. It then blocks again, waiting for more data to arrive from another connection. As long as the CPU is fast enough to satisfy the load presented to the server, the single thread version handles requests as well as a version with multiple threads. In fact, because a singly-threaded implementation requires less switching between thread contexts, it may be able to handle a slightly higher load than an implementation that uses multiple threads.

The key to programming a singly-threaded, concurrent server lies in the use of asynchronous I/O through the Windows Sockets function *select*. A server creates a socket for each of the connections it must manage, and then calls *select* to wait for data to arrive on any of them. In fact, because *select* can wait for I/O on all possible sockets, it can also wait for new connections at the same time. Algorithm 8.5 lists the detailed steps a singly-threaded server uses.

12.4 Thread Structure Of A Singly-Threaded Server

Figure 12.1 illustrates the thread and socket structure of a singly-threaded, concurrent server. One thread manages all sockets.

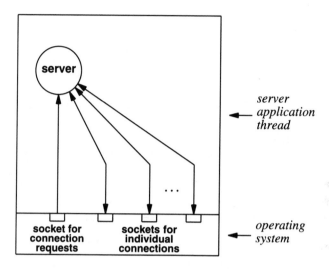

Figure 12.1 The thread structure of a connection-oriented server that achieves
concurrency with a single thread. The thread manages multiple
sockets.

In essence, a single thread server must perform the duties of both the master and slave threads. It maintains a set of sockets, with one socket in the set bound to the well-known port at which the master would accept connections. The other sockets in the set each correspond to a connection over which a slave would handle requests. The server passes the set of socket descriptors as an argument to *select*, and waits for activity on any of them. When *select* returns, it passes back a bit mask that specifies which of the descriptors in the set is ready. The server uses the order in which descriptors become ready to decide how to proceed.

To distinguish between master and slave operations, a singly-threaded server uses the descriptor. If the descriptor that corresponds to the master socket becomes ready, the server performs the same operation the master would perform: it calls *accept* on the socket to obtain a new connection. If a descriptor that corresponds to a slave socket becomes ready, the server performs the operation a slave would perform: it calls *recv* to obtain a request, and then answers it.

12.5 An Example Singly-Threaded ECHO Server

An example will help clarify the ideas and explain how a singly-threaded, concurrent server works. Consider file *TCPmechd.cpp*, which contains the code for a
singly-threaded server that implements the ECHO service.

```
/* TCPmechd.cpp - main, echo */

#include <winsock.h>
#include <string.h>

#define QLEN            5    /* maximum connection queue length    */

#define BUFSIZE         4096
#define WSVERS          MAKEWORD(2, 0)


void    errexit(const char *, ...);
SOCKET  passiveTCP(const char *, int);
int     echo(SOCKET);


/*------------------------------------------------------------------
 * main - Concurrent TCP server for ECHO service
 *------------------------------------------------------------------
 */
void
main(int argc, char *argv[])
{
        char    *service = "echo";      /* service name or port number  */
        struct  sockaddr_in fsin;       /* the from address of a client */
        SOCKET  msock;                  /* master server socket         */
        fd_set  rfds;                   /* read file descriptor set     */
        fd_set  afds;                   /* active file descriptor set   */
        int     alen;                   /* from-address length          */
        WSADATA wsdata;
        unsigned int    fndx;

        switch (argc) {
        case    1:
                break;
        case    2:
                service = argv[1];
                break;
```

```
            default:
                    errexit("usage: TCPmechod [port]\n");
            }

            if (WSAStartup(WSVERS, &wsdata) != 0)
                    errexit("WSAStartup failed\n");

    msock = passiveTCP(service, QLEN);

    FD_ZERO(&afds);
    FD_SET(msock, &afds);

    while (1) {
            memcpy(&rfds, &afds, sizeof(rfds));

            if (select(FD_SETSIZE, &rfds, (fd_set *)0, (fd_set *)0,
                (struct timeval *)0) == SOCKET_ERROR)
                    errexit("select error: %d\n", GetLastError());
            if (FD_ISSET(msock, &rfds)) {
                    SOCKET  ssock;

                    alen = sizeof(fsin);
                    ssock = accept(msock, (struct sockaddr *)&fsin,
                            &alen);
                    if (ssock == INVALID_SOCKET)
                            errexit("accept: error %d\n",
                                    GetLastError());
                    FD_SET(ssock, &afds);
            }

            for (fdndx=0; fdndx<rfds.fd_count; ++fdndx){
                    SOCKET fd = rfds.fd_array[fdndx];

                    if (fd != msock && FD_ISSET(fd, &rfds))
                            if (echo(fd) == 0) {
                                    (void) closesocket(fd);
                                    FD_CLR(fd, &afds);
                            }
            }
    }
}
```

```
/*------------------------------------------------------------------------
 * echo - echo one buffer of data, returning byte count
 *------------------------------------------------------------------------
 */
int
echo(SOCKET fd)
{
        char    buf[BUFSIZE];
        int     cc;

        cc = recv(fd, buf, sizeof buf, 0);
        if (cc == SOCKET_ERROR)
                errexit("echo recv error %d\n", GetLastError());
        if (cc && send(fd, buf, cc, 0) == SOCKET_ERROR)
                errexit("echo send error %d\n", GetLastError());
        return cc;
}
```

The singly-threaded server begins, like the master server in a multithreaded implementation, by opening a passive socket at the well-known port. It uses *FD_ZERO* and
FD_SET to create a vector that corresponds to the socket descriptors that it wishes to
test. The server then enters an infinite loop in which it calls *select* to wait for one or
more of the descriptors to become ready.

If the master descriptor becomes ready, the server calls *accept* to obtain a new connection. It adds the descriptor for the new connection to the set it manages, and continues to wait for more activity. If a slave descriptor becomes ready, the server calls procedure *echo* which calls *recv* to obtain data from the connection and *send* to send it
back to the client. If one of the slave descriptors reports an end-of-file condition, the
server closes the descriptor and uses macro *FD_CLR* to remove it from the set of
descriptors *select* uses.

12.6 Summary

Execution in concurrent servers is often driven by the arrival of data and not by the
timeslicing mechanism in the underlying operating system. In cases where the service
requires little processing, a singly-threaded implementation can use asynchronous I/O to
manage connections to multiple clients as effectively as an implementation that uses
multiple threads or processes.

The singly-threaded implementation performs the duties of the master and slave
threads. When the master socket becomes ready, the server accepts a new connection.
When any other socket becomes ready, the server receives a request and sends a reply.
An example singly-threaded server for the ECHO service illustrates the ideas and shows
the programming details.

FOR FURTHER STUDY

A good protocol specification does not constrain the implementation. For example, the singly-threaded server described in this chapter implements the ECHO protocol defined by Postel [RFC 862]. Chapter *11* shows an example of a multithreaded, concurrent server built from the same protocol specification.

EXERCISES

12.1 Conduct an experiment that proves the example ECHO server can handle connections concurrently.

12.2 Does it make sense to use the implementation discussed in this chapter for the DAYTIME service? Why or why not?

12.3 Read the Windows documentation to find out the exact representation of descriptors in the list passed to *select*. Write the *FD_SET* and *FD_CLR* macros.

12.4 Compare the performance of singly-threaded and multithreaded server implementations on a computer with multiple processors. Under what circumstances will a singly-threaded version perform better than (or equal to) a multithreaded version?

12.5 Suppose a large number of clients (e.g., *100*) access the example server in this chapter at the same time. Explain what each client might observe.

12.6 Can a singly-threaded server ever deprive one client of service while it repeatedly honors requests from another? Can a multithreaded implementation ever exhibit the same behavior? Explain.

13

Multiprotocol Servers (TCP, UDP)

13.1 Introduction

The previous chapter describes how to construct a singly-threaded server that uses asynchronous I/O to provide apparent concurrency among multiple connections. This chapter expands the concept. It shows how a singly-threaded server can accommodate multiple transport protocols. It illustrates the idea by showing a singly-threaded server that provides the DAYTIME service through both UDP and TCP. While the example server handles requests iteratively, the basic idea generalizes directly to servers that handle requests concurrently.

13.2 The Motivation For Reducing The Number Of Servers

In most cases, a given server handles requests for one particular service accessed through one particular transport protocol. For example, a computer system that offers the DAYTIME service often runs two servers – one server handles requests that arrive via UDP, while the other handles requests that arrive via TCP.

The chief advantage of using a separate server for each protocol lies in control: a system manager can easily control which protocols a computer offers by controlling which of the servers the system runs. The chief disadvantage of using one server per protocol lies in replication. Because many services can be accessed through either UDP or TCP, each service can require two servers. Furthermore, because both UDP and TCP servers use the same basic algorithm to compute a response, they both contain the code needed to perform the computation. If two programs both contain code to perform a given service, software management and debugging can become tedious. The programmer must ensure that both server programs remain the same when correcting bugs or when changing servers to accommodate new releases of system software. Furthermore, the system manager must coordinate execution carefully to ensure that the TCP and UDP servers executing at any time both supply exactly the same version of the service. Another disadvantage of running separate servers for each protocol arises from the use of resources: multiple server threads unnecessarily consume thread table entries and other system resources. The magnitude of the problem becomes clear when one remembers that the TCP/IP standards define dozens of services.

13.3 Multiprotocol Server Design

A multiprotocol server consists of a single thread that uses asynchronous I/O to handle communication over either UDP or TCP. The server initially opens two sockets: one that uses a connectionless transport (UDP) and one that uses a connection-oriented transport (TCP). The server then uses asynchronous I/O to wait for one of the sockets to become ready. If the TCP socket becomes ready, a client has requested a TCP connection. The server uses *accept* to obtain the new connection, and then communicates with the client over that connection. If the UDP socket becomes ready, a client has sent a request in the form of a UDP datagram. The server uses *recvfrom* to receive the request and record the sender's endpoint address. Once it has computed a response, the server sends the response back to the client using *sendto*.

13.4 Thread Structure

Figure 13.1 illustrates the thread structure of an iterative, multiprotocol server.

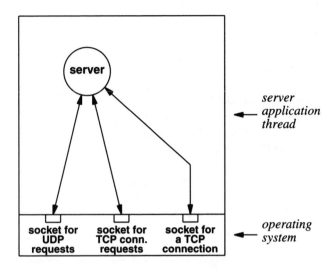

Figure 13.1 The thread structure of an iterative, multiprotocol server. At any time, the server has at most three sockets open: one for UDP requests, one for TCP connection requests, and a temporary one for an individual TCP connection.

An iterative, multiprotocol server has at most three sockets open at any given time. Initially, it opens one socket to accept incoming UDP datagrams and a second socket to accept incoming TCP connection requests. When a datagram arrives on the UDP socket, the server computes a response and sends it back to the client using the same socket. When a connection request arrives on the TCP socket, the server uses *accept* to obtain the new connection. *Accept* creates a third socket for the connection, and the server uses the new socket to communicate with the client. Once it finishes interacting, the server closes the third socket and waits for activity on the other two.

13.5 An Example Multiprotocol DAYTIME Server

Program *daytimed* illustrates how a multiprotocol server operates. It consists of a single thread that provides the DAYTIME service for both UDP and TCP.

```
/* daytimed.cpp - main, daytime */

#include <stdio.h>
#include <time.h>
#include <winsock.h>

void    daytime(char buf[]);
void    errexit(const char *, ...);
SOCKET  passiveTCP(const char *, int);
SOCKET  passiveUDP(const char *);

#define WSVERS          MAKEWORD(2, 0)
#define QLEN            5

#define LINELEN         128

/*------------------------------------------------------------------
 * main - Iterative server for DAYTIME service
 *------------------------------------------------------------------
 */
void
main(int argc, char *argv[])
{
        char    *service = "daytime";   /* service name or port number */
        char    buf[LINELEN+1];         /* buffer for one line of text */
        struct  sockaddr_in fsin;       /* the request from address    */
        int     alen;                   /* from-address length         */
        SOCKET  tsock;                  /* TCP master socket           */
        SOCKET  usock;                  /* UDP socket                  */
        fd_set  rfds;                   /* readable file descriptors   */
        int     rv;
        WSADATA wsadata;

        switch (argc) {
        case    1:
                break;
        case    2:
                service = argv[1];
                break;
        default:
                errexit("usage: daytimed [port]\n");
        }

        if (WSAStartup(WSVERS, &wsadata) != 0)
```

```
                    errexit("WSAStartup failed\n");

          tsock = passiveTCP(service, QLEN);
          usock = passiveUDP(service);

          FD_ZERO(&rfds);

          while (1) {
                    FD_SET(tsock, &rfds);
                    FD_SET(usock, &rfds);

                    if (select(FD_SETSIZE, &rfds, (fd_set *)0, (fd_set *)0,
                                    (struct timeval *)0) == SOCKET_ERROR)
                              errexit("select error: %d\n", GetLastError());
                    if (FD_ISSET(tsock, &rfds)) {
                              SOCKET  ssock;                /* TCP slave socket     */

                              alen = sizeof(fsin);
                              ssock = accept(tsock, (struct sockaddr *)&fsin,
                                        &alen);
                              if (ssock == INVALID_SOCKET)
                                        errexit("accept failed: error %d\n",
                                                  GetLastError());
                              daytime(buf);
                              (void) send(ssock, buf, strlen(buf), 0);
                              (void) closesocket(ssock);
                    }
                    if (FD_ISSET(usock, &rfds)) {
                              alen = sizeof(fsin);
                              rv = recvfrom(usock, buf, sizeof(buf), 0,
                                  (struct sockaddr *)&fsin, &alen);
                              if (rv == SOCKET_ERROR)
                                        errexit("recvfrom: error number %d\n",
                                                  GetLastError());
                              daytime(buf);
                              (void) sendto(usock, buf, strlen(buf), 0,
                                        (struct sockaddr *)&fsin, sizeof(fsin));
                    }
          }
}


/*------------------------------------------------------------------------
 * daytime - fill the given buffer with the time of day
 *------------------------------------------------------------------------
```

```
 */
void
daytime(char buf[])
{
        time_t  now;

        (void) time(&now);
        sprintf(buf, "%s", ctime(&now));
}
```

Daytimed takes an optional argument that allows the user to specify a service name or protocol port number. If the user does not supply an argument, *daytimed* uses the port for service *daytime*.

After parsing its arguments, *daytimed* calls *passiveTCP* and *passiveUDP* to create two passive sockets for use with TCP and UDP. Both sockets use the same service and, for most services, both will use the same protocol port number. Think of these as the master sockets – the server keeps them open forever, and all initial contact from a client arrives through one of them. The call to *passiveTCP* specifies that the system must enqueue up to *QLEN* connection requests.

After the server creates the master sockets, it prepares to use *select* by initializing the read file descriptor list, *rfds*. The server then enters an infinite loop. In each iteration of the loop, it uses macro *FD_SET* to build a set of the descriptors that correspond to the two master sockets. It then uses *select* to wait for input activity on either of the sockets.

When the *select* call returns, one or both of the master sockets is ready. The server uses macro *FD_ISSET* to check the TCP socket and again to check the UDP socket. The server must check both because if a UDP datagram happened to arrive at exactly the same time as a TCP connection request, both sockets would be ready.

If the TCP socket becomes ready, it means that a client initiated a connection request. The server uses *accept* to establish the connection. *Accept* returns the descriptor of a new, temporary socket used only for the new connection. The server calls procedure *daytime* to compute the response, *send* to send the response across the new connection, and *closesocket* to terminate the connection and release resources.

If the UDP socket becomes ready, it means that a client sent a datagram to prompt for a DAYTIME response. The server calls *recvfrom* to receive the incoming datagram and record the client's endpoint address. It uses procedure *daytime* to compute the response, and then calls *sendto* to send the response back to the client. Because it uses the master UDP socket for all communication, the server does not issue a *closesocket* after sending the UDP response.

13.6 The Concept Of Shared Code

Our example server illustrates an important idea:

A multiprotocol server design permits the designer to create a single procedure that responds to requests for a given service and to call that procedure regardless of whether requests arrive via UDP or TCP.

In the DAYTIME example, of course, the shared code occupies only a few lines. It has been placed in a single procedure, *daytime*. In most practical servers, however, the code needed to compute a response can span hundreds or thousands of lines and usually involves many procedures. It should be obvious that keeping the code in a single place where it can be shared makes maintenance easier and guarantees that the service offered by both transport protocols will be identical.

13.7 Concurrent Multiprotocol Servers

Like the single-protocol DAYTIME server shown earlier, the example multiprotocol DAYTIME server uses an iterative method to handle requests. The reason for using an iterative solution is the same as for the earlier server that supplies the DAYTIME service: an iterative server suffices because the DAYTIME service performs minimal computation for each request.

An iterative implementation may not suffice for other services that require more computation per request. In such cases, the multiprotocol design can be extended to handle the requests concurrently. In the simplest case, a multiprotocol server can create a new thread to handle each TCP connection concurrently, while it handles UDP requests iteratively. The multiprotocol design can also be extended to use the singly-threaded implementation described in Chapter *12*. Such an implementation provides apparent concurrency among requests that arrive over multiple TCP connections or via UDP.

13.8 Summary

A multiprotocol server allows the designer to encapsulate all the code for a given service in a single program, eliminating replication and making it easier to coordinate changes. The multiprotocol server consists of a single thread. The thread opens master sockets for both UDP and TCP, and uses *select* to wait for either or both of them to become ready. If the TCP socket becomes ready, the server accepts the new connection and handles requests using it. If the UDP socket becomes ready, the server receives the request and responds.

The multiprotocol server design illustrated in this chapter can be extended to allow concurrent TCP connections or to use a singly-threaded implementation that handles requests concurrently regardless of whether they arrive via TCP or UDP. Multiprotocol servers eliminate replication of code by using a single procedure to compute the response for the service. They also eliminate unnecessary use of system resources, especially threads.

FOR FURTHER STUDY

Reynolds and Postel [RFC 1700] specifies a list of application protocols along with the UDP and TCP protocol ports assigned to each.

EXERCISES

13.1 Extend the example server in this chapter to handle requests concurrently.

13.2 Study some of the most common services defined for TCP/IP. Can you find examples where a multiprotocol server cannot use shared code to compute the responses? Explain.

13.3 The example code allows the user to specify a service name or protocol port number as an argument, and uses the argument when creating passive sockets for the service. Is there an example of a service that uses a different protocol port number for UDP than for TCP? Change the code to allow the user to specify a separate protocol port number for each protocol.

13.4 The example server does not allow the system manager to control which protocols it uses. Modify the server to include arguments that allow a manager to specify whether to offer the service for TCP, UDP, or both.

13.5 Consider a site that decides to implement security through an authorization scheme. The site provides each server with a list of authorized client machines, and makes the rule that the server must disallow requests that originate from machines other than those on the list. Implement the authorization scheme for the example multiprotocol server. (Hint: look carefully at the socket functions to see how to do it for TCP.)

14

Multiservice Servers (TCP, UDP)

14.1 Introduction

Chapter *12* describes how to construct a singly-threaded server that uses asynchronous I/O to provide apparent concurrency among multiple connections, and Chapter *13* shows how a multiprotocol server supplies a service over both the TCP and UDP transport protocols. This chapter expands the concepts and combines them with some of the iterative and concurrent server designs discussed in earlier chapters. It shows how a single server can supply multiple services, and illustrates the idea using a singly-threaded server that handles a set of services.

14.2 Consolidating Servers

In most cases, programmers design an individual server to handle each service. The example servers in previous chapters illustrate the single-service approach – each waits at a well-known port and answers requests for the service associated with that port. Thus, a computer usually runs one server for the DAYTIME service, another for the ECHO service, and so on. The previous chapter discusses how a server that uses multiple protocols helps conserve system resources and makes maintenance easier. The same advantages that motivate multiprotocol servers motivate consolidating multiple services into a single, multiservice server.

When it begins execution, the multiservice server creates one socket for each service it offers, binds each socket to the well-known port for the service, and uses *select* to wait for an incoming connection request on any of them. When one of the sockets becomes ready, the server calls *accept* to obtain the new connection that has arrived. *Accept* creates a new socket for the incoming connection. The server uses the new socket to interact with a client, and then closes it. Thus, besides one master socket for each service, the server has at most one additional socket open at any time.

As in the connectionless case, the server keeps a table of mappings so it can decide how to handle each incoming connection. When the server begins, it allocates master sockets. For each master socket, the server adds an entry to the mapping table that specifies the socket number and a procedure that implements the service offered by that socket. After it has allocated a master socket for each service, the server calls *select* to wait for a connection. Once a connection arrives, the server uses the mapping table to decide which of many internal procedures to call to handle the service that the client requested.

14.5 A Concurrent, Connection-Oriented, Multiservice Server

The procedure called by a multiservice server when a connection request arrives can accept and handle the new connection directly (making the server iterative), or it can create a slave thread to handle it (making the server concurrent). In fact, a multiservice server can choose to handle some services iteratively and other services concurrently; the programmer does not need to choose a single style for all services. Figure 14.3 shows the thread structure for a multiservice server that uses a concurrent, connection-oriented implementation.

In an iterative implementation, once the procedure finishes communicating with the client, it closes the new connection. In a concurrent implementation, the slave thread works exactly like a slave in a conventional, concurrent, connection-oriented server. It communicates with the client over the connection, honoring requests and sending replies. When it finishes the interaction, the slave closes the socket, breaks the communication with the client, and ceases execution.

14.6 A Singly-Threaded, Multiservice Server Implementation

It is possible, although uncommon, to manage all activity in a multiservice server with a single thread, using a design exactly like the singly-threaded server discussed in Chapter *12*. Instead of creating a slave thread for each incoming connection, a singly-threaded server adds the socket for each new connection to the set it uses with *select*. If one of the master sockets becomes ready, the server calls *accept*; if one of the slave sockets becomes ready, the server calls *recv* to obtain an incoming request from the client, forms a response, and calls *send* to transmit the response back to the client.

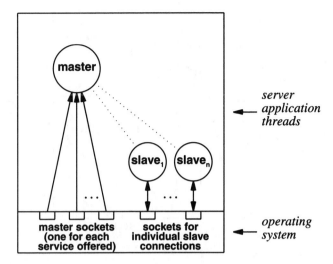

Figure 14.3 The thread structure for a concurrent, connection-oriented, multiservice server. The master thread handles incoming connection requests, while a slave thread handles each connection.

14.7 Invoking Separate Programs From A Multiservice Server

One of the chief disadvantages of most of the designs discussed so far is their inflexibility: changing the code for any single service requires recompilation of the entire multiservice server. The disadvantage does not become important until one considers a server that handles many services. Any small change requires the programmer to recompile the server, terminate the executing server program, and restart the server using the newly compiled code.

If a multiservice server offers many services, the chances are higher that at least one client will be communicating with it at any given time. Thus, terminating the server may cause a problem for some clients. In addition, the more services a given server offers, the higher the probability that it will need to be modified.

Designers often choose to break a large, monolithic, multiservice server into independent components by using independently compiled programs to handle each service. The idea is easiest to understand when applied to a concurrent, connection-oriented design.

Consider the concurrent, connection-oriented server illustrated in Figure 14.3. The master server thread waits for a connection request from a set of master sockets. Once a connection request arrives, the master thread calls _*beginthread* to create a slave thread that will handle the connection. The server must have the code for all services compiled into the master program. Figure 14.4 illustrates how the design can be modified to break the large server into separate pieces.

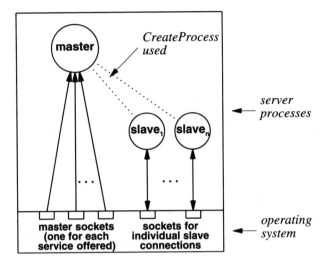

Figure 14.4 The structure of a connection-oriented, multiservice server that uses *CreateProcess* to execute a separate program to handle each connection.

As the figure shows, the master server uses *CreateProcess* to create a new process (not just a new thread) to handle each connection. One of the arguments to *CreateProcess* specifies the name of a new program to run. The master process arranges for the connection to remain open when the new process is created, allowing the new program to use the socket to handle all client communication.

Because *CreateProcess* retrieves the new program from a file, the design described above allows a system manager to replace the file without recompiling the multiservice server, terminating the server process, or restarting it. Conceptually, using *CreateProcess* separates the programs that handle each service from the master server code that sets up connections.

> *In a multiservice server, the Windows* CreateProcess *call makes it possible to separate the code that handles an individual service from the code that manages initial requests from clients.*

14.8 Multiservice, Multiprotocol Designs

Although it may seem natural to think of a multiservice server as either connectionless or connection-oriented, a multiprotocol design is also possible. As described in Chapter *13*, a multiprotocol design allows a single server thread to manage both a UDP socket and a TCP socket for the same service. In the case of a multiservice server, the server can manage UDP and TCP sockets for some or all of the services it offers.

Many networking experts use the term *super server* to refer to a multiservice, multiprotocol server. In principle, a super server operates much the same as a conventional multiservice server. Initially, the server opens one or two master sockets for each service it offers. The master sockets for a given service correspond to connectionless transport (UDP) or connection-oriented transport (TCP). The server uses *select* to wait for any socket to become ready. If a UDP socket becomes ready, the server calls a procedure that reads the next request (datagram) from the socket, computes a response, and sends a reply. If a TCP socket becomes ready, the server calls a procedure that accepts the next connection from the socket and handles it. The server can handle the connection directly, making it iterative, or it can create a new thread (or a new process) to handle the connection, making it concurrent.

14.9 An Example Multiservice Server

The multiservice server in file *superd.cpp* extends the singly-threaded server implementation in Chapter *12*. After initializing data structures and opening sockets for each of the services it offers, the main program enters an infinite loop. Each iteration of the loop calls *select* to wait for a socket to become ready. The *select* call returns when one or more requests arrive.

Each entry in array *svent* contains a structure of type *service* that specifies the mapping between a service and a socket descriptor. When *select* returns, the server iterates through *svent* and uses macro *FD_ISSET* to test whether the descriptor recorded in field *sv_sock* is ready. If it finds a ready descriptor, the server invokes a function to handle the request.

Field *sv_func* contains the address of a function to handle the service. After finding an entry in *svent* that corresponds to a descriptor that is ready, the program calls the selected function. For a UDP socket, the server calls the service handler directly; for a TCP socket, the server calls the service handler indirectly through procedure *doTCP*.

TCP services require the additional procedure because a TCP socket corresponds to the master socket in a connection-oriented server. When such a socket becomes ready, it means that a connection request has arrived at the socket. The server needs to create a new thread to manage the connection. Thus, procedure *doTCP* calls *accept* to accept the new connection. It then calls *_beginthread* to create a new slave thread that invokes the service handler function (*sv_func*). When the service function returns, the slave thread terminates.

service, the server does not abort connections already in progress. Thus, a request from a client is either refused altogether or handled completely.

Making a super server dynamically configurable adds considerable flexibility. The executable program that handles a given service can be changed without changing the super server itself. Furthermore, because the set of services available through the server can be changed without recompiling code or restarting the server, a programmer can test new services without disrupting production service. More important, because reconfiguring does not require changes to source code, nonprogrammers can learn to configure a server. To summarize:

> *A super server that can be reconfigured dynamically is flexible because the set of services offered can be changed without recompiling the server program or restarting the server.*

14.11 An Example Super Server, Inetd

Many computer systems run a super server that handles a large set of services. Called *inetd*, the super server was originally designed for UNIX; many vendors who sell server software include inetd or a similar program.

The original motivation for inetd arose from a desire for an efficient mechanism that could offer many services without using excessive system resources. In particular, although the TCP/IP services such as *ECHO* and *CHARGEN* are useful for testing or debugging, they are seldom used in a production system. Creating a server for each of the services takes system resources (e.g., entries in operating system tables). Furthermore, separate applications compete for memory if they run concurrently. Therefore, combining the servers into a single super server reduces the overhead, without eliminating the functionality.

Inetd is dynamically configurable. That is, a system administrator can instruct the *inetd* program to read a file that contains configuration information, and to handle the services specified in the file. Moreover, the administrator can force *inetd* to reconfigure at any time; the program does not need to stop and restart.

Each entry in the file has six or more fields as Figure 14.5 illustrates.

socket and a TCP socket for the same service. In the case of a multiservice server, the server can manage UDP and TCP sockets for some or all of the services it offers.

Many networking experts use the term *super server* to refer to a multiservice, multiprotocol server. In principle, a super server operates much the same as a conventional multiservice server. Initially, the server opens one or two master sockets for each service it offers. The master sockets for a given service correspond to connectionless transport (UDP) or connection-oriented transport (TCP). The server uses *select* to wait for any socket to become ready. If a UDP socket becomes ready, the server calls a procedure that reads the next request (datagram) from the socket, computes a response, and sends a reply. If a TCP socket becomes ready, the server calls a procedure that accepts the next connection from the socket and handles it. The server can handle the connection directly, making it iterative, or it can create a new thread (or a new process) to handle the connection, making it concurrent.

14.9 An Example Multiservice Server

The multiservice server in file *superd.cpp* extends the singly-threaded server implementation in Chapter *12*. After initializing data structures and opening sockets for each of the services it offers, the main program enters an infinite loop. Each iteration of the loop calls *select* to wait for a socket to become ready. The *select* call returns when one or more requests arrive.

Each entry in array *svent* contains a structure of type *service* that specifies the mapping between a service and a socket descriptor. When *select* returns, the server iterates through *svent* and uses macro *FD_ISSET* to test whether the descriptor recorded in field *sv_sock* is ready. If it finds a ready descriptor, the server invokes a function to handle the request.

Field *sv_func* contains the address of a function to handle the service. After finding an entry in *svent* that corresponds to a descriptor that is ready, the program calls the selected function. For a UDP socket, the server calls the service handler directly; for a TCP socket, the server calls the service handler indirectly through procedure *doTCP*.

TCP services require the additional procedure because a TCP socket corresponds to the master socket in a connection-oriented server. When such a socket becomes ready, it means that a connection request has arrived at the socket. The server needs to create a new thread to manage the connection. Thus, procedure *doTCP* calls *accept* to accept the new connection. It then calls *_beginthread* to create a new slave thread that invokes the service handler function (*sv_func*). When the service function returns, the slave thread terminates.

```cpp
/* superd.cpp - main, doTCP */

#include <process.h>
#include <winsock.h>

#define UDP_SERV        0
#define TCP_SERV        1

struct service {
        char    *sv_name;
        char    sv_useTCP;
        SOCKET  sv_sock;
        void    (*sv_func)(SOCKET);
};

void    TCPechod(SOCKET), TCPchargend(SOCKET), TCPdaytimed(SOCKET),
        TCPtimed(SOCKET);

SOCKET  passiveTCP(const char *, int);
SOCKET  passiveUDP(const char *);
void    errexit(const char *, ...);
void    doTCP(struct service *);

struct service svent[] =
        {       { "echo", TCP_SERV, INVALID_SOCKET, TCPechod },
                { "chargen", TCP_SERV, INVALID_SOCKET, TCPchargend },
                { "daytime", TCP_SERV, INVALID_SOCKET, TCPdaytimed },
                { "time", TCP_SERV, INVALID_SOCKET, TCPtimed },
                { 0, 0, 0, 0 },
        };


#define WSVERS          MAKEWORD(2, 0)
#define QLEN            5
#define LINELEN         128

extern  u_short portbase;       /* from passivesock() */
```

```
/*------------------------------------------------------------------------
 * main - Super-server main program
 *------------------------------------------------------------------------
 */
void
main(int argc, char *argv[])
{
        struct service  *psv;           /* service table pointer        */
        fd_set          afds, rfds;     /* readable file descriptors    */
        WSADATA         wsdata;

        switch (argc) {
        case 1:
                break;
        case 2:
                portbase = (u_short) atoi(argv[1]);
                break;
        default:
                errexit("usage: superd [portbase]\n");
        }
        if (WSAStartup(WSVERS, &wsdata))
                errexit("WSAStartup failed\n");

        FD_ZERO(&afds);
        for (psv = &svent[0]; psv->sv_name; ++psv) {
                if (psv->sv_useTCP)
                        psv->sv_sock = passiveTCP(psv->sv_name, QLEN);
                else
                        psv->sv_sock = passiveUDP(psv->sv_name);
                FD_SET(psv->sv_sock, &afds);
        }

        while (1) {
                memcpy(&rfds, &afds, sizeof(rfds));
                if (select(FD_SETSIZE, &rfds, (fd_set *)0, (fd_set *)0,
                    (struct timeval *)0) == SOCKET_ERROR)
                        errexit("select error: %d\n", GetLastError());
                for (psv=&svent[0]; psv->sv_name; ++psv) {
                        if (FD_ISSET(psv->sv_sock, &rfds)) {
                                if (psv->sv_useTCP)
                                        doTCP(psv);
```

```
                                    else
                                            psv->sv_func(psv->sv_sock);
                        }
                }
        }
}


/*------------------------------------------------------------------------
 * doTCP - handle a TCP service connection request
 *------------------------------------------------------------------------
 */
void
doTCP(struct service *psv)
{
        struct sockaddr_in fsin;        /* the request from address     */
        int             alen;           /* from-address length          */
        SOCKET          ssock;

        alen = sizeof(fsin);
        ssock = accept(psv->sv_sock, (struct sockaddr *)&fsin, &alen);
        if (ssock == INVALID_SOCKET)
                errexit("accept: %d\n", GetLastError());
        if (_beginthread((void (*)(void *))psv->sv_func, 0, (void *)ssock)
            == (unsigned long) -1)
                errexit("_beginthread: %s\n", strerror(errno));
}
```

The example super server supplies four services: ECHO, CHARGEN, DAYTIME, and TIME. The services other than CHARGEN appear in examples in earlier chapters. Programmers use the CHARGEN service to test client software. Once a client forms a connection to a CHARGEN server, the server generates an infinite sequence of characters and sends it to the client.

File *sv_funcs.cpp* contains the code for the functions that handle each of the individual services.

```
/* sv_funcs.cpp - TCPechod, TCPchargend, TCPdaytimed, TCPtimed */

#include <stdio.h>
#include <time.h>
#include <winsock.h>
```

```
#define BUFFERSIZE      4096             /* max read buffer size */

void    TCPechod(SOCKET), TCPchargend(SOCKET), TCPdaytimed(SOCKET),
        TCPtimed(SOCKET);
void    errexit(const char *, ...);

/*------------------------------------------------------------------------
 * TCPecho - do TCP ECHO on the given socket
 *------------------------------------------------------------------------
 */
void
TCPechod(SOCKET fd)
{
        char    buf[BUFFERSIZE];
        int     cc;

        while (cc = recv(fd, buf, sizeof buf, 0)) {
                if (cc == SOCKET_ERROR)
                        errexit("echo recv: errnum %d\n", GetLastError());
                if (send(fd, buf, cc, 0) == SOCKET_ERROR)
                        errexit("echo send: errnum %d\n", GetLastError());
        }
        closesocket(fd);
}

#define LINELEN         72

/*------------------------------------------------------------------------
 * TCPchargend - do TCP CHARGEN on the given socket
 *------------------------------------------------------------------------
 */
void
TCPchargend(SOCKET fd)
{
        char    c, buf[LINELEN+2];        /* print LINELEN chars + \r\n */

        c = ' ';
        buf[LINELEN] = '\r';
        buf[LINELEN+1] = '\n';
        while (1) {
                int     i;

                for (i=0; i<LINELEN; ++i) {
                        buf[i] = c++;
```

```
                        if (c > '~')
                                c = ' ';
                }
                if (send(fd, buf, LINELEN+2, 0) == SOCKET_ERROR)
                        break;
        }
        closesocket(fd);
}


/*------------------------------------------------------------------------
 * TCPdaytimed - do TCP DAYTIME protocol
 *------------------------------------------------------------------------
 */
void
TCPdaytimed(SOCKET fd)
{
        char    buf[LINELEN];
        time_t  now;

        (void) time(&now);
        sprintf(buf, "%s", ctime(&now));
        (void) send(fd, buf, strlen(buf), 0);
        closesocket(fd);
}


#define WINEPOCH        2208988800      /* Windows epoch, in UCT secs  */


/*------------------------------------------------------------------------
 * TCPtimed - do TCP TIME protocol
 *------------------------------------------------------------------------
 */
void
TCPtimed(SOCKET fd)
{
        time_t  now;

        (void) time(&now);
        now = htonl((u_long)(now + WINEPOCH));
        (void) send(fd, (char *)&now, sizeof(now), 0);
        closesocket(fd);
}
```

Code for most of the individual functions should seem familiar; it has been derived from the example servers in earlier chapters. The code for the CHARGEN service can be found in procedure *TCPchargend*; it is straightforward. The procedure consists of a loop that repeatedly creates a buffer filled with ASCII characters and calls *send* to send the contents of the buffer to the client. The loop terminates when the client closes the connection, causing *send* to return *SOCKET_ERROR*.

14.10 Static and Dynamic Server Configuration

In practice, many systems supply the skeleton of a super server to which system administrators can add additional services. To increase ease of use, super servers are often configurable – the set of services that the server handles can be changed without recompiling source code. Two types of configuration are possible: *static* and *dynamic*. Static configuration occurs when the server program begins execution. Typically, configuration information is placed in a file that the server reads when it starts. The configuration file specifies a set of services the server should handle as well as an executable program to be used for each service. To change the services being handled, a system administrator merely needs to change the configuration file and restart the server.

Dynamic configuration occurs while a super server is running. Like a statically configured server, a dynamically configured server reads a configuration file when it begins execution. The configuration file determines the initial set of services the server handles. Unlike a statically configured server, a dynamically configured server can redefine the services that it offers without restarting. To change services, a system administrator alters the configuration file, and then informs the server that reconfiguration is required. The server examines the configuration file, and changes its behavior accordingly.

How does an administrator inform a server that reconfiguration is needed? The answer depends on the operating system. In Windows, dynamic reconfiguration relies on conventional communication – the programmer must establish an additional input to permit the administrator to enter commands. For example, the server can be programmed to open an extra socket that is used for control. When reconfiguration is required, the administrator uses the control connection to inform the program. In systems that have an interprocess communication mechanism, the server can use that mechanism. For example, a server running under the UNIX system can use the *signal* mechanism. The administrator sends the server a signal; the server must catch the signal and interpret its arrival as a request to reconfigure.

When an administrator forces a server to dynamically reconfigure, the server reads the configuration file and changes the services it offers. If the configuration file contains one or more services that did not appear in the previous configuration, the server opens sockets to accept requests for the new services. If one or more services have been deleted from the configuration file, the server closes the sockets that correspond to the services it no longer handles. Of course, a well-designed super server handles reconfiguration gracefully – although it stops accepting new requests for a discontinued service, the server does not abort connections already in progress. Thus, a request from a client is either refused altogether or handled completely.

Making a super server dynamically configurable adds considerable flexibility. The executable program that handles a given service can be changed without changing the super server itself. Furthermore, because the set of services available through the server can be changed without recompiling code or restarting the server, a programmer can test new services without disrupting production service. More important, because reconfiguring does not require changes to source code, nonprogrammers can learn to configure a server. To summarize:

> *A super server that can be reconfigured dynamically is flexible because the set of services offered can be changed without recompiling the server program or restarting the server.*

14.11 An Example Super Server, Inetd

Many computer systems run a super server that handles a large set of services. Called *inetd*, the super server was originally designed for UNIX; many vendors who sell server software include inetd or a similar program.

The original motivation for inetd arose from a desire for an efficient mechanism that could offer many services without using excessive system resources. In particular, although the TCP/IP services such as *ECHO* and *CHARGEN* are useful for testing or debugging, they are seldom used in a production system. Creating a server for each of the services takes system resources (e.g., entries in operating system tables). Furthermore, separate applications compete for memory if they run concurrently. Therefore, combining the servers into a single super server reduces the overhead, without eliminating the functionality.

Inetd is dynamically configurable. That is, a system administrator can instruct the *inetd* program to read a file that contains configuration information, and to handle the services specified in the file. Moreover, the administrator can force *inetd* to reconfigure at any time; the program does not need to stop and restart.

Each entry in the file has six or more fields as Figure 14.5 illustrates.

Field	Meaning
service name	The name of a service to be offered (the name must appear in the system's service database).
socket type	The type of socket to use (must be a valid socket type such as *stream* or *dgram*).
protocol	The name of a protocol to use with the service (must be a valid protocol such as *tcp* or *udp*).
wait status	The value *wait* to specify that inetd should wait for the service program to finish one request before handling another, or *nowait* to allow concurrency.
userid	The login id under which the service program should be run.
server program	The name of the service program to execute or the string *internal* to use the version of the code compiled into inetd.
arguments	Zero or more arguments to be passed to the service program that inetd executes.

Figure 14.5 An example of fields found in each entry of an inetd configuration file. The first six fields are required and consist of contiguous nonblank characters; remaining words on the line comprise *arguments*.

When it first starts or after reconfiguration, inetd must create a master socket for each new service in the configuration file. To do so, inetd parses the configuration file and extracts individual fields. The *socket type* field is used to determine whether the master socket uses the *stream* or *dgram* socket type. Inetd must also bind a local protocol port to the socket. To find a protocol port number, inetd extracts the *service name* and *protocol* fields, and uses them in a query to the system's service database. The database returns a protocol port number to use for the service; if the service database does not contain an entry for the combination of the *service name* and *protocol* fields, inetd cannot handle the service.

Once a master socket has been created for each service, inetd records the remaining information from the configuration file, and waits for a request to arrive on one of the master sockets. When a client contacts one of the specified services, inetd uses the recorded information to determine how to proceed. For example, field *wait status* determines whether inetd runs multiple copies of the service program concurrently. If the configuration specifies *nowait*, inetd creates a new process† for each request that arrives, and allows all requests to be handled concurrently. Because inetd creates a new process to execute a service program, one new process is created each time a request arrives. The singly-threaded inetd process, which always remains running, continues to wait for requests on the master sockets.

---

†Although it is possible for *inetd* to achieve concurrency with *_beginthread* instead of *CreateProcess*, most implementations use processes because threads do not permit dynamic reconfiguration.

Conceptually, the value *wait* means that inetd should handle requests for the service iteratively (i.e., the service program should finish handling a request before inetd starts another process to run the program). Interestingly, most implementations of *inetd* use a form of concurrency for all requests. When a request first arrives for a service that specifies *wait*, inetd creates a separate slave to handle the service. To understand why, observe that the main inetd process cannot block while waiting for a service because other services may need to continue concurrent execution. After starting a process for a given service, inetd uses the *wait status* to determine how to proceed. If the wait status specifies *wait*, inetd temporarily stops accepting further requests for a service until the slave finishes. To do so, inetd removes the master socket for the service from the set to which it listens. After the process running the service finishes, inetd adds the socket back into its active set, and becomes willing to accept a request for the service again.

Although the wait status field provides a conceptual distinction between iterative and concurrent execution, there is also a practical reason for choosing *wait*. In particular, UDP services use *wait* for services that require a client and server to exchange multiple datagrams. The *wait* status prevents inetd from using the socket until the service program finishes. Thus, the client can send datagrams to the slave without interference. Once the slave finishes, inetd resumes use of the socket.

For either form of waiting, inetd uses the *server program* field in the configuration file to determine which service program to execute. If the field specifies *internal*, inetd calls an internal procedure to handle the service†. Otherwise, inetd treats the string as the name of a file to be executed. When it invokes a server, inetd passes the contents of the *arguments* field to the program.

14.12 Summary

When designing a server, a programmer can choose among a myriad of possible implementations. While most servers offer only a single service, the programmer can choose a multiservice implementation to reduce the number of servers needed. Most multiservice servers use a single transport protocol. However, multiple transport protocols can be used to combine connectionless and connection-oriented services into a single server. Finally, the programmer can choose to implement the controlling part of a concurrent, multiservice server with concurrent threads or with a single thread that uses asynchronous I/O to provide apparent concurrency.

The example server presented in this chapter illustrates how a multiservice server uses asynchronous I/O to replace a set of master servers. The server calls the socket function *select* to wait for activity on any of the master sockets.

Servers can be statically or dynamically configurable. Static configuration occurs when the server begins execution; dynamic configuration occurs while the server is running. Dynamic configuration allows a system administrator to change the set of services without recompiling or restarting the server. The super server *inetd* is a multiprotocol, multiservice server available on many computers.

---

†Code for a few trivial services is built into inetd to improve efficiency.

FOR FURTHER STUDY

Versions of *inetd* are available for many computer systems; the vendor's documentation describes the list of internal functions and calling conventions.

EXERCISES

14.1   If a connection-oriented, concurrent, multiservice server handles K services, what is the maximum number of sockets it will use?

14.2   Experiment to find out what limits your operating system places on the number of sockets that can be opened simultaneously. How many sockets can a single thread open? A single process with multiple threads? Multiple processes owned by a single user?

14.3   In the previous exercise, experiment to determine if the limits depend on the size of physical memory or the size of available memory.

14.4   Consider a singly-threaded implementation of a multiservice server. Write an algorithm that shows how the server manages connections.

14.5   Read RFC 1288 to find out about the FINGER service. Add FINGER to the example multiservice server described in this chapter.

14.6   Design a super server that allows new services to be added without recompiling or restarting the server.

14.7   For each of the iterative and concurrent multiservice server designs discussed in this chapter, write an expression for the maximum number of sockets the server allocates. Express your answer as a function of the number of services offered and the number of requests handled concurrently.

14.8   What is the chief disadvantage of a super server that calls *CreateProcess* to create a new process for each request? What is the chief disadvantage of one that calls *_beginthread*?

14.9   Look at the configuration file on a computer that runs *inetd* to find out which services it offers.

14.10   Does it make sense to run a World Wide Web service from a super server? Why or why not?

14.11   Consult a vendor's manual that describes an *inetd* configuration file. If the file permits %A in the argument field, what does it mean? When is it important?

15

Uniform, Efficient Management Of Server Concurrency

15.1 Introduction

Earlier chapters present specific server designs, and show how each design uses iterative or concurrent processing. The previous chapter considers how some of the designs can be combined to create a multiservice server.

This chapter considers concurrent servers in a broader sense. It examines the issues underlying server design and several techniques for managing concurrency that can apply to many of the previous designs. The techniques increase design flexibility and allow a designer to optimize server performance. Although the iterative and concurrent designs presented in earlier chapters may seem contradictory, they can each improve server performance in some circumstances. Furthermore, we will see that both techniques arise from a single concept.

15.2 Choosing Between An Iterative And A Concurrent Design

The server designs discussed so far have been partitioned into two categories: those that handle requests iteratively and those that handle them concurrently. The discussions in previous chapters imply that the designer must make a clear choice between the two basic approaches before the server is constructed.

The choice between iterative and concurrent implementations is fundamental be-cause it influences the entire program structure, the perceived response time, and the ability of a server to handle multiple requests. If the designer makes an incorrect deci-sion early in the design process, the cost to change can be high; much of the program may need to be rewritten.

How can a programmer know whether concurrency is warranted? How can a pro-grammer know which server design is optimal? More important, how can a program-mer estimate demand or service times? These questions are not easy to answer because conditions change. Once users hear about the available services, they want access. As the set of connected users increases, the demand on individual servers increases. Furth-ermore, demand can shift rapidly as a particular service becomes popular or unpopular. At the same time, new technologies and products continually improve communication and processing speeds. However, increases in communication and processing capabili-ties do not usually occur at the same rate. First one, then the other, becomes faster.

One might wonder exactly how a designer can make a fundamental design choice in a world that is constantly changing. The answer usually comes from experience and intuition: a designer makes the best estimate possible by looking at recent trends. In essence, the designer extrapolates from recent history to formulate an estimate for the near future. Of course, designers can only provide an approximation: as technologies and user demands change, the designer must reevaluate the decisions, and possibly change the design. The point is:

> *Choosing between iterative and concurrent server designs can be dif-ficult because user demands, processing speeds, and communication capabilities change rapidly. Most designers extrapolate from recent trends when making a choice.*

15.3 Level Of Concurrency

Consider one of the details of concurrent server implementation: the level of con-currency permitted. We define the *level of concurrency* for a server to be the total number of processes or threads the server has running at a given time†. The level of concurrency varies over time as the server creates a slave to handle an incoming request or as a slave completes a request and exits. Programmers and system administrators are not concerned with tracking the level of concurrency at any given instant, but they do care about the maximum level of concurrency a server exhibits over its lifetime.

Only a few of the designs presented so far require the designer to specify the max-imum level of concurrency for a server. Most of the designs permit the master server thread to create as many concurrent slaves as needed to handle incoming requests.

Usually, a concurrent, connection-oriented server creates one slave for each con-nection it receives from a client. Of course, a practical server cannot handle arbitrarily many connections. Each implementation of TCP places a bound on the number of ac-tive connections possible, and each operating system places a bound on the number of

---

†Although a few details vary, the concurrency concepts presented in this chapter apply to concurrency achieved with either processes or threads.

processes or threads available (the system must restrict either the concurrency available per user or the total number available). When the server reaches one of these limits, the system will deny requests from functions like *_beginthread* or *CreateProcess*.

To increase server flexibility, many programmers avoid placing a fixed upper bound on the maximum level of concurrency in the program. If the server code does not have a predefined maximum level of concurrency, the single implementation can operate either in an environment that does not demand much concurrency or in an environment that has much demand. The programmer does not need to change the code or recompile when moving a server from the former type of environment to the latter. However, servers that do not bound concurrency are at risk in an environment that presents a heavy load. Concurrency can increase until the server's operating system becomes swamped with processes or threads.

15.4 Demand-Driven Concurrency

To achieve flexibility, most of the concurrent server designs presented in earlier chapters use incoming requests to trigger an increase in concurrency. We call such schemes *demand-driven*, and say that the level of concurrency increases *on demand*†.

Servers that increase concurrency on demand may seem optimal because they do not use system resources (e.g., tables in the system or buffers) unless needed. Thus, demand-driven servers do not use resources unnecessarily. In addition, demand-driven servers provide low observed response times because they can handle multiple requests without waiting for processing to complete on an existing request.

15.5 The Cost Of Concurrency

While the general motivation for demand-driven concurrency is laudable, the implementations presented in earlier chapters may not produce optimal results. To understand why, we must consider the subtleties of thread creation and scheduling as well as the details of server operation. The central issue is one of how to measure the costs and benefits. In particular, one must consider the cost of concurrency as well as its benefits.

15.6 Overhead And Delay

The server designs presented in earlier chapters all use incoming requests as a measure of demand and as a trigger for increased concurrency. The master server waits for a request, and creates a new slave to handle it immediately after the request arrives. Thus, the level of concurrency at any instant reflects the number of requests the server has received, but has not finished processing.

---

†The term *request-driven concurrency* can also be used with servers, because demand is measured by the number of requests being serviced.

Despite the apparent simplicity of the demand-driven scheme, creating a new thread for each request can be expensive. Whether the server uses connectionless or connection-oriented transport, the operating system must inform the master server that a message or a connection has arrived. The master must then ask the system to create a slave.

Receiving a request from a network and creating a new thread can take considerable time. In addition to delaying request processing, creating a thread consumes system resources. Thus, on a conventional uniprocessor, the server will not execute while the operating system creates a new thread and switches thread context.

15.7 Small Delays Can Matter

Does the short delay incurred while creating a new process or thread matter? Figure 15.1 shows how it can.

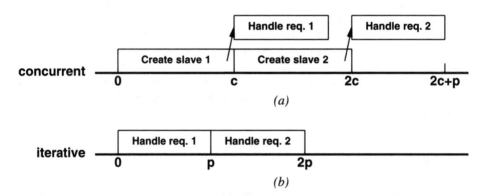

Figure 15.1 (a) The time required to handle two requests in a concurrent server and (b) in an iterative version of the server. The iterative version has lower delay because the time required to handle a request, p, is less than the time required to create a thread, c.

The figure shows an example in which the time required to handle a request is less than the time required to create a new thread. Let p denote the processing time, and let c denote the time required to create a thread. Assume that two requests arrive in a burst at time 0. The concurrent version completes processing the first request after $c + p$ time units, and it finishes processing the second after $2c + p$ time units. Thus, it requires an average of $3c/2 + p$ time units per request. An iterative server completes processing the first request at time p and the second at time $2p$, yielding an average of only $3p/2$ time units per request. Thus, the iterative server design exhibits lower average delay than the concurrent version.

The small additional delay may seem unimportant when considering only a few requests. However, the delay can be significant if one considers the continuous operation
of a server under heavy load. If many requests arrive close to the same time, they must
wait while the server creates threads to handle them. If additional requests arrive faster
than the server can process them, the delays accumulate.

In the short term, small delays in the server affect the observed response time but
not the overall throughput. If a burst of requests arrives at or near the same time, protocol software in the operating system will place them in a queue until the server can extract and process them. For example, if the server uses a connection-oriented transport,
TCP will enqueue connection requests. If the server uses a connectionless transport,
UDP will enqueue incoming datagrams.

In the long term, extra delays can cause requests to be lost. To see how, imagine a
server that takes c time units to create a thread, but only p time units ($p < c$) to process a
request. A concurrent implementation of the server can handle an average of $1/c$ requests per unit time, while an iterative version can handle $1/p$ requests per unit time.

A problem arises when the rate at which requests arrive exceeds $1/c$, but remains
less than $1/p$. An iterative implementation can handle the load, but a concurrent implementation spends too much time creating threads. In the concurrent version, queues in
the protocol software eventually become full, and the software begins rejecting further
requests.

In practice, few servers operate close to their maximum throughput. Furthermore,
few designers use concurrent servers when the cost of creating a thread exceeds the cost
of processing. Thus, request delay or loss does not occur in many applications. However, servers designed to provide optimum response under heavy load must consider alternatives to demand-driven concurrency.

15.8 Thread Preallocation

A straightforward technique can be used to control delay, limit the maximum level
of concurrency, and maintain high throughput in concurrent servers when thread creation time is significant. The technique consists of preallocating concurrent threads to
avoid the cost of creating them.

To use the preallocation technique, a designer programs the master server to create
N slave threads when it begins execution. Each thread uses facilities available in the
operating system to wait for a request to arrive. When a request arrives, one of the
waiting slave threads begins execution and handles the request. When it finishes handling a request, the slave does not terminate. Instead, it returns to the code that waits
for another request.

The chief advantage of preallocation arises from lower operating system overhead.
Because the server does not need to create a thread when a request arrives, it can handle
requests faster. The technique is especially important when request processing involves
more I/O than computation. Preallocation allows the server system to switch to another

thread and begin to handle the next request while waiting for I/O activity associated with the previous request. To summarize:

> *When using preallocation, a server creates concurrent slave threads at startup. Preallocation can lower server delay because it avoids the cost of creating a thread each time a request arrives and allows processing of one request to overlap I/O activity associated with another.*

15.8.1 Preallocation Techniques

The details of preallocation depend on the facilities available in the underlying operating system and the type of concurrency used. In Windows systems, preallocated threads can use shared memory to coordinate with the master; preallocated processes often rely on message passing facilities. In systems that do not offer shared memory, preallocation may still be possible because the master and slaves can use socket functions to coordinate.

> *Socket functions can be used to coordinate concurrency in systems that allow a child thread or process to inherit access to socket descriptors that the parent has opened.*

To take advantage of socket sharing, a master server opens the necessary socket before it preallocates any slave. In particular, when it starts, the master server opens a socket for the well-known port at which requests will arrive. The master then uses the appropriate operating system function to create as many slaves as desired. Because each slave inherits copies of socket descriptors from the parent, all slaves have access to the socket for the well-known port. The next sections discuss how the socket functions can be used to handle preallocation in connection-oriented and connectionless servers.

15.8.2 Preallocation In A Connection-Oriented Server

If a concurrent server uses TCP for communication, the level of concurrency depends on the number of active connections. Each incoming connection request must be handled by an independent process or thread. Fortunately, in most systems, the socket functions provide mutual exclusion for multiple slaves that all attempt to accept a connection from the same socket. Each slave calls *accept*, which blocks awaiting receipt of an incoming connection request to the well-known port. When a connection request arrives, the system unblocks exactly one of the slaves. In an individual slave, when the call to *accept* returns, it provides a new file descriptor used for the incoming connection. The slave handles the connection, closes the new socket, and then calls *accept* to wait for the next request. Figure 15.2 shows the thread structure.

As the figure shows, all slaves inherit access to the socket for the well-known port. An individual slave receives a new socket used for an individual connection when its call to *accept* returns. Although the master creates the socket that corresponds to the well-known port, it does not use the socket for other operations. The dashed line in the diagram denotes the difference between the master's use of the socket and the slaves' use.

Although Figure 15.2 shows a master thread running at the same time as the slaves, the distinction between master and slave is somewhat blurred. In practice, the master has no role after it preallocates the slaves. Thus, the master can simply terminate once the slaves have been started†. A clever programmer can even arrange for the master to create all except the last slave thread. The master then becomes the last slave, thereby saving the cost of one extra thread creation. In Windows, the code required to do so is trivial.

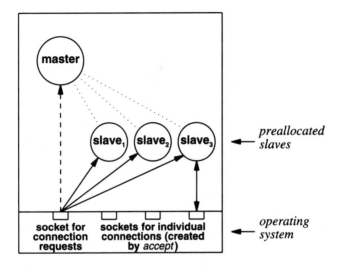

Figure 15.2 The thread structure in a concurrent, connection-oriented server that preallocates slaves. The example shows three preallocated slaves with one of them actively handling a connection. The master opens the socket for the well-known port, but does not use it.

15.8.3 Preallocation In A Connectionless Server

If a concurrent server uses connectionless transport, the level of concurrency depends on the number of requests that arrive. Each incoming request arrives in a separate UDP datagram, and each must be given to a separate thread. Concurrent, connectionless designs usually arrange for a master server to create a separate slave when a request arrives.

Windows permits a connectionless server to preallocate slaves using the same preallocation strategy as is used in connection-oriented servers. Figure 15.3 shows the thread structure.

---

†In practice, some systems require the master to remain allocated because it "owns" the slaves.

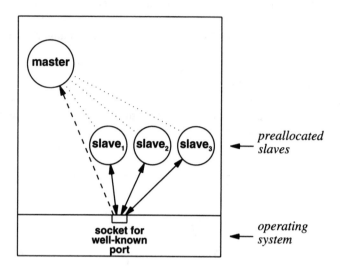

Figure 15.3 The thread structure for a concurrent, connectionless server that
preallocates slaves. The diagram shows three slaves that all read
from the socket for the well-known port. Only one slave receives each incoming request.

As the figure shows, each slave shares access to the socket for the well-known
port. Because communication is connectionless, the slaves can use a single socket to
send responses as well as to receive incoming requests. A slave calls *recvfrom* to obtain the sender's address as well as a datagram from that sender; it calls *sendto* to
transmit a reply.

As in a connection-oriented server that uses preallocation, the master for the connectionless case has little to do after it opens the socket for the well-known port and
preallocates the slaves. Thus, it can either terminate or choose to transform itself into
the last slave to avoid the overhead of creating the last thread.

15.8.4 Preallocation, Bursty Traffic, And NFS

Experience has shown that because most implementations of UDP do not provide
large queues for arriving datagrams, bursts of incoming requests can easily overrun a
queue. UDP merely discards datagrams that arrive after the receiver's queue has filled,
so bursts of traffic can cause loss.

The problem of overrun is especially difficult because UDP software often resides
in the operating system. Thus, application programmers cannot always modify it easily.
However, application programmers can preallocate slave threads. The preallocation is
usually sufficient to eliminate loss.

Many implementations of NFS use preallocation to avoid datagram loss. If one examines a system running NFS, one often finds a set of preallocated servers all reading from the same UDP socket. In fact, preallocation can mean the difference between a usable and an unusable implementation of NFS.

15.8.5 Preallocation On A Multiprocessor

Preallocation on a multiprocessor has a special purpose. It permits the designer to relate the level of concurrency in a server to the hardware's capability. If the machine has K processors, the designer can preallocate K slaves. Because multiprocessor operating systems give each process or thread to a separate processor, a preallocation can ensures that the level of concurrency matches the hardware. When a request arrives, the operating system passes it to one of the preallocated slaves, and assigns that slave to a processor. Because the slave has been preallocated, little time is required to start it running. Thus, the system will distribute requests quickly. If a burst of requests arrives, each processor will handle one request, giving the maximum possible speed.

15.9 Delayed Thread Allocation

Although preallocation can improve efficiency, it does not solve all problems. Surprisingly, in some circumstances efficiency can be improved by using the opposite approach: namely, delaying slave allocation.

To understand how delay can help, recall that thread creation requires time and resources. Creating additional threads can only be justified if doing so will somehow increase the system throughput or lower delay. Creating a thread not only takes time, it also adds overhead to the operating system component that must manage threads. In addition, preallocating threads that all attempt to receive incoming requests may add overhead to the networking code.

We said that concurrency will lower delay if the cost of creating a thread is smaller than the cost of processing a request. An iterative solution works best if the cost of processing a request is smaller. However, a programmer cannot always know how the costs will compare because the time required may depend on the request (e.g., the time required to search a database may depend on the query).

In addition, the programmer cannot know whether an error will be found quickly. To understand why, consider how most server software works. When a request arrives, the server software checks the message to verify that the fields contain appropriate values and that the client is authorized to make a request. Verification can take a few microseconds, or it may involve further network communication that can take several orders of magnitude longer. On one hand, if the server detects an error in the message, it will reject the request quickly, making the total time required to process the message negligible. On the other hand, if the server receives a valid request, it may take considerable processing time. In cases where processing time is short, concurrent processing is unwarranted; an iterative server exhibits lower delay and higher throughput.

How can designers optimize delay and throughput when they do not know whether concurrent processing is justified? The answer lies in a technique for *delayed concurrency*. The idea is straightforward: instead of choosing an iterative or concurrent design, allow a server to measure processing cost and choose between iterative handling or concurrent handling dynamically. The choice is dynamic because it can vary from one request to the next.

To implement dynamic, delayed allocation, servers usually estimate processing cost by measuring elapsed time. The master server receives a request, sets a timer, and begins processing the request iteratively. If the server finishes processing the request before the timer expires, the server cancels the timer. If the timer expires before the server finishes processing the request, the server creates a slave and allows the slave to handle the request. To summarize:

> *When using dynamic, delayed allocation, a server begins processing each request iteratively. The server creates a concurrent thread to handle the request only if processing takes substantial time. Doing so allows the master to check for errors and handle short requests before it creates a thread or switches context.*

In most systems, delayed allocation is easy. The operating system offers mechanisms that permit a running program to set an asynchronous timer. When it begins to handle a request, the master sets a timer. When the timer expires, the master creates a slave, and arranges for the slave to continue processing exactly at the point where the master was executing before the timer expired. If the master created a socket for the request, the slave takes control of the socket.

15.10 The Uniform Basis For Both Techniques

It may seem that the techniques of slave preallocation and delayed slave allocation have nothing in common. In fact, they seem to be exact opposites. However, they share much in common because they both arise from the same conceptual principle: it is possible to improve the performance of some concurrent servers by relaxing the interval between request arrival and slave creation. Preallocation increases the level of server concurrency before requests arrive; delayed allocation increases server concurrency after requests arrive. The idea can be summarized:

> *Preallocation and delayed allocation arise from a single principle: by detaching the level of server concurrency from the number of currently active requests, the designer can gain flexibility and improve server efficiency.*

15.11 Combining Techniques

The techniques of delayed allocation and preallocation can be combined. A server can begin with no preallocated threads and can use delayed allocation. It waits for a request to arrive, and only creates a slave if processing takes a long time (i.e., if its timer expires). Once a slave has been created, however, the slave need not exit immediately; it can consider itself permanently allocated and persist. After processing one request, the slave can wait for the next incoming request to arrive.

The biggest problem with a combined system arises from the need to control concurrency. It is easy to know when to create an additional slave, but more difficult to know when a slave should cease execution instead of persisting. One possible solution arranges for the master to specify a maximum propagation value, M, when creating a slave. The slave can create up to M additional slaves, each of which can create zero more. Thus, the system begins with only a single master thread, but eventually reaches a fixed maximum level of concurrency. Another technique for controlling concurrency involves arranging for a slave to terminate after a period of inactivity. The slave starts a timer before it waits for the next request. If the timer expires before a request arrives, the slave terminates.

In systems like Windows, the slaves can use facilities like shared memory to coordinate their activities. They create a shared integer that records the level of concurrency at any instant, and use the value to determine whether to persist or terminate after handling a request. In systems that permit an application to find out the number of requests enqueued at a socket, a slave can also use the queue length to help it decide the level of concurrency.

15.12 Summary

Two main techniques permit a designer to improve concurrent server performance: preallocation and delayed allocation of slaves.

Preallocation optimizes delay by arranging to create slaves before they are needed. The master server opens a socket for the well-known port it will use and then preallocates all slaves. Because the slaves share access to the socket, they can all wait for a request to arrive. The system hands each incoming request to exactly one slave. Preallocation is important for concurrent, connectionless servers because the time required to process a request is usually small, making the overhead of thread or process creation significant. Preallocation also makes concurrent, connectionless designs efficient on multiprocessor systems.

Delayed allocation uses a lazy approach to concurrency management. A master server begins processing each request iteratively, but sets a timer. It creates a concurrent slave to handle the request if the timer expires before the master finishes. Delayed allocation works well in cases where processing times vary among requests or when a server must check a request for correctness (e.g., to verify that the client is authorized). Delayed allocation eliminates thread creation overhead for short requests or requests that contain errors.

Although they appear to be opposite, both optimization techniques arise from the same basic principle: they relax the strict coordination between the level of concurrency in the server and the number of pending requests. Doing so can improve server performance.

FOR FURTHER STUDY

Chapters *23* and *24* describe the *Network File System* (NFS). Many implementations of NFS use preallocation to help avoid loss of requests.

Beveridge and Weiner [1997] describes multithreaded applications that use Win32. Further details about the functions available for process and timer management can be found in the documentation that vendors supply with standard compilers.

EXERCISES

15.1   Modify one of the example servers in previous chapters to use preallocation. How does the performance change?

15.2   Modify one of the example servers in previous chapters to use delayed allocation. How does the performance change?

15.3   Test a connectionless server that uses preallocation on a multiprocessor. Be sure to arrange for clients to transmit bursts of requests. How does the useful level of concurrency relate to the number of processors? If the two are not the same, explain why.

15.4   Write a server algorithm that combines delayed allocation with preallocation. What scheme did you choose to limit the maximum level of concurrency? Why?

15.5   In the previous question, if your operating system offered a message passing facility, how could you use it to control the level of concurrency?

15.6   What advantages can one obtain by combining the techniques discussed in this chapter with a concurrent, singly-threaded server?

15.7   How can a designer use the techniques discussed in this chapter with a multiservice server?

16

Concurrency In Clients

16.1 Introduction

The previous chapters show how servers can handle requests concurrently. This chapter considers the issue of concurrency in client software. It discusses how a client can benefit from concurrency and how a concurrent client operates. Finally, it shows an example client that illustrates concurrent operation.

16.2 The Advantages Of Concurrency

Servers use concurrency for two main reasons:

- Concurrency can improve the observed response time (and therefore the overall throughput to all clients).
- Concurrency can eliminate potential deadlocks.

In addition, a concurrent implementation permits the designer to create multiprotocol or multiservice servers easily. Finally, concurrent implementations that use multiple processes or threads are extremely flexible because they operate well on a variety of hardware platforms. When ported to a computer that has a single CPU, they work correctly. When ported to a computer that has multiple processors, they operate more efficiently because they take advantage of the additional processing power without any changes to the code.

It may seem that clients could not benefit from concurrency, primarily because a client usually performs only one activity at a time. Once it sends a request to a server, the client cannot proceed until it receives a response. Furthermore, the issue of client efficiency and deadlock are not as serious as the issue of server deadlock because if a client slows or ceases to execute, it stops only itself – other clients continue to operate.

Despite appearances, concurrency does have advantages in clients. First, concurrent implementations can be easier to program because they separate functionality into conceptually separate components. Second, concurrent implementations can be easier to maintain and extend because they make the code modular. Third, concurrent clients can contact several servers at the same time, either to compare response times or to merge the results the servers return. Fourth, concurrency can allow the user to change parameters, inquire about the client status, or control processing dynamically. This chapter will focus on the idea of interacting with multiple servers at the same time.

> *The key advantage of using concurrency in clients lies in asynchrony.*
> *It allows a client to handle multiple tasks simultaneously without im-*
> *posing a strict execution order on them.*

16.3 The Motivation For Exercising Control

One possible use of asynchrony arises from the need to separate control functions from normal processing. For example, consider a client used to query a large demographic database. Assume a user can generate queries like:

Find all people who live on Elm Street.

If the database contains information for a single town, the response could include fewer than *100* names. If the database contains information about all people in the United States, however, the response could contain hundreds of thousands of names. Furthermore, if the database system consists of many servers distributed across a wide geographic area, the look up could take many minutes.

The database example illustrates an important idea underlying many client-server interactions: a user who invokes a client may have little or no idea how long it will take to receive a response or how large that response will be.

Most client software merely waits until a response arrives. Of course, if the server malfunctions, deadlock occurs and the client will block attempting to read a response that will never arrive. Unfortunately, the user cannot know if a true deadlock has occurred or if processing is merely slow because network delays are high or the server is overloaded. Furthermore, the user cannot know whether the client has received any messages from the server.

If a user becomes impatient or decides that a particular response requires too much time, the user has only one option: abort the client program and try again later. In such situations, concurrency can help because an appropriately designed concurrent client can permit the user to continue to interact with the client while the client waits for a response. The user can find out whether any data has been received, choose to send a different request, or terminate the communication gracefully.

As an example, consider the hypothetical database client described above. A concurrent implementation can read and process commands from the user's keyboard concurrently with the database search. Thus, a user can type a command like *status* to determine whether the client has successfully opened a connection to the server and whether the client has sent a request. The user can type *abort* to stop communication, or the user can type *newserver* to instruct the client to terminate the existing communication and attempt to communicate with another server.

Separating client control from normal processing allows a user to interact with a client even if the normal input for the client comes from a file. Thus, even after the user starts a client handling a large input file, he or she can interact with the running client program to find out how processing has progressed. Similarly, a concurrent client can proceed to place responses in an output file while keeping its interaction with the user separate.

16.4 Concurrent Contact With Multiple Servers

Concurrency can allow a single client to contact several servers at the same time and to report to the user as soon as it receives a response from any of them. For example, a concurrent client for the TIME service can send to multiple servers and either accept the first response that arrives or take the average of several responses.

Consider a client that uses the ECHO service to measure the throughput to a given destination. Assume the client forms a TCP connection to an ECHO server, sends a large volume of data, reads the echo back, computes the total time required for the task, and reports the time. A user can invoke such a client to determine the current network throughput.

Now consider how concurrency can enhance a client that uses ECHO to measure throughput. Instead of measuring one connection at a time, a concurrent client can access multiple destinations at the same time. It can send to any of them and read from any of them concurrently. Because it performs all measurements concurrently, it executes faster than a non-concurrent client. Furthermore, because it makes all measurements at the same time, they are all affected equally by the loads on the CPU and the local network.

16.5 Implementing Concurrent Clients

Like concurrent servers, most concurrent client implementations follow one of two basic approaches:

- The client divides into two or more threads that each handle one function,

  or

- The client consists of a single thread that uses *select* to handle multiple input and output events asynchronously.

Systems like Windows have support for threads that share memory. On such systems, multiple threads can be used to create a concurrent client when the application uses a connection-oriented protocol. Figure 16.1 illustrates the thread structure of such a program.

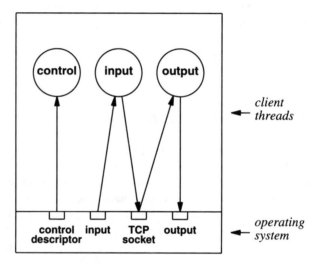

Figure 16.1 One possible thread structure for a connection-oriented client that uses multiple threads to achieve concurrent processing. One thread handles input and sends requests to the server, while another retrieves responses and handles output.

As Figure 16.1 illustrates, multiple threads allow the client to separate input and output processing. The figure shows how the threads interact with I/O device sockets. An *input thread* reads from the keyboard, formulates requests, and sends them to the server over the TCP connection, while a separate *output thread* receives responses from the server and displays them on the user's screen. Meanwhile, a third *control thread* accepts commands from the user or system administrator that control processing.

16.6 Singly-Threaded Implementations

Some operating systems do not support threads that share memory. For example, the multithreaded implementation described above does not work under some versions of UNIX. Concurrent clients built for such systems usually implement concurrency with a singly-threaded algorithm similar to Algorithm 8.5† and the examples in Chapters *12* through *14*. Figure 16.2 illustrates the thread structure of such clients.

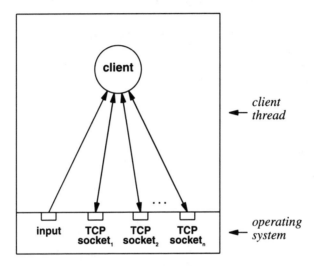

Figure 16.2 The thread structure of a connection-oriented client that provides apparent concurrency with a single thread. The client uses *select* to handle multiple connections concurrently.

A singly-threaded client uses asynchronous I/O like a singly-threaded server. The client creates socket descriptors for its TCP connections to multiple servers. It may also have a connection to an input device such as a keyboard. The body of a client program consists of a loop that checks the input device and then uses *select* to wait for one of its socket descriptors to become ready‡. If the input device is ready, the client reads the input and either stores it for later use or acts on it immediately. If a TCP connection becomes ready for output, the client prepares and sends a request across the TCP connection. If a TCP connection becomes ready for input, the client reads the response that the server has sent and handles it.

Of course, a singly-threaded concurrent client shares many advantages and disadvantages with a singly-threaded server implementation. The client reads input or responses from the server at whatever rate they are generated. Local processing will continue even if the server delays for a short time. Thus, the client will continue to read and honor control commands even if the server fails to respond.

---

†See page 114 for a description of Algorithm 8.5.

‡The client can use the timeout feature of *select* to ensure that it checks the input device frequently.

A singly-threaded client can become deadlocked if it invokes a system function
that blocks. Thus, the programmer must be careful to ensure that the client thread does
not block indefinitely waiting for an event that will not occur. Of course, the programmer may choose to ignore some cases and to allow the user to detect that deadlock
problems have occurred. It is important for the programmer to understand the subtleties
and to make conscious decisions about each case.

16.7 An Example Concurrent Client That Uses ECHO

An example client that achieves concurrency with a single thread will clarify the
ideas presented above. The example concurrent client shown below in file
TCPtecho.cpp uses the ECHO service described in Chapter 7 to measure network
throughput to a set of machines.

```
/* TCPtecho.cpp - main, TCPtecho, reader, writer, mstime */

#include <stdio.h>
#include <string.h>
#include <time.h>
#include <winsock.h>


#define BUFSIZE          4096            /* write buffer size        */
#define CCOUNT           64*1024         /* default character count  */
#define WSVERS           MAKEWORD(2, 0)

#define MIN(x, y)        ((x)>(y) ? (y) : (x))

#define USAGE     "usage: TCPtecho [ -c count ] host1 host2...\n"

struct hdat {
        char            *hd_name;       /* host name                */
        SOCKET          hd_sock;        /* host socket descriptor   */
        unsigned        hd_rc;          /* recv character count     */
        unsigned        hd_wc;          /* send character count     */
} hdat[FD_SETSIZE];                     /* fd to host name mapping  */
char    buf[BUFSIZE];                   /* read/write data buffer   */

void    TCPtecho(fd_set *, int);
int     reader(struct hdat *, fd_set *);
void    writer(struct hdat *, fd_set *);
void    errexit(const char *, ...);
SOCKET  connectTCP(const char *, const char *);
long    mstime(u_long *);
```

```
/*------------------------------------------------------------------------
 * main - concurrent TCP client for ECHO service timing
 *------------------------------------------------------------------------
 */
void
main(int argc, char *argv[])
{
        int             ccount = CCOUNT;
        int             i, hcount, fd;
        unsigned long   one = 1;
        fd_set          afds;
        WSADATA         wsdata;

        hcount = 0;
        if (WSAStartup(WSVERS, &wsdata))
                errexit("WSAStartup failed\n");
        FD_ZERO(&afds);
        for (i=1; i<argc; ++i) {
                if (strcmp(argv[i], "-c") == 0) {
                        if (++i < argc && (ccount = atoi(argv[i])))
                                continue;
                        errexit(USAGE);
                }
                /* else, a host */


                fd = connectTCP(argv[i], "echo");

                if (ioctlsocket(fd, FIONBIO, &one)) {
                        fprintf(stderr,
                            "can't mark nonblocking (host %s): %d\n",
                            argv[i], GetLastError());
                        continue;
                }

                hdat[hcount].hd_name = argv[i];
                hdat[hcount].hd_sock = fd;
                hdat[hcount].hd_rc = hdat[hcount].hd_wc = ccount;
                ++hcount;
                FD_SET(fd, &afds);
        }
        TCPtecho(&afds, hcount);
        WSACleanup();
        exit(0);
}
```

```
/*------------------------------------------------------------------------
 * TCPtecho - time TCP ECHO requests to multiple servers
 *------------------------------------------------------------------------
 */
void
TCPtecho(fd_set *pafds, int hcount)
{
        fd_set  rfds, wfds;               /* read/write fd sets        */
        fd_set  rcfds, wcfds;             /* read/write fd sets (copy) */
        int     fd, hndx, i;

        for (i=0; i<BUFSIZE; ++i)         /* echo data     */
                buf[i] = 'D';
        memcpy(&rcfds, pafds, sizeof(rcfds));
        memcpy(&wcfds, pafds, sizeof(wcfds));

        (void) mstime((u_long *)0);       /* set the epoch */

        while (hcount) {
                memcpy(&rfds, &rcfds, sizeof(rfds));
                memcpy(&wfds, &wcfds, sizeof(wfds));

                if (select(FD_SETSIZE, &rfds, &wfds, (fd_set *)0,
                                (struct timeval *)0) == SOCKET_ERROR)
                        errexit("select failed: error %d\n",
                                GetLastError());
                for (hndx=0; hndx<hcount; ++hndx) {
                        fd = hdat[hndx].hd_sock;
                        if (FD_ISSET(fd, &rfds))
                                if (reader(&hdat[hndx], &rcfds) == 0) {
                                        /* this host is done */
                                        for (i=hndx+1; i<hcount; ++i)
                                                hdat[i-1]=hdat[i];
                                        hcount--;
                                        continue;
                                }
                        if (FD_ISSET(fd, &wfds))
                                writer(&hdat[hndx], &wcfds);
                }
        }
}
```

```
/*-----------------------------------------------------------------------
 * reader - handle ECHO reads
 *-----------------------------------------------------------------------
 */
int
reader(struct hdat *phd, fd_set *pfdset)
{
        u_long  now;
        int     cc;

        cc = recv(phd->hd_sock, buf, sizeof(buf), 0);
        if (cc == SOCKET_ERROR)
                errexit("recv: error %d\n", GetLastError());
        if (cc == 0)
                errexit("recv: premature end of file\n");
        phd->hd_rc -= cc;
        if (phd->hd_rc > 0)
                return 1;
        (void) mstime(&now);
        printf("%s: %d ms\n", phd->hd_name, now);
        (void) closesocket(phd->hd_sock);
        FD_CLR(phd->hd_sock, pfdset);
        return 0;
}


/*-----------------------------------------------------------------------
 * writer - handle ECHO writes
 *-----------------------------------------------------------------------
 */
void
writer(struct hdat *phd, fd_set *pfdset)
{
        int     cc;

        cc = send(phd->hd_sock, buf, MIN(sizeof(buf), phd->hd_wc), 0);
        if (cc == SOCKET_ERROR)
                errexit("send: error number %d\n", GetLastError());
        phd->hd_wc -= cc;
        if (phd->hd_wc == 0) {
                (void) shutdown(phd->hd_sock, 1);
                FD_CLR(phd->hd_sock, pfdset);
        }
}
```

```
/*-------------------------------------------------------------------------
 * mstime - report the number of clock ticks elapsed since mstime(0) call
 *-------------------------------------------------------------------------
 */
long
mstime(u_long *pms)
{
        static unsigned long    epoch;
        unsigned long           now;

        now = clock();
        if (pms == 0) {
                epoch = now;
                return 0;
        }
        *pms = now - epoch;
        return *pms;
}
```

16.8 Execution Of The Concurrent Client

The *TCPtecho* program accepts multiple machine names as arguments. For each machine, it opens a TCP connection to the ECHO server on that machine, sends *ccount* characters (bytes) across the connection, reads the bytes it receives back from each server, and prints the total time required to complete the task. Thus, the program can be used to measure the current throughput to a set of machines.

The main program begins by initializing the character count variable to the default value, *CCOUNT*. It then parses its arguments to see if they include the *-c* option. If so, it converts the specified count to an integer and stores it in variable *ccount* to replace the default.

The program assumes all arguments other than *-c* specify the name of a machine. For each such argument, it calls *connectTCP* to form a connection to the ECHO server on the named machine, and allocates an entry in array *hdat* to store information about the connection. It records the name of the remote machine in field *hd_name* and the descriptor for the socket in field *hd_sock*. Finally, it uses macro *FD_SET* to add the socket to the descriptor set.

Once it has established a TCP connection for each machine specified in the arguments, the main program calls procedure *TCPtecho* to handle the transmission and reception of data. *TCPtecho* handles all connections concurrently. It fills buffer *buf* with data to be sent (the letter *D*), and then calls *select* to wait for any TCP connection to become ready for input or for output. When the *select* call returns, *TCPtecho* iterates through all descriptors to see which are ready.

When it finds that a connection is ready for output, *TCPtecho* calls procedure *writer*, which sends as much data from the buffer as TCP will accept in a single call to *send*. If *writer* finds that all data has been sent, it calls *shutdown* to close the descriptor for output and removes the descriptor from the output set used by *select*.

When a connection is ready for input, *TCPtecho* calls procedure *reader*, which accepts as much data from the connection as TCP can deliver and place in the buffer. Procedure *reader* receives data, places it in the buffer, and decrements the count of characters remaining. If the count reaches zero (i.e., the server has received as many characters as it sent), procedure *reader* computes how much time has elapsed since data transmission started, prints a message, and closes the connection. It also removes the descriptor from the input set used by *select*. Thus, a message that reports the total time required to echo data appears on the output each time a connection completes.

After performing a single input or output operation on a connection, procedures *reader* and *writer* each return and the loop in *TCPtecho* continues to iterate, calling *select* again. *Reader* returns a value of *0* if it detected an end of file condition and closed a connection, and a value of *1*, otherwise. *TCPtecho* uses *reader*'s return code to determine whether it should remove the record of the connection. When the count of connections reaches zero, the loop in *TCPtecho* terminates, *TCPtecho* returns to the main program, and the main program returns, causing the client to cease execution.

16.9 Managing A Timer

To compute the time that elapses while sending and receiving data, *TCPtecho* calls procedure *mstime*. In principle, computing elapsed time is straightforward. However, because the *clock* function in Windows returns the time in milliseconds, the elapsed time for an event must be computed by subtracting the time at which the task starts from the time it finishes. Thus, at least two procedure calls are required – one to record the value from *clock* before starting, and another to subtract the initial value from the current time.

Mstime is used both to record the starting time and to compute elapsed time. It takes a single argument, *pms*, and uses the value to determine how to proceed. If the argument is zero, *mstime* records the current time in static variable *epoch*. If the argument is nonzero, *mstime* computes the difference between the current time and the stored *epoch* value, stores the result in the location given by *pms*, and returns the result as the value of the function.

16.10 Example Output

Figure 16.3 shows sample output from three separate executions of *TCPtecho*.

```
% TCPtecho localhost
localhost: 311 ms

% TCPtecho ector arthur merlin
arthur:   601 ms
merlin: 4921 ms
ector: 11791 ms

% TCPtecho -c 1000 sage
sage: 80 ms
```

Figure 16.3 An example of the output from three separate executions of
TCPtecho. A destination requires more time if it is further away
from the client or has a slower processor.

The first invocation shows that *TCPtecho* only requires *311* milliseconds to send
data to the ECHO server on the local machine. The command line has a single argument, *localhost*. Because the second invocation has three arguments (*ector*, *arthur*, and
merlin), it causes *TCPtecho* to interact with all three machines concurrently. The third
invocation measures the time required to reach machine *sage*, but the command line
specifies that *TCPtecho* should only send *1000* characters instead of the default (64K).

16.11 Concurrency In The Example Code

A concurrent implementation of *TCPtecho* improves the program in two ways.
First, a concurrent implementation obtains a more accurate measure of the time required
for each connection because it measures the throughput on all connections during the
same time interval. Thus, congestion affects all connections equally. Second, a concurrent implementation makes *TCPtecho* more appealing to users. To understand why,
look again at the times reported in the sample output for the second trial. The output
message for machine *arthur* appears in a little over one half of a second, the message
for machine *merlin* appears after about five seconds, and the final message, for *ector*,
appears after about twelve seconds. If the user had to wait for all tests to run sequentially, the total execution would require approximately eighteen seconds. When measuring machines further away on the Internet, individual times can be substantially longer,
making the concurrent version much faster. In many circumstances, using a sequential
client implementation to measure N machines can take approximately N times longer
than a concurrent version.

16.12 Summary

Concurrent execution provides a powerful tool that can be used in clients as well as servers. Concurrent client implementations can offer faster response time and can avoid deadlock problems. Finally, concurrency can help designers separate control and status processing from normal input and output.

We studied an example connection-oriented client that measures the time required to access the ECHO server on one or more machines. Because the client executes concurrently, it can avoid the differences in throughput caused by network congestion by making all measurements during the same time interval. The concurrent implementation also appeals to users because it overlaps the measurements instead of making the user wait to perform them sequentially.

EXERCISES

16.1   Notice that the example client checks ready socket descriptors sequentially. If many descriptors become ready simultaneously, the client will handle the descriptors with lowest indexes first, and then iterate through the others. After handling all ready descriptors, it again calls *select* to wait until another descriptor becomes ready. Consider the time that elapses between handling a ready descriptor and calling *select*. Less time elapses after operations on descriptors with higher indexes than elapses after operations on descriptors with low indexes. Can the difference lead to starvation? Explain.

16.2   Modify the example client to avoid the unfairness discussed in the previous exercise.

16.3   For each of the iterative and concurrent client designs discussed in this chapter, write an expression that gives the maximum number of sockets used.

16.4   Consider a browser used to access Web pages. Can a concurrent version of a browser appear to operate faster than a nonconcurrent version? Explain.

17

Tunneling At The Transport
And Application Levels

17.1 Introduction

Previous chapters describe the design of client and server software for cases where a TCP/IP internet interconnects all communicating machines. Many of the designs presented assume that clients and servers will run on reasonably powerful computers that have operating system support for concurrent processes or threads as well as full support for TCP/IP protocols.

This chapter begins to explore the techniques system managers and programmers use to exploit alternative topologies. In particular, it examines techniques that allow computers to use a high-level protocol service to carry IP traffic and designs that use IP to carry traffic for other protocol systems.

17.2 Multiprotocol Environments

In an ideal world, programmers using TCP/IP only need to build client and server software for computers that connect directly to a TCP/IP internet and provide full support for TCP/IP protocols. In reality, however, not all machines provide complete TCP/IP support, and not all organizations use TCP/IP exclusively to interconnect computers. For example, an organization may have small personal computers with insufficient capacity to run server software, or it may have groups of machines connected to networks that use protocols like *DECNET*, *SNA*, or *ATM*. In fact, networking in most organizations has grown over time as the organization has added new networks to interconnect existing groups of computers. Usually, network managers choose a hardware technology and a protocol suite for each group of computers independently. They use factors such as cost, distance, desired speed, and vendor availability when making a choice. Organizations that installed networks before TCP/IP protocols were available may have selected a vendor-specific protocol suite. As a result of such network evolution, most large organizations have several groups of machines, with each group using its own protocol suite. The point is:

> *Because networking has evolved slowly over many years, because vendors promoted proprietary network systems, and because TCP/IP was not always available, large organizations often have groups of computers using alternative protocol systems to communicate. Furthermore, to minimize expense, organizations often continue to use older network systems until they can phase in new technologies.*

For example, Figure 17.1 illustrates an organization that uses three networks at its two sites. Each site has its own Ethernet. A single wide area network uses *Asynchronous Transfer Mode (ATM)* to interconnect hosts at the two sites. As the figure shows, a subset of machines connect to each network.

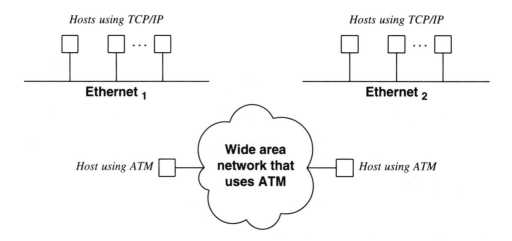

Figure 17.1 An example organization with three networks. All computers connected to the wide area network use ATM while all computers connected to the local area networks use TCP/IP.

The chief disadvantages of having multiple network systems arise from duplication of effort and limitations on interoperability. Applications on hosts that connect to an ATM wide area network can choose to interact directly with ATM facilities. Thus, if a client and server run on hosts connected to the ATM network shown in Figure 17.1, they must use an ATM virtual circuit for communication. Meanwhile, clients and servers running on an Ethernet use TCP virtual circuits.

17.3 Mixing Network Technologies

Usually, a TCP/IP internet consists of a set of host computers attached to physical networks that are interconnected by IP gateways (routers). All hosts and gateways in the internet must use TCP/IP protocols. Similarly, a network running the DECNET protocols consists of physical links and computers that use DECNET exclusively, while a network running SNA protocols usually consists of physical links and computers that use SNA exclusively. However, because a transport-level service can deliver packets from one point to another as easily as packet-switching hardware can, it should be possible to substitute any transport-level switching service in place of a single physical link in another packet switching system.

Many internets have been built that use switched technology instead of physical networks. For example, consider the networks shown in Figure 17.1 again. Assume the organization decides to interconnect its two Ethernets to form a single TCP/IP internet that will allow all the hosts attached to the Ethernets to communicate. The most obvious strategy involves installing two IP gateways between them. However, if a large geographic distance separates the two Ethernets, the cost of adding a dedicated leased line to interconnect the two networks may be prohibitive. The additional cost may be especially difficult to justify because the organization already has an ATM network connecting the two sites.

Figure 17.2 illustrates how the organization shown in Figure 17.1 can use existing ATM network connectivity to provide a TCP/IP internet connection between its two sites.

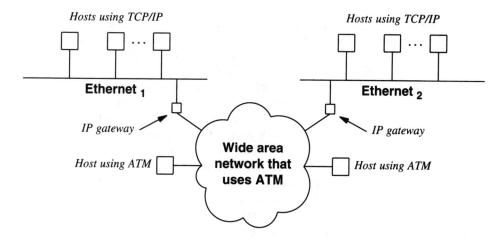

Figure 17.2 IP gateways using an ATM service.

The organization installs a new IP gateway at each site. Each of the new IP gateways connects to the ATM network and to the local Ethernet at its site. When the IP gateways boot, they use ATM to form a virtual circuit to one another across the ATM wide area network. Each IP gateway arranges its routing table so it routes nonlocal traffic across the ATM circuit. The IP gateways use the ATM network to send IP datagrams to one another. From the viewpoint of the IP gateways, ATM merely provides a link over which datagrams can be sent. From the viewpoint of the ATM network, software on the two IP gateways acts exactly like application software on other hosts. The ATM service does not know that the data being sent across the virtual circuit consists of IP datagrams.

With the two IP gateways in place, a user on any host can invoke standard TCP/IP client software that contacts a server on any other host. Client-server interactions may cross a single Ethernet or may traverse the ATM network to reach the other site. Neither the user nor the client-server applications needs to know that datagrams pass across an ATM network when they travel from the Ethernet at one site to the Ethernet at the other. The two Ethernets merely form part of a TCP/IP internet. Furthermore, hosts using ATM protocols on the wide area network do not need to change. They can continue to communicate without interference from the TCP/IP traffic because the virtual circuits they use will remain independent of the new connection between the IP gateways.

17.4 Dynamic Circuit Allocation

In the example topology that Figure 17.2 illustrates, the TCP/IP internet traffic needs only one ATM virtual circuit through the ATM network because the organization only has two sites. If the organization expands by adding additional sites, it can extend the topology by placing an IP gateway at each new site and creating additional circuits through the ATM network to interconnect each new IP gateway to the IP gateways at existing sites.

The static scheme for circuits described above can expand to an arbitrary number of sites if the ATM network does not limit the number of circuits that a single computer can allocate simultaneously. An organization with N sites will need $(N*(N-1))/2$ circuits to interconnect all of them. Thus, an IP gateway needs *15* connections for *6* sites, and *45* connections when the organization reaches *10* sites. Unfortunately, each circuit requires both hardware and software resources. For example, the routing software must store the mapping between the address of a remote IP gateway and the ATM circuit that connects to that gateway, and the network interface must allocate buffer space for the data being sent and received. More important, because communication is often intermittent, a connection may not be used for long periods.

To conserve resources, some implementations limit the number of simultaneous ATM circuits that can be open. Instead of arbitrarily choosing which connections are allowed, the implementations take a different approach – they allocate circuits on demand and close circuits that are not being used. When a datagram arrives at an IP gateway, the IP gateway looks up the destination address to determine the route the datagram will follow. The routing lookup produces a *next-hop address*, the address of the next IP gateway to which the datagram should be sent. If the next hop address specifies a site connected to the ATM network, the IP gateway consults its table of active ATM virtual circuits. If a circuit exists to the next-hop, the IP gateway forwards the datagram across the circuit. If no circuit exists, the IP gateway opens a new circuit to the desired destination dynamically.

If the limit of ATM circuits has been reached when an IP gateway needs to open a new circuit, the gateway must close an existing circuit to make one available. The problem becomes one of choosing which circuit to close. Usually, a gateway follows the same policy that a demand paging system uses: it closes the *least recently used* (LRU) circuit. After sending its datagram across the new circuit, the gateway leaves the circuit open. Often the outgoing datagrams will cause the receiver to reply, so keeping the circuit open helps minimize delay and cost.

By dynamically opening and closing virtual circuits, an IP gateway can limit the number of simultaneous connections it needs without losing the ability to communicate with all sites. The gateway only needs to have one circuit open for each site with which communication is currently in progress.

17.5 Encapsulation And Tunneling

The term *encapsulation* describes the process of placing an IP datagram inside a network packet or frame so that it can be sent across an underlying network. Encapsulation refers to how the network interface uses packet switching hardware. For example, two hosts that communicate across an Ethernet, using IP, encapsulate each datagram in a single Ethernet packet for transmission. The encapsulation standard for TCP/IP specifies that an IP datagram occupies the data portion of the Ethernet packet and that the Ethernet packet type must be set to a value that specifies IP.

By contrast, the term *tunneling* refers to the use of a transport network service to carry packets or messages from another service. For example, if the ATM network in Figure 17.2 is replaced by a transport service (e.g., an X.25 network system), the gateways would use a tunnel to communicate. In both tunneling and encapsulation, two computers attached to a network system use the system to send packets. The key difference between tunneling and encapsulation lies in whether IP transmits datagrams in hardware packets or uses a high-level transport service to deliver them.

> *IP encapsulates each datagram in a packet when it uses the hardware directly. It creates a tunnel when it uses a high-level transport delivery service to send datagrams from one point to another.*

17.6 Tunneling Through An IP Internet

After TCP/IP was first defined, researchers experimented to see how they could make IP software tunnel through existing networks to deliver datagrams. The motivation should be clear: many organizations had existing networks in place. Surprisingly, the trend has turned around. Most tunneling now occurs because vendors use IP protocols to deliver packets from non-TCP/IP protocols†.

Understanding the change in tunneling requires us to understand a change in networking. As the Internet became popular, it became the universal packet delivery mechanism for many groups. In fact, IP now provides the widest connectivity among the computers at most organizations.

To see how the availability of IP affects other protocols, suppose two computers in an organization need to communicate using a vendor-specific protocol. Instead of adding additional physical network connections between the two computers, a manager can think of the organization's intranet as a large network, and can allow the protocol software on the two computers to exchange messages by sending them in IP datagrams. Software is currently available that uses IP to carry IPX traffic (Novell), SNA traffic (IBM), and traffic from other high-level protocols. In addition, engineers have devised ways to allow IP networks to carry traffic from new protocols, allowing designers to build and debug new high-level protocols before they have working implementations of lower layers.

17.7 Application-Level Tunneling Between Clients And Servers

Although the general notion of tunneling refers to the use of one transport-level protocol suite by another, programmers can extend the idea to client-server interactions. The programmer can use *application-level tunneling* to provide a communication path between a client and a server.

To understand how application-level tunneling works, think of two computers that attach to a network that uses a protocol other than IP. Suppose a programmer wishes to run a UDP client application on one and a UDP server application on the other. Often, application programmers cannot make changes to the operating system software because they do not have access to system source code. Therefore, if the operating systems on the two computers do not support the UDP protocol, a programmer may find it inconvenient or impossible to use UDP or to make individual IP datagrams tunnel through the underlying network.

In such cases, application-level tunneling makes it possible for clients and servers to use IP protocols to communicate across a non-IP network. To use such a tunnel, the programmer must build a library of procedures that simulates the socket interface. The simulation library must allow an application to create an active or passive UDP socket and to send or receive UDP datagrams. Procedures in the socket simulation library translate calls to the standard socket routines (e.g., *socket*, *send*, and *recv*) into operations that allocate and manipulate local data structures and transmit the message across

---

†As one of the exercises suggests, tunneling can also be used to pass experimental IP traffic across the Internet.

the available network. When the client calls a function like *socket* or *bind*, the *socket* library routine records the information. When the client or server calls *send* to transmit a message, the *send* library routine consults the recorded information to determine the destination, and uses the underlying network system to transfer the UDP datagram.

Once a socket simulation library has been created, programmers can compile any UDP client or server program, link the compiled program using the simulation library, and then run the resulting application. Figure 17.3 illustrates the resulting software structure.

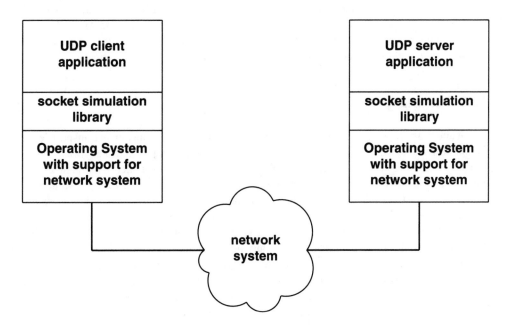

Figure 17.3 Conceptual organization of software in a client and server using application-level tunneling through a network. The socket simulation library allows the client and server to exchange UDP datagrams across a non-TCP/IP transport service.

17.8 Tunneling, Encapsulation, And Dialup Phone Lines

Modems are available that allow two computers to communicate across the dialup telephone system at speeds of 56 Kbps. A set of protocols, including *Serial Line IP* (*SLIP*) and the *Point-to-Point Protocol* (*PPP*) have been designed to send IP across a dialup channel.

Should IP transmission across a dialup connection be viewed as a form of tunneling or encapsulation? Certainly, the use of dialup is analogous to the notion of tunneling discussed in this chapter. The phone system can be viewed as a transport system over which IP datagrams are tunneled. In fact, dialup connections can be managed much like ATM circuits.

Although there is some debate, most experts agree that the dialup phone system should not be viewed as a transport system. Instead, the phone system should be viewed as a connection-oriented physical network. Thus, protocols such as SLIP and PPP define a form of encapsulation – they each define a link-level framing format that specifies how to encapsulate datagrams for transmission. Similar to a dedicated serial line, the phone system can be used to connect an IP gateway at one site to an IP gateway at another site. The next chapter explains how SLIP and PPP can be extended to accommodate dialup connections in a heterogeneous addressing environment.

17.9 Summary

Tunneling consists of sending packets between computers using a transport-level packet delivery system instead of sending them directly across physical networks. Early work on tunneling IP through existing network systems was motivated by organizations that already had large wide area networks in place. These organizations wanted to avoid the cost of adding new physical connections to run IP. Researchers devised ways to allow IP to use the existing networks to transfer packets without changing the networks. IP treats the transport service as a single hardware link; the transport service treats IP traffic the same as traffic sent by any application.

IP has become the delivery system that provides the most interoperability. Consequently, current work on tunneling concentrates on finding ways to use IP as a packet delivery system that carries packets for other network protocols. Many vendors have announced software that enables their proprietary networking systems to communicate across an underlying IP internet.

Programmers can apply the idea of tunneling to application software by building a library that simulates a socket interface but uses a non-TCP/IP transport service to deliver messages. In particular, it is easy to build a socket simulation library that allows clients and servers to communicate using UDP, even if the only connection between the client and server computers consists of a non-IP network.

The general concept of tunneling described in this chapter seems to apply to communication through the telephone system. Two IP gateways can use the phone system if they have dialup modems and they agree on a link-level protocol. When being precise, such communication is classified as encapsulation rather than tunneling.

FOR FURTHER STUDY

Cole et. al. [RFC 1932] provides a general description of IP over an ATM network. Laubach [RFC 1577] describes how the ARP protocol can be used to bind addresses when using IP over ATM.

Comer and Korb [1983] describes how to tunnel IP through an X.25 network, including how to manage X.25 virtual circuits when the hardware imposes a fixed limit on simultaneous connections. Malis et. al. [RFC 1356] describes tunneling over X.25 and ISDN. Provan [RFC 1234] describes tunneling IPX protocol traffic through an IP Internet. Simpson [RFC 1853] discusses tunneling IP in IP.

EXERCISES

17.1 Read RFC 877. How does an IP gateway that tunnels through an X.25 network map a destination IP address to an equivalent X.25 address?

17.2 Many transport-level services use their own retransmission scheme to provide reliable delivery. What can happen if both TCP and the underlying network protocols retransmit messages?

17.3 We said that many IP gateways use dynamic virtual circuit allocation, and that a gateway usually applies an LRU heuristic when it needs to close an existing circuit to make one available. Explain what happens in an IP gateway if the network interface allows K simultaneous circuits and the gateway attempts to communicate with $K+1$ other sites simultaneously.

17.4 Build a socket simulation library that allows client and server applications to exchange UDP datagrams over a non-TCP/IP transport-level protocol. Test it by arranging for a UDP ECHO client to communicate with a UDP ECHO server.

17.5 Suppose researchers at two sites decide to experiment with IP audio multicast. Although each researcher can assign multicast addresses and routes locally, they cannot change routes in Internet gateways that separate the two sites. Explain how the researchers can use tunneling to send multicast packets from one site to the other (hint: think of IP-in-IP).

18

Application Level Gateways

18.1 Introduction

The previous chapter examines tunneling, a technique that allows one protocol suite to use the transport-level delivery service from another protocol suite in place of a physical network. From an application programmer's viewpoint, tunneling makes it possible for a client and server to communicate using TCP/IP even if the only path between them includes a non-TCP/IP network.

This chapter continues the exploration of techniques that clients and servers use to communicate across environments that do not provide full TCP/IP connectivity. It shows how clients operating on systems with limited protocol support can use an application program on an intermediate machine to forward requests, and how the use of such intermediaries can expand the range of available services.

18.2 Clients And Servers In Constrained Environments

18.2.1 The Reality Of Multiple Technologies

Not all computer systems have direct access to the Internet. Furthermore, access limitations can complicate client and server software because they arise for economic and political reasons as well as technical ones. Chapter *17* points out that networking has evolved slowly in many organizations. As a result, subgroups may each have their own network and the networks may each use a different protocol suite. More important, a group of users may become accustomed to the application software available from a particular vendor or a particular computer. If the application software only operates with one set of protocols, the users may want to keep the network in place.

Network technologies can also gain inertia as managers gain expertise. As a technology becomes entrenched, an organization invests in training for personnel who install, manage, or operate the network. In addition to people who plan and manage the physical network, programmers invest time learning how to write software that uses the network. Once a manager learns the details and subtleties of a given technology, it becomes easier to expand the existing network than to replace it with a new technology. Thus, organizations that have multiple groups, each managing an independent network, often find that the initial cost of consolidation can be high because many groups must retrain their personnel.

For programmers, multiple network technologies often result in incompatible systems that do not provide interoperability. Unless the organization provides tunneling, programmers cannot depend on end-to-end transport-level connectivity. Thus, they cannot use a single transport protocol, nor can they easily communicate between clients and servers on arbitrary machines. Finally, programmers often build and maintain programs that duplicate functionality for each network technology. For example, programmers must maintain multiple electronic mail systems.

18.2.2 Computers With Limited Functionality

In addition to contending with multiple networks, programmers must sometimes create software for computers that offer limited network functionality. For example, many organizations have groups of small personal computers that lack operating system facilities for concurrent processing or asynchronous I/O. Such computers cannot support the concurrent server algorithms discussed in Chapter *8* or the concurrent client algorithms discussed in Chapter *16*.

18.2.3 Connectivity Constraints That Arise From Security

Organizations may institute security policies that also constrain how clients and servers communicate. Some organizations partition computers into *secure* and *unsecure* subsets. To prevent client and server programs from compromising security, the network manager places policy constraints on connectivity. The manager restrains computers in the secure partition so they can communicate among themselves, but they can neither initiate contact to servers nor accept requests from clients on computers in the unsecure partition. Although such policies ensure security, they can make it difficult for programmers to design applications that use client-server interactions. In particular, computers in one partition cannot directly access services available on computers in the other partition.

18.3 Using Application Gateways

Programmers who need to design client-server interactions in restricted environments usually rely on a single, powerful technique to overcome connectivity constraints. The technique consists of adding application programs that run on intermediate machines, and enabling the applications to relay information between a client and the desired server. An intermediate program that provides the service is known as an *application gateway*†. If the intermediate machine has been dedicated to running one particular application gateway program, programmers or network managers sometimes refer to the machine as a *gateway machine*. For example, a computer dedicated to running a program that passes electronic mail between two groups may be called a *mail gateway*. Technically, of course, the term *application gateway* refers to the running program – programmers stretch the terminology when they refer to a machine as an application gateway.

Figure 18.1 illustrates a common use of an application gateway as an intermediary between two electronic mail systems.

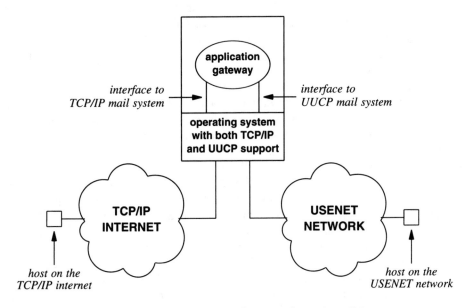

Figure 18.1 An application program used to pass electronic mail between two network systems. The application gateway understands the syntax and semantics of both mail systems, and translates messages between them.

---

†Use of the term *gateway* can be confusing because the term is also applied to systems that forward IP packets. To avoid confusion, one should distinguish the two carefully.

The organization depicted in Figure 18.1 has access to two main network systems: the USENET network and the Internet. Each network system has its own electronic mail system. In a broad conceptual sense, the two mail systems provide the same services. Each system allows a user to compose and transmit an outgoing message or to receive and read an incoming message. However, the two systems cannot interoperate directly because each has its own destination address syntax and its own mail transport protocol.

To allow users on one network system to send mail to users on the other, the organization has installed an application program that serves as a mail gateway. In the example, the mail gateway program runs on a computer that attaches to both networks. The mail gateway must be designed carefully so it can communicate with any host in the organization. It must understand how to send messages using either of the two mail systems, and it must have logical connections to both networks.

18.4 Interoperability Through A Mail Gateway

For the organization shown in Figure 18.1, a single mail gateway program can provide all the facilities the organization needs to establish interoperability for electronic mail. As usual, each host throughout the organization checks the destination address of outgoing mail, and chooses a next-hop machine. If an outgoing memo is destined for a machine on the same network as the sending machine, the sending machine uses the electronic mail system available on its local network to deliver the message. However, if a host encounters outgoing mail destined for a machine that attaches to a nonlocal network, the sending machine cannot deliver the message directly. Instead, the sender transmits the message to the mail gateway program. All machines can reach the mail gateway directly because it runs on a computer that attaches to both networks and communicates using either of the two mail delivery protocols.

Once a mail message arrives at the mail gateway, it must be routed again. The mail gateway examines the destination mail address to determine how to proceed. It may also consult a database of destinations to help make the decision. Once it knows the intended destination and the network over which it must deliver the message, the mail gateway selects the appropriate network and mail transport protocols.

The gateway may need to reformat a mail message or change the message header when forwarding it from one network to another. In particular, a mail gateway usually modifies the reply field in the mail header so the receiver's mail interface can correctly construct a reply address. The reply address modification may be trivial (e.g., adding a suffix that identifies the sender's network), or it may be complicated (e.g., adding information that identifies the mail gateway as an intermediate machine that will lead back to the source).

18.5 Implementation Of A Mail Gateway

In theory, a single thread suffices to implement a mail gateway. In practice, however, most implementations divide the functionality into two threads. One thread handles incoming mail messages, while the other manages outgoing mail. The thread that handles incoming mail never sends a message. It computes a reply address, routes the mail to its destination, and then deposits the outgoing message in a queue to await transmission. The thread that handles outgoing messages does not accept incoming messages directly. Instead, it scans the output queue periodically. For each message it finds in the output queue, the output thread makes a network connection to the destination, and sends the message. If it cannot make a connection to the destination (e.g., because the destination machine has crashed), the output thread leaves the message in the output queue and continues processing with the next message in the queue. Later, when it rescans the queue, the output thread will try again to contact the destination and deliver the message. If a message remains in the output queue for an extended time (e.g., three days), the output thread reports a delivery error to the user who originally sent the message.

Separating the mail gateway into input and output components allows each component to proceed independently. The output thread can try to deliver a message, wait to see if the connection attempt succeeds, and then go on to the next message without coordinating its activities with those of the input thread. If the connection attempt succeeds, the output thread can send a message without regard to its length. It does not need to interrupt transmission to accept incoming messages because the input thread handles them. Meanwhile, the input thread can continue to accept incoming messages, route them, and store them for later transmission. Because the components operate independently, a long output message does not block input processing, nor does a long input message interfere with output processing.

18.6 A Comparison Of Application Gateways And Tunneling

The previous chapter showed that designers could choose tunneling to provide interoperability in a heterogeneous environment. It may be difficult to choose between tunneling and application gateways because neither technique solves all problems well and each technique provides advantages in some situations.

The chief advantage of using an application gateway instead of tunneling arises because programmers can create application gateways without modifying the computer's operating system. In many circumstances, programmers cannot modify the system either because they do not have access to the source code or because they do not have the expertise required. An application gateway can be built using conventional programming tools; the gateway does not require any change to the underlying protocol software. Furthermore, once an application gateway is in place, the site can use standard client and server programs.

The operating systems on small personal computers often provide limited facilities that do not include support for concurrent processing. The lack of concurrent processing limits client-server interactions because the computer must be dedicated to a single task at any time. In particular, it is often impossible for a user to run a server in the background while using the computer for other processing.

To understand how the lack of background processing limits client-server interaction, consider electronic mail. A personal computer can support mail client software because it can wait until the user decides to send a message before executing client software. Furthermore, once the user composes a message, the client program can make the user wait while it transmits the message to its destination. However, a computer system that does not support concurrent processing cannot run server software in the background. Thus, it cannot have a server ready to accept incoming mail until the user decides to run the server. Unfortunately, users cannot run any other application while the mail server operates because the machine must stop receiving mail while performing any other task. As a result, users seldom use such computers to run electronic mail servers.

An organization that has many personal computers can use an application gateway to solve the server problem. Consider the computers in Figure 18.2 again. The organization has purchased one large, powerful computer on which it runs a standard server that accepts incoming electronic mail. The server, which runs in the background, remains available to accept mail at all times. When a message arrives, the server places it in a file on disk. Files that store mail are often called *mailbox files* or *mailboxes*. The system may have one mailbox file for each user, or may place each message in a separate file. Usually, implementations that use a separate file for each message collect the files together into directories, where each directory corresponds to a single user.

In addition to the standard mail server, the computer must also run a specialized application gateway that allows users on personal computers to access their mailboxes. To read mail, a user on one of the personal computers invokes a client that contacts the special application gateway. The gateway retrieves each message from the user's mailbox, and sends it to the personal computer for the user to read.

Using a powerful machine to run a conventional server that accepts incoming mail solves the server problem because it means that small personal computers do not need to run a mail server continuously. Using a mail gateway program to provide users with access to their mailboxes eliminates the need for users to log into the mail server machine.

18.8 Application Gateways Used For Security

Many organizations choose application gateways to solve the problem of security. For example, suppose an organization needs to restrict remote login. Imagine that the organization classifies its employees as either authorized or unauthorized for remote login. Figure 18.3 illustrates how the organization can use an application gateway to implement its security policy.

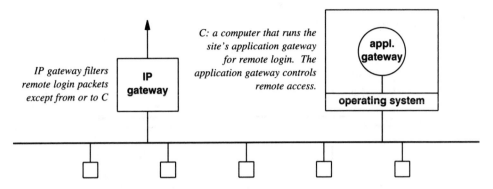

conventional hosts prohibited from sending remote login packets except through application gateway

Figure 18.3 An application gateway used to implement a remote login security policy. A user must communicate with remote machines through the application gateway which enforces authorization controls.

The organization depicted in the figure uses a conventional IP gateway filter to block all datagrams that contain remote login connection requests unless they originate from the host that runs the application gateway. To form a remote login connection, a user on any host in the organization invokes a client that first connects to the application gateway. After the user obtains authorization, the application gateway connects the user to the desired destination.

18.9 Application Gateways And The Extra Hop Problem

The *extra hop problem* refers to a situation in which datagrams pass across the same network twice on their way to a final destination. The problem is usually caused by incorrect routing tables.

Introduction of an application gateway into an existing network can also create a form of the extra hop problem. To understand why, consider the network topology that Figure 18.4a illustrates. The figure shows the path a message would travel from a host to a remote server if the host supported the same transport protocol as the server. Now assume that the existing host wishes to access a service that is only available through some protocol other than the one the host uses. Interoperability can be achieved by introducing an application gateway as Figure 18.4b shows. The application gateway accepts requests using one protocol system and sends them to the remote server using another. Unfortunately, each message traverses the network twice. The figure is realistic: network managers often acquire a new physical computer for each application gateway program because they want to avoid overloading existing machines.

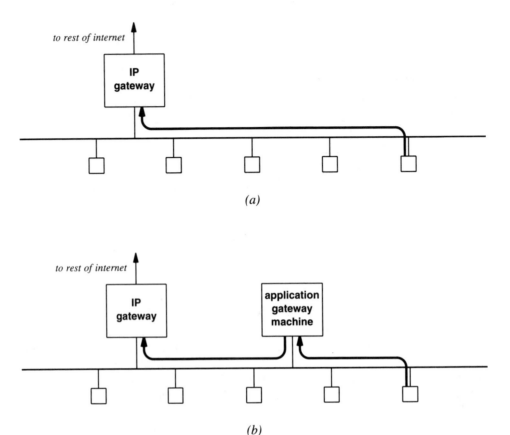

(a)

(b)

Figure 18.4 (a) A set of hosts and a gateway. The darkened arrow shows the
path a message takes from a host to a remote server and (b) the
path of a message after an application gateway is introduced.
The new gateway causes each message to traverse the network
twice.

Once the application gateway has been introduced, clients executing on existing
hosts use the application gateway to access the service it offers. A client sends its request to the application gateway using one protocol, which forwards the request on to
the remote server using another protocol. When the server returns its result to the application gateway, the gateway sends a response back to the client. The system appears to
work well. Existing protocol software on the hosts need not be changed. After the application gateway has been installed, a client executing on an arbitrary host will be able
to access the desired service through the gateway.

Unfortunately, close examination of the underlying network reveals that the configuration in Figure 18.4b does not make good use of network resources. It creates the extra hop problem. Each request must pass across the local area network twice: once when it travels from the original host to the application gateway machine, and once when it travels from the application gateway machine on toward the ultimate server. If the server lies in the Internet beyond the IP gateway, the second transmission occurs when the message passes from the application gateway machine to the IP gateway. If the server lies on the local net, the second transmission occurs when the message passes from the application gateway machine to the machine running the server.

For services that do not require much network traffic, the extra hop may be unimportant. Indeed, several vendors build products that use the topology Figure 18.4b illustrates. If the network is heavily loaded, however, or if the service requires significant network traffic, the extra hop may make such a solution too expensive. Thus, designers need to calculate expected load carefully before they adopt the application gateway approach.

18.10 An Example Application Gateway

An application gateway can extend services by providing access to client machines that do not run all protocols. For example, consider a user on a host that has access to the Web but has no access to file transfer protocols like FTP. Such restrictions may arise from economic considerations (e.g., the cost of FTP software is too high), commercial realities (e.g., no one sells FTP client software for the computer in question), or security reasons (e.g., the site decides to reduce its security risk by prohibiting file transfers)†.

Suppose a user on a restricted machine needs access to the *Request For Comments* documents (RFCs). The application gateway technique can solve the access problem by allowing the organization to interconnect electronic mail and FTP services, while controlling access and ensuring authorization.

To provide RFC access from a Web browser, an application gateway must connect to both services. To use the gateway, a user must visit a Web page on the gateway that corresponds to the desired RFC. The application gateway verifies that the user is authorized to access RFCs, makes an FTP connection, obtains a copy of the RFC, and displays the RFC document as a Web page.

For example, imagine an application gateway identified by the *Uniform Resource Locator (URL)*:

http://www.gateway.somewhere.com

Further imagine that a user who visits the page is presented with a list of all the RFC documents, each of which is a selectable item. RFCs are numbered consecutively, so one possible presentation lists all the integers that correspond to RFC documents.

---

†In reality, security considerations are the most likely reason; Web browsers contain FTP client code, meaning that a user who can obtain software to access the Web can also obtain an FTP client.

Another possible presentation displays one line per RFC; the line includes the RFC number along with the title.

To use such a gateway, a user specifies the gateway's URL to a Web browser that uses the *HyperText Transfer Protocol* (*HTTP*) to contact the gateway. The Web server running on the gateway machine responds to the browser's request by sending the list of RFCs to the browser for display. The user scans the list of RFCs and uses the mouse to select one of them.

So far, we have described conventional Web access; no application gateway is used to access the initial Web page. In fact, if the Web server on the gateway had a copy of each RFC in a local file, conventional Web access could be used to obtain an RFC. However, we will assume that RFCs are not prestored on the gateway's Web server. Instead, we will assume that an application gateway is used to fetch an RFC in response to the user's request. Thus, when the user selects an item from the initial Web page, the browser uses HTTP to send the application gateway a request that identifies the desired RFC. The application gateway uses FTP to obtain the RFC, and then uses HTTP to return the RFC to the browser.

18.11 Details Of A Web-Based Application Gateway

To implement the example application gateway described above, four facilities are required: a computer that has access to both HTTP and FTP, a conventional Web server, the application gateway program, and a mechanism that passes incoming RFC requests from the Web server to the gateway program. Fortunately, most Web servers include the necessary facilities. In particular, Web servers use the *Common Gateway Interface* (*CGI*) technology to permit the server to invoke a program.

A Web server that includes CGI programs must handle two types of requests. When it receives a request for a conventional Web page, the server retrieves a copy of the page from disk, and sends the copy to the browser that made the request. When it receives a request for information managed by a CGI program, the server invokes the program, passes it the request, and waits for the program. When it runs, the CGI program generates output, which the Web server passes back to the browser that sent the request. For example, Figure 18.5 illustrates the architecture of an application gateway that uses a CGI program to access RFCs.

To make the scheme work, the application gateway must return a valid document. In the case of a CGI program, the output from the program must be a document that a browser can display. Fortunately, browsers are designed to accept multiple formats. If the gateway returns ASCII text, the browser will display it in a fixed-width font. Thus, if the CGI program sends the browser an exact copy of the file obtained via FTP, the browser will display the RFC as ASCII text. If the gateway modifies the document to insert HTML commands, the browser will interpret formatting commands when it displays the document.

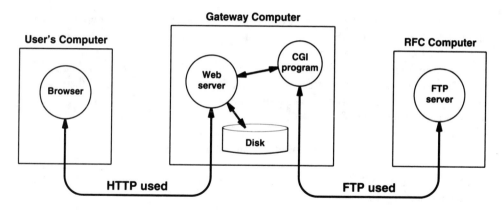

Figure 18.5 Communication from a browser through an application gateway
to an FTP server. An intermediate gateway is used in situations
where the user's computer is restricted from direct FTP access.

Note that from a browser's perspective, it cannot distinguish between conventional
Web pages and documents produced by CGI programs. In either case, the browser
sends a request, receives a document, and displays the document for the user.

18.12 Invoking A CGI Program

How can the Web server know whether a request corresponds to a conventional
Web page or an application gateway? The server uses the URL that arrives in the request from the browser to determine whether to retrieve a conventional page or run a
CGI program. In fact, most servers manage multiple CGI programs just as they manage
multiple Web pages. Each URL that invokes a CGI program must identify a particular
program to run, and supply arguments to the program.

On most computer systems, the CGI programs that a Web server can invoke are
placed in a single folder. For example, the system administrator in charge of the server
might choose to place all CGI programs in folder *C:\www-cgi*. The system administrator then configures the server to associate URLs with programs in the folder. A prefix
is used to identify the URL as a CGI request, and the next piece of the URL identifies a
particular CGI program. For example, a site might choose to associate URLs that begin:

http://www.somewhere.com/cgi-bin/

with the CGI folder†. If a program in the folder is named *pgm*, the program is invoked
with the URL:

http://www.somewhere.com/cgi-bin/pgm

---

†In practice, many Web administrators select a term that is easier to remember than *cgi-bin* (e.g., *gateway*).

When the request arrives, the server extracts the name of the requested item and checks the prefix. For any name that begins *cgi-bin/*, the server extracts the next component, and uses that as the name of a program.

In addition to a prefix that identifies the item as a CGI request and the name of a specific CGI program, a request can contain a string that will be passed to the program as an argument. The syntax uses a question mark to separate the program name from the argument string†. Thus, the URL:

http://www.somewhere.com/cgi-bin/pgm?arg-string

causes the server to pass one argument to program *pgm*. The argument consists of the character string *arg-string*.

18.13 URLs For The RFC Application Gateway

The implementation of an application gateway to fetch RFCs should now be clear. The initial Web page contains a large set of selectable links. The URL for each link begins with a prefix that specifies the application gateway program followed by an argument that specifies the number of the RFC. For example, if the program is named *retrieve-rfc* and resides in the CGI directory on the Web server at *somewhere.com*, the URL associated with RFC *2000* would be:

http://www.somewhere.com/cgi-bin/retrieve-rfc?2000

If a user selects the link, the browser sends the URL to the Web server in a request. The Web server invokes program *retrieve-rfc*, passing *2000* as an argument.

18.14 A General-Purpose Application Gateway

An interesting application gateway has been developed for use with dialup telephone lines. Called *SLIRP*, the gateway is unusual because it allows access to multiple services. In particular, SLIRP was built to allow an application program running on a home computer to access an arbitrary application on the Internet.

To appreciate the design of SLIRP, it is necessary to know that SLIRP solves a different problem than SLIP or PPP. Instead of defining an encapsulation protocol for use over a serial line, SLIRP solves an important IP address problem. The problem arises when users with home computers desire dialup access to the Internet. In the traditional IP addressing model, each computer must be assigned a unique IP address. Unfortunately, dialup access makes it difficult to verify the owner of a given IP address and difficult to use the address to enforce restrictions on access. Thus, for security reasons, many companies restrict dialup access to conventional terminal login, and do not assign IP addresses to remote computers.

---

†The advantage of using a different delimiter for the argument string is that the program name can contain a path.

The chief disadvantage of restricting dialup access is that it limits functionality: although a dialup terminal session can be used with character-oriented protocols such as FTP and TELNET, a user cannot access services such as the World Wide Web that require clients to have full IP access. SLIRP overcomes the limitation with a mechanism that provides IP access over dialup phone lines without assigning an IP address to each computer.

18.15 Operation Of SLIRP

SLIRP operates as an application gateway on a computer that has both Internet access and a dialup telephone modem. To use SLIRP, one must first establish a conventional terminal session. That is, when a user on a home computer first dials in to a machine, G, that runs a SLIRP gateway, the user establishes a terminal session by sending a login identifier and a password. Once the user has established a terminal session on G, the user performs two steps in quick succession. First, the user invokes SLIRP on computer G. Second, the user deletes the terminal session on the home computer, and allows PPP† to use the connection. In fact, software exists that automates the steps of dialing in, starting SLIRP, and then starting PPP on the local computer.

When PPP runs across a dialup connection, it treats the connection like a serial line. IP routing on the home computer uses the dialup connection as a default route for all traffic. PPP at one end of the connection encapsulates datagrams in a PPP frame for transmission, and PPP at the other end removes the datagram.

Because it understands PPP encapsulation, SLIRP can send or receive datagrams across the dialup connection. Furthermore, SLIRP contains the code needed to process incoming TCP segments as well as the code needed to handle IP datagrams. For example, SLIRP can generate or verify an IP checksum, and it can send an acknowledgement in response to a TCP segment. In essence, SLIRP contains software for the entire TCP/IP protocol stack in an application program.

18.16 How SLIRP Handles Connections

Because SLIRP is an application program, the TCP/IP code in SLIRP does not interact directly with TCP/IP protocol software in the operating system of the gateway computer. Instead, SLIRP only uses its TCP/IP code to interpret datagrams that arrive across the dialup connection; SLIRP uses the socket interface to communicate with the Internet.

SLIRP maps between events that occur on the dialup connection and events that occur on the Internet. For example, suppose the home computer establishes a TCP connection to destination D. As segments arrive from the home computer, SLIRP impersonates D. That is, when the home computer sends a *SYN*, SLIRP responds as if D answered. Meanwhile, SLIRP creates a socket and connects to D. Similarly, SLIRP transfers data between the home machine and the Internet. For example, if data arrives

---

†Although we refer to PPP in the example, versions of SLIRP exist that use SLIP.

across the TCP connection from the home machine, SLIRP receives the data, returns a
TCP acknowledgement, and then uses the socket interface to send the data to its destination, *D*.

18.17 IP Addressing And SLIRP

How does using SLIRP differ from the conventional use of PPP? The answer lies
in IP addressing as Figure 18.6 illustrates.

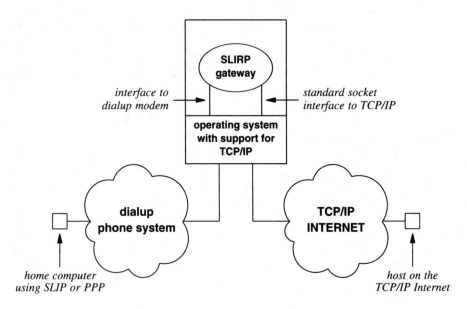

Figure 18.6 Illustration of a SLIRP gateway. Although the home computer
can use an arbitrary IP address, SLIRP uses a valid address
when communicating with a host on the Internet.

Whenever SLIRP interacts with a host on the Internet, SLIRP uses the socket interface. Thus, SLIRP operates like any other application running on the gateway machine.
In particular, all communication from SLIRP across the Internet uses the IP address assigned to the gateway computer; remote destinations cannot distinguish between communication with SLIRP and communication with any other application on the gateway
computer.

In contrast to the addressing it uses on the Internet, the addressing SLIRP uses on
the dialup connection is nonstandard. Because SLIRP intercepts all datagrams from the
home machine, the IP address used by the home machine does not need to be valid –
any address can be used provided that the address is not used elsewhere†. Thus, SLIRP
users often choose an IP address like *10.0.0.1*, that is not assigned to an Internet host
and is easy to remember.

---

†If a valid Internet address is used, the home machine cannot communicate with the computer that owns
the address.

18.18 Summary

Although tunneling allows one protocol system to use another high-level protocol as a transport device, conventional tunneling is restricted to cases where the designer has access to the operating system code. The application gateway technique, an alternative to tunneling, permits application programmers to interconnect heterogeneous systems without changing the operating system.

An application gateway is a program that accepts requests using one high-level protocol and fulfills requests using another high-level protocol. In essence, each application gateway is a server for one service and a client of another.

We saw that an application gateway can be associated with a Web server. The Web server uses a technology like CGI to invoke the application gateway program when a request arrives, and forwards output from the program back to the browser that sent the request. The Web server uses the prefix of a URL to determine whether the URL refers to a CGI program or a conventional Web page; the server must be configured to associate a specific prefix with a folder of CGI programs. In addition to specifying a CGI program, a URL can contain a suffix that is passed to the program as an argument.

Many sites use application gateways to implement authorization and security checks. Because the gateway operates as a conventional application program, little effort is required to program the gateway to filter unwanted access or to keep a record of each request.

A gateway, called SLIRP, exists that supports multiple services. Intended for use over a dialup telephone line, SLIRP allows a home computer to access IP services without requiring the home computer to be assigned a valid IP address. The home computer runs PPP or SLIP software, which sends IP datagrams across a dialup connection. SLIRP receives incoming datagrams, sends acknowledgements that impersonate the destination, and uses conventional Internet software to communicate with the destination.

FOR FURTHER STUDY

Simpson [RFC 1661] documents the PPP protocol, and Romkey [RFC 1055] describes SLIP. Consult Web server documentation to learn more about CGI.

The Web site:

> http://ucnet.canberra.edu.au/slirp

has information about the *SLIRP* program as well as source code. Note especially file *slirp.doc* in the source code.

The Post Office Protocol (POP) provides a standard application gateway service that allows a personal computer to access e-mail from a server. Myers and Rose [RFC 1939] describes version *3* of the POP protocol (*POP3*).

EXERCISES

18.1   What authorization checks should an application gateway perform? Why?

18.2   Many application gateways implement caching in which the gateway keeps a local copy of the last N items fetched to avoid fetching the items for subsequent requests. Under what conditions is caching beneficial? Not beneficial?

18.3   In the previous question, consider a concurrent application gateway. For example, suppose a Web server creates a new thread to execute a CGI program each time a user sends a request. Explain how the threads might interfere with one another.

18.4   Can a sender request a copy of the RFC index with a CGI program? Why or why not?

18.5   Read about CGI. How does CGI use the environment variable *QUERY_STRING*?

18.6   Can *SLIRP* be used to run client software on a home machine? Can it be used to run a server? Explain.

19

External Data Representation (XDR)

19.1 Introduction

Previous chapters describe algorithms, mechanisms, and implementation techniques for client and server programs. This chapter begins a discussion of the concepts and techniques that help programmers use the client-server paradigm and the mechanisms that provide programming support for these concepts. In particular, it examines a *de facto* standard for external data representation and presentation as well as a set of library procedures used to perform data conversion.

The chapter describes the general motivations for using an external data representation and the details of one particular implementation. The next chapter shows how an external data representation standard helps simplify client and server communication, and illustrates how a standard makes it possible to use a single, uniform remote access mechanism for client-server communication.

19.2 Representations For Data In Computers

Each computer architecture provides its own definition for the representation of data. Some computers store the least significant byte of an integer at the lowest memory address, others store the most significant byte at the lowest address, and others do not store bytes contiguously in memory. For example, Figure 19.1 shows the two most popular representations for 32-bit integers.

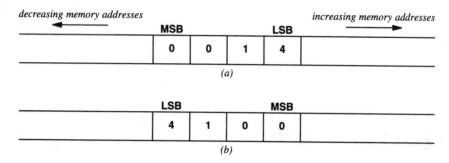

Figure 19.1 Two representations for the value *260* stored as a 32-bit binary integer: (a) "big endian" order with the most significant byte at the lowest memory address and (b) "little endian" order with the least significant byte at the lowest memory address. Numbers give the decimal value of each 8-bit byte.

Programmers who write programs for a single computer do not need to think about data representation because a given computer usually only permits one representation. When a programmer declares a variable to be an integer (e.g., by using Pascal's *integer* declaration or C's *int* declaration), the compiler uses the computer's *native data representation* when it allocates storage for the integer or when it generates code to fetch, store, or compare values.

Programmers who create client and server software must contend with data representation, however, because both endpoints must agree on the exact representation for all data sent across the communication channel between them. If the native data representations on two machines differ, data sent from a program on one machine to a program on the other must be converted.

19.3 The N-Squared Conversion Problem

The central issue underlying data representation is software portability. At one extreme, a programmer could choose to embed knowledge of the computers' architectures in each client-server pair so the client and server agree on which side will convert the data. Designs that convert directly from the client's representation to the server's representation use *asymmetric data conversion* because one side or the other performs conversion. Unfortunately, using asymmetric data conversion means that the programmer must write a different version of the client-server pair for each pair of architectures on which they will be used.

To understand why building separate client-server pairs for each architecture combination can be costly, consider a set of *N* computers. If each computer uses a different data representation to store floating point numbers, a programmer must construct

$$(N^2 - N) / 2$$

versions of any client-server program that exchanges floating point values. We call this the *n-squared conversion problem*† to emphasize that the programming effort is proportional to the square of the number of different data representations.

Another way to view the n-squared conversion problem is to imagine the effort required to add a new architecture to an existing set of N machines. Each time a new computer arrives, the programmer must build N new versions of each client-server pair before the new computer can interoperate with each of the existing computers.

Even if the programmer uses conditional compilation (e.g., the C preprocessor's *if-def* construct), creating, testing, maintaining, and managing N^2 versions of a program can be difficult. Furthermore, users may need to distinguish among versions when they invoke a client. To summarize:

> If client-server software is designed to convert from the client's native data representation directly to the server's native data representation asymmetrically, the number of versions of the software grows as the square of the number of architectures.

To avoid the problems inherent in maintaining N-squared versions of a client-server program, programmers try to avoid asymmetric data conversion. Instead, they write client and server software in such a way that each source program can be compiled and executed on a variety of machines without change. Doing so makes programming easier because it results in a highly portable program. It also makes accessing a service easier because users only need to remember how to invoke one version of the client.

19.4 Network Standard Byte Order

How can a single source program compile and execute correctly on a variety of architectures if the architectures use multiple representations for data? More important, how can a client or server program send data to a program on another machine if the two machines use a different data representation? Chapter 5 describes how TCP/IP solves the representation problem for simple integer data by using functions that convert from the computer's native byte order to a network standard byte order and vice versa.

Conceptually, the use of a standard representation for data sent across a network in protocol headers means the TCP/IP protocol software employs *symmetric data conversion*. Both ends perform the required conversion. As a result, only one version of the protocol software is needed because all protocol headers represent data in a standard, machine-independent form.

Most programmers adopt the same symmetric data conversion technique when they build client-server application software. Instead of converting directly from one machine's representation to the other's, both client and server perform a data conver-

---

†Some literature refers to the problem as the $n * m$ problem to emphasize that clients can operate on n architectures while servers operate on m architectures.

sion. Before sending across the network, they convert data from the sending computer's native representation into a standard, machine-independent representation. Likewise, they convert from the machine-independent representation to the receiving computer's native representation after receiving data from the network. The standard representation used for data traversing the network is known as the *external data representation*.

Using a standard external data representation has both advantages and disadvantages. The chief advantage lies in flexibility: neither the client nor the server needs to understand the architecture of the other. A single client can contact a server on an arbitrary machine without knowing the machine architecture. The total programming effort required will be proportional to the number of machine architectures instead of the square of that number.

The chief disadvantage of symmetric conversion is computational overhead. In cases where the client and server both operate on computers that have the same architecture, the cost seems unwarranted. One end converts all data from the native architecture's representation to the external representation before sending it, and the other end converts from the external representation back to the original representation after receiving it.

Even if the client and server machines do not share a common architecture, using an intermediate form introduces additional computation. Instead of converting directly from the sender's representation to the receiver's, the client and server must each spend CPU time converting between their local representations and the external representation. Furthermore, because the external representation may add information to the data or align it on word boundaries, the conversion may result in a larger stream of bytes than necessary.

Despite the additional overhead and network bandwidth required, most programmers agree that using symmetric conversion is worthwhile. It simplifies programming, reduces errors, and increases interoperability among programs. It also makes network management and debugging easier because the network manager can interpret the contents of packets without knowing the architectures of the sending and receiving machines.

19.5 A De Facto Standard External Data Representation

Sun Microsystems, Incorporated devised an external data representation that specifies how to represent common forms of data when transferring data across a network. Known by the initials *XDR*, Sun's *eXternal Data Representation* has become a *de facto* standard for most client-server applications.

XDR specifies data formats for most of the data types that clients and servers exchange. For example, XDR specifies that 32-bit binary integers should be represented in ''big endian'' order (i.e., with the most significant byte in the lowest memory address).

19.6 XDR Data Types

The table in Figure 19.2 lists the data types for which XDR defines a standard representation.

Data Type	Size	Description
int	32 bits	32-bit signed binary integer
unsigned int	32-bits	32-bit unsigned binary integer
bool	32 bits	Boolean value (*false* or *true*) represented by *0* or *1*
enum	arb.	Enumeration type with values defined by integers (e.g., *RED=1, WHITE=2, BLUE=3*)
hyper	64 bits	64-bit signed binary integer
unsigned hyper	64-bits	64-bit unsigned binary integer
float	32 bits	Single precision floating point number
double	64 bits	Double precision floating point number
opaque	arb.	Unconverted data (i.e., data in the sender's native representation)
string	arb.	String of ASCII characters
fixed array	arb.	A fixed-size array of any other data type
counted array	arb.	Array in which the type has a fixed upper limit, but individual arrays may vary up to that size
structure	arb.	A data aggregate, like C's *struct*
discriminated union	arb.	A data structure that allows one of several alternative forms, like C's *union* or Pascal's variant record
void	0	Used if no data is present where a data item is optional (e.g., in a structure)
symbolic constant	arb.	A symbolic constant and associated value
optional data	arb.	Optional item (can be absent)

Figure 19.2 The types for which XDR defines an external representation. The standard specifies how data items for each type should be encoded when sent across a network.

The types in Figure 19.2 cover most of the data structures found in application programs because they allow the programmer to compose aggregate types from other types. For example, in addition to allowing an array of integers, XDR allows an array of structures, each of which can have multiple fields that can each be an array, structure, or union. Thus, XDR provides representations for most of the structures that a C programmer can specify.

19.7 Implicit Types

The XDR standard specifies how a data object should be encoded for each of the data types listed in Figure 19.2. However, the encodings contain only the data items and not information about their types. For example, XDR specifies using "big-endian" order for 32-bit binary integers (the same encoding used in TCP/IP protocol headers). If an application program uses XDR representation to encode a 32-bit integer, the result occupies exactly 32 bits; the encoding does not contain additional bits to identify it as an integer or to specify its length. Thus, clients and servers using XDR must agree on the exact format of messages they will exchange. A program cannot interpret an XDR-encoded message unless it knows the exact format and the types of all data fields.

19.8 Software Support For Using XDR

Programmers who choose to use the XDR representation for symmetric data conversion must be careful to place each data item in external form before sending it across a network. Similarly, a receiving program must be careful to convert each incoming item to native representation. Chapter 5 shows one method programmers can use to perform the conversion: insert a function call in the code to convert each data item in a message to external form before sending the message, and insert a function call to convert each data item to internal form when a message arrives.

Most programmers could write the required XDR conversion functions with little effort. However, some conversions require considerable expertise (e.g., converting from a computer's native floating point representation to the XDR standard without losing precision may require an understanding of basic numerical analysis). To eliminate potential conversion errors, an implementation of XDR includes library routines that perform the necessary conversions.

19.9 XDR Library Routines

XDR library routines for a given machine can convert data items from the computer's native representation to the XDR standard representation and vice versa. Most implementations of XDR use a *buffer paradigm* that allows a programmer to create a complete message in XDR form.

19.10 Building A Message One Piece At A Time

The buffer paradigm XDR uses requires a program to allocate a buffer large enough to hold the external representation of a message and to add items (i.e., fields) one at a time. For example, the version of XDR available under the SunOS operating system provides conversion routines that each append an external representation to the end of a buffer in memory. A program first invokes procedure *xdrmem_create* to allocate a buffer in memory and inform XDR that it intends to compose an external representation in it. *Xdrmem_create* initializes the memory so it represents an *XDR stream* that can be used to encode (convert to standard representation) or decode (convert to native representation) data. The call initializes the XDR stream to be empty by assigning the address of the beginning of the buffer to an internal pointer. *Xdrmem_create* returns a pointer to the stream, which must then be used in successive calls to XDR routines. The declarations and calls needed to create an XDR stream using C are:

```
#include <rpc/xdr.h>
#define BUFSIZE 4000          /* size of memory for encoding  */

    XDR    *xdrs;             /* pointer to an XDR "stream"   */
    char   buf[BUFSIZE];      /* memory area to hold XDR data */

    xdrmem_create(xdrs, buf, BUFSIZE, XDR_ENCODE);
```

Once a program has created an XDR stream, it can call individual XDR conversion routines to convert native data objects into external form. Each call encodes one data object and appends the encoded information on the end of the stream (i.e., places the encoded data in the next available locations in the buffer and then updates the internal stream pointer). For example, procedure *xdr_int* converts a 32-bit binary integer from the native representation to the standard XDR representation and appends it to an XDR stream. A program invokes *xdr_int* by passing it a pointer to an XDR stream and a pointer to an integer:

```
    int    i;         /* integer in native representation      */
    . . .             /* assume stream initialized for ENCODE */
    i = 260;          /* assign integer value to be converted */
    xdr_int(xdrs, &i); /* convert integer and append to stream */
```

Figure 19.3 illustrates how the call to *xdr_int* shown in the sample code adds four bytes of data to the XDR stream.

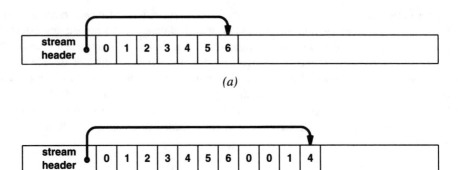

Figure 19.3 (a) An XDR stream that has been initialized for encoding and already contains *7* bytes of data, and (b) the same XDR stream after a call to *xdr_int* appends a 32-bit integer with value *260*.

19.11 Conversion Routines In The XDR Library

The table in Figure 19.4 lists the XDR conversion routines.

Procedure	arguments	Data Type Converted
xdr_bool	xdrs, ptrbool	Boolean (*int* in C)
xdr_bytes	xdrs, ptrstr, strsize, maxsize	Counted byte string
xdr_char	xdrs, ptrchar	Character
xdr_double	xdrs, ptrdouble	Double precision floating point
xdr_enum	xdrs, ptrint	Variable of enumerated data type (an *int* in C)
xdr_float	xdrs, ptrfloat	Single precision floating point
xdr_int	xdrs, ip	32-bit integer
xdr_long	xdrs, ptrlong	64-bit integer
xdr_opaque	xdrs, ptrchar, count	Bytes sent without conversion
xdr_pointer	xdrs, ptrobj, objsize, xdrobj	A pointer (used in linked data structures like lists or trees)
xdr_short	xdrs, ptrshort	16-bit integer
xdr_string	xdrs, ptrstr, maxsize	A C string
xdr_u_char	xdrs, ptruchar	Unsigned 8-bit integer
xdr_u_int	xdrs, ptrint	Unsigned 32-bit integer
xdr_u_long	xdrs, ptrulong	Unsigned 64-bit integer
xdr_u_short	xdrs, ptrushort	Unsigned 16-bit integer
xdr_union	xdrs, ptrdiscrim, ptrunion, choicefcn, default	Discriminated union
xdr_vector	xdrs, ptrarray, size, elemsize, elemproc	Fixed length array
xdr_void	-none-	Not a conversion (used to denote empty part of a data structure)

Figure 19.4 The XDR data conversion routines found in an XDR library. The routines can convert in either direction because most arguments are pointers to data objects and not data values.

To form a message, the application calls XDR conversion routines for each data item in the message. After encoding each data item and placing it in an XDR stream, the application can send the message by sending the resulting stream. The receiving application must reverse the entire process. It calls *xdrmem_create* to create a memory buffer that will hold an XDR stream, and places the incoming message in a buffer area. XDR records the direction of conversion in the stream itself where the conversion routines can access it. The receiver specifies *XDR_DECODE* as the third argument of *xdrmem_create* when creating an XDR stream that will be used for input. As a result, whenever the receiver calls an individual conversion routine on an input stream, the routine extracts an item from the stream and converts it to native mode. For example, if the receiver has established an XDR stream used for input (i.e., the call specified

XDR_DECODE), it can extract a 32-bit integer and convert it to the native representation by calling *xdr_int*:

```
int      i;            /* integer using native representation  */
. . .                  /* assume stream initialized for DECODE */


xdr_int(xdrs, &i);   /* extract integer from stream             */
```

Thus, unlike the conversion routines *htons* and *ntohs* found in Windows Sockets, individual XDR conversion routines do not specify the direction of conversion. Instead, they require the program to specify the direction when creating the XDR stream. To summarize:

> *Individual XDR conversion routines do not specify the direction of conversion. Instead, a single routine that can convert in either direction determines the direction of the conversion by examining the XDR stream being used.*

19.12 XDR Streams, I/O, and TCP

The code fragments above create an XDR stream associated with a buffer in memory. Using memory to buffer data can make a program efficient because buffering allows the application to convert large amounts of data to external form before sending it across a network. After items have been converted to external form and placed in the buffer, the application must call an I/O function like *send* to transmit it across a TCP connection.

On UNIX systems, it is possible to arrange to have XDR conversion routines send data across a TCP connection automatically each time they convert a data item to external form†. To do so, an application program first creates a TCP socket, and then calls function *fdopen* to attach a *standard I/O stream* to the socket. Instead of calling *xdrmem_create*, the application calls *xdrstdio_create* to create an XDR stream and connect it to the existing I/O descriptor. XDR streams attached to a TCP socket do not require explicit calls to *send* or *recv*. Each time the application calls an XDR conversion routine, the conversion routine automatically performs a buffered *send* or *recv* operation using the underlying descriptor. A *send* causes TCP to transmit outgoing data to the socket; a *recv* causes TCP to receive incoming data from the socket. The application can also call conventional functions from the I/O library to act on the I/O stream. For example, if output is desired, the application can use *fflush* to flush the output buffer after only a few bytes of data have been converted.

---

†Under Windows, it is not possible to associate an XDR stream with a TCP connection because Windows does not permit standard I/O functions to be used with sockets.

19.13 Records, Record Boundaries, And Datagram I/O

As described, the XDR mechanism works well when connected to a TCP socket because both XDR and TCP implementations use the stream abstraction. To make XDR work with UDP as easily as it works with TCP, the designers added a second interface. The alternative design provides an application with a *record-oriented interface*.

To use the record-oriented interface, a program calls function *xdrrec_create* when creating an XDR stream. The call includes two arguments, *inproc* and *outproc*, that specify an input procedure and an output procedure. When converting to external form, each conversion routine checks the buffer. If the buffer becomes full, the conversion routine calls *outproc* to send the existing buffer contents and make space for the new data. Similarly, each time the application calls a conversion routine to convert from external form to the native representation, the routine checks the buffer to see if it contains data. If the buffer is empty, the conversion routine calls *inproc* to obtain more data.

To use XDR with UDP, an application creates a record-oriented XDR stream. It arranges for the input and output procedures associated with the stream to call *recv* and *send*. When the application fills a buffer, the conversion routines call *send* to transmit the buffer in a single UDP datagram. Similarly, when an application calls a conversion routine to extract data, the conversion routine calls *recv* to obtain the next incoming datagram and place it in the buffer.

XDR streams created by *xdrrec_create* differ from other XDR streams in several ways. Record-oriented streams allow an application to mark record boundaries. Furthermore, the sender can specify whether to send the record immediately or to wait for the buffer to fill before sending data. The receiver can detect record boundaries, skip a fixed number of records in the input, or find out whether additional records have been received.

19.14 Summary

Because computers do not use a common data representation, client and server programs must contend with representation issues. To solve the problem, client-server interaction can be *asymmetric* or *symmetric*. Asymmetric conversion requires either the client or the server to convert between its own representation and the other machine's native representation. Symmetric conversion uses a standard network representation, and requires both the client and server to convert between the network standard and the local representation.

The chief problem with asymmetric interaction arises because multiple versions of each program are required. If the network supports N architectures, asymmetric interaction requires programming effort proportional to N^2. While symmetric designs may require slightly more computational overhead, they provide interoperability with one program per architecture. Thus, most designers choose symmetric solutions because they require programming effort proportional to N.

Sun Microsystems, Incorporated has defined an external data representation that has become, *de facto*, a standard. Known as XDR, the Sun standard provides definitions for data aggregates (e.g., arrays and structures) as well as for basic data types (e.g., integers and character strings). XDR library routines provide conversion from a computer's native data representation to the external standard and vice versa. Client and server programs can use XDR routines to convert data to external form before sending it and to internal form after receiving it. The conversion routines can be associated with input and output using TCP or UDP.

FOR FURTHER STUDY

Sun Microsystems, Incorporated [RFC 1014] defines the XDR encoding and the standard XDR conversion routines. Srinivasan [RFC 1832] contains a new version that is a proposed standard. Additional information can be found in the documentation that accompanies each vendor's software. For example, the *Network Programming Guide* accompanies the SunOS operating system.

International Organization for Standardization [1987a and 1987b] defines an alternative external data representation known as *Abstract Syntax Notation One (ASN.1)*. Although some protocols in the TCP/IP suite use the ASN.1 representation, most application programmers prefer XDR. Partridge and Rose [1989] shows that XDR and ASN.1 have equivalent expressive power.

Padlipsky [1983] discusses the problem of asymmetric conversion and points out that it requires $n * m$ possible conversions.

EXERCISES

19.1   Construct a version of *ntohs* and conduct an experiment that compares the execution time of your version to the execution time of the version in your system's library or *include* files. Explain the results.

19.2   How does XDR's use of the buffer paradigm make programming easier?

19.3   Design an external data representation that includes a type field before each data item. What is the chief advantage of such a solution? What is the chief disadvantage?

19.4   Read the vendor's documentation to find out more about the format of an XDR stream. What information is kept in the header?

19.5   Argue that programs would be easier to read if the designers of XDR had chosen to use separate conversion routines for encoding and decoding instead of recording the conversion direction in the stream header. What is the disadvantage of keeping separate conversion routines?

19.6   Under what circumstances might a programmer need to pass *opaque* data objects between a client and a server?

20

Remote Procedure Call Concept (RPC)

20.1 Introduction

The previous chapter begins a discussion of techniques and mechanisms that help programmers use the client-server paradigm†. It considers the advantages of using symmetric data conversion, and describes how the XDR external data representation standard and associated library routines provide symmetric conversion.

This chapter continues the discussion. It introduces the remote procedure call concept in general, and describes a particular implementation of a remote procedure call that uses the XDR standard for data representation. It shows how the remote procedure concept simplifies the design of client-server software and makes the resulting programs easier to understand. The next two chapters complete the discussion of remote procedure call by describing a tool that generates much of the C code needed to implement a program that uses remote calls. Chapter 22 contains a complete working example that shows how the tool can generate a client and a server that use remote procedure calls.

20.2 Remote Procedure Call Model

So far, we have described client-server programs by examining the structure of the client and server components separately. However, when programmers build a client-server application, they cannot focus exclusively on one component at a time. Instead, they must consider how the entire system will function and how the two components will interact.

---

†Such mechanisms are often called *middleware*.

To help programmers design and understand client-server interaction, researchers have devised a conceptual framework for building distributed programs. Known as the *remote procedure call model* or *RPC model*, the framework uses familiar concepts from conventional programs as the basis for the design of distributed applications.

20.3 Two Paradigms For Building Distributed Programs

A programmer can use one of two approaches when designing a distributed application:

- **Communication-Oriented Design**
  Begin with the communication protocol. Design a message format and syntax. Design the client and server components by specifying how each reacts to incoming messages and how each generates outgoing messages.

- **Application-Oriented Design**
  Begin with the application. Design a conventional application program to solve the problem. Build and test a working version of the conventional program that operates on a single machine. Divide the program into two or more pieces, and add communication protocols that allow each piece to execute on a separate computer.

A communication-oriented design sometimes leads to problems. First, by focusing on the communication protocol, the programmer may miss important subtleties in the application and may find that the protocol does not provide all the needed functionality. Second, because few programmers have experience and expertise with protocol design, they often produce awkward, incorrect, or inefficient protocols. Small oversights in protocol design can lead to fundamental errors that remain hidden until the programs run under stress (e.g., the possibility of deadlock). Third, because the programmer concentrates on communication, it usually becomes the centerpiece of the resulting programs, making them difficult to understand or modify. In particular, because the server is specified by giving a list of messages and the actions required when each message arrives, it may be difficult to understand the intended interaction or the underlying motivations.

The remote procedure call model uses the application-oriented approach, which emphasizes the problem to be solved instead of the communication needed. Using the remote procedure call model, a programmer first designs a conventional program to solve the problem, and then divides the program into pieces that run on two or more computers. The programmer can follow good design principles that make the code modular and maintainable.

In an ideal situation, the remote procedure call model provides more than an abstract concept. It allows a programmer to build, compile, and test a conventional version of the program to ensure that it solves the problem correctly before dividing the program into pieces that operate on separate machines. Furthermore, because RPC divides programs at procedure boundaries, the split into local and remote parts can be made without major modifications to the program structure. In fact, it may be possible to move some of the procedures from a program to remote machines without changing or even recompiling the main program itself. Thus, RPC separates the solution of a problem from the task of making the solution operate in a distributed environment.

> *The remote procedure call paradigm for programming focuses on the application. It allows a programmer to concentrate on devising a conventional program that solves the problem before attempting to divide the program into pieces that operate on multiple computers.*

20.4 A Conceptual Model For Conventional Procedure Calls

The remote procedure call model draws heavily from the procedure call mechanism found in conventional programming languages. Procedures offer a powerful abstraction that allows programmers to divide programs into small, manageable, easily-understood pieces. Procedures are especially useful because they have a straightforward implementation that provides a conceptual model of program execution. Figure 20.1 illustrates the concept.

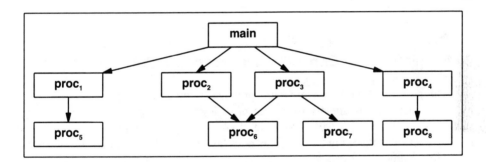

Figure 20.1 The procedure concept. A conventional program consists of one or more procedures, usually arranged in a hierarchy of calls. An arrow from procedure *n* to procedure *m* denotes a call from *n* to *m*.

20.5 An Extension Of the Procedural Model

The remote procedure call model uses the same procedural abstraction as a conventional program, but allows a procedure call to span the boundary between two computers. Figure 20.2 illustrates how the remote procedure call paradigm can be used to divide a program into two pieces that each execute on a separate computer. Of course, a conventional procedure call cannot pass from one computer to another. Before a program can use remote procedure calls, it must be augmented with protocol software that allows it to communicate with the remote procedure.

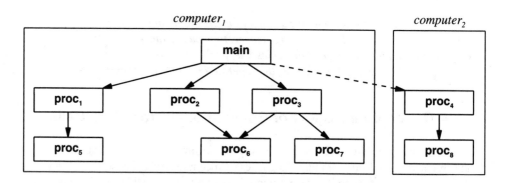

Figure 20.2 A distributed program that shows how the program from Figure 20.1 can be extended to use the remote procedure call paradigm. The division occurs between the main program and procedure *4*. A communication protocol is required to implement the remote call.

20.6 Execution Of Conventional Procedure Call And Return

The procedural model for programs provides a conceptual explanation of program execution that extends directly to remote procedure calls. The concept can be understood best by considering the relationship of control flow to compiled program code in memory. For example, Figure 20.3 illustrates how control flows from a main program through two procedures and back.

According to the procedural execution model, a single *thread of control* or *thread of execution* flows through all procedures. The computer begins execution in a *main* program and continues until it encounters a *procedure call*. The call causes execution to branch to code in the specified procedure and continue. If it encounters another call, the computer branches to a second procedure.

Execution continues in the called procedure until the computer encounters a *return* statement. The return statement causes execution to resume at a point just after the last call. For example, in Figure 20.3, executing the return in procedure *B* causes control to pass back to procedure *A* at a point just after the call to *B*.

bitrary amounts of data (i.e., it can accept or return an arbitrary stream over a TCP connection).

Although it would be ideal if local and remote procedure calls behaved identically, several practical constraints prevent it. First, network delays can make a remote procedure call several orders of magnitude more expensive than a conventional procedure call. Second, because the called procedure operates in the same address space as the calling procedure, conventional programs can pass pointers as arguments. A remote procedure call cannot have pointers as arguments because the remote procedure operates in a completely different address space than the caller. Third, because a remote procedure does not share the caller's environment, it does not have direct access to the caller's I/O descriptors or operating system functions. For example, a remote procedure cannot write error messages directly to the caller's standard error file.

20.9 Distributed Computation As A Program

The key to appreciating remote procedure call is to understand that, despite its practical limitations, the paradigm helps programmers design distributed programs easily. To see how, imagine that each distributed computation consists of an individual program that runs in a distributed environment. Instead of thinking about the client and server software that implements communication, imagine how easy it would be to build distributed programs if a program simply invoked a procedure when it needed access to a remote service. Imagine that the program's thread of execution could pass across the network to the remote machine, execute the remote procedure on that machine, and then return back to the caller. From the programmer's point of view, remote services would be as easy to access as local procedures or local operating system services. In short, distributed programs would become as easy to construct as conventional programs because they could draw on the programmer's intuition and experience with conventional procedure calls. Furthermore, programmers familiar with the procedure parameter mechanism could define client-server communication precisely without any need for a special notation or language. To summarize:

> *Thinking of a distributed computation as a single program in which control passes across the network to a remote procedure and back helps programmers specify client-server interactions; it relates the interaction of distributed computations to the familiar notions of procedure call and return.*

20.10 Sun Microsystems' Remote Procedure Call Definition

Sun Microsystems, Incorporated has defined a specific form of remote procedure call. Known as *Sun RPC*, *Open Network Computing (ONC) RPC*, or simply *RPC*†, the remote procedure call definition has received wide acceptance in the industry. It has been used as an implementation mechanism for many applications, including the Network File System (NFS‡).

RPC defines the format of messages that the caller (client) sends to invoke a remote procedure on a server, the format of arguments, and the format of results that the called procedure returns to the caller. It permits the calling program to use either UDP or TCP to carry messages, and uses XDR to represent procedure arguments as well as other items in an RPC message header. Finally, in addition to the protocol specification, RPC includes a compiler system that helps programmers build distributed programs automatically.

20.11 Remote Programs And Procedures

RPC extends the remote procedure call model by defining a remote execution environment. It defines a *remote program* as the basic unit of software that executes on a remote machine. Each remote program corresponds to what we think of as a server, and contains a set of one or more remote procedures plus global data. The procedures inside a remote program all share access to its global data. Thus, a set of cooperative remote procedures can share state information. For example, one can implement a simple remote database by constructing a single remote program that includes data structures to hold shared information and three remote procedures to manipulate it: *insert*, *delete*, and *lookup*. As Figure 20.5 illustrates, all remote procedures inside the remote program can share access to the single database.

a single remote program

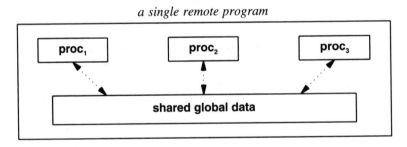

Figure 20.5 Conceptual organization of three remote procedures in a remote program. All three procedures share access to global data in the program, just as conventional procedures share access to global data in a conventional program.

---

†Throughout the remainder of this text, the term *RPC* will refer to ONC RPC unless otherwise noted.
‡Chapter *23* discusses NFS in detail.

20.12 Reducing The Number Of Arguments

Because most programming languages use positional notation to represent arguments, a procedure call that contains more than a handful of arguments can be difficult to read. Programmers can reduce the problem by collecting many arguments into a single data aggregate (e.g., a C *struct*) and passing the resulting aggregate as a single argument. The caller assigns each field in the structure a value before passing the structure to the called procedure; the caller extracts return values from the structure after the call returns. To summarize:

> *Using a structure instead of multiple arguments makes the program more readable because the structure field names serve as keywords that tell the reader how each argument will be used.*

Because we will assume throughout the remainder of this discussion that all programs using RPC collect their arguments into a structure, each remote procedure will need only a single argument.

20.13 Identifying Remote Programs And Procedures

The ONC RPC standard specifies that each remote program executing on a computer must be assigned a unique 32-bit integer that the caller uses to identify it. Furthermore, ONC RPC assigns an integer identifier to each remote procedure inside a given remote program. The procedures are numbered sequentially: *1, 2, ..., N*†. Conceptually, a specific remote procedure on a given remote computer can be identified by a pair:

$$(prog, proc)$$

where *prog* identifies the remote program and *proc* identifies a remote procedure within the program. To help ensure that program numbers defined by separate organizations do not conflict, RPC has divided the set of program numbers into eight groups as Figure 20.6 shows.

---

†By convention, the number *0* is always reserved for an echo procedure that can be used to test whether the remote program can be reached.

From		To	Values Assigned By
0x00000000	-	0x1fffffff	Sun Microsystems, Inc.
0x20000000	-	0x3fffffff	The system manager at a user's site
0x40000000	-	0x5fffffff	Transient (temporary)
0x60000000	-	0x7fffffff	Reserved
0x80000000	-	0x9fffffff	Reserved
0xa0000000	-	0xbfffffff	Reserved
0xc0000000	-	0xdfffffff	Reserved
0xe0000000	-	0xffffffff	Reserved

Figure 20.6 The division into eight groups of 32-bit numbers that RPC uses
to identify remote programs. Each remote program is assigned a
unique number.

Sun Microsystems, Incorporated administers the first group of identifiers, allowing
anyone to apply for a standard RPC program number. Because Sun publishes the assignments, all computers that run RPC use the standard values. Of the 2^{29} program
numbers available in the first group, Sun has only assigned a handful of numbers. Figure 20.7 summarizes some of the assignments.

20.14 Accommodating Multiple Versions Of A Remote Program

In addition to a program number, RPC includes an integer *version number* for each
remote program. Usually, the first version of a program is assigned version *1*. Later
versions each receive a unique version number.

Version numbers provide the ability to change the details of a remote procedure
call without obtaining a new program number. In practice, each RPC message identifies the intended recipient on a given computer by a triple:

$$(prog, vers, proc)$$

where *prog* identifies the remote program, *vers* specifies the version of the program to
which the message has been sent, and *proc* identifies a remote procedure within that remote program. The RPC specification permits a computer to run multiple versions of a
remote program simultaneously, allowing for graceful migration during changes. The
idea can be summarized:

> Because all RPC messages identify a remote program, the version of
> that program, and a remote procedure in the program, it is possible
> to migrate from one version of a remote procedure to another grace-
> fully and to test a new version of the server while an old version con-
> tinues to operate.

Name	assigned number	Description
portmap	100000	port mapper
rstatd	100001	rstat, rup, and perfmeter
rusersd	100002	remote users
nfs	100003	network file system
ypserv	100004	yp (now called NIS)
mountd	100005	mount, showmount
dbxd	100006	DBXprog (debugger)
ypbind	100007	NIS binder
walld	100008	rwall, shutdown
yppasswdd	100009	yppasswd
etherstatd	100010	ethernet statistics
rquotad	100011	rquotaprog, quota, rquota
sprayd	100012	spray
selection_svc	100015	selection service
dbsessionmgr	100016	unify, netdbms, dbms
rexd	100017	rex, remote_exec
office_auto	100018	alice
lockd	100020	klmprog
lockd	100021	nlmprog
statd	100024	status monitor
bootparamd	100026	bootstrap
pcnfsd	150001	NFS for PC

Figure 20.7 Example RPC program numbers currently assigned by Sun Microsystems, Inc.

20.15 Mutual Exclusion For Procedures In A Remote Program

The RPC mechanism specifies that at most one remote procedure in a remote program can be invoked at a given time. Thus, RPC provides automatic mutual exclusion among procedures within a given remote program. Such exclusion can be important for remote programs that maintain shared data accessed by several procedures. For example, if a remote database program includes remote procedures for *insert* and *delete* operations, the programmer does not need to worry about the two remote procedure calls interfering with one another because the mechanism only permits one call to execute at a time. The system blocks other calls until the current call finishes. To summarize:

RPC provides mutual exclusion among remote procedures within a
single remote program; at most one remote procedure call can exe-
cute in a remote program at one time.

20.16 Communication Semantics

When choosing the semantics for RPC, the designers had to choose between two
possibilities. On one hand, to make a remote procedure call behave as much like a local procedure call as possible, RPC should use a reliable transport like TCP and should
guarantee reliability to the programmer. The remote procedure call mechanism should
either transfer the call to the remote procedure and receive a reply, or it should report
that communication is impossible. On the other hand, to allow programmers to use efficient, connectionless transport protocols, the remote procedure call mechanism should
support communication through a datagram protocol like UDP.

RPC does not enforce reliable semantics. It allows each application to choose TCP
or UDP as a transport protocol. Furthermore, the standard does not specify additional
protocols or mechanisms to achieve reliable delivery. Instead, it defines RPC semantics
as a function of the semantics of the underlying transport protocol. For example, because UDP permits datagrams to be lost or duplicated, RPC specifies that remote procedure calls using UDP may experience loss or duplication.

20.17 At Least Once Semantics

RPC defines the semantics of a remote procedure call in the simplest way by specifying that a program should only draw the weakest possible conclusion from any interaction. For example, when using UDP, a request or reply message (call to a remote
procedure or return from one) can be lost or duplicated. If a remote procedure call does
not return, the caller cannot conclude that the remote procedure has not been called because the reply could have been lost, even if the request was not. If a remote procedure
call does return, the caller can conclude that the remote procedure was called *at least
once*. However, the calling procedure cannot conclude that the remote procedure was
called exactly once because the request could have been duplicated or a reply message
could have been lost.

The ONC RPC standard uses the term *at least once semantics* to describe RPC execution when the caller receives a reply, and *zero or more semantics* to describe the
behavior of a remote procedure call when the caller does not receive a reply.

RPC's zero-or-more semantics imposes an important responsibility on the programmer:

> *Programmers who choose to use UDP as the transport protocol for*
> *an ONC RPC application must build the application to tolerate zero-*
> *or-more execution semantics.*

In practice, zero-or-more semantics usually means that a programmer makes each remote procedure call *idempotent†*. For example, consider a remote file access application. A remote procedure that appends data to a file is not idempotent because repeated executions of the procedure will append data repeatedly. On the other hand, a remote procedure that writes data to a specified position in a file is idempotent because repeated executions will always write data to the same position.

20.18 RPC Retransmission

The library software supplied with the ONC RPC implementation includes a simple timeout and retransmission strategy, but does not guarantee reliability in the strict sense. The default timeout mechanism implements a fixed (nonadaptive) timeout with a fixed number of retries. When the RPC library software sends a message that corresponds to a remote procedure call, it starts a timer. The software retransmits the request if the timer expires before a response arrives. Programmers can adjust the timeout and retry limits for a given application, but the software does not adapt automatically to long network delays or to changes in delay over time.

Of course, a simple retransmission strategy does not guarantee reliability, nor does it guarantee that the calling application can draw a correct conclusion about execution of the remote procedure. For example, if the network loses all responses, the caller may retransmit the request several times and each request may result in an execution of the remote procedure. Ultimately, however, library software on the caller's machine will reach its retry limit and declare that the remote procedure cannot be executed. Most important, an application cannot interpret failure as a guarantee that the remote procedure was never executed (in fact, it may have executed several times).

20.19 Mapping A Remote Program To A Protocol Port

UDP and TCP transport protocols use 16-bit protocol port numbers to identify communication endpoints. Earlier chapters describe how a server creates a passive socket, binds the socket to a well-known protocol port, and waits for client programs to contact it. To make it possible for clients and servers to rendezvous, we assume that each service is assigned a unique protocol port number and that the assignments are well-known. Thus, both the server and client agree on the protocol port at which the server accepts requests because they both consult a published list of port assignments.

---

†The term is taken from mathematics, where an operation is said to be idempotent if repeated applications of the operation produce the same result.

RPC introduces an interesting problem: because it uses 32-bit numbers to identify remote programs, RPC programs can outnumber protocol ports. Thus, it is impossible to map RPC program numbers onto protocol ports directly. More important, because RPC programs cannot all be assigned a unique protocol port, programmers cannot use a scheme that depends on well-known protocol port assignments.

Although the potential number of RPC programs rules out well-known port assignments, RPC does not differ dramatically from other services. At any given time, a single computer executes only a small number of remote programs. Thus, as long as the port assignments are temporary, each RPC program can obtain a protocol port number and use it for communication.

If an RPC program does not use a reserved, well-known protocol port, clients cannot contact it directly. To see why, think of the server and client components. When the server (remote program) begins execution, it asks the operating system to allocate an unused protocol port number. The server uses the newly allocated protocol port for all communication. The system may choose a different protocol port number each time the server begins (i.e., the server may have a different port assigned each time the system boots).

The client (the program that issues the remote procedure call) knows the machine address and RPC program number for the remote program it wishes to contact. However, because the RPC program (server) only obtains a protocol port after it begins execution, the client cannot know which protocol port the server obtained. Thus, the client cannot contact the remote program directly.

20.20 Dynamic Port Mapping

To solve the port identification problem, a client must be able to map from an RPC program number and a machine address to the protocol port that the server obtained on the destination machine when it started. The mapping must be dynamic because it can change if the machine reboots or if the RPC program starts execution again.

To allow clients to contact remote programs, the RPC mechanism includes a dynamic mapping service. Each machine that offers an RPC program (i.e., that runs a server) maintains a database of port mappings and provides a mechanism that allows a caller to map RPC program numbers to protocol ports. Called the *RPC port mapper* or sometimes simply the *port mapper*, the RPC port mapping mechanism uses a server to maintain a small database on each machine. Figure 20.8 illustrates that the port mapper operates as a separate server process.

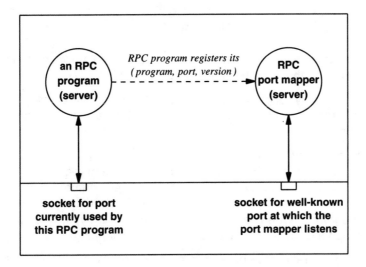

Figure 20.8 The RPC port mapper. Each RPC program registers its program
number, protocol port number, and version number with the port
mapper on the local machine. A caller contacts the port mapper
on a machine to find the protocol port to use for a given RPC
program on that machine.

20.21 RPC Port Mapper Algorithm

One port mapper operates on each machine using Algorithm 20.1. The port
mapper allows clients to reach remote programs even though the remote programs
dynamically allocate protocol ports. Whenever a remote program (i.e., a server) begins
execution, it allocates a local protocol port that it will use for communication. The remote program then contacts the port mapper on its local machine and adds a triple of
integers to the database:

$$(RPC\ prog\ number,\ version\ number,\ protocol\ port\ number)$$

Once an RPC program has registered itself, callers on other machines can find its protocol port by sending a request to the port mapper.

Algorithm 20.1

1. Create a passive socket bound to the well-known port assigned to the ONC RPC port mapper service (*111*).

2. Repeatedly accept requests to register an RPC program number or to look up a protocol port given an RPC program number.

   Registration requests come from RPC programs on the same machine as the port mapper. Each registration request specifies a triple consisting of the RPC program number, version number, and the protocol port currently used to reach that program. When a registration request arrives, the port mapper adds the triple to its database of mappings.

   Look-up requests come from arbitrary machines. They each specify a remote program number and version number, and request the number of a protocol port that can be used to reach the remote program. The port mapper looks up the remote program in its database, and responds by returning the corresponding protocol port for that program.

Algorithm 20.1 The RPC port mapper algorithm. One port mapper server runs on each machine that implements the server side of an RPC program.

The port mapper on a given machine works like directory assistance in the U.S. telephone system: a caller can ask the port mapper how to reach a particular RPC program on that machine. To contact a remote program, a caller must know the address of the machine on which the remote program executes as well as the RPC program number assigned to the program, and the version number. The caller first contacts the RPC port mapper on the target machine, and then sends the port mapper an RPC program number and a version number. The port mapper returns the protocol port number that the specified program is currently using. A caller can always reach the port mapper because the port mapper communicates using the well-known protocol port, *111*. Once a caller knows the protocol port number the target program is using, it can contact the remote program directly.

20.22 RPC Message Format

Unlike many TCP/IP protocols, RPC does not use a fixed format for messages. The protocol standard defines the general format of RPC messages as well as the data items in each field using a language known as the *XDR Language*. Because XDR language resembles data structure declarations in C, programmers familiar with C can usually read and understand the language without much explanation. In general, the language specifies how to assemble a sequence of data items that comprise a message. Each item is encoded using the XDR representation standard.

A message type field in the RPC message header distinguishes between messages that a client uses to initiate a remote procedure call and messages that a remote procedure uses to reply. Constants used in the message type field can be defined using XDR language. For example, the declarations:

```
enum msg_type {                 /* RPC message type constants */
    CALL  = 0;
    REPLY = 1;
};
```

declare the symbolic constants *CALL* and *REPLY* to be the values of an enumerated type, *msg_type*.

Data structures in XDR language can be considered a sequence of XDR types, and can be interpreted as instructions for assembling a message by composing data using XDR. For example, once values have been declared for symbolic constants, the XDR language can define the format of an RPC message:

```
struct rpc_msg {                 /* Format of an RPC message      */
    unsigned int mesgid;     /* used to match reply to call  */
    union switch (msg_type mesgt) {
        case CALL:
            call_body cbody;
        case REPLY:
            rply_body rbody;
    } body;
};
```

The declaration specifies that an RPC message, *rpc_msg* consists of an integer message identifier, *mesgid*, followed by the XDR representation of a discriminated union. Using the XDR representation, each union begins with an integer, *mesgt* in this case. *Mesgt* determines the format of the remainder of the RPC message; it contains a value that defines the message to be either a *CALL* or a *REPLY*. A CALL message contains further information in the form of a *call_body*; a REPLY contains information in the form of a *rply_body*. The declarations for *call_body* and *rply_body* must be given elsewhere. For example, RPC defines a *call_body* to have the form:

```
struct call_body {              /* format of RPC CALL             */
     unsigned int rpcvers;      /* which version of RPC?          */
     unsigned int rprog;        /* number of remote program       */
     unsigned int rprogvers;    /* version number of remote prog*/
     unsigned int rproc;        /* number of remote procedure     */
     opaque_auth  cred;         /* credentials for called auth.   */
     opaque_auth  verf;         /* authentication verifier        */
     /* ARGS */                 /* arguments for remote proc.     */
};
```

The first few items in the body of a remote procedure call present no surprises. The caller must supply the RPC protocol version number in field *rpcvers* to ensure that both client and server are using the same message format. Integer fields *rprog*, *rprogvers*, and *rproc* identify the remote program being called, the desired version of that program, and the remote procedure within that program. Fields *cred* and *verf* contain information that the called program can use to authenticate the caller's identity.

20.23 Marshaling Arguments For A Remote Procedure

Fields in an RPC message following the authentication information contain arguments for the remote procedure. The number of arguments and the type of each depend on the remote procedure being called.

RPC must represent all arguments in an external form that allows them to be transferred between computers. In particular, if any of the arguments passed to the remote procedure consists of a complex data structure like a linked list, it must be encoded into a compact representation that can be sent across the network. We use the terms *marshal*, *linearize*, or *serialize* to denote the task of encoding arguments. We say that the client side of RPC marshals arguments into the message and the server side unmarshals them. A programmer must remember that although RPC allows an RPC call to contain complex data objects, marshaling and unmarshaling large data structures can require significant CPU time and network bandwidth. Thus, most programmers avoid passing linked structures as arguments.

20.24 Authentication

RPC defines several possible forms of authentication, including a simple authentication scheme derived from UNIX and a more complex scheme that uses the *Data Encryption Standard* (*DES*) published by the National Institute For Standards and Technology (*NIST*)†. Authentication information can have one of the four types shown in the following declaration:

---

†NIST was known as The National Bureau Of Standards (NBS) when the DES standard was originally published.

```
enum auth_type  {              /* possible forms of auth.       */
    AUTH_NULL  = 0;            /* no authentication             */
    AUTH_UNIX  = 1;            /* UNIX machine name authentic.  */
    AUTH_SHORT = 2;            /* Used for short form auth. in  */
                              /*   messages after the first    */
    AUTH_DES   = 3;            /* NIST's (NBS's) DES standard   */
};
```

In each case, RPC leaves the format and interpretation of the authentication information up to the authentication subsystem. Therefore, the declaration of the authentication structure in an RPC message uses the keyword *opaque* to indicate that it appears in the message without any interpretation:

```
struct opaque_auth {           /* structure for authent. info. */
    auth_type atype;           /* which type of authentication */
    opaque body<400>;          /* data for the type specified  */
};
```

Of course, each authentication method uses a specific format for encoding data. For example, whether a computer uses Windows, UNIX, or another operating system, the computer can be configured to use UNIX authentication, which defines the structure of its authentication information to contain five fields:

```
struct auth_unix {             /* format of UNIX authentication*/
    unsigned int timestamp;    /* integer timestamp            */
    string smachine<255>;      /* name of sender's machine     */
    unsigned int userid;       /* user id of user making req.  */
    unsigned int grpid;        /* group id of user making req. */
    unsigned int grpids<10>;   /* other group ids for the user */
};
```

UNIX authentication relies on the client machine to supply its name in field *smachine* and the numeric identifier of the user making the request in field *userid*. The client also specifies its local time in field *timestamp*, which can be used to sequence requests. Finally, the client sends a main numeric group identifier and secondary group identifiers of the sending user in fields *grpid* and *grpids*.

20.25 An Example Of RPC Message Representation

XDR defines the size and external format of each field in an RPC message. For example, XDR specifies that an integer (either signed or unsigned) occupies 32 bits and is stored in big-endian byte order.

Figure 20.9 shows an example RPC *CALL* message. The size of each field is determined by its RPC definition and the XDR specification of sizes. For example, the *MESSAGE TYPE* field is defined to be enumerated, which XDR stores as a 32-bit integer.

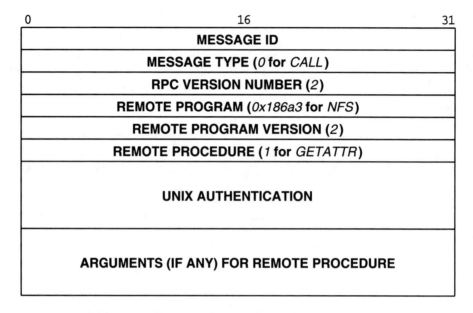

0	16	31

Figure 20.9 An example of the external format used for an RPC *CALL* message. The first fields of the message have a fixed size, but the sizes of later fields vary with their content.

20.26 An Example Of An Authentication Field

The size of the authentication field in an RPC message depends on its contents. For example the second field in a UNIX authentication structure is a machine name in a variable-length format. XDR represents a variable-length string as a 4-byte integer length followed by the bytes of the string itself. Figure 20.10 shows an example of the representation for a UNIX authentication field. In the example, the computer's name, *merlin.cs.purdue.edu*, contains *20* characters.

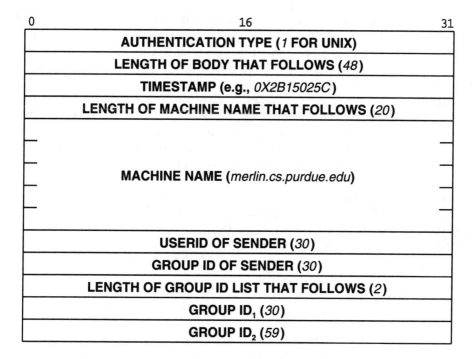

Figure 20.10 Example representation for UNIX authentication within an RPC message. The example values are taken from a message sent by a user with numeric login identifier *30* on machine *merlin.cs.purdue.edu*.

20.27 Summary

The remote procedure model helps make distributed programs easy to design and understand because it relates client-server communication to conventional procedure calls. The remote procedure call model views each server as implementing one or more procedures. A message sent from a client to a server corresponds to a "call" of a remote procedure, and a response from the server to the client corresponds to a "return" from a procedure call.

Like conventional procedures, remote procedures accept arguments and return one or more results. The arguments and results passed between the caller and the called procedure provide a precise definition of the communication between the client and the server.

Using the remote procedure call model helps programmers focus on the application instead of the communication protocol. The programmer can build and test a conventional program that solves a particular problem, and then can divide the program into parts that execute on two or more computers.

Sun Microsystems, Incorporated defined a particular form of remote procedure call that has become a *de facto* standard. ONC RPC specifies a scheme for identifying remote procedures as well as a standard for the format of RPC messages. The standard uses the external data representation, XDR, to keep message representations machine independent.

RPC programs do not use well-known protocol ports like conventional clients and servers. Instead, they use a dynamic binding mechanism that allows each RPC program to choose an arbitrary, unused protocol port when it begins. Called the RPC port mapper, the binding mechanism requires each computer that offers RPC programs to also run a port mapper server at a well-known protocol port. Each RPC program registers with the port mapper on its local machine after it obtains a protocol port. When an RPC client wants to contact an RPC program, it first contacts the port mapper on the target machine. The port mapper responds by telling the client which port the target RPC program is using. Once a client obtains the correct protocol port for a target RPC program, it contacts the target RPC program directly using that port.

FOR FURTHER STUDY

Sun Microsystems, Incorporated [RFC 1057] defines the standard for ONC RPC and describes most of the ideas presented in this chapter. Srinivasan [RFC 1831] contains a new version that is a proposed standard. Additional information can be found in the documentation that accompanies each vendor's RPC software.

EXERCISES

20.1   Read the RPC specification and create a diagram that shows the size of the fields in a typical return message.

20.2   Conduct an experiment to measure the overhead that using a port mapper introduces.

20.3   A client can avoid needless overhead by caching protocol port bindings. That is, after a client contacts the port mapper to obtain a protocol port for the target RPC program, it can store the binding in a cache to avoid looking it up again. How long will a binding remain valid?

20.4   Can the port mapper concept be extended to services other than RPC? Explain your answer.

20.5   What are the major advantages and disadvantages of using a port mapper instead of well-known ports?

20.6   When an RPC client contacts a port mapper, it must either specify or learn whether the target program has opened a UDP port or a TCP port. Read the specification carefully to find out how an RPC client distinguishes between the two.

20.7   If your computer has the utility program *rpcinfo*, read the manual pages to determine its capabilities. Use *rpcinfo* to obtain a list of the RPC programs and versions that are available on your computer.

20.8   Read about other vendor's designs for RPC. Are there concepts that are not present in ONC RPC?

20.9   Consider the authentication scheme used in ONC RPC. Is the scheme completely secure for use within an organization? For use between two organizations?

20.10 Compare DCE RPC to ONC RPC. How do the two differ?

20.11 Read about the *Common Object Request Broker Architecture, CORBA*. What new facilities does such an architecture provide for RPC?

21

Distributed Program Generation (Rpcgen Concept)

21.1 Introduction

The previous chapter presents the principles underlying the remote procedure call model. It describes the remote procedure call concept, and explains how programmers can use remote procedure calls to build programs that operate in the client-server paradigm. Finally, it describes the ONC RPC mechanism.

This chapter continues the discussion. It focuses on the structure of programs that use RPC, and shows how programs can be divided along procedural boundaries. It introduces the stub procedure concept and a program generator tool that automates much of the code generation associated with ONC RPC. It also discusses a library of procedures that makes it easy to build servers that offer remote procedures and clients that call them.

The next chapter completes the discussion of the generator. It shows the sequence of steps a programmer takes to create a conventional program and then to divide the program into local and remote components. It presents a simple example application, and then uses the example to follow through the process of constructing a distributed program. The example in the next chapter complements the conceptual description in this chapter by illustrating many of the details and showing the code that the generator produces.

21.2 Using Remote Procedure Calls

The remote procedure call model is general. A programmer can choose to use the remote procedure paradigm in any of the following ways:

- As a program specification technique only. To do so, the programmer follows the RPC model and specifies all interaction between a client and server as either a remote procedure call or a return. Procedure arguments specify the data passed between the client and server. The programmer can ignore the procedural structure when designing the client and server, but use the procedural specification to verify the correctness of the resulting system.

- For both program specification and as an abstraction during program design. To implement this approach, think about remote procedure calls when designing the application programs and the communication protocol. Design a communication protocol in which each message corresponds closely to one of the remote procedure calls.

- For the conceptual design and explicitly in the implementation. To include RPC in the implementation, the programmer designs a generalized RPC message format and a protocol for passing control to a remote procedure. The programmer follows the procedural specification precisely when passing data between the client and server. The program uses a standard external data representation to encode arguments, and follows the exact data type specifications given in the design. It calls standard library routines to convert between the computer's native representation and the external representation used when crossing a network.

- For design and implementation, constructing all software from scratch. The programmer builds a conventional application that solves the problem, and then divides it into pieces along procedural boundaries, moving the pieces to separate machines. The program uses the ONC RPC message format (including the XDR data representation) and program numbering scheme when calling a remote procedure. The programmer builds the implementation from the ONC RPC specifications alone, using the port mapper to bind a remote program number to the corresponding protocol port.

- For design and implementation, using standard libraries. The programmer builds an application and divides it into pieces using the ONC RPC specification, but relies on existing RPC library routines whenever possible. For example, the programmer uses library routines to register with the port mapper, to compose and send a remote procedure call message, and to compose a reply.

- For an automated implementation. The programmer follows the ONC RPC specification completely, and uses an automatic program generator tool to help automate construction of the necessary pieces of client and server code and the calls to RPC library routines that perform tasks like registering a program with the port mapper, constructing a message, and dispatching a call to the appropriate remote procedure in a remote program.

21.3 Programming Mechanisms To Support RPC

ONC RPC specifications are both extensive and complicated. Building an application that implements RPC without using any existing software can be tedious and time consuming. Most programmers prefer to avoid duplicating the effort for each application. Instead, they rely on library routines and programming tools to handle much of the work.

Implementations of ONC RPC provide significant help for those who wish to avoid unnecessary programming. Assistance comes in four forms:

1. XDR library routines that convert individual data items from internal form to the XDR standard external representation
2. XDR library routines that format the complex data aggregates (e.g., arrays and structures) used to define RPC messages
3. RPC run-time library routines that allow a program to call a remote procedure, register a service with the port mapper, or dispatch an incoming call to the correct remote procedure inside a remote program
4. A program generator† tool that produces many of the C source files needed to build a distributed program that uses RPC

The RPC run-time library has procedures that supply most of the functionality needed for RPC. For example, procedure *callrpc* sends an RPC message to a server. It has the form:

```
callrpc (host, prog, progver, procnum, inproc, in, outproc, out);
```

Argument *host* points to a character string that contains the name of a machine on which the remote procedure executes. Arguments *prog*, *progver*, and *procnum* identify the remote program number, the version of the program to use, and the remote procedure number. Argument *inproc* gives the address of a local procedure that can be called to marshal arguments into an RPC message, and argument *in* gives the address of the arguments for the remote procedure. Argument *outproc* gives the address of a local procedure that can be called to decode the results, and *out* gives the address in memory where the results should go.

While *callrpc* handles many of the chores required to send an RPC message, the ONC RPC library contains many other procedures. For example, a client calls function:

```
handle = clnt_create (host, prog, vers, proto);
```

to create an integer identifier that can be used to send RPC messages. RPC calls the integer identifier a *handle*; several RPC library procedures take a handle as one of their arguments. Arguments to *clnt_create* specify the name of a remote host, a remote program on that host, the version of that program, and a protocol (TCP or UDP).

---

†Programmers often refer to the program generator as a *stub generator*. The reason that such terminology has become popular will become apparent when we review how the generator works.

The library also contains routines that create, store, and manipulate authentication information. For example, if the program is using UNIX authentication, procedure:

authunix_create (host, uid, gid, len, aup_gids);

creates an authentication handle for a given user on a given host computer. Arguments specify a remote host, the user's login and primary group identifiers, and a set of groups to which the user belongs, *aup_gids*. Argument *len* specifies the number of items in the set.

Although programmers can write applications that call the RPC library routines directly, few programmers do. Most rely on the program generator tool discussed later in this chapter. The code it generates contains many calls to the library procedures.

21.4 Dividing A Program Into Local And Remote Procedures

To understand how the RPC programming tools work, it is necessary to understand how a program can be divided into local and remote procedures. Think of the procedure calls in a conventional application. Figure 21.1 illustrates one such call.

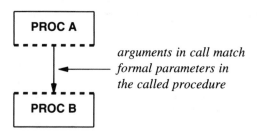

Figure 21.1 An example procedure call that illustrates the procedural interface used by a calling procedure and a called procedure. The dashed lines denote a match between arguments in the procedure call and parameters in the called procedure.

Each procedure has a set of formal parameters, and each procedure call specifies a set of arguments. The total number of arguments in the caller must equal the total number of formal parameters in the called procedure, and the type of each argument must match the declared type of the corresponding formal parameter. In other words, the parameters define the interface between a calling procedure and a called procedure.

21.5 Adding Code For RPC

Moving one or more procedures to a remote machine requires a programmer to add code between the procedure call and the remote procedure. On the client side, the new code must marshal arguments and translate them to a machine-independent representation, create an RPC *CALL* message, send the message to the remote program, wait for the results, and translate the resulting values back to the client's native representation. On the server side, the new code must accept an incoming RPC request, translate arguments to the server's native data representation, dispatch the message to the appropriate procedure, form a reply message by translating values to the machine-independent data representation, and send the result back to the client.

To keep the program structure intact and to isolate the code that handles RPC from the code that handles the application, the additional code required for RPC can be added in the form of two extra procedures that completely hide the communication details. The new procedures can add the required functionality without changing the interface between the original calling and called procedures. Preserving the original interface helps reduce the chance for errors because it keeps the communication details separate from the original application.

21.6 Stub Procedures

The additional procedures added to a program to implement RPC are called *stub procedures*. The easiest way to understand stub procedures is to imagine a conventional program being divided into two programs with an existing procedure being moved to a remote machine. On the caller's (client) side, a stub procedure replaces the called procedure. On the remote procedure's (server) side, a stub procedure replaces the caller. The two stubs implement all the communication required for the remote procedure call, leaving the original calling and called procedures unchanged. Figure 21.2 illustrates the stub concept, showing how stub procedures allow the procedure call shown in Figure 21.1 to be separated into local and remote parts.

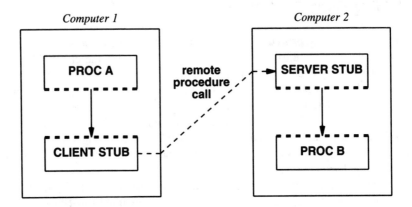

Figure 21.2 Stub procedures added to a program implement a remote procedure call. Because stubs use the same interface as the original
call, adding them does not require a change to either the original
calling procedure or the called procedure.

21.7 Multiple Remote Procedures And Dispatching

Figure 21.2 presents a simplified view of RPC because it only shows a single remote procedure call. In practice, a given server usually includes several remote procedures in a single remote program. Each RPC call consists of a message that identifies
a specific remote procedure. When an RPC message arrives, the server uses the remote
procedure number in the message to *dispatch* the call to the correct procedure. Figure
21.3 illustrates the concept.

The figure shows how RPC relates to a conventional client-server implementation.
The remote program consists of a singly-threaded server that must be running before
any messages arrive. A remote procedure call, which can originate from any client,
must specify the address of the machine on which the server operates, the number of the
remote program on that machine, and the remote procedure to call. The server program
consists of a dispatcher routine plus the remote procedures and server-side stub procedures. The dispatcher understands how the remote procedure numbers correspond to
the server-side stubs, and uses the correspondence to forward each incoming remote
procedure call to an appropriate stub.

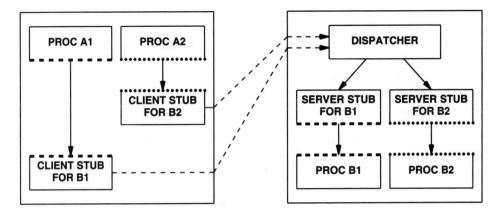

Figure 21.3 Message dispatch in an RPC server. Clients send RPC requests
to a single server program. The server uses the remote procedure number in a message to decide which procedure should
receive the call. In the example, procedure *A1* calls procedure
B1, and *A2* calls *B2*. Dashed and dotted lines show which interface each procedure uses.

21.8 Name Of The Client-Side Stub Procedure

The transition from a conventional application to a distributed program can be
trivial if the programmer chooses to name the client stub the same as the called procedure. To see why, consider again the stub procedures shown in Figure 21.3. The original caller, procedure *A1*, contains a call to procedure *B1*. After the program has been
divided, *A1* becomes part of the client and must call a stub to communicate with the remote procedure. If the programmer names the client-side stub *B1* and builds it to have
exactly the same interface as the original procedure *B1*, the calling procedure (*A1*) does
not need to change. In fact, it may even be possible to make the change without recompiling procedure *A1*. The original compiled binary for *A1* can be linked with the new
client-side stub for *B1* to produce a valid client. Adding a client-side stub without
changing the original caller isolates the RPC code from the original application program
code, making programming easier and reducing the chance of introducing errors.

Of course, naming the client stub *B1* makes source code management more difficult because it means that the distributed version of the program will have two procedures named *B1*: the client-side stub and the original procedure that becomes part of
the server. The two versions of *B1* are never part of the same linked program. In most
cases, they will not execute on the same computer. Thus, as long as the programmer
exercises caution when building object programs, the stub approach works well. To
summarize:

To build a distributed version of an application program, a program-
mer must move one or more procedures to a remote machine. When
doing so, the addition of stub procedures allows the original calling
and called procedures to remain unchanged as long as the client-side
stub has the same name as the original called procedure.

21.9 Using Rpcgen To Generate Distributed Programs

It should be obvious that much of the code needed to implement an RPC server
does not change. For example, if the mapping between remote procedure numbers and
server-side stubs is kept in a data structure, all servers can use the same dispatcher routine. Similarly, all servers can use the same code to register their services with the port
mapper.

To avoid unnecessary programming, implementations of ONC RPC include a tool
that generates much of the code needed to implement a distributed program automatically. Called *rpcgen*, the tool reads a specification file as input and generates files of C
source code as output. The specification file contains the declarations for constants,
global data types, global data, and remote procedures (including the procedure argument
and result types). The files that rpcgen produces contain most of the source code needed to implement the client and server programs that provide the specified remote procedure calls. In particular, rpcgen generates code for the client-side and server-side stub
procedures, including the code to marshal arguments, to send an RPC message, to
dispatch an incoming call to the correct procedure, to send a reply, and to translate arguments and results between the external representations and native data representations. When combined with an application program and a few files that the programmer
writes, the rpcgen output produces complete client and server programs.

Because rpcgen produces source code as output, the programmer can choose to edit
the code (e.g., to hand-optimize the code to improve performance) or to combine it with
other files. In most cases, programmers use rpcgen to handle as many of the details as
possible. They try to avoid changing the output by hand to keep the entire process of
generating a client and server automated. If the program specifications change or new
remote procedure calls are needed, the programmer can modify the specifications and
use rpcgen again to produce a new client and server without manual intervention.

21.10 Rpcgen Output And Interface Procedures

To maintain flexibility and to allow automatic generation of significant portions of
the stub code, rpcgen separates each stub procedure into two parts. One part, common
to almost all applications that use RPC, provides basic client-server communication; the
other part provides an interface to the application program. Rpcgen produces the communication portion of the stub automatically from a description of the remote procedure

and its arguments. Because rpcgen produces code for the communication stub, it specifies the arguments required on the client side and the calling sequence on the server side. The programmer must accept rpcgen calling conventions when using the communication stubs that rpcgen generates.

The idea behind separating the stub into communication and interface routines is simple: it allows rpcgen to choose the calling conventions the communication stubs use, while it allows the programmer to choose the calling conventions the remote procedures use. The programmer creates interface stubs to map between the remote procedure calling conventions and the conventions provided by the communication stub procedures that rpcgen generates. Figure 21.4 illustrates how all the routines interact.

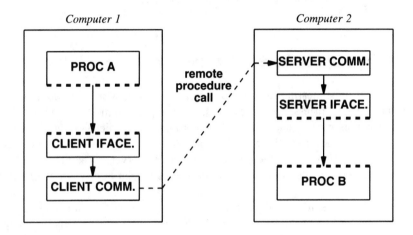

Figure 21.4 The form of a distributed program created using rpcgen. Rpcgen generates the basic communication stubs automatically; the programmer supplies the two interface procedures.

As Figure 21.4 illustrates, the two parts of a stub each consist of two separate procedures. On the client side, the interface procedure calls the communication procedure. On the server side, the communication procedure calls the interface procedure. If the stub interface procedures are defined carefully, the original caller and the original called procedure can remain unchanged.

21.11 Rpcgen Input And Output

Rpcgen reads an input file that contains a specification of a remote program. It produces four output files, each of which contains source code. Rpcgen derives names for the output files from the name of the input file. If the specification file has name Q.x, all output files will begin with Q. The table in Figure 21.5 lists the output files and describes their contents.

File Name	Contents
Q.h	Declarations of constants and types used in the code generated for both the client and server
*Q*_xdr.cpp	XDR procedure calls used in the client and server to marshal arguments
*Q*_clnt.cpp	Client-side communication stub procedure
*Q*_svc.cpp	Server-side communication stub procedure

Figure 21.5 The output files produced by rpcgen for an input file named *Q*.x. As their names imply, the output files contain the C source code for both programs and data declarations.

21.12 Using Rpcgen To Build A Client And Server

Figure 21.6 illustrates the files that a programmer must write to build a client and server using rpcgen. In essence, rpcgen requires the programmer to write an application, the procedures it calls, and the interface portions of the client-side and server-side stubs. The programmer divides the application into a driver program (the client) and a set of procedures that comprise the remote program (the server). The programmer then writes a specification for the remote program and uses rpcgen to generate the remaining pieces.

When rpcgen runs, it reads the specification and generates C source code that must be compiled and linked to produce running programs. After rpcgen runs, two separate compile-and-link steps occur. One produces the executable client program and the other produces an executable server.

Figure 21.6 only provides an overview of rpcgen input and output. The next chapter provides additional details on its use. The chapter presents a simple example application, and shows the steps a programmer takes to transform it into a distributed program. The chapter describes the specification file rpcgen takes as input as well as the code rpcgen produces.

21.13 Summary

RPC is a broad concept that can help programmers design client-server software. A programmer can use RPC to help specify or implement a distributed program. When using ONC RPC, the programmer can choose to follow the specification while building code from scratch, to use procedures found in the RPC library, or to use an automatic program generation tool called *rpcgen*.

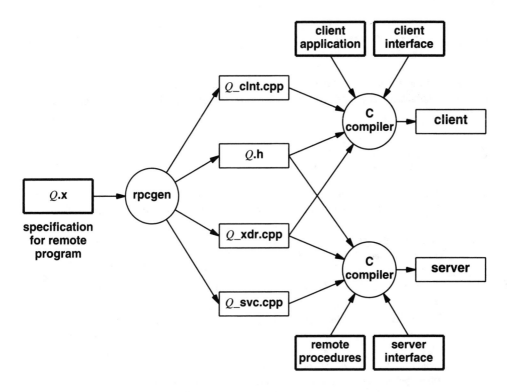

Figure 21.6 The files required to build a client and server from the output of rpcgen, and the compilation steps required to process them. Darkened boxes show the input that the programmer supplies.

RPC allows a programmer to construct a conventional program and then to transform it into a distributed program by moving some procedures to a remote machine. When doing so, the programmer can minimize changes and reduce the chance of introducing errors by adding stub procedures to the program. The stub procedures implement the necessary communication. Using stubs allows the original calling and called procedures to remain unchanged.

Because most distributed programs using ONC RPC follow the same general architecture, rpcgen can generate much of the required code automatically. In addition to creating a specification file, the programmer only needs to supply a pair of interface procedures and the procedures associated with the application. Rpcgen generates the rest of the client and server programs, including procedures that register the server with the port mapper, provide communication between client and server, and dispatch incoming calls to the correct remote procedure.

FOR FURTHER STUDY

Additional information on *rpcgen* can be found in the documentation that accompanies the software. Stevens [1990] describes the details of RPC exception handling.

EXERCISES

21.1   Write down the sequence of steps a server takes when an RPC CALL message arrives. Be sure to specify when data values are converted from the external representations to native representations.

21.2   Read about the RPC library routines in the documentation. What are the arguments for function *svc_sendreply*? Why is each needed?

21.3   The RPC library includes routines that allow a server to register with the port mapper. Read the documentation to find out what procedure *pmap_unset* does. Why is it necessary?

21.4   If you have access to the source code for RPC library routines, find out how many lines of code they occupy. Compare the library size to the size of the source code for the rpcgen program. Why is rpcgen as large as it is?

21.5   Rpcgen produces C source code instead of object code. The documentation that accompanies rpcgen suggests that having source code allows a programmer to modify the generated code. Why might a programmer make such modifications?

21.6   Refer to the previous question. What are the disadvantages of modifying the rpcgen output?

21.7   It is possible to design a remote procedure call mechanism that combines all procedures from a remote program into a single procedure by using an additional argument to decide which procedure to call (e.g., the remote procedure consists of a C *switch* statement that uses the new argument to make a choice among alternative actions). What are the chief advantages of such an approach compared to the ONC RPC approach? What are the chief disadvantages?

21.8   If the server side of a ONC RPC program uses sockets, what are the possible methods it can use to implement mutual exclusion (i.e., how can it guarantee that only one remote procedure will be called at any time)? What are the advantages and disadvantages of each method? Hint: consider the socket options.

22

Distributed Program Generation (Rpcgen Example)

22.1 Introduction

The previous chapters present the principles underlying the remote procedure call model and the ONC RPC mechanism. They discuss the remote procedure call concept and explain how programs can be divided along procedure call boundaries. They also describe how the rpcgen tool and associated library routines automate much of the code generation for programs that use ONC RPC.

This chapter completes the discussion of rpcgen. It presents the sequence of steps a programmer takes to first create a conventional program and then divide the program into local and remote components. It uses an example application to follow through each step of the process. It shows the output from rpcgen and the additional code required to create the client and server components of a distributed program that uses RPC.

22.2 An Example To Illustrate Rpcgen

An example will clarify how rpcgen works and will illustrate most of the details. Because the point of the example is to explain how rpcgen works, we have selected an extremely simple application. In practice, of course, few RPC programs are as trivial or easy to follow as our example. Thus, one should think of the example as a tutorial and not question whether the application warrants a distributed solution.

22.3 Dictionary Look Up

As an example of using rpcgen, consider an application that implements a simple database. The database offers four basic operations: *initialize* to initialize the database (i.e., erase all previously stored values), *insert* to insert a new item, *delete* to remove an item, and *lookup* to search for an item. We will assume that items in the database are individual words. Thus, the database will function as a dictionary. The application inserts a set of valid words, and then uses the database to check new words to see if each is in the dictionary.

To keep the example simple, we will assume that input to the application is a text file, where each line contains a one-letter command followed by a word. The table in Figure 22.1 lists the commands, and gives the meaning of each:

one-letter command	Argument	Meaning
I	-none-	Initialize the database by removing all words
i	word	insert word into the database
d	word	delete word from the database
l	word	look up word in the database
q	-none-	quit

Figure 22.1 Input commands for the example database application and their meanings. Some commands must be followed by a word that can be thought of as an argument to the command.

For example, the following input contains a sequence of data commands. The commands initialize the dictionary, insert names of computer vendors, delete some of the names, and look up three names:

```
I
i  Navy
i  IBM
i  RCA
i  Encore
```

```
i  Digital
d  RCA
d  Navy
l  IBM
d  Encore
l  CDC
l  Encore
q
```

When this file of commands is presented as input, the dictionary application should find *IBM* in the dictionary, but it should not find *Encore* or *CDC*.

22.4 Eight Steps To A Distributed Application

Figure 21.6† shows the input required for rpcgen and the output files it generates. To create the required files and combine them into a client and server, a programmer takes the following eight steps:

1. Build and test a conventional application that solves the problem.

2. Divide the program by choosing a set of procedures to move to a remote machine. Place the selected procedures in a separate file.

3. Write an rpcgen specification for the remote program, including names and numbers for the remote procedures and the declarations of their arguments. Choose a remote program number and a version number (usually *1*).

4. Run rpcgen to check the specification and, if valid, generate the four source code files that will be used in the client and server.

5. Write stub interface routines for the client side and server side.

6. Compile and link together the client program. It consists of four main files: the original application program (with the remote procedures removed), the client-side stub (generated by rpcgen), the client-side interface stub, and the XDR procedures (generated by rpcgen). When all these files have been compiled and linked together, the resulting executable program becomes the client.

7. Compile and link together the server program. It consists of four main files: the procedures taken from the original application that now comprise the remote program, the server-side stub (generated by rpcgen), the server-side interface stub, and the XDR procedures (generated by rpcgen). When all these files have been compiled and linked together, the resulting executable program becomes the server.

8. Start the server on the remote machine, and then invoke the client on the local machine.

---

†Figure 21.6 can be found on page 277.

The next sections examine each step in more detail and use the dictionary application to illustrate the subtleties.

22.5 Step 1: Build A Conventional Application Program

The first step in building a distributed version of the example dictionary application requires the programmer to construct a conventional program that solves the problem. File *dict.cpp* contains an application program for the dictionary problem written in the C language.

```
/* dict.cpp - main, initw, nextin, insertw, deletew, lookupw */

#include <stdlib.h>
#include <stdio.h>
#include <ctype.h>
#include <string.h>

#define MAXWORDLEN      50       /* maximum length of a command or word  */
#define DICTSIZ 100              /* maximum number of entries in diction.*/
char    dict[DICTSIZ][MAXWORDLEN+1];/* storage for a dictionary of words*/
int     nwords = 0;             /* number of words in the dictionary    */

int     nextin(char *, char *), initw(), insertw(const char *);
int     deletew(const char *), lookupw(const char *);

/*------------------------------------------------------------------------
 * main - insert, delete, or lookup words in a dictionary as specified
 *------------------------------------------------------------------------
 */
int
main(int argc, char argv[])
{
        char    word[MAXWORDLEN+1]; /*space to hold word from input line*/
        char    cmd;
        int     wrdlen;         /* length of input word                 */

        while (1) {
                wrdlen = nextin(&cmd, word);
                if (wrdlen < 0)
                        exit(0);
                word[wrdlen] = '\0';
                switch (cmd) {
```

```
                case 'I':          /* "initialize" */
                        initw();
                        printf("Dictionary initialized to empty.\n");
                        break;
                case 'i':          /* "insert" */
                        insertw(word);
                        printf("%s inserted.\n",word);
                        break;
                case 'd':          /* "delete" */
                        if (deletew(word))
                                printf("%s deleted.\n",word);
                        else
                                printf("%s not found.\n",word);
                        break;
                case 'l':          /* "lookup" */
                        if (lookupw(word))
                                printf("%s was found.\n",word);
                        else
                                printf("%s was not found.\n",word);
                        break;
                case 'q':          /* quit */
                        printf("program quits.\n");
                        exit(0);
                default:           /* illegal input */
                        printf("command %c invalid.\n", cmd);
                        break;
                }
        }
}


/*------------------------------------------------------------------------
 * nextin - read a command and (possibly) a word from the next input line
 *------------------------------------------------------------------------
 */
int
nextin(char *cmd, char *word)
{
        int     i, ch;

        ch = getc(stdin);
        while (isspace(ch))
                ch = getc(stdin);
        if (ch == EOF)
                return -1;
```

```
        *cmd = (char) ch;
        ch = getc(stdin);
        while (isspace(ch))
                ch = getc(stdin);
        if (ch == EOF)
                return -1;
        if (ch == '\n')
                return 0;
        i = 0;
        while (!isspace(ch)) {
                if (++i > MAXWORDLEN) {
                        printf("error: word too long.\n");
                        exit(1);
                }
                *word++ = ch;
                ch = getc(stdin);
        }
        return i;
}


/*-------------------------------------------------------------------------
 * initw - initialize the dictionary to contain no words at all
 *-------------------------------------------------------------------------
 */
int
initw()
{
        nwords = 0;
        return 1;
}


/*-------------------------------------------------------------------------
 * insertw - insert  a word in the dictionary
 *-------------------------------------------------------------------------
 */
int
insertw(const char *word)
{
        strcpy(dict[nwords], word);
        nwords++;
        return nwords;
}
```

```
/*------------------------------------------------------------------------
 * deletew - delete  a word from the dictionary
 *------------------------------------------------------------------------
 */
int
deletew(const char *word)
{
        int     i;

        for (i=0 ; i<nwords ; i++)
                if (strcmp(word, dict[i]) == 0) {
                        nwords--;
                        strcpy(dict[i], dict[nwords]);
                        return 1;
                }
        return 0;
}


/*------------------------------------------------------------------------
 * lookupw - look up a word in the dictionary
 *------------------------------------------------------------------------
 */
int
lookupw(const char *word)
{
        int     i;

        for (i=0 ; i<nwords ; i++)
                if (strcmp(word, dict[i]) == 0)
                        return 1;
        return 0;
}
```

To keep the application simple and easy to understand, the conventional program in file *dict.cpp* uses a two-dimensional array to store words. A global variable, *nwords*, counts the number of words in the dictionary at any time. The main program contains a loop that reads and processes one line of input on each iteration. It calls procedure *nextin* to read a command (and possibly a word) from the next input line, and then uses a C *switch* statement to select one of six possible cases. The cases correspond to the five valid commands plus a default case that handles illegal input.

Each case in the main program calls a procedure to handle the details. For example, the case that corresponds to an insertion command, *i*, calls procedure *insertw*. Procedure *insertw* inserts a new word at the end of the array and increments *nwords*.

The other procedures operate as expected. Procedure *deletew* searches for the word to be deleted. If it finds the word, *deletew* replaces it with the last word in the dictionary and decrements *nwords*. Finally, *lookupw* searches the array sequentially to determine if the specified word is present. It returns *1* if the word is present in the dictionary and *0* otherwise.

To produce an executable binary for the application, the programmer compiles the C code. For example, to produce an executable binary file for the *dict* program, the programmer must compile the source program found in file *dict.cpp*

22.6 Step 2: Divide The Program Into Two Parts

Once a conventional application has been built and tested, it can be partitioned into local and remote components. Programmers must have a conceptual model of a program's procedure call graph before they can partition the program. For example, Figure 22.2 shows the procedural organization of the original dictionary application.

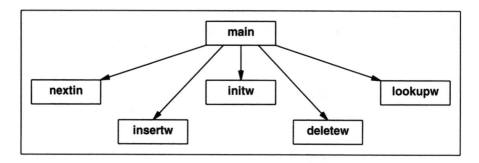

Figure 22.2 The procedure call graph for the original, conventional program that solves the dictionary problem. A call graph represents a program's procedural organization.

When considering which procedures can be moved to a remote machine, the programmer must consider the facilities that each procedure needs. For example, procedure *nextin* reads and parses the next input line each time it is called. Because it needs access to the program's standard input file, *nextin* must be kept with the main program. To summarize:

> *Procedures that perform I/O or otherwise access file descriptors cannot be moved to a remote machine easily.*

The programmer must also consider the location of data that each procedure accesses. For example, procedure *lookupw* needs to access the entire database of words. If *lookupw* executes on a machine other than the machine where the dictionary resides, the RPC call to *lookupw* must pass the entire dictionary as an argument.

Passing large data structures as arguments to remote procedures is extremely inefficient because the RPC mechanism must read and encode the entire data structure for each remote procedure call. In general:

> *Procedures should execute on the same machine as the data they access. Passing large data structures as arguments to remote procedures is inefficient.*

After considering the original dictionary program and the data each procedure accesses, it should be obvious that procedures *insertw*, *deletew*, *initw*, and *lookupw* belong on the same machine as the dictionary itself.

Assume that the programmer decides to move the dictionary storage and associated procedures to a remote machine. To help understand the consequences of moving some procedures to a remote machine, programmers usually create a mental image, or even a sketch, of the distributed program and data structures. Figure 22.3 illustrates the new structure of the dictionary application with the data and access procedures moved to a remote machine.

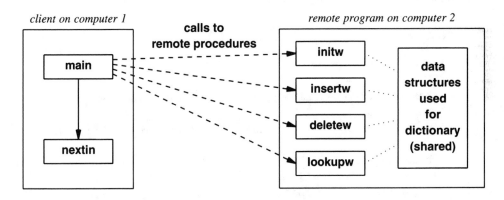

Figure 22.3 The conceptual division of the dictionary program into local and remote components. The remote component contains the data for the dictionary and the procedures that access and search it.

A simple drawing like the one in Figure 22.3 can help a programmer think about the division of a program into local and remote components. The programmer must consider whether each procedure has access to the data and services it needs, and must consider the arguments that each remote procedure will require along with the cost of passing that information across a network. Finally, the diagram helps the programmer assess how network delays will affect program performance.

Assuming the programmer chooses a conceptual division and decides to proceed, the next step is to divide the source program into two components. The programmer identifies the constants and data structures used by each component, and places each component in a separate file. In the dictionary example, the division is straightforward because the original source file can be divided between procedure *nextin* and procedure *initw*. File *dict1.cpp* contains the main program and procedure *nextin*:

```
/* dict1.cpp - main, nextin */

#include <stdlib.h>
#include <stdio.h>
#include <ctype.h>

#define MAXWORDLEN       50       /* maximum length of a command or word  */

int     nextin(char *, char *), initw(void), insertw(char *),
        deletew(char *), lookupw(char *);

/*--------------------------------------------------------------------------
 * main - insert, delete, or lookup words in a dictionary as specified
 *--------------------------------------------------------------------------
 */
int
main(int argc, char *argv[])
{
        char    word[MAXWORDLEN+1]; /*space to hold word from input line*/
        char    cmd;
        int     wrdlen;            /* length of input word                */

        while (1) {
                wrdlen = nextin(&cmd, word);
                if (wrdlen < 0)
                        exit(0);
                switch (cmd) {
                case 'I':       /* "initialize" */
                        initw();
                        printf("Dictionary initialized to empty.\n");
                        break;
                case 'i':       /* "insert" */
                        insertw(word);
                        printf("%s inserted.\n",word);
                        break;
```

```
            case 'd':        /* "delete" */
                    if (deletew(word))
                            printf("%s deleted.\n",word);
                    else
                            printf("%s not found.\n",word);
                    break;
            case 'l':        /* "lookup" */
                    if (lookupw(word))
                            printf("%s was found.\n",word);
                    else
                            printf("%s was not found.\n",word);
                    break;
            case 'q':        /* quit */
                    printf("program quits.\n");
                    exit(0);
            default:         /* illegal input */
                    printf("command %c invalid.\n", cmd);
                    break;
            }
        }
}


/*-------------------------------------------------------------------------
 * nextin - read a command and (possibly) a word from the next input line
 *-------------------------------------------------------------------------
 */
int
nextin(char *cmd, char *word)
{
        int     i, ch;

        ch = getc(stdin);
        while (isspace(ch))
                ch = getc(stdin);
        if (ch == EOF)
                return -1;
        *cmd = (char) ch;
        ch = getc(stdin);
        while (isspace(ch))
                ch = getc(stdin);
        if (ch == EOF)
                return -1;
        if (ch == '\n')
                return 0;
```

```
                i = 0;
                while (!isspace(ch)) {
                        if (++i > MAXWORDLEN) {
                                printf("error: word too long.\n");
                                exit(1);
                        }
                        *word++ = ch;
                        ch = getc(stdin);
                }
                return i;
}
```

File *dict2.cpp* contains the procedures from the original application that will become part of the remote program. In addition, it contains declarations for the global data that the procedures will share. At this point, the file does not contain a complete program – the remaining code will be added later.

```
/* dict2.cpp - initw, insertw, deletew, lookupw */

#include <string.h>

#define MAXWORDLEN      50      /* maximum length of a command or word  */
#define DICTSIZ 100             /* maximum number of entries in diction.*/
char    dict[DICTSIZ][MAXWORDLEN+1];/* storage for a dictionary of words*/
int     nwords = 0;             /* number of words in the dictionary    */

/*------------------------------------------------------------------------
 * initw - initialize the dictionary to contain no words at all
 *------------------------------------------------------------------------
 */
int
initw()
{
        nwords = 0;
        return 1;
}

/*------------------------------------------------------------------------
 * insertw - insert  a word in the dictionary
 *------------------------------------------------------------------------
 */
int
insertw(char *word)
```

```
{
        strcpy(dict[nwords], word);
        nwords++;
        return nwords;
}


/*-------------------------------------------------------------------
 * deletew - delete  a word from the dictionary
 *-------------------------------------------------------------------
 */
int
deletew(char *word)
{
        int     i;

        for (i=0 ; i<nwords ; i++)
                if (strcmp(word, dict[i]) == 0) {
                        nwords--;
                        strcpy(dict[i], dict[nwords]);
                        return 1;
                }
        return 0;
}


/*-------------------------------------------------------------------
 * lookupw - look up a word in the dictionary
 *-------------------------------------------------------------------
 */
int
lookupw(char *word)
{
        int     i;

        for (i=0 ; i<nwords ; i++)
                if (strcmp(word, dict[i]) == 0)
                        return 1;
        return 0;
}
```

Note that the definition of symbolic constant *MAXWORD* appears in both components because they both declare variables used to store words. Only file *dict2.cpp* contains the declarations for data structures used to store the dictionary, however, because only the remote program will include the dictionary data structures.

From a practical point of view, separating the application into two files makes it possible to compile the client and server pieces separately. The compiler checks for problems like symbolic constants referenced by both parts, and the linker checks to see that all data structures have been collected together with the procedures that reference them.

Although a compiler appears to read a source program and produce an executable binary program in a single step, most compilers have at least two distinct internal steps. In the first step, the computer checks the syntax and produces intermediate object files (i.e., files with the suffix *.obj*). In the second step, the compiler invokes a *linkage editor*† to combine object files into an executable binary. At this step, a programmer usually requests the compiler to produce object files (not complete programs) for the two components. The components must be linked together to produce an executable program, but that is not the immediate reason to compile them: the compiler checks that both files are syntactically correct.

When thinking about the utility of having a compiler check the code, remember that most distributed programs are much more complex than our trivial example. A compilation may find problems in a large program that escape the programmer's attention. Catching such problems before additional code has been inserted makes them easier to repair.

22.7 Step 3: Create An Rpcgen Specification

Once the programmer selects a structure for the distributed program, he or she can prepare an rpcgen specification. In essence, an rpcgen specification file contains a declaration of a remote program, including the data structures it uses.

The specification file contains constants, type definitions, and declarations for the client and server programs. More precisely, the specification file contains:

- declarations for constants used in the client or, more often, in the server (remote program),
- declarations of data types used (especially in arguments to remote procedures), and
- declarations of remote programs, the procedures contained in each program, and the types of their parameters.

Recall that RPC uses numbers to identify remote programs and the remote procedures within them. The program declaration in a specification file defines such details as a program's RPC number, its version number, and the numbers assigned to each procedure within the program.

All specifications must be given in the RPC programming language, not C. While the differences are minor, they can be frustrating. For example, RPC language uses the keyword *string* to denote null-terminated character strings, while C uses *char **. Even

---

†The term is often abbreviated *linker*.

experienced programmers may require multiple iterations to produce a correct specification.

File *rdict.x* illustrates an rpcgen specification. It contains example declarations for the RPC version of the dictionary program.

```
/* dict.x */

/* RPC declarations for dictionary program */

const    MAXWORD = 50;          /* maximum length of a command or word */
const    DICTSIZ = 100;         /* number of entries in dictionary     */


struct example {                /* unused structure declared here to   */
        int     exfield1;       /* illustrate how rpcgen builds XDR     */
        char    exfield2;       /* routines to convert structures.      */
};


/*-------------------------------------------------------------------
 * RDICTPROG - remote program that provides insert, delete, and lookup
 *-------------------------------------------------------------------
 */
program RDICTPROG {             /* name of remote program (not used)    */
    version RDICTVERS {         /* declaration of version (see below)   */
        int INITW(void)    = 1;/* first procedure in this program       */
        int INSERTW(string) = 2;/* second procedure in this program     */
        int DELETEW(string) = 3;/* third procedure in this program      */
        int LOOKUPW(string) = 4;/* fourth procedure in this program     */
    } = 1;                      /* definition of the program version    */
} = 0x30090949;                 /* remote program number (must be       */
                                /*  unique)                             */
```

An rpcgen specification file does not contain entries for all declarations found in the original program. Instead, it only defines those constants and types shared across the client and server or needed to specify arguments.

The example specification file begins by defining constants *MAXWORD* and *DICTSIZE*. In the original application, both were defined to be symbolic constants using a C preprocessor *define* statement. RPC language does not use C symbolic constant declarations. Instead it requires symbolic constants to be declared with the *const* keyword and assigned a value using the equal symbol (=).

Following suggested conventions, the specification file uses upper case names to define procedures and programs. As we will see later, the names become symbolic constants that can be used in C programs. Using upper case is not absolutely required, but it helps avoid name conflicts.

22.8 Step 4: Run Rpcgen

After the specification has been completed, the programmer runs rpcgen to check for syntax errors and generate four† files of code as Figure 21.6 shows‡. On most Windows systems, the command syntax is:

```
rpcgen rdict.x
```

Rpcgen uses the name of the input file when generating the names of the four output files. For example, because the input file began with *rdict*, the output files will be named: *rdict.h*, *rdict_clnt.cpp*, *rdict_svc.cpp*, and *rdict_xdr.cpp*.

22.9 The .h File Produced By Rpcgen

Figure 22.4 shows the contents of file *rdict.h*, which contains valid C declarations for any constants and data types declared in the specification file. In addition, rpcgen adds definitions for the remote procedures. In the example code, rpcgen defines upper case *INSERTW* to be *2* because the specification declared procedure *INSERTW* to be the second procedure in the remote program.

The external procedure declarations in *rdict.h* require an explanation. The declared procedures comprise the interface portion of the server-side stub. Procedure names have been generated by taking the declared procedure names, mapping them to lower case, and appending an underscore followed by the program version number. For example, the sample specification file declares that the remote program contains procedure *DELETEW*, so *dict.h* contains an *extern* declaration for procedure *deletew_1*. To understand why rpcgen declares these interface routines, recall the purpose of the interface portion of the stub: it allows rpcgen to choose its own calling conventions, while allowing the original called procedure to remain unchanged.

As an example of interface stub naming, consider procedure *insertw*. The original procedure will become part of the server and will remain unchanged. Thus, the server will have a procedure named *insertw* that has the same arguments as in the original application. To avoid a naming conflict, the server must use a different name for the interface stub procedure. Rpcgen arranges for the server-side communication stub to call an interface stub procedure named *insertw_1*. The call uses rpcgen's choice of arguments, and allows the programmer to design *insertw_1* so that it calls *insertw* using the correct arguments.

---

†If a particular output file would be empty, rpcgen will not create it. Therefore, some specifications produce fewer than four files.

‡Figure 21.6 can be found on page 277.

```
#define MAXWORD 50
#define DICTSIZ 100

struct example {
        int exfield1;
        char exfield2;
};
typedef struct example example;
bool_t xdr_example();


#define RDICTPROG ((u_long)0x30090949)
#define RDICTVERS ((u_long)1)

#ifdef RPC_CLNT
#define INITW ((u_long)1)
extern int *initw_1(void *, CLIENT *);
#define INSERTW ((u_long)2)
extern int *insertw_1(char **, CLIENT *);
#define DELETEW ((u_long)3)
extern int *deletew_1(char **, CLIENT *);
#define LOOKUPW ((u_long)4)
extern int *lookupw_1(char **, CLIENT *);
#endif

#ifdef RPC_SVC
#define INITW ((u_long)1)
extern int *initw_1(void *, struct svc_req *);
#define INSERTW ((u_long)2)
extern int *insertw_1(void *, struct svc_req *);
#define DELETEW ((u_long)3)
extern int *deletew_1(void *, struct svc_req *);
#define LOOKUPW ((u_long)4)
extern int *lookupw_1(void *, struct svc_req *);
#endif
```

Figure 22.4 File *rdict.h* – an example *.h* file that rpcgen produces.

22.10 The XDR Conversion File Produced By Rpcgen

Rpcgen produces a file that contains calls to routines that perform XDR conversions for all data types declared in the remote program. For example, file *rdict_xdr.cpp* contains calls to conversion routines for the data types declared in the dictionary program.

```
#include <rpc/rpc.h>
#include "rdict.h"


bool_t
xdr_example(XDR *xdrs, example *objp)
{
        if (!xdr_int(xdrs, &objp->exfield1)) {
                return (FALSE);
        }
        if (!xdr_char(xdrs, &objp->exfield2)) {
                return (FALSE);
        }
        return (TRUE);
}
```

Figure 22.5 File *rdict_xdr.cpp* – an example file of XDR conversion routines
that rpcgen produces.

In our example, the only type declaration that appears in the specification file has the name *example*. It defines a structure that has one integer field and one character field. File *rdict_xdr.cpp* contains the code needed to convert a structure of type *example* between the native data representation and the external data representation. The code, which has been generated automatically by rpcgen, calls routines from the XDR library for each field of the structure. Once a declaration has been given, the declared type can be used for arguments to remote procedures. If one of the remote procedures did use an *example* structure as an argument, rpcgen would generate code in both the client and server to call procedure *xdr_example* to convert the representation.

22.11 The Client Code Produced By Rpcgen

For the example dictionary application, rpcgen produces file *rdict_clnt.cpp*, a source program that will become the client-side communication stub in the distributed version of the program.

```cpp
#include <string.h>
#include <rpc/rpc.h>

#define RPC_CLNT
#include "rdict.h"

/* Default timeout can be changed using clnt_control() */
static struct timeval TIMEOUT = { 25, 0 };

int *
initw_1(void *argp, CLIENT *clnt)
{
        static int res;

        memset((char *)&res, 0, sizeof(res));
        if (clnt_call(clnt, INITW, (xdrproc_t)xdr_void, (caddr_t)argp,
            (xdrproc_t)xdr_int, (caddr_t)&res, TIMEOUT) != RPC_SUCCESS) {
                return (NULL);
        }
        return (&res);
}


int *
insertw_1(char **argp, CLIENT *clnt)
{
        static int res;

        memset((char *)&res, 0, sizeof(res));
        if (clnt_call(clnt, INSERTW, (xdrproc_t)xdr_wrapstring, (caddr_t)argp,
            (xdrproc_t)xdr_int, (caddr_t)&res, TIMEOUT) != RPC_SUCCESS) {
                return (NULL);
        }
        return (&res);
}
```

```
int *
deletew_1(char **argp, CLIENT *clnt)
{
        static int res;

        memset((char *)&res, 0, sizeof(res));
        if (clnt_call(clnt, DELETEW, (xdrproc_t)xdr_wrapstring, (caddr_t)argp,
            (xdrproc_t)xdr_int, (caddr_t)&res, TIMEOUT) != RPC_SUCCESS) {
                return (NULL);
        }
        return (&res);
}



int *
lookupw_1(char **argp, CLIENT *clnt)
{
        static int res;

        memset((char *)&res, 0, sizeof(res));
        if (clnt_call(clnt, LOOKUPW, (xdrproc_t)xdr_wrapstring, (caddr_t)argp,
            (xdrproc_t)xdr_int, (caddr_t)&res, TIMEOUT) != RPC_SUCCESS) {
                return (NULL);
        }
        return (&res);
}
```

Figure 22.6 File *rdict_clnt.cpp* – an example of the client stub that rpcgen
produces.

The file contains a communication stub procedure for each of the procedures in the remote program. As with the server, names have been chosen to avoid conflicts.

22.12 The Server Code Produced By Rpcgen

For the dictionary example, rpcgen produces a fourth file, *rdict_svc.cpp*, that contains the code needed for a server. The file contains a main program that executes
when the server begins. It obtains UDP and TCP protocol ports, registers the RPC program with the port mapper, and then waits to receive RPC calls. It dispatches each call
to the appropriate server-side stub interface routine. When the called procedure
responds, the server creates an RPC reply and sends it back to the client.

```
#include <stdlib.h>
#include <string.h>
#include <stdio.h>
#include <rpc/rpc.h>
#include <rpc/pmap_clnt.h>

#define RPC_SVC
#include "rdict.h"

#define WSVERS   MAKEWORD(2, 0)

static void rdictprog_1(struct svc_req *, SVCXPRT *);


main()
{
        SVCXPRT *transp;
        WSADATA wsdata;

        if (WSAStartup(WSVERS, &wsdata) < 0) {
                fprintf(stderr, "WSAStartup failed.\n");
                exit(1);
        }

        (void)pmap_unset(RDICTPROG, RDICTVERS);

        transp = svcudp_create(RPC_ANYSOCK);
        if (transp == NULL) {
                (void)fprintf(stderr, "cannot create udp service.\n");
                exit(1);
        }
        if (!svc_register(transp, RDICTPROG, RDICTVERS, rdictprog_1, IPPROTO_UDP)) {
                (void)fprintf(stderr,
                        "unable to register (RDICTPROG, RDICTVERS, udp).\n");
                exit(1);
        }

        transp = svctcp_create(RPC_ANYSOCK, 0, 0);
        if (transp == NULL) {
                (void)fprintf(stderr, "cannot create tcp service.\n");
                exit(1);
        }
```

```
        if (!svc_register(transp, RDICTPROG, RDICTVERS, rdictprog_1, IPPROTO_TC
                (void)fprintf(stderr,
                        "unable to register (RDICTPROG, RDICTVERS, tcp).\n");
                exit(1);
        }
        svc_run();
        (void)fprintf(stderr, "svc_run returned\n");
        exit(1);
}

static void
rdictprog_1(struct svc_req *rqstp, SVCXPRT *transp)
{
        union {
                char *insertw_1_arg;
                char *deletew_1_arg;
                char *lookupw_1_arg;
        } argument;
        char *result;
        xdrproc_t xdr_argument, xdr_result;
        char *(*local)(void *, struct svc_req *);

        switch (rqstp->rq_proc) {
        case NULLPROC:
                (void)svc_sendreply(transp, (xdrproc_t)xdr_void, (char *)NULL);
                return;

        case INITW:
                xdr_argument = (xdrproc_t)xdr_void;
                xdr_result = (xdrproc_t)xdr_int;
                local = (char *(*)(void *, struct svc_req *)) initw_1;
                break;

        case INSERTW:
                xdr_argument = (xdrproc_t)xdr_wrapstring;
                xdr_result = (xdrproc_t)xdr_int;
                local = (char *(*)(void *, struct svc_req *)) insertw_1;
                break;

        case DELETEW:
                xdr_argument = (xdrproc_t)xdr_wrapstring;
                xdr_result = (xdrproc_t)xdr_int;
                local = (char *(*)(void *, struct svc_req *)) deletew_1;
                break;
```

```
        case LOOKUPW:
                xdr_argument = (xdrproc_t)xdr_wrapstring;
                xdr_result = (xdrproc_t)xdr_int;
                local = (char *(*)(void *, struct svc_req *)) lookupw_1;
                break;

    default:
                svcerr_noproc(transp);
                return;
    }
    memset((char *)&argument, 0, sizeof(argument));
    if (!svc_getargs(transp, xdr_argument, (caddr_t)&argument)) {
                svcerr_decode(transp);
                return;
    }
    result = (*local)(&argument, rqstp);
    if (result != NULL && !svc_sendreply(transp, xdr_result, result)) {
                svcerr_systemerr(transp);
    }
    if (!svc_freeargs(transp, xdr_argument, (caddr_t)&argument)) {
                (void)fprintf(stderr, "unable to free arguments\n");
                exit(1);
    }
}
```

Figure 22.7 File *rdict_svc.cpp* – an example server stub that rpcgen produces.

Once the files have been generated, they can be compiled and kept in object form. Three separate compilation steps are needed; each takes a C source file and produces a corresponding object file. Object file names have ".obj" in place of the ".cpp" suffix. For example, the compiled version of *rdict_clnt.cpp* will be placed in file *rdict_clnt.obj*.

22.13 Step 5: Write Stub Interface Procedures

22.13.1 Client-Side Interface Routines

The files that rpcgen produces do not form complete programs. They require client-side and server-side interface routines that the programmer must write. One interface procedure must exist for each remote procedure in the remote program.

On the client side, the original application program controls processing. It calls interface procedures using the same procedure names and argument types as it originally used to call those procedures which have become remote in the distributed version. Each interface procedure must convert its arguments to the form used by rpcgen, and must then call the corresponding client-side communication procedure. For example, because the original program contained a procedure named *insertw* that takes a pointer to a character string as an argument, the client-side interface must contain such a procedure. The interface procedure calls *insertw_1*, the client-side communication stub generated by rpcgen.

The chief difference between conventional procedure parameters and the parameters used by the communication stubs is that the arguments for all procedures produced by rpcgen use indirection. For example, if the original procedure had an integer argument, the corresponding argument in the communication stub for that procedure must be a pointer to an integer. In the dictionary program, most procedures require a character string argument, declared in C to be a character pointer (*char **). The corresponding communication stubs all require that their arguments be a pointer to a character pointer (*char ***).

File *rdict_cif.cpp* illustrates how interface routines convert arguments to the form expected by the code produced by rpcgen. The file contains one client-side interface procedure for each of the remote procedures in the program.

```
/* rdict_cif.cpp - initw, insertw, deletew, lookupw */

#include <rpc/rpc.h>

#include <stdio.h>

#define RPC_CLNT
#include "rdict.h"

/* Client-side stub interface routines written by programmer */

extern  CLIENT  *handle;          /* handle for remote procedure  */
static  int     *ret;             /* tmp storage for return code  */

/*--------------------------------------------------------------------
 * initw - client interface routine that calls initw_1
 *--------------------------------------------------------------------
 */
int
initw()
{
        ret = initw_1(0, handle);
        return ret==0 ? 0 : *ret;
}
```

```
/*-----------------------------------------------------------------
 * insertw - client interface routine that calls insertw_1
 *-----------------------------------------------------------------
 */
int
insertw(char *word)
{
        char    **arg;                  /* pointer to argument */
        arg = &word;
        ret = insertw_1(arg, handle);
        return ret==0 ? 0 : *ret;
}


/*-----------------------------------------------------------------
 * deletew - client interface routine that calls deletew_1
 *-----------------------------------------------------------------
 */
int
deletew(char *word)
{
        char    **arg;                  /* pointer to argument */

        arg = &word;
        ret = deletew_1(arg, handle);
        return ret==0 ? 0 : *ret;
}


/*-----------------------------------------------------------------
 * lookupw - client interface routine that calls lookupw_1
 *-----------------------------------------------------------------
 */
int
lookupw(char *word)
{
        char    **arg;                  /* pointer to argument */

        arg = &word;
        ret = lookupw_1(arg, handle);
        return ret==0 ? 0 : *ret;
}
```

22.13.2 Server-Side Interface Routines

On the server side, the interface routines accept calls from the communication stubs that rpcgen produces, and pass control to the procedure that implements the specified call. As with the client side, server-side interface routines must translate from argument types chosen by rpcgen to the argument types that the called procedures use. In most cases, the difference lies in an extra indirection – rpcgen passes a pointer to an object instead of the object itself. To convert an argument, an interface procedure only needs to apply the C indirection operator (*). File *rdict_sif.cpp* illustrates the concept. It contains the server-side interface routines for the dictionary program.

```
/* rdict_sif.cpp - init_1, insert_1, delete_1, lookup_1 */

#include <rpc/rpc.h>

#define RPC_SVC
#include "rdict.h"

/* Server-side stub inteface routines written by hand */

static  int retcode;

int     initw(void), insertw(char *), deletew(char *), lookupw(char *);

/*-------------------------------------------------------------------------
 * insertw_1 -  server side interface to remote procedure insertw
 *-------------------------------------------------------------------------
 */
int     *
insertw_1(void *w, struct svc_req *rqstp)
{
        retcode = insertw(*(char **)w);
        return &retcode;
}


/*-------------------------------------------------------------------------
 * initw_1 -  server side interface to remote procedure initw
 *-------------------------------------------------------------------------
 */
int     *
initw_1(void *w, struct svc_req *rqstp)
{
        retcode = initw();
        return &retcode;
```

```
}

/*---------------------------------------------------------------------------
 * deletew_1 -  server side interface to remote procedure deletew
 *---------------------------------------------------------------------------
 */
int     *
deletew_1(void *w, struct svc_req *rqstp)
{
        retcode = deletew(*(char **)w);
        return &retcode;
}


/*---------------------------------------------------------------------------
 * lookupw_1 -  server side interface to remote procedure lookupw
 *---------------------------------------------------------------------------
 */
int     *
lookupw_1(void *w, struct svc_req *rqstp)
{
        retcode = lookupw(*(char**)w);
        return &retcode;
}
```

22.14 Step 6: Compile And Link The Client Program

Once the client interface routines have been written and placed in a source file, they can be compiled. For example, file *rdict_cif.cpp* contains all the client interface routines for the dictionary example. The compiler will produce object file *rdict_cif.obj*. To complete the client, the programmer needs to add a few details to the original main program. Because the new version uses RPC, it needs the C *include* file for RPC declarations. It also needs to include file *rdict.h* because that file contains definitions for constants used by both the client and server.

The client program also needs to declare and initialize a *handle* that the RPC communication routines can use to communicate with the server. Most clients declare the handle using the defined type *CLIENT*, and initialize the handle by calling the RPC library routine, *clnt_create*. File *rdict.cpp* shows an example of the necessary code:

```
/* rdict.cpp - main, nextin */

#include <rpc/rpc.h>

#include <stdlib.h>
#include <stdio.h>
#include <ctype.h>

#include "rdict.h"

#define WSVERS          MAKEWORD(2, 0)

#define MAXWORDLEN      50      /* maximum length of a command or word  */

#define RMACHINE        "localhost"    /* name of remote machine       */
CLIENT  *handle;                       /* handle for remote procedure  */

int     nextin(char *, char *), initw(void), insertw(char *);
int     deletew(char *), lookupw(char *);

/*-----------------------------------------------------------------------
 * main - insert, delete, or lookup words in a dictionary as specified
 *-----------------------------------------------------------------------
 */
int
main(int argc, char *argv[])
{
        char    word[MAXWORDLEN+1]; /*space to hold word from input line*/
        char    cmd;
        int     wrdlen;         /* length of input word                */
        WSADATA wsdata;

        if (WSAStartup(WSVERS, &wsdata)) {
                fprintf(stderr, "WSAStartup failed\n");
                exit(1);
        }
     /* set up connection for remote procedure call  */

        handle = clnt_create(RMACHINE, RDICTPROG, RDICTVERS, "tcp");
        if (handle == 0) {
                printf("Could not contact remote program.\n");
                exit(1);
        }
```

```
        while (1) {
                wrdlen = nextin(&cmd, word);
                if (wrdlen < 0)
                        exit(0);
                word[wrdlen] = '\0';
                switch (cmd) {
                case 'I':        /* "initialize" */
                        initw();
                        printf("Dictionary initialized to empty.\n");
                        break;
                case 'i':        /* "insert" */
                        insertw(word);
                        printf("%s inserted.\n",word);
                        break;
                case 'd':        /* "delete" */
                        if (deletew(word))
                                printf("%s deleted.\n",word);
                        else
                                printf("%s not found.\n",word);
                        break;
                case 'l':        /* "lookup" */
                        if (lookupw(word))
                                printf("%s was found.\n",word);
                        else
                                printf("%s was not found.\n",word);
                        break;
                case 'q':        /* quit */
                        printf("program quits.\n");
                        exit(0);
                default:         /* illegal input */
                        printf("command %c invalid.\n", cmd);
                        break;
                }
        }
}


/*-------------------------------------------------------------------------
 * nextin - read a command and (possibly) a word from the next input line
 *-------------------------------------------------------------------------
 */
int
nextin(char *cmd, char *word)
{
        int     i, ch;
```

```
ch = getc(stdin);
while (isspace(ch))
        ch = getc(stdin);
if (ch == EOF)
        return -1;
*cmd = (char) ch;
ch = getc(stdin);
while (isspace(ch))
        ch = getc(stdin);
if (ch == EOF)
        return -1;
if (ch == '\n')
        return 0;
i = 0;
while (!isspace(ch)) {
        if (++i > MAXWORDLEN) {
                printf("error: word too long.\n");
                exit(1);
        }
        *word++ = ch;
        ch = getc(stdin);
}
return i;
}
```

Compare *rdict.cpp* with *dict1.cpp*† from which it was derived to see how little code has been added. The sample code uses symbolic constant *RMACHINE* to specify the domain name of the remote machine. To make testing easy *RMACHINE* has been defined to be *localhost*, which means the client and server will operate on the same machine. Of course, once testing has been completed on a distributed program, the programmer will change the definition to specify the permanent location of the server.

Clnt_create attempts to make a connection to a specified remote computer. If the connection attempt fails, *clnt_create* returns the value *NULL*, allowing the application to report an error to the user. Our sample code exits if *clnt_create* reports an error. In practice, a client may choose to try repeatedly, or may maintain a list of machines and try each of them.

Like other C source files, *rdict.cpp* can be compiled to produce an object program. Once the object program for *rdict.cpp* has been compiled, all files that comprise the client can be linked together into an executable program. When invoking the linker, one can specify the name of a file into which the resulting executable image should be placed. The choice is arbitrary (i.e., there is no relationship between the name of the object files that are linked and the name of the resulting executable). We chose the name *rdict.exe*, but could have just as easily used another name.

---

†File *dict1.cpp* can be found on page 288.

22.15 Step 7: Compile And Link The Server Program

The output generated by rpcgen includes most of the code needed for a server. The programmer supplies two additional files: the server interface routines (which we have chosen to place in file *rdict_sif.cpp*) and the remote procedures themselves. For the dictionary example, the final version of the remote procedures appears in file *rdict_srp.cpp*. The code for the procedures has been derived from the code in the original application.

```
/* rdict_srp.cpp - initw, insertw, deletew, lookupw */

#include <rpc/rpc.h>

#include <string.h>

#include "rdict.h"

/* Server-side remote procedures and the global data they use */

char    dict[DICTSIZ][MAXWORDLEN+1];/* storage for a dictionary of words*/
int     nwords = 0;                 /* number of words in the dictionary    */

/*-------------------------------------------------------------------------
 * initw - initialize the dictionary to contain no words at all
 *-------------------------------------------------------------------------
 */
int
initw()
{
        nwords = 0;
        return 1;
}


/*-------------------------------------------------------------------------
 * insertw - insert  a word in the dictionary
 *-------------------------------------------------------------------------
 */
int
insertw(char *word)
{
        strcpy(dict[nwords], word);
        nwords++;
        return nwords;
}
```

```
/*------------------------------------------------------------------
 * deletew - delete  a word from the dictionary
 *------------------------------------------------------------------
 */
int
deletew(char *word)
{
        int     i;

        for (i=0 ; i<nwords ; i++)
                if (strcmp(word, dict[i]) == 0) {
                        nwords--;
                        strcpy(dict[i], dict[nwords]);
                        return 1;
                }
        return 0;
}


/*------------------------------------------------------------------
 * lookupw - look up a word in the dictionary
 *------------------------------------------------------------------
 */
int
lookupw(char *word)
{
        int     i;

        for (i=0 ; i<nwords ; i++)
                if (strcmp(word, dict[i]) == 0)
                        return 1;
        return 0;
}
```

Once the file containing remote procedures has been compiled, the object programs that comprise the server can be linked together into an executable file. Once again, the name assigned to the executable file is arbitrary. We chose *rdictd.exe*.

22.16 Step 8: Start The Server And Execute The Client

The first serious test of the entire system occurs when both the client and server components operate together on the same machine. The server must begin execution before the client attempts to contact it. Otherwise, the client will print the message:

Could not contact remote program.

and halt. Once the server has been started, the client can be run.

22.17 Summary

Constructing a distributed program using rpcgen consists of eight steps. The programmer begins with a conventional application program to solve the problem, decides how to partition the program into components that execute locally and remotely, divides the application into two physical parts, creates a specification file that describes the remote program, and runs rpcgen to produce needed files. The programmer then writes client-side and server-side interface routines and combines them with the code produced by rpcgen. Finally, the programmer compiles and links the client-side files and the server-side files to produce executable client and server programs.

Although rpcgen eliminates much of the coding required for RPC, building a distributed program requires careful thought. When considering how to partition a program into local and remote components, the programmer must examine the data accessed by each piece to minimize data movement. The programmer must also consider the delay that each remote procedure call will introduce as well as how each piece will access I/O facilities.

The example dictionary application in this chapter shows how much effort is required to transform a trivial application into a distributed program. More complicated applications require substantially more complex specifications and interface procedures. In particular, applications that pass structured data to remote procedures or that check client authorizations can require substantially more code.

FOR FURTHER STUDY

Additional information on *rpcgen* can be found in the documentation that accompanies the software.

EXERCISES

22.1   Modify the example program from this chapter so the client interface routine keeps a cache of recently referenced words and searches the cache before making a remote procedure call. How much additional computational overhead does the cache require? How much time does the cache save when an entry can be found locally?

22.2   Build a distributed application that provides access to files on the remote machine. Include remote procedures that permit the client to *read* or *write* data to a specified location in a specified file.

22.3   Build a distributed program that passes a linked list as an argument to a remote procedure. Hint: use relative pointers instead of absolute memory addresses.

22.4   Try to modify the example dictionary program so the remote procedures can write error messages on the client's terminal. What problems did you encounter? How did you solve them?

22.5   Rpcgen could have been designed so it automatically assigns each remote procedure a unique number, 1, 2, and so on. What are the advantages of having the programmer assign remote procedure numbers manually in the specification file instead of assigning them automatically? What are the disadvantages?

22.6   What limitations does rpcgen have? Hint: consider trying to build a server that is also a client for another service.

22.7   Try building and testing two versions of the distributed dictionary program simultaneously. Would it be possible to test new versions if the server side used a well-known port number? Explain.

22.8   The example dictionary program recognizes blanks as separator characters in the input. Revise procedure *nextin* to allow tabs as well as blanks.

22.9   Is it possible to make the server side of the dictionary program concurrent? Why or why not?

23

Network File System
Concepts (NFS)

23.1 Introduction

The previous chapters describe remote procedure call, explain the relationship between RPC and client-server interaction, and show how RPC can be used to create a distributed version of an application program. This chapter and the next focus on an application and a protocol that is specified, designed, and implemented using ONC RPC. This chapter describes the general concept of remote file access, and reviews the concepts underlying the NFS remote file access mechanism. Although the mechanism can be used with a variety of operating systems, including Windows, many of the ideas and details are derived directly from the UNIX system. Consequently, this chapter reviews the UNIX file system and the semantics of file operations. It discusses hierarchical directory structures and path names, and shows how a remote file access mechanism implements operations on hierarchies. The next chapter provides additional details about the protocol, and shows how the NFS and mount protocol specifications use RPC to define remote file operations.

23.2 Remote File Access Vs. Transfer

Many early network systems provided *file transfer* services that permitted users to move a copy of a file from one machine to another. More recent network systems provide *file access* services that permit an application program to access a file from a remote machine. A remote file access mechanism keeps one copy of each file, and allows one or more application programs to access the copy on demand.

Applications that use a remote file mechanism to access a file can execute on the machine where the file resides or on a remote machine. When an application accesses a file that resides on a remote machine, the program's operating system invokes client software that contacts a server on the remote machine and performs the requested operations on the file. Unlike a file transfer service, the application's system does not retrieve or store an entire file at once. Instead, it requests transfers of one small block of data at a time.

To provide remote access to some or all of the files that reside on a computer, the system manager must arrange for the computer to run a server that responds to access requests. The server checks each request to verify that the client is authorized to access the specified file, performs the specified operation, and returns a result to the client.

Sun Microsystems, Incorporated defined a remote file access mechanism that has become widely accepted throughout the computer industry. Known as Sun's *Network File System*, or simply *NFS*, the mechanism allows a computer to run a server that makes some or all of its files available for remote access, and allows applications on other computers to access those files.

23.3 Operations On Remote Files

NFS provides the same operations on remote files that one expects to use on local files. Conceptually, an application can *open* a remote file to obtain access, *read* data from the file, *write* data to the file, *seek* to a specified position in the file (e.g., to the beginning of the file, the end of the file, or a specific location in the file), and *close* the file when finished using it.

23.4 File Access Among Heterogeneous Computers

Providing remote file access can be nontrivial. In addition to the basic mechanisms for reading and writing files, a file access service must provide ways to create and destroy files, peruse directories, authenticate requests, honor file protections, and translate information among the representations used on various computers. Because a remote file access service connects two machines, it must handle differences in the way the client and server systems name files, denote paths through directories, and store information about files. More important, the file access software must accommodate differences in the semantic interpretation of file operations.

NFS was designed to accommodate heterogeneous computer systems. From the beginning, the NFS protocol, operations, and semantics were chosen to allow a variety of systems to interact. Of course, NFS cannot provide all the file system subtleties available in all possible operating systems. Instead, it tries to define file operations that accommodate as many systems as possible without becoming inefficient or hopelessly complex. In practice, most of the choices work well.

23.5 Stateless Servers

The NFS design stores state information at the client site, allowing servers to remain stateless. Because the server is stateless, disruptions in service will not affect client operation. In theory, for example, a client will be able to continue file access after a stateless server crashes and reboots; the application program, which runs on the client system, can remain unaware of the server reboot. Furthermore, because a stateless server does not need to allocate resources for each client, a stateless design can scale to handle many more clients than a stateful design.

The NFS stateless server design affects both the protocol and its implementation. Most important, a server cannot keep any notion of *position*, whether in a file or directory. We will see how NFS achieves a stateless design after examining the operations that NFS provides.

23.6 NFS And UNIX File Semantics

Although NFS was designed to accommodate heterogeneous file systems, the UNIX file system strongly influenced its overall design, the terminology used, and many of the protocol details. The NFS designers adopted UNIX file system semantics when defining the meaning of individual operations. Thus, to understand NFS, one must begin with the UNIX file system.

The next section discusses UNIX file storage and access, concentrating on the concepts and details that are most pertinent to NFS. Later sections show how NFS borrowed many ideas from the UNIX file system directly and adopted other details with only slight modifications. To summarize:

> *Understanding the UNIX file system is essential to understanding NFS because NFS uses the UNIX file system terminology and semantics.*

23.7 Review Of The UNIX File System

23.7.1 Basic Definitions

From the user's point of view, UNIX defines a *file* to consist of a sequence of bytes. In theory, a UNIX file can grow arbitrarily large; in practice, a file is limited by the space available on the physical storage device. UNIX files can grow dynamically. The file system does not require predeclaration of the expected size or preallocation of space. Instead, a file grows automatically to accommodate whatever data an application writes into it.

Conceptually, UNIX numbers the bytes in a file starting at zero. At any time, the *size* of a file is defined to be the number of bytes in it. The UNIX file system permits random access to any file, using the byte numbers as a reference. It allows an application to move to any byte position in a file and to access data at that position.

23.7.2 A Byte Sequence Without Record Boundaries

Each UNIX file is a sequence of bytes; the system does not provide any additional structure for a file beyond the data itself. In particular, UNIX does not have notions of *record boundaries*, *record blocking*, *indexed files*, or *typed files* found in other systems. Of course, it is possible for an application to create a file of records and to access them later. The point is that the file system itself does not understand the file contents: applications that use a file must agree on the format.

23.7.3 A File's Owner And Group Identifiers

UNIX systems provide accounts for multiple users, and assign each user a numeric user identifier used for accounting and authentication throughout the system. Each UNIX file has a single *owner*, represented by the numeric identifier of the user who created the file. Ownership information is stored with the file (i.e., as opposed to the directory system).

In addition to user identifiers, UNIX provides for file sharing among groups of users by allowing the system manager to assign a subset of users a numeric *group identifier*. At any time, a given user can belong to one or more UNIX groups. When a user runs an application program (e.g., a spreadsheet program or a text editor), the running program inherits the user's owner and group identifiers. Each UNIX file belongs to one group and has its numeric group identifier stored with it. The system compares the owner and group identifiers stored with a file to the user and group identifiers of a particular application process to determine what operations that program can perform on the file.

23.7.4 Protection And Access

The UNIX access protection mechanism allows a file's owner to control file access separately for the owner, members of the file's group, and all other users. For each of the three sets, the protection mechanism allows the owner to specify whether the users in that set have permission to *read*, *write*, or *execute* the file. Figure 23.1 shows that the UNIX file access permissions can be viewed as a matrix of protection bits.

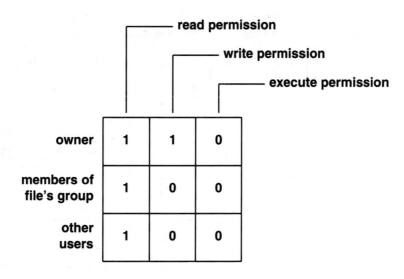

Figure 23.1 UNIX file access permissions viewed as a matrix of protection
bits.

UNIX encodes the file access protection matrix in the low-order bits of a single
binary integer, and uses the terms *file mode* or *file access mode* when referring to the
integer that encodes the protection bits. Figure 23.2 illustrates how UNIX encodes file
protection bits into the 9 low-order bits of a file mode integer. In addition to the protection bits illustrated in Figure 23.2, UNIX defines additional bits of the mode integer
to specify other properties of the file (e.g., mode bits specify whether the file is a regular file or a directory).

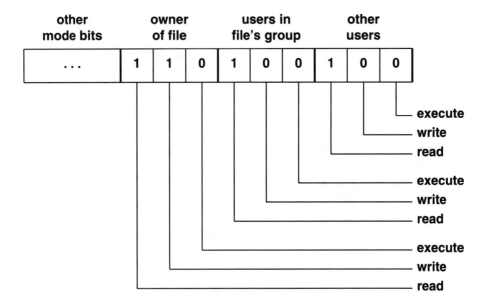

Figure 23.2 UNIX file access permissions stored in the low-order nine bits of
the mode integer. A value of *1* grants permission; a value of *0*
denies it. When written in octal, the protections illustrated have
the value *0644*.

When the value of the mode integer is written in octal, the rightmost three digits
give the protections for the owner, members of the file's group, and other users. Thus,
a protection value of *0700* specifies that the owner can read, write, or execute the file,
but no other users can have access. A protection mode value of *0644* specifies that all
users can read the file, but only the owner can write to it.

23.7.5 The UNIX Open-Read-Write-Close Paradigm

Under UNIX, applications use the *open-read-write-close* paradigm to access files.
To establish access to a file, an application must call function *open*, passing it the name
of the file and an argument that describes the desired access. *Open* returns an integer
file descriptor that the application uses for all further operations on the file. For example, the code:

```
fdesc = open("filename", O_CREAT | O_RDWR, 0644);
```

opens a file with name *filename*. The value *O_CREAT* in the second argument specifies
that the file should be created if it does not already exist, and the value *O_RDWR* specifies that the file should be created for both reading and writing. The octal value *0644*
specifies protection mode bits to assign to the file if it is created. Other values for the

second argument can be used to specify whether the file should be truncated and whether it should be opened for reading, writing, or both.

23.7.6 UNIX Data Transfer

Under UNIX, an application calls *read* to transfer data from a file into memory, and calls *write* to transfer data from memory to a file. The *read* function takes three arguments: the descriptor for an open file, a buffer address, and the number of bytes to read. For example, the following code requests that the system read *24* bytes of data from the file with descriptor *fdesc*:

```
n = read(fdesc, buff, 24);
```

Both *read* and *write* begin transfer at the current file position, and both operations update the file position when they finish. For example, if an application opens a file, moves to position *0*, and reads *10* bytes from the file, the file position will be *10* after the *read* operation completes. Thus, a program can extract all data from a file sequentially by starting at position zero and calling *read* repeatedly.

If an application attempts to *read* more bytes than the file contains, the *read* function extracts as many bytes as the file contains and returns the number read as its result. If the file is positioned at the end of a file when an application calls *read*, the *read* call returns zero to indicate an *end-of-file* condition.

23.7.7 Permission To Search A Directory

UNIX organizes files into a *hierarchy* using *directories*† to hold files and other directories. The system uses the same *9*-bit protection mode scheme for directories as it uses for regular data files. The *read* permission bits on a directory determine whether an application can obtain a list of the files in a directory, and the *write* permission bits determine whether an application can insert or delete files in the directory. Each individual file has a separate set of permission bits that determine which operations are allowed on the contents of the file. The directory permissions only specify which operations are allowed on the directory itself.

Directories can contain application programs, but a directory is not a program. Thus, the normal meaning of *execute* permission does not apply to a directory. UNIX interprets the *execute* permission bit for a directory to mean *search permission*. If an application has search permission, it can reference a file that lies in a directory; otherwise, the system will not permit any references to the file. Search permission can be used to hide or uncover an entire subtree of the file hierarchy without modifying the permissions on individual files in the subtree. Separation of execute permission and read permission means that it is possible to allow others to access files in the directory, while denying them the right to list the names of files in the directory.

---

†Some operating systems and application programs use the term *folder* instead of *directory*.

23.7.8 UNIX Random Access

When a file is opened, the position can be set to the beginning of the file (e.g., to access the file sequentially) or to the end of the file (e.g., to append data to an existing file). After a file has been opened, the position can be changed by calling function *lseek*. *Lseek* takes three arguments that specify a file descriptor, an offset, and a measure for the offset. The third argument allows an application to specify whether the offset gives an absolute location in the file (e.g., byte *512*), a new location relative to the current position (e.g., a byte that is *64* beyond the current position), or a position relative to the end of the file (e.g., *2* bytes before the end of the file). For example, the constant *L_SET* specifies that the system should interpret the offset as an absolute value. Thus, the call:

```
lseek(fdesc, 100L, L_SET);
```

specifies that the current position of the file with descriptor *fdesc* should be moved to byte number *100*.

23.7.9 Seeking Beyond The End Of A UNIX File

The UNIX file system permits an application to move to any position in a file, even if the specified position lies beyond the current end of the file. If the application seeks to an existing byte position and writes new data, the new data replaces the old data at that position. If the application seeks beyond the end of the file and writes new data, the file system extends the file size. From the user's point of view, the system appears to fill any gap between existing data and new data with null bytes (bytes with value zero). Later, if an application attempts to read from the byte positions that comprise the gap, the file system will return bytes with zeros in them. Figure 23.3 illustrates the concept:

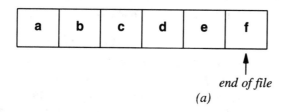

end of file

(a)

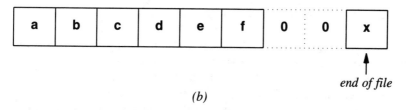

end of file

(b)

Figure 23.3 (a) a UNIX file that contains 6 bytes consisting of the characters
a through *f* and (b) the file after an application seeks to position
8 and writes a byte containing the character *x*. Unwritten bytes
appear to contain zeroes.

Although the file system appears to fill gaps with null bytes, the storage structure makes
it possible to simulate null bytes without representing them on the physical medium.
Thus, the file size records the highest byte position into which data has been written,
not the total number of bytes written.

23.7.10 UNIX File Position And Concurrent Access

The UNIX file system permits multiple application programs to access a file concurrently. The descriptor for each open file references a data structure that records a
current position in the file. When a process calls *fork*†, the new child process inherits
copies of all file descriptors the parent had open at the time of the fork. The descriptors
in both the original process and the new process point to a common underlying data
structure used to access the file. Thus, if one of the two processes changes the file position, the position changes for the other process as well.

Each call to *open* generates a new descriptor with a file position that is independent of that obtained by previous calls to *open*. Thus, if two applications both call *open*
on the same file, they can each maintain an independent position in the file. One application can move to the end of the file, while the other remains at the beginning. Programmers must decide when designing an application whether it needs to share the file
position with another process or have a separate position.

---

†Recall that fork is the UNIX system function that creates a new process.

Understanding that multiple applications can each maintain an independent position in the same file will be important when we examine operations on remote files. The concept can be summarized:

> *Each call to* open *produces a new file descriptor that stores a file offset. Separating the current file position from the file itself permits multiple applications to access a file concurrently without interference. It also allows an* lseek *operation to modify an application's position in a file without changing the file itself.*

23.7.11 Semantics Of Write During Concurrent Access

When two programs write a file concurrently, they may introduce conflicts. For example, suppose two concurrent programs each read the first two bytes of a file, exchange the bytes, and write them back into the file. If the scheduler chooses to run one program and then the other, the first program will swap the two bytes and write them back to the file. The second program will read the bytes in reversed order, swap them back to their original positions, and write them back to the file. However, if the scheduler starts both programs running, and allows them each to read from the file before either writes to it, they will both read the bytes in original order and then both write the bytes in reverse order. As a consequence, the ultimate order of bytes in the file depends on how the system scheduler chooses to delegate the CPU to the two programs.

UNIX does not provide mutual exclusion or define the semantics of concurrent access except to specify that a file always contains the data written most recently. Responsibility for correctness falls to the programmer†. A programmer must be careful to construct concurrent programs in such a way that they always produce the same results.

23.7.12 UNIX File Names And Paths

UNIX provides a hierarchical file name space. Each file and directory in a UNIX file system has an individual name that can be represented by an ASCII string. In addition, each directory or file has a *full path name* that denotes the position of the file within the hierarchy. Figure 23.4 illustrates the names of files and directories for a small example of a UNIX hierarchy.

---

†Some versions of UNIX offer an advisory lock mechanism such as *flock* or *lockf*; others offer exclusive access with argument *O_EXCL* in the *open* call.

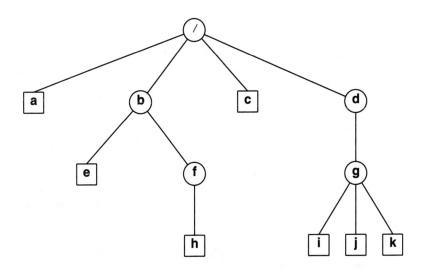

Figure 23.4 An example hierarchical file system. Circles denote directories and squares denote files. In this example, the top level directory contains two files (*a* and *c*) and two directories (*b* and *d*). In practice, UNIX files seldom have single-character names.

As the figure shows, the top directory of the file system, called the *root*, has full path name / (usually pronounced "slash"). The full path name of a file can be thought of as the concatenation of labels on the path in the hierarchy from the root to the file, using / as a separator character. For example, the file with name *a* that appears in the root directory has full path name */a*. The file with name *e* that appears in directory *b* has full path name */b/e*, and the file with name *k* has full path name */d/g/k*.

23.7.13 The UNIX Inode: Information Stored With A File

In addition to the data itself, UNIX stores information about each file on stable storage. The information is kept in a structure known as the file's *inode†*. The inode contains many fields, including: the owner and group identifiers, the mode integer (described in Section 23.7.4), the time of last access, the time of last modification, the file size, the disk device and file system on which the file resides, the number of directory entries for the file, the number of disk blocks currently used by the file, and the basic type (e.g., regular file or directory).

The inode concept helps explain several features of the UNIX file system that are also used in NFS. First, UNIX separates information such as ownership and file protection bits from the directory entry for a file. Doing so makes it possible to have two directory entries that point to the same file. UNIX uses the term *link* or *hard link* to refer to a directory entry for a file. As Figure 23.5 illustrates, when a file has more than one hard link, it appears in more than one directory.

---

†*Inode*, usually pronounced "eye-node," is an abbreviation for *index node*.

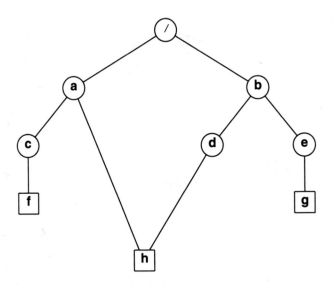

Figure 23.5 An illustration of hard links. File *h* has two links, one from
directory *a* and one from directory *d*. File *h* can be accessed by
path name */a/h* or path name */b/d/h*.

Files with multiple hard links can be accessed by more than one full path name.
For example, in Figure *23.5*, file *h* can be accessed by full path name */a/h* because it appears in directory *a*. It can also be accessed by full path name */b/d/h* because it appears in directory *d*. As the example shows, the path names for a file with multiple links can differ in length.

Because UNIX stores information about a file in its inode and not in the directory, ownership and protection information for file *h* remain consistent no matter which name an application uses to access the file. If the owner changes the protection mode of file */a/h*, the protection mode will also change on file */b/d/h*.

23.7.14 The UNIX Stat Operation

The UNIX system function *stat* extracts information about a file from its inode and returns the information to the caller. The call takes two arguments: the path name of a file and the address of a structure into which it places the results:

```
stat( pathname, &result_struct );
```

The second argument must be the address of an area in memory large enough to hold the following structure:

```
struct stat {                    /* structure returned by stat   */
        dev_t    st_dev;         /* device on which inode resides*/
        ino_t    st_ino;         /* file's inode number          */
        u_short  st_mode;        /* protection bits              */
        short    st_nlink;       /* total hard links to the file */
        short    st_uid;         /* user id of file's owner      */
        short    st_gid;         /* group id assigned to file    */
        dev_t    st_rdev;        /* used for devices, not files  */
        long     st_size;        /* total size of file in bytes  */
        time_t   st_atime;       /* time of last file access     */
        int      st_unused1;     /* not used                     */
        time_t   st_mtime;       /* time of last modification    */
        int      st_unused2;     /* not used                     */
        time_t   st_ctime;       /* time of last inode change    */
};
```

Any user can call *stat* to obtain information about a file, even if the file itself is not readable. However, the caller must have permission to search all the directories along the path to the specified file or *stat* will return an error.

23.7.15 The UNIX File Naming Mechanism

Although users imagine all files and directories to be part of a single hierarchy, the hierarchy is achieved through a file naming mechanism. The naming mechanism allows a system manager to piece together a single, conceptual hierarchy out of several smaller hierarchies. Users seldom understand the underlying file system structure or how the various components form the UNIX hierarchy because the naming mechanism hides the structure completely. We will see that when NFS runs under UNIX, it takes advantage of the UNIX naming mechanism to integrate remote files with local ones.

The original motivation for the UNIX naming mechanism arose because computer systems have multiple physical storage devices (i.e., multiple hard disks). Instead of forcing users to identify a disk as well as a file, the UNIX designers invented the idea of allowing the system manager to attach the hierarchy on one disk to the hierarchy on another. The result is a single, unified file namespace that permits the user to work without knowing the location of files. The naming mechanism operates as follows:

- The manager designates the hierarchy on one of the disks to be the root.
- The manager creates an empty directory in the root hierarchy. Let the full path name of the empty directory be given by a string /α.
- The manager instructs the naming mechanism to overlay a new hierarchy (usually one from some other disk) over directory /α.

Once the manager has attached the new hierarchy, the naming mechanism automatically maps names of the form /α/β to the file or subdirectory with path β in the attached hierarchy. The important concept is:

> *The UNIX naming mechanism provides users and application programs with a single, uniform file hierarchy even though the underlying files span multiple physical disks.*

In fact, the UNIX system is more general than a system that attaches entire disks as part of the hierarchy. It allows a system manager to partition a single physical disk into one or more *file systems*. Each file system is an independent hierarchy; it includes both files and directories. A file system can be attached to the unified hierarchy at any point. The example in the next section will clarify the naming mechanism.

23.7.16 UNIX File System Mounts

The UNIX naming mechanism relies on the *mount* system call to construct the unified hierarchy. The system manager uses *mount* to specify how a file system on one disk should be attached in the hierarchy. Usually, the manager arranges to perform necessary mounts automatically at system startup. Figure 23.6 illustrates three file systems that have been mounted to form a single hierarchy.

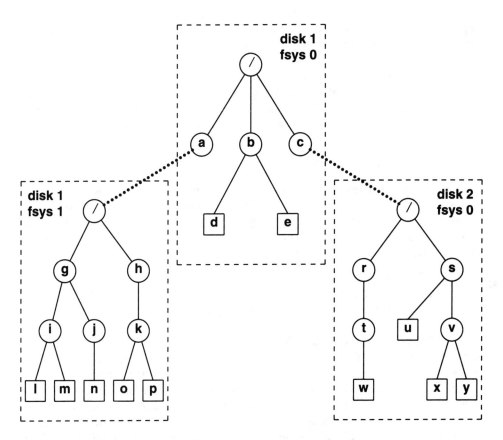

Figure 23.6 Three UNIX file systems mounted to form a single, uniform
hierarchy. After the mounts, the boundaries between disks become invisible. For example, file system *0* on disk *2* appears to
be directory */c*.

In the figure, file system *0* on disk *1* has been mounted on the root of the hierarchy. File system *1* on the same disk has been mounted on directory */a*, and file system
0 on disk *2* has been mounted on directory */c*. A mount completely overlays an original
directory with a new file system. Usually, the system administrator creates a directory
to be used for mounting. However, if the directory on which a file system is mounted
contains any files before the mount occurs, they will be completely hidden (i.e., inacces-
sible, even to system administrators) until the file system is unmounted again.

From the user's point of view, the mounts are completely invisible†. If the user
lists the contents of directory */*, the system reports three subdirectories: *a*, *b*, and *c*. If
the user lists the contents of directory */a*, the system reports two directories: *g* and *h*. If
the user lists the contents of directory */c/s*, the system reports a file, *u*, and a directory,
v.

---

†Users cannot create hard links that cross file system boundaries.

Path names do not denote the boundaries between file systems; users do not know where files reside. For example, the file named *n* (located in file system *1* on disk *1*) can be accessed using the full path name */a/g/j/n*.

> *Once a UNIX file system hierarchy has been constructed using the* mount *system function, attachments between individual file systems become transparent. Some files and directories can reside on one disk, while other files and directories reside on another disk. The user cannot distinguish among them because mounting hides all the boundaries under a uniform naming scheme.*

In practice, users can find out how the file systems have been mounted if they are interested. The system includes an executable application named *mount* that queries the system, and then displays the list of mounted file systems. A manager can also use the *mount* command to create new mounts. For example, running the *mount* command on one computer produced the following output:

```
/dev/ra0a on /          type ufs  (rw,noquota)
/dev/ra1h on /usr       type ufs  (rw,noquota)
/dev/ra0b on /usr/src   type ufs  (rw,noquota)
```

The first line of output shows that file system *ra0a* (the first file system on disk *0*) has been mounted on / and forms the root of the hierarchy. The words *type ufs* indicate that the mount refers to a *UNIX File System*, and the items in parentheses mean that the file system has been mounted for both reading and writing and that it does not have accounting quotas. File system *ra1h* (the main file system on disk *1*) has been mounted on */usr*. Thus, files that appear in directory */usr* reside on a different disk than those in */*. Finally, file system *ra0b* (the second file system on disk *0*) has been mounted on */usr/src*. The third mount provides an interesting twist because it means that although most files in */usr* reside on disk *1*, files in the subtree */usr/src* reside on disk *0*. The point is that the *mount* mechanism permits a manager to combine many file systems on many disks into a single, uniform directory hierarchy; a user or an application program uses the uniform hierarchy without knowing the location of files.

The concept of mounting file systems to form a single hierarchy provides incredible flexibility. It allows managers to choose an allocation of files to disks for economy, to reduce access contention, or to keep directories isolated in case of accidental loss. As we will see, it also provides a convenient way to introduce remote files into a UNIX hierarchy.

23.7.17 UNIX File Name Resolution

When presented with a full path name, the UNIX file system mechanism traces through the conceptual hierarchy to *resolve* the name. In UNIX, name resolution means finding the inode that identifies a file. To resolve a full path name, the file system begins at the root of the hierarchy and traces through directories one at a time. For example, given a name like */a/b/c/d*, the file system opens the root directory and searches in it for a subdirectory named *a*. Once it finds */a*, it opens that directory and searches it for a subdirectory named *b*. Similarly, it searches in *b* for a directory named *c*, and searches in *c* for a file or subdirectory named *d*. The name resolution software can extract one component of the full path name at each step because the slash character always separates individual components.

While the details of UNIX file name resolution are unimportant, the concept is essential:

> *UNIX resolves a path name one component at a time. It begins at the root of the hierarchy and at the beginning of the path. It repeatedly extracts the next component from the path and finds a file or subdirectory with that name.*

We will see that NFS takes the same approach as UNIX when resolving a name.

23.7.18 UNIX Symbolic Links

Most UNIX file systems permit a special file type known as a *symbolic link*. A symbolic link is a special text file that contains the name of another file. For example, one can create a file named */a/b/c* that contains a symbolic link with value */a/q*. If a program opens file */a/b/c*, the system finds that it contains a symbolic link and automatically switches to file */a/q*.

The chief advantage of symbolic links lies in their generality: because a symbolic link can contain an arbitrary string, it can name any file or directory. For example, although the file system forbids making a hard link to a directory, it permits a user to create a symbolic link to a directory. Furthermore, because a symbolic link can refer to an arbitrary path, it can be used to abbreviate a long path name or to make a directory in a distant part of the hierarchy appear to be much closer.

The chief disadvantage of symbolic links arises from their lack of consistency and reliability. One can create a symbolic link to a file and then remove the file, leaving the symbolic link naming a nonexistent object. In fact, one can create a symbolic link to a nonexistent file because the system does not check the contents of a symbolic link when creating it. One can also create a set of symbolic links that forms a cycle or two symbolic links that point to one another. Calling *open* on such a link results in a run-time error.

23.8 Files Under NFS

NFS uses many of the UNIX file system definitions. It views a file as a sequence of bytes, permits files to grow arbitrarily large, and allows random access using byte positions in the file as a reference. It honors the same *open-read-write-close* paradigm as UNIX, and offers most of the same services.

Like UNIX, NFS assumes a hierarchical naming system. The NFS hierarchy uses UNIX terminology; it considers the file hierarchy to be composed of *directories* and *files*. A directory can contain files and other directories.

NFS has also adopted many of the UNIX file system details, leaving some unchanged, and making minor modifications to others. The next sections describe several features of NFS and show how they relate to the UNIX file system described earlier.

23.9 NFS File Types

NFS uses the same basic file types as UNIX. It defines enumerated values that a server can use when specifying a file type:

```
enum ftype {
         NFNON = 0,              /* Specified name is not a file */
         NFREG = 1,              /* Regular data file            */
         NFDIR = 2,              /* Directory                    */
         NFBLK = 3,              /* Block-oriented device        */
         NFCHR = 4,              /* Character-oriented device    */
         NFLNK = 5               /* Symbolic link                */
};
```

The set of types, including *NFBLK* and *NFCHR*, come directly from UNIX. In particular, UNIX permits system managers to configure I/O devices in the file system namespace, making it possible for application programs to open an I/O device and transfer data to or from it using the conventional *open-read-write-close* paradigm. NFS has adopted UNIX's terminology that divides I/O devices into block-oriented (e.g., a disk that always transfers data in 512-byte blocks) and character-oriented (e.g., an ASCII terminal device that transfers data one character at a time) devices. NFS literature sometimes uses the UNIX term *special file* to denote device names. A file name that corresponds to a block-oriented device has type *block-special*, while a name that corresponds to a character-oriented device has type *character-special*.

23.10 NFS File Modes

Like UNIX, NFS assumes that each file or directory has a *mode* that specifies its type and access protection. Figure 23.7 lists individual bits of the NFS mode integer and gives their meanings. The table uses octal values to represent bits; the definitions correspond directly to those returned by the UNIX *stat* function.

Mode Bit	Meaning
0040000	This is a directory; the "type" should be *NFDIR*.
0020000	This is a character-special file; the "type" should be *NFCHR*.
0060000	This is a block-special file; the type should be *NFBLK*
0100000	This is a regular file; the type should be *NFREG*
0120000	This is a symbolic link; the type should be *NFLNK*
0140000	This is a named socket; the type should be *NFNON*
0004000	Set user id on execution
0002000	Set group id on execution
0001000	Save swapped text after use
0000400	Read permission for owner
0000200	Write permission for owner
0000100	Execute or directory search permission for owner
0000040	Read permission for group
0000020	Write permission for group
0000010	Execute or directory search permission for group
0000004	Read permission for others
0000002	Write permission for others
0000001	Execute or directory search permission for others

Figure 23.7 The meaning of bits in the NFS *mode* integer. The definitions have been taken directly from UNIX.

Although NFS defines file types for devices, it does not permit remote device access (e.g., a client may not *read* or *write* a remote device). Thus, while it is possible for a client to obtain information about a file name, it is not possible for a client to manipulate devices, even if the protection modes permit it.

Although NFS defines file protection bits that determine whether a client can read or write a particular file, NFS denies a remote machine access to all devices, even if the protection bits specify that access is allowed.

23.11 NFS File Attributes

Similar to UNIX, NFS has a mechanism to obtain information about a file. NFS uses the term *file attributes* when referring to file information. Structure *fattr* describes the file attributes that NFS provides:

```
struct fattr {                    /* NFS file attributes       */
        ftype        type;        /* type: file, directory, etc */
        unsigned int mode;        /* file's protection bits    */
        unsigned int nlink;       /* total hard links to the file */
```

```
                unsigned int userid;      /* user id of file's owner       */
                unsigned int groupid;     /* group id assigned to file     */
                unsigned int size;        /* total size of file in bytes   */
                unsigned int blocksize;   /* block size used to store file*/
                unsigned int devnum;      /* dev. num. if file is device   */
                unsigned int blocks;      /* number of blocks file uses    */
                unsigned int fsid;        /* file system id for file       */
                unsigned int fileid;      /* unique id for file            */
                timeval      atime;       /* time of last file access      */
                timeval      mtime;       /* time of last modification     */
                timeval      ctime;       /* time of last inode change     */
    };
```

As the structure shows, the concept and most of the details have been derived from the information that the UNIX *stat* function returns.

23.12 NFS Client And Server

An *NFS server* runs on a machine that has a local file system. The server makes some of the local files available to remote machines. An *NFS client* runs on an arbitrary machine, and accesses the files on machines that run NFS servers. Often, an organization will choose to dedicate a computer that has large disks to the server function. Such a machine is often called a *file server*. Forbidding users from running application programs on an NFS file server machine helps keep the load low and guarantees faster response to access requests. Dedicating a computer to the file server function also guarantees that remote file access traffic will not reduce the CPU time available for application programs.

Most NFS client implementations integrate NFS files with the computer's native file system, hiding file locations from application programs and users. For example, consider a *Windows 95* environment. File names have the form: $X{:}\alpha$, where X is a single-character disk identifier and α denotes a path name on that disk. Windows 95 uses the backslash character (\) to separate components in the path. Thus, the file name $C{:}\backslash D\backslash E\backslash F$ denotes file F in subdirectory E in directory D on the system's hard disk. If an NFS client is added to the system and configured to access files on a remote server, it can use the Windows 95 naming scheme. For example, the manager might choose names of the form $R{:}\beta$ for all remote files, where β denotes a path on the remote file system.

When an application program calls *open* to obtain access to a file, the operating system uses the syntax of the path name to choose between local and remote file access procedures. If the path refers to a remote file, the system uses NFS client software to access the remote file. If the path refers to a local file, the system uses the computer's standard file system software to access the file. Figure 23.8 illustrates how the modules in an operating system interact when making the choice.

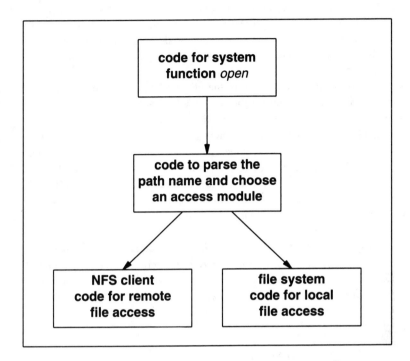

Figure 23.8 Procedures in an operating system that are called when an application opens a file. The system uses the path name syntax to choose between NFS, which will open a remote file, or the standard file system, which will open a local one.

23.13 NFS Client Operation

Recall that NFS was designed to accommodate heterogeneous computer systems. When system managers install NFS client code in an operating system, they try to integrate it into the system's file naming scheme. However, the path name syntax used by the remote file system may differ from that of the client machine. For example, when NFS client code running on a machine that uses Windows 95 connects to an NFS server running on a machine that uses UNIX, the client's system uses backslash (\) as a separator character, while the server's file system uses slash (/).

To accommodate potential differences between the client and server path name syntax, NFS follows a simple rule: only the client side interprets full path names. To trace a full path name through the server's hierarchical directory system, the client sends each individual path name component one at a time. For example, if a client that uses slash as a separator needs to look up path name /a/b/c on a server, it begins by obtaining information about the server's root directory. It then asks the server to look up name *a* in that directory. The server sends back information about *a*. Presumably, the information will show that *a* is a directory. The client then asks the server to look up name *b* in that directory. When the server replies, the client verifies that *b* is a directory, and if it is, asks the server to look up name *c* in it. Finally, the server will respond by sending information about *c*.

The chief disadvantage of requiring the client to parse path names should be obvious: it requires an exchange across the network for each component in the path. The chief advantage should also be obvious: applications on a given computer can access remote files using the same path name syntax they use for local files. More important, both the applications and the client code can be written to access remote files without knowing where files will be located or the naming conventions used by the file systems on the servers. Thus, none of the client applications needs to change when the system manager upgrades one of the server machines, even if the new computer uses a different operating system or a different file naming scheme than the original. To summarize:

> *To keep applications on client machines independent of file locations and server computer systems, NFS requires that only clients interpret full path names. A client traces a path through the server's hierarchy by sending the server one component at a time and receiving information about the file or directory it names.*

23.14 NFS Client And UNIX

Recall that UNIX uses the *mount* mechanism to construct a single, unified naming hierarchy from individual file systems on multiple disks. UNIX implementations of NFS client code use an extended version of the *mount* mechanism to integrate remote file systems into the naming hierarchy along with local file systems. From the application program's perspective, the chief advantage of using the *mount* mechanism is consistency: all file names have the same form. An application program cannot tell whether a file is local or remote from the name syntax alone. When an application opens a remote file, it receives an integer descriptor for the file exactly as it would for a local file. Internal information associated with the descriptor specifies that the file is a remote file accessible through NFS.

Whenever an application performs an operation on a file descriptor (e.g., *read*), the system checks to see whether the descriptor refers to a local file or a remote file. If the file is local, the operating system handles the operation as usual. If the file is remote, the operating system calls NFS client code that translates the operation into an equivalent NFS operation and places a remote procedure call to the server.

23.15 NFS Mounts

When managers add NFS mount entries to a UNIX mount table, they must specify a remote machine that operates an NFS server, a hierarchy on that server, a local directory onto which the mount will be added, and information that specifies details about the mount. For example, the following output from the UNIX *mount* command shows some of the NFS mounts used on a UNIX system at Purdue University (non-NFS mounts have been deleted):

```
arthur:/p1 on /p1    type nfs (rw,grpid,intr,bg,noquota)
arthur:/p4 on /p4    type nfs (rw,grpid,intr,bg,noquota)
ector:/u4  on /u4    type nfs (rw,grpid,soft,bg,noquota)
gwen:/     on /gwen type nfs (rw,grpid,soft,bg,noquota)
gwen:/u5   on /u5    type nfs (rw,grpid,soft,bg,noquota)
```

In this output, each line corresponds to a single NFS file system mount. The first field of each line specifies a machine that runs an NFS server and a hierarchy on that server, while the third field specifies a local directory on which the remote file system has been mounted. For example, *arthur:/p1* specifies the */p1* hierarchy on machine *arthur*. It has been mounted on the local directory named */p1*. The system manager chose to mount arthur's */p1* file system on a local directory with the same name so users on both machines could access the files using identical names.

All mounts shown in the example above have type *nfs*, which means they refer to remote file systems available via NFS. In addition, the parenthesized parameters on each line specify further details about the mount. Like mounts for local file systems, the remote file system mounts can specify whether to allow *reading* and *writing* (*rw*) or reading only (*r*).

NFS defines two basic paradigms for remote mounts in UNIX. Using a *soft mount* specifies that an NFS client should implement a timeout mechanism and consider the server off-line if the timeout expires. Using a *hard mount* specifies that an NFS client should not use a timeout mechanism.

UNIX administrators usually arrange to have all mounts created automatically at system startup. Once an NFS mount has been created, application programs and users cannot distinguish between local and remote files. The user can use a conventional application program to manipulate a remote file as easily as the program can manipulate a local file. For example, a user can run a standard text editor to edit a remote file; the editor operates on the file the same way it operates on a local file. Furthermore, the user can change to a remote directory or back to a local directory simply by giving a path name that crosses one of the mount points.

23.16 File Handle

Once a client has identified and opened a file, it needs a way to identify that file for subsequent operations (e.g., *read* and *write*). Furthermore, a client needs a way to identify an individual directory or file as it traces through the server's hierarchy. To solve these problems, NFS arranges for a server to assign each file a unique *file handle* that it uses as an identifier. The server makes up a handle and sends it to the client when the client first *opens* the file. The client sends the handle back to the server when it requests operations on the file.

From the client's point of view, the file handle consists of a 32-byte string that the server uses to identify a file. From the server's point of view, a file handle can be chosen to be any convenient set of bytes that uniquely identify an individual file. For example, a file handle can encode information that allows the server to decode a handle and locate a file quickly.

In NFS terminology, a file handle is *opaque* to the client, meaning that a client cannot decode the handle or fabricate a handle itself. Only servers create file handles, and servers only recognize handles that they create. Furthermore, secure implementations of NFS servers use a sophisticated encoding to prevent a client from guessing the handle for a file. In particular, servers choose some of the bits in a handle at random to help ensure that clients cannot fabricate a valid handle.

To improve security, servers can also limit the time a handle can be used. Doing so makes it impossible for a client to keep a handle forever. To limit a handle's lifetime, the server encodes a *timestamp* in the handle. If the handle expires, the server refuses to perform further operations on a file using it. The client must obtain a fresh handle before it can continue access. In practice, NFS timestamps are usually long enough to permit any reasonable access. Applications that have legitimate use of a file can always obtain a fresh handle (the transactions required can be hidden from the application completely).

23.17 NFS Handles Replace Path Names

To understand why handles are needed, consider naming files in a remote directory hierarchy. Recall that to isolate clients from the server's path name syntax and to allow heterogeneous machines to access hierarchical files, NFS requires that the client perform all path name interpretation. As a consequence, a client cannot use a full path name to specify a file when requesting an operation on that file. Instead, the client must obtain a handle that it can use to reference the file.

Having the server provide handles for directories as well as files permits a client to trace a path through the server's hierarchy. To see how, consider Figure 23.9, which illustrates the exchange between a client and server as the client looks up a file with path */a/b/c* in the server's hierarchy.

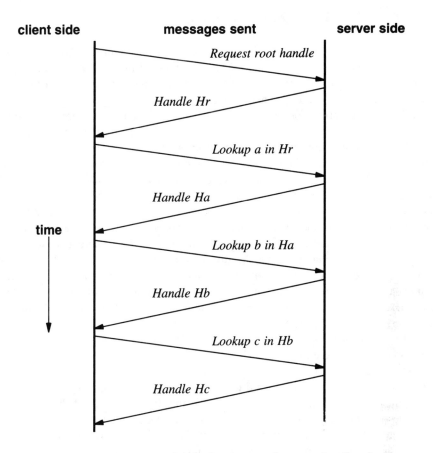

Figure 23.9 The messages a client and a server exchange as the client looks
up a file that has full path name */a/b/c*, where ''/'' denotes the
client's component separator. The handle for a file or directory
named *x* is denoted *Hx*. In practice, a separate protocol provides
the root handle.

The figure shows that the server returns a handle for each directory along the path.
The client uses each handle in the next remote procedure call. For example, once the
client obtains a handle for directory *a*, it sends that handle back to the server and requests that the server search for *b* in directory *a*. The client cannot reference the file as
/a/b, nor can it reference the directory as */a*, because the client does not know the
server's path name syntax.

23.18 An NFS Client Under Windows

When NFS client code is installed in a system such as Windows 95, it must be associated with an unused device identifier. For example, if the letter *F* has not been used for an existing device, one might choose to associate the client code with that device identifier. The NFS client code operates like a device driver for the device.

Whenever an application program opens a file, the operating system begins by examining the device identifier in the file name, and calling the appropriate device driver. If the device is a disk, control passes to the disk device driver code, which uses the path name to locate the correct file on the disk. If the device is a remote file system, control passes to the NFS client code, which uses the path name to locate a remote file. Because the directories in the path reside on a remote machine, the NFS client code cannot search them directly. Instead, it must look up one component of the path at a time. To look up a component, the client sends the component name to the appropriate NFS server; if the component is valid, the server returns a handle. The client then uses the handle to ask the server to search the directory for the next component. The search continues one component at a time until the client asks for information about the last component in the path. If the path is valid (i.e., corresponds to a file on the remote system), the server returns a handle for the remote file. The NFS client code stores the handle, creates a descriptor that corresponds to the remote file, and returns the descriptor to the application. The application uses the descriptor for subsequent *read* or *write* operations on the remote file.

Whenever an application performs an operation on a file descriptor, the operating system uses the descriptor to forward the operation to a device driver. If the descriptor corresponds to a local file, control will pass to the driver for a local disk, which performs the operation as usual. If the descriptor corresponds to a remote file, control will pass to the NFS client code, which uses the file handle it received from the server when the file was opened. The client sends the handle to the server along with the *read* or *write* request.

23.19 File Positioning With A Stateless Server

Because NFS uses a stateless server design, the server cannot store a file position for each application that is using a file. Instead, the client stores all file position information, and each request sent to the server must specify the file position to use. Storing position information at the client also helps optimize operations that change the file position. In most implementations, NFS uses the same mechanism to store the position of a remote file as is used to store the position of a local file. If an application changes the position of a file (i.e., by using a *seek* operation), the client records the new file position without sending a message to the server. Whenever an application requests a *read* or *write*, the client sends the current position to the server along with the *read* or *write* request. Thus, because *lseek* does not send any messages across the network, seeking in a remote file is as efficient as seeking in a local one.

23.20 Operations On Directories

Conceptually, NFS defines a directory to consist of a set of pairs, where each pair contains a file name and a pointer to the named file. A directory can be arbitrarily large; there is no preset limit on its size. NFS provides operations that permit a client to: *insert* a file in a directory, *delete* a file from a directory, *search* a directory for a name, and *read* the contents of a directory.

23.21 Reading A Directory Statelessly

Because directories can be arbitrarily large and communication networks impose a fixed limit on the size of a single message, reading the contents of a directory may require multiple requests. Because NFS servers are stateless, the server cannot keep a record of each client's position in the directory.

The NFS designers chose to overcome the limitations of stateless servers by arranging for an NFS server to return a *position identifier* when it answers a request for an entry from a directory. The client uses the position identifier in the next request to specify which entries it has already received and which it still needs. Thus, when a client wishes to read entries from a remote directory, it steps through the directory by making repeated requests that each specify the position identifier returned in the previous request.

Using informal terminology popular among systems programmers, NFS calls its directory position identifier a *magic cookie*. The term is meant to imply that the client does not interpret the identifier, nor can it fabricate an identifier itself. Only a server can create a magic cookie (hence the term *magic*); a client can only use a magic cookie that has been supplied by a server.

A magic cookie does not guarantee atomicity, nor does it lock the directory. Thus, two applications that perform operations on a directory may interfere with one another. For example, imagine a server that is handling requests from two or more clients concurrently. Suppose that after reading three directory entries from some directory, *D*, the first client receives a magic cookie that refers to a position before the fourth entry. Then suppose another client performs a series of operations that *insert* and *delete* files in directory *D*. If the first client attempts to read remaining entries from *D* using the old magic cookie, it may not receive all the changes.

In practice, the potential problems of concurrent directory access seldom affect users because they do not depend on instantaneous insertion or deletion of files. In fact, many conventional operating systems exhibit the same behavior as NFS; users seldom understand the details of how the system interprets concurrent directory operations because they rarely need to know.

23.22 Multiple Hierarchies In An NFS Server

Recall that to make NFS interoperate across heterogeneous machines, the designers chose to have the client parse all path names. Doing so allows both the client and server to each use the file naming scheme native to its operating system without requiring either of them to understand the other's environment.

Restricting the use of full path names has little effect on most file operations. However, it does introduce a serious problem because it means that a client cannot use a full path name to identify a remote file system or directory.

Early versions of the NFS protocol assumed that each server only provided access to a single remote hierarchy. The original protocol included a function named *NFSPROC_ROOT* that a client could call to obtain the handle for the root directory in the server's hierarchy. Once the client had a handle for the root, it could read directory entries and follow an arbitrary path through the hierarchy.

Later versions of NFS allow a single server to provide remote access to files located in several hierarchies. In such cases, a procedure that returns the handle of a single root directory does not suffice. To enable a single server to handle multiple hierarchies, NFS requires an additional mechanism. The additional mechanism, described in the next section, allows a client to specify one of the possible hierarchies and obtain a handle for its root.

23.23 The Mount Protocol

The current version of NFS uses a separate protocol to handle the problem of finding a root directory. Called the *mount protocol*, it is defined using RPC. However, the mount protocol is not part of the NFS remote program. Although it is required for an NFS server, the mount protocol operates as a separate remote program.

The mount protocol provides four basic services that clients need before they can use NFS. First, it allows the client to obtain a list of the directory hierarchies (i.e., file systems) that the client can access through NFS. Second, it accepts full path names that allow the client to identify a particular directory hierarchy. Third, it authenticates each client's request and validates the client's permission to access the requested hierarchy. Fourth, it returns a file handle for the root directory of the hierarchy a client specifies. The client uses the root handle obtained from the mount protocol when making NFS calls.

The name and idea for the mount protocol come from UNIX: a UNIX system uses the mount protocol when it creates a remote file system mount in its namespace. A client system uses the mount protocol to contact a server and verify access to the remote file system before adding the remote mount to its local hierarchical namespace. If the mount protocol denies access, the client code reports an error to the system manager. If the mount protocol approves access, the client code stores the handle for the root of the remote file system so it can use the handle when an application tries to open a file on that file system.

23.24 Summary

Sun Microsystems, Incorporated defined a remote file access mechanism called *NFS* that has become an industry standard. To allow many clients to access a server and to keep the servers isolated from client crashes, NFS uses stateless servers.

Because NFS is designed for a heterogeneous environment, a client cannot know the path name syntax on all servers. To accommodate heterogeneity, NFS requires the client to parse path names and look up each component individually. When a client looks up a particular component name, the server returns a 32-byte file handle that the client uses as a reference to the file or directory in subsequent operations.

Most of the NFS definitions and file system semantics have been derived from UNIX. NFS supports a hierarchical directory system, views a file as a sequence of bytes, allows files to grow dynamically, provides sequential or random access, and provides information about files almost identical to the information provided by the UNIX *stat* function.

Many of the conceptual file operations used in NFS have been derived from operations provided by the UNIX file system. NFS adopted the *open-read-write-close* paradigm used in UNIX, along with basic file types and file protection modes.

A companion to NFS, the mount protocol makes it possible for a single NFS server to provide access to multiple directory hierarchies. The mount protocol implements access authentication, and allows a client to obtain the handle for the root of a particular directory hierarchy. Once the client obtains a handle for the root, it can use NFS procedures to access directories and files in that hierarchy. UNIX systems use the mount protocol when the system manager installs remote mounts in the UNIX hierarchical namespace.

FOR FURTHER STUDY

Ritchie and Thompson [1974] explains the original UNIX file system, and discusses the implementation of files using inodes and descriptors. Bach [1986] covers UNIX file system semantics. McKusick *et al.* [August 1984] describes the fast file system used in later releases of BSD UNIX. Sun Microsystems, Incorporated [RFC 1094] specifies the details of both NFS and the mount protocol. It mentions most of the concepts presented here. Callahan *et al.* [RFC 1813] describes version *3* of the NFS protocol.

EXERCISES

23.1   Build a program that obtains a magic cookie from an NFS server. Use the program to obtain magic cookies for several directories on several servers and print their contents in hexadecimal. Try to guess what information the cookie contains and how the server encodes it.

23.2 Use a network analyzer to watch messages exchanged between an NFS client and a server. How many packets are exchanged for each of the following operations: *open* a file not in the top level directory, *read 10* bytes from the file, and *close* the file?

23.3 Suppose the network that connects an NFS client and an NFS server delivers packets out of order. What errors can result from reordering NFS operations?

23.4 Suppose the network that connects an NFS client and an NFS server can duplicate packets as well as deliver packets out of order. What errors can result from duplicating and reordering NFS operations? Compare your answer to your response for the previous exercise. Does packet duplication introduce any additional error conditions? Why or why not?

23.5 Examine the specifications for NFS versions *2* and *3*. What are the chief differences? Does version *3* make any changes that are visible or important to a programmer?

23.6 Although NFS was designed to be stateless, the file handle mechanism adds state to the protocol. What problems, if any, do file handles introduce? How can such problems be overcome? (Hint: Many implementations of NFS require all active clients to reboot after a server crashes and reboots.)

24

Network File System
Protocol (NFS, Mount)

24.1 Introduction

The previous chapter describes the concepts underlying Sun's Network File System (NFS), and shows that much of the terminology and many of the details were derived from the UNIX file system. This chapter continues the discussion of NFS by describing the protocol. It shows how NFS is defined to be a remote program using ONC RPC and how each operation on a file corresponds to a remote procedure call.

24.2 Using RPC To Define A Protocol

Chapters *20* through *22* show how RPC can be used to divide a program into components that execute on separate machines. Most programmers use RPC in the exact way described in those chapters: they first write a conventional program, and then use RPC to form a distributed version. This chapter takes another approach. It shows how RPC can be used to define a protocol without tying it to any particular program.

The chief difference between using RPC to construct a distributed version of a program and a general-purpose protocol arises in the way the designer thinks about the issues. When building a distributed version of a program, the programmer starts from an existing program that includes both procedures and data structures. When devising a protocol, the programmer starts from a set of desired services and devises abstract procedures that support them.

Designing a protocol requires thought about how services will be used as well as thought about how programmers will implement programs that supply those services. The designer must choose a protocol definition that strikes a balance between precision and freedom. The protocol must be precise enough to guarantee interoperability among programs that adhere to it, but it must be general enough to permit a wide variety of implementations.

Thinking about protocol design in a vacuum is seldom sufficient. Successful protocol specification requires the designer to be proficient with the technical details of communication and to have good intuition about the design. The intuition required usually arises from extensive experience with computer systems, application programs, and other communication protocols. Thus, protocol design can be more difficult than it appears. In particular, one should not confuse the apparent simplicity of a protocol like NFS with the notion that the design did not take much thought. The point is:

> *Although RPC provides a convenient way to specify a protocol, it does not make protocol design easier nor does it guarantee efficiency.*

24.3 Defining A Protocol With Data Structures And Procedures

To specify a protocol using RPC, one must:

- provide declarations for the constants, types, and data structures used as procedure arguments or function results,
- provide a declaration for each remote procedure that specifies the arguments, results, and semantics of the action it performs, and
- define the semantics for each remote procedure by specifying how it processes its arguments and computes a return value.

Conceptually, a protocol specified using RPC defines a server to be a single remote program. An operation sent from the client to the server corresponds to a remote procedure call, and a message returned from the server to the client corresponds to a procedure return. Thus, in any RPC-defined protocol, the client must initiate all operations; a server can only respond to individual client requests.

For NFS, requiring the client to initiate each operation makes sense because a file access protocol can be designed to be driven from the client. A server offers procedures that permit a client to: *create* or *delete* files, directories, and symbolic links; *read* or *write* data; *search* a directory for a named file; and obtain *status* information about an entire remote file system or about an individual file or directory. Although other application protocols may not lend themselves to RPC specification as directly as NFS, experience shows that most client-server interactions can be cast into the remote procedure call paradigm with modest effort.

NFS provides an interesting example of RPC specification because the protocol is sufficiently complex to require several remote procedures and data types, yet it is intuitive and conceptually simple enough to understand. The next section describes examples of the basic constant and type declarations used in the NFS protocol. Later sections show how the procedure declarations use the constants and types to specify arguments and results.

24.4 NFS Constant, Type, And Data Declarations

The NFS protocol standard defines constants, type names, and data structures that are used throughout the procedural declarations. All declarations are given using RPC declaration syntax.

24.4.1 NFS Constants

NFS defines six basic constants that specify the sizes of arrays used by the protocol. The declarations are given using the RPC language:

```
const MAXDATA     = 8192; /* Maximum bytes in a data transfer    */
const MAXPATHLEN = 1024; /* Maximum characters in a path name   */
const MAXNAMLEN  =  255; /* Maximum characters in a name        */
const COOKIESIZE =    4; /* Octets in an NFS magic cookie       */
const FHSIZE     =   32; /* Octets in an NFS file handle        */
```

In addition to the basic constants, the protocol also defines an enumerated set of constants used to report error status. Each remote procedure call returns one of these status values. The set is named *stat*, and is declared as:

```
enum stat {
    NFS_OK              = 0   /* Successful call                     */
    NFSERR_PERM         = 1,  /* Ownership mismatch or error         */
    NFSERR_NOENT        = 2,  /* File does not exist                 */
    NFSERR_IO           = 5,  /* I/O device error occurred           */
    NFSERR_NXIO         = 6,  /* Device or address does not exist    */
    NFSERR_ACCES        = 13, /* Permission to access was denied     */
    NFSERR_EXIST        = 17, /* Specified file already exists       */
    NFSERR_NODEV        = 19, /* Specified device does not exist     */
    NFSERR_NOTDIR       = 20, /* Specified item not a directory      */
    NFSERR_ISDIR        = 21, /* Specified item is a directory       */
    NFSERR_FBIG         = 27, /* File is too large for server        */
    NFSERR_NOSPC        = 28, /* No space left on device (disk)      */
    NFSERR_ROFS         = 30, /* Write to read-only file system      */
    NFSERR_NAMETOOLONG= 63, /* File name was too long              */
    NFSERR_NOTEMPTY     = 66, /* Directory not empty                 */
    NFSERR_DQUOT        = 69, /* Disk quota exceeded                 */
    NFSERR_STALE        = 70, /* File handle is stale                */
    NFSERR_WFLUSH       = 99  /* Write cache was flushed to disk     */
};
```

Each of these error values makes sense in the context of some call. For example, if a client attempts to perform a directory operation on a regular file, the server returns error code *NFSERR_NOTDIR*. If the client attempts to perform a regular file operation on a directory, the server returns error code *NFSERR_ISDIR*.

24.4.2 NFS Typedef Declarations

To make its structure declarations clearer, the NFS protocol standard defines names for types used in multiple structures. For example, the type *filename* is defined to be an array of characters large enough to contain a component name. In RPC syntax, the keyword *string* must be used to declare an array of characters. Thus, the declaration is:

```
typedef string filename<MAXNAMLEN>;
```

Similarly, the standard defines *fhandle* to be the type of a *32*-byte array that contains a file handle. The type is declared to be *opaque* because the client does not know the internal structure:

```
typedef opaque fhandle[FHSIZE];
```

24.4.3 NFS Data Structures

With constant and type definitions in place, a protocol designer can specify the types of all data structures used. NFS follows the convention of combining all the arguments for a remote procedure call into a single structure. Thus, the standard defines an argument structure for each remote procedure and a separate structure for each procedure result. In addition, the standard defines a few structures shared by several procedures. For example, Chapter *22* describes the *fattr* structure that NFS uses to specify file attributes. *Fattr* was derived from the data returned by the UNIX *stat* structure.

Some fields in the *fattr* structure record the time at which a file was last modified or accessed. Such fields are declared to be of type *timeval*, a structure:

```
struct timeval {          /* date and time used by NFS      */
       unsigned int seconds;  /* seconds past epoch (1/1/70)   */
       unsigned int useconds; /* additional microseconds       */
};
```

The declaration specifies that NFS stores a time value in two *32*-bit integers. The first integer records the number of seconds past an epoch date, and the second integer records additional microseconds (allowing for more precision). NFS uses the epoch date of January 1, 1970† to measure time values.

Most of the remaining declarations define the type of arguments passed to a remote procedure or the result the procedure returns. For example, when calling a procedure that performs an operation on a directory (e.g., *delete* a file), the client must pass the name of a file. NFS declares the argument type to be a structure, *diropargs* (*di*rectory *op*eration *arg*ument*s*):

---

†The designers chose the NFS time epoch to be the same as that used by UNIX.

```
struct diropargs {       /* directory operation arguments    */
      fhandle dir;       /* handle for directory file is in  */
      filename name;     /* name of file in that directory   */
};
```

The structure shows that the argument consists of a file handle for the directory and the name of a file in that directory. To understand why *diropargs* is needed, recall that the NFS client parses all path names. Thus, a client cannot use a full path name to identify a file. Instead, NFS requires all operations on files to be specified by giving the handle for the directory in which the file resides and the name of the file in that directory.

In addition to declarations for argument types, the standard defines the types returned by remote procedures. For example, a directory operation returns a union type named *diropres*:

```
union diropres switch (stat status) { /* result of dir. op  */
case NFS_OK:              /* If operation was successful      */
     struct {            /*     structure for success results */
          fhandle file;  /*     file handle for new file      */
          fattr   attributes;/* status of the file           */
     } diropok;          /* end of structure for success     */
default:                 /* If operation failed              */
     void;               /*     get nothing back             */
};
```

The union allows two possible forms of a return value, with the choice depending on the status. If the operation succeeds, the status will have value *NFS_OK*, and the return value will consist of a file handle for the newly created file (or the file that changed) and a structure that contains the file's attributes. If the operation fails, the call will not return anything.

The arguments for other remote procedures sometimes include one or more file specifications. For example, the remote procedure used to rename a file requires two file names: the name of an existing file and the new name for that file. The arguments for the *rename* procedure are declared to be of type *renameargs*, a structure:

```
struct renameargs {       /* arguments to RENAME             */
      diropargs from;     /* an existing file                */
      diropargs to;       /* new location/name for file      */
};
```

Individual fields that give the old and new file names are declared to be of type *diropargs*.

Most other NFS argument types correspond to remote procedures. For example, NFS defines structure *writeargs* to specify arguments used in a call to *write* data to a file:

```
struct writeargs {                   /* arguments to WRITE     */
        fhandle  file;               /* file to be written     */
        unsigned beginoffset;        /* obsolete (ignore)       */
        unsigned offset;             /* where to write data     */
        unsigned totalcount;         /* obsolete (ignore)       */
        nfsdata  data;               /* data to put into file   */
};
```

Similarly, structure *readargs* specifies the arguments for the *read* operation:

```
struct readargs {                    /* arguments to READ      */
        fhandle  file;               /* file to be read        */
        unsigned offset;             /* where to read data     */
        unsigned count;              /* num. of bytes requested */
        unsigned totalcount;         /* obsolete (ignore)       */
};
```

Procedure *readlink* allows the client to read the contents of a symbolic link. Its results are defined by the union *readlinkres*:

```
union readlinkres switch (stat status) { /* READLINK result */
case NFS_OK:                 /* If operation was successful   */
    path data;               /*      path name found in link  */
default:                     /* If operation failed           */
    void;                    /*      nothing                   */
};
```

24.5 NFS Procedures

Once constants and data types have been declared, one only needs to specify the remote procedures that implement the protocol. An NFS server provides a remote program that implements *18* procedures. Using RPC language, the program can be declared:

```
program NFS_PROGRAM {
        version NFS_VERSION {
            void        NFSPROC_NULL(void)           = 0;

            attrstat    NFSPROC_GETATTR(fhandle)     = 1;

            attrstat    NFSPROC_SETATTR(sattrargs)   = 2;

            void        NFSPROC_ROOT(void)           = 3;

            diropres    NFSPROC_LOOKUP(diropargs)    = 4;

            readlinkres NFSPROC_READLINK(fhandle)    = 5;

            readres     NFSPROC_READ(readargs)       = 6;

            void        NFSPROC_WRITECACHE(void)     = 7;

            attrstat    NFSPROC_WRITE(writeargs)     = 8;

            diropres    NFSPROC_CREATE(createargs)   = 9;

            stat        NFSPROC_REMOVE(diropargs)    = 10;

            stat        NFSPROC_RENAME(renameargs)   = 11;

            stat        NFSPROC_LINK(linkargs)       = 12;

            stat        NFSPROC_SYMLINK(symlinkargs) = 13;

            diropres    NFSPROC_MKDIR(createargs)    = 14;

            stat        NFSPROC_RMDIR(diropargs)     = 15;

            readdirres  NFSPROC_READDIR(readdirargs) = 16;

            statfsres   NFSPROC_STATFS(fhandle)      = 17;

        } = 2;          /* current version of NFS protocol    */
    } = 100003;         /* RPC program number assigned to NFS */
```

24.6 Semantics Of NFS Operations

The semantics for most NFS operations follow the semantics of file operations in UNIX. The following sections each describe how one of the NFS remote procedures operates.

24.6.1 NFSPROC_NULL (Procedure 0)

By convention, procedure *0* in any RPC program is termed *null* because it does not perform any action. An application can call it to test whether a given server is responding.

24.6.2 NFSPROC_GETATTR (Procedure 1)

A client calls procedure *1* to obtain the attributes of a file, which include such items as the protection mode, owner, size, and time of last access.

24.6.3 NFSPROC_SETATTR (Procedure 2)

Procedure *2* permits a client to set some of the attributes of a file. The client cannot set all attributes (e.g., it cannot change the recorded file size except by adding bytes to the file or truncating it). If the call succeeds, the result returned contains the file's attributes after the changes have been applied.

24.6.4 NFSPROC_ROOT (Procedure 3) [Obsolete in NFS3]

Procedure *3* was defined for earlier versions of NFS, but is now obsolete. It has been replaced by the mount protocol.

24.6.5 NFSPROC_LOOKUP (Procedure 4)

Clients call procedure *4* to search for a file in a directory. If successful, the returned value consists of a file handle and the attributes for the specified file.

24.6.6 NFSPROC_READLINK (Procedure 5)

Procedure *5* permits the client to read the value from a symbolic link.

24.6.7 NFSPROC_READ (Procedure 6)

Procedure *6* provides one of the most important functions because it permits a client to read data from a file. The result returned by the server is a union, *readres*. If the operation succeeds, the result contains attributes for the file as well as the data requested. If the operation fails, the status value contains an error code.

24.6.8 NFSPROC_WRITECACHE (Procedure 7) [Obsolete in NFS3]

Procedure *7* is not used in the current protocol.

24.6.9 NFSPROC_WRITE (Procedure 8)

Procedure *8* provides another of the basic functions: it permits a client to write data into a remote file. The call returns a union, *attrstat*, that either contains an error code, if the operation fails, or the attributes of the file, if the operation succeeds.

24.6.10 NFSPROC_CREATE (Procedure 9)

A client calls procedure *9* to create a file in a specified directory. The file must not exist or the call will return an error. The call returns a union of type *diropres* that either contains an error status or a handle for the new file along with its attributes.

24.6.11 NFSPROC_REMOVE (Procedure 10)

A client invokes procedure *10* to delete an existing file. The call returns a status value. The status either indicates that the operation succeeded or provides an error code that tells why it failed.

24.6.12 NFSPROC_RENAME (Procedure 11)

Procedure *11* permits a client to rename a file. Because the arguments allow the client to specify a new directory for the file as well as a new name, the *rename* operation corresponds to the UNIX *mv (move)* command. NFS guarantees that *rename* will be atomic on the server (i.e., it cannot be interrupted). The guarantee of atomicity is important because it means the old name for the file will not be removed until the new name has been installed. Thus, the file will not appear to be missing during a *rename* operation.

24.6.13 NFSPROC_LINK (Procedure 12)

Clients call procedure *12* to form a hard link to an existing file. NFS guarantees that if a file has multiple hard links, the attributes visible for the file will be identical no matter which link is used to access it.

24.6.14 NFSPROC_SYMLINK (Procedure 13)

Procedure *13* creates a symbolic link. The arguments specify a directory handle and the name of a file to be created as well as a string that will become the contents of the symbolic link. The server creates the symbolic link, and then returns a status value that either indicates success or gives a reason for the failure.

24.6.15 NFSPROC_MKDIR (Procedure 14)

A client calls procedure *14* to create a directory. If the call succeeds, the server returns a handle for the new directory along with a list of its attributes. If the call fails,
the returned status value indicates the reason for the failure.

24.6.16 NFSPROC_RMDIR (Procedure 15)

A client can use procedure *15* to remove a directory. As in UNIX, a directory
must be empty before it can be removed. Thus, to remove an entire subtree, a client
must traverse the subtree removing all files, and then remove the empty directories that
remain. Usually, the removal of files and empty directories is accomplished in a single
pass by using a post-order traversal of the directory tree.

24.6.17 NFSPROC_READDIR (Procedure 16)

A client calls procedure *16* to read entries from a directory. The argument structure, *readdirargs*, specifies a handle for the directory to be read, a magic cookie, and a
maximum count of characters to read. On the initial call, the client specifies a magic
cookie containing zero, which causes the server to read entries from the beginning of
the directory. The value returned, of type *readdirres*, contains a linked list of zero or
more directory entries and a Boolean value to indicate whether the last entry returned
lies at the end of the directory.

After a successful return, each directory entry on the linked list contains the name
of a file, a unique identifier for the file, a magic cookie that gives the file's position in
the directory, and a pointer to the next entry on the list.

To read the sequence of entries in a directory, the client begins by calling
NFSPROC_READDIR with a magic cookie value of zero and a character count equal to
its internal buffer size. The server returns as many directory entries as fit into the
buffer. The client iterates through the list of entries and processes each file name. If
the returned value shows that the client has reached the end of the directory, it stops
processing. Otherwise, the client uses the magic cookie in the last entry to make another call to the server and obtain more entries. The client continues reading groups of entries until it reaches the end of the directory.

24.6.18 NFSPROC_STATFS (Procedure 17)

Procedure *17* permits a client to obtain information about the remote file system on
which a file resides. The returned result, a structure of type *statfsres*, contains fields
that specify the optimum transfer size (i.e., the size of data in *read* or *write* requests that
produces optimal transfer rates), the size of data blocks on the storage device, the
number of blocks on the device, the number of blocks currently unused, and the number
of unused blocks available to nonprivileged users.

A sophisticated client program can use *NFSPROC_STATFS* to optimize transfers or to estimate whether sufficient space remains on a disk to accommodate a *write* request.

24.7 The Mount Protocol

The mount protocol described in Chapter *22* is also defined using RPC. Although an NFS server must have a companion mount server, the two have been defined as separate remote programs. Thus, the protocol standard for mount specifies constants, types, and a set of remote procedures that comprise the server.

24.7.1 Mount Constant Definitions

Although the two protocols are defined separately, the values for many of the constants and types defined for the mount protocol have been derived from corresponding constants used in the NFS protocol. Indeed, the two protocols could not work together well unless they both used a common representation for objects like file handles. For example, mount defines the sizes of a file name, a path name, and a file handle as follows:

```
const MNTNAMLEN = 255;

const MNTPATHLEN = 1024;

const FHSIZE = 32;
```

The declarations use RPC syntax; each expresses a length as a number of bytes.

24.7.2 Mount Type Definitions

The mount protocol also specifies type definitions that agree with their counterparts found in the NFS protocol. For example, mount specifies the type of a file handle:

```
typedef opaque fhandle[FHSIZE];
```

Similarly, the mount protocol specifies that a path name consists of an array of characters:

```
typedef string dirpath<MNTPATHLEN>;
```

24.7.3 Mount Data Structures

Because the mount protocol has been defined using RPC, it follows the convention of declaring a structure for the argument and result of each remote procedure. For example, one of the basic procedures in the protocol returns a file handle for the root directory in a named hierarchy. The value returned consists of a union, *fhstatus*, declared to be:

```
union fhstatus switch (unsigned status) {
case 0:                  /* If successful               */
    fhandle directory;   /*    handle for specified root */
default:                 /* Otherwise                   */
    void;                /*    nothing                  */
};
```

As in the NFS protocol, each remote procedure in the mount protocol returns a status value along with other information. If the operation fails, the status value indicates the reason.

In addition to a procedure that returns a file handle, the mount protocol provides a procedure that allows a client to determine which file systems are available for access. The procedure returns the results in a linked list called an *export list*†. The type of a node on the export list is declared with structure *exportlist*:

```
struct *exportlist {     /* list of available hierarchies */
        dirpath filesys; /* path name for this hierarchy  */
        groups groups;   /* groups allowed to access it   */
        exportlist next; /* pointer to next item in list  */
};
```

Field *groups* in an *exportlist* node contains a pointer to a linked list that specifies which protection groups are allowed to access the named hierarchy. Nodes on the list are defined to be a structure of type *groups*:

```
struct *groups {         /* list of group names          */
        name grname;     /* name of one group            */
        groups grnext;   /* pointer to next item on list */
};
```

The mount protocol also allows a client to determine which remote file systems a given machine is accessing. Thus, it is possible to construct an NFS cross-reference list for a set of machines. To do so, one asks each of the machines in the set for a list of the remote file systems that the machine is accessing. Note that the set of remote file systems a given machine is accessing will be disjoint from the set of local file systems that the machine has exported for others to access.

†The term *export* refers to the idea that a server *exports* some of its files to other machines.

A reply from the mount protocol that lists remote accesses is a linked list where each node has type *mountlist*:

```
struct *mountlist {          /* list of remote mounts          */
        name      hostname;  /* machine on which files reside  */
        dirpath   directory; /* path name of hierarchy         */
        mountlist nextentry; /* pointer to next item on the list*/
};
```

24.8 Procedures In The Mount Protocol

Like NFS, the mount protocol defines all operations as procedures in a remote program. The RPC declaration of the mount program is:

```
program MOUNTPROG {
        version MOUNTVERS {

        void        MOUNTPROC_NULL(void)      = 0;

        fhstatus    MOUNTPROC_MNT(dirpath)    = 1;

        mountlist   MOUNTPROC_DUMP(void)      = 2;

        void        MOUNTPROC_UMNT(dirpath)   = 3;

        void        MOUNTPROC_UMNTALL(void)   = 4;

        exportlist  MOUNTPROC_EXPORT(void)    = 5;
        } = 1;          /* mount version 1 matches NFS vers. 2 */
} = 100005;             /* RPC program number assigned to mount*/
```

24.9 Semantics of Mount Operations

The mount protocol defines the semantics of each of the operations listed above. The following sections give a brief summary of each.

24.9.1 MNTPROC_NULL (Procedure 0)

Following the RPC convention, procedure *0* does not perform any action.

24.9.2 MNTPROC_MNT (Procedure 1)

A client calls procedure *1* to obtain the handle for a particular hierarchy. The argument contains a path name that the server uses to distinguish among the hierarchies it exports for access; the result has type *fhstatus*. Names for the hierarchies available on a given server can be obtained by calling *MNTPROC_EXPORT* (see below).

24.9.3 MNTPROC_DUMP (Procedure 2)

Procedure *2* permits a client to obtain a list of the remote file systems that a particular machine is using. The information provided by *MNTPROC_DUMP* has little value to conventional applications; it is intended for system administrators.

24.9.4 MNTPROC_UMNT (Procedure 3)

A client can use procedure *3* to inform another machine that it will be out of service. For example, if machine *A* has mounted one or more file systems from the server on machine *B*, machine *B* can use *MNTPROC_UMNT* to inform *A* that a particular file system will be out of service (e.g., for disk maintenance). Doing so keeps *A* from sending additional requests to *B* while the files are off-line.

24.9.5 MNTPROC_UMNTALL (Procedure 4)

Procedure *4* allows one machine to tell another that all of its NFS file systems will be unavailable. For example, a server can tell clients to unmount all its file systems before it reboots.

24.9.6 MNTPROC_EXPORT (Procedure 5)

Procedure *5* provides an important service: it allows a client to obtain the names of all the hierarchies accessible on a given server. The call returns a linked list that contains a single node of type *exportlist* for each available file system. The client must use one of the directory path names found in the export list when calling *MNTPROC_MNT* (procedure *1*).

24.10 NFS And Mount Authentication

NFS relies on the mount protocol to provide authentication. The mount protocol authenticates a client's request for the handle of a root directory, but NFS does not authenticate each individual client request.

Surprisingly, the mount protocol does not offer much protection. It uses RPC's *AUTH_UNIX* or *AUTH_NONE* to authenticate the client. Once a client has obtained a handle for a root directory, protections on individual files mean little. For example, if programmers obtain privilege on their private workstations, they may be able to access arbitrary files on NFS servers as well as on their local machines. Furthermore, if a programmer can guess the contents of an opaque file handle, the programmer can manufacture handles for arbitrary directories.

Early versions of NFS created handles by combining information about a file or directory in fixed ways. For example, Figure 24.1 shows how one UNIX implementation divides the *32*-byte handle into ten fields:

Field	Size	Contents
Fileid	4	UNIX's major and minor device numbers for the file
one	1	Always *1*
length$_1$	2	Total length of next three fields
zero$_1$	2	Always *0*
inode	4	UNIX's internal number for the file
igener	4	Generation number for file (randomized for security)
length$_2$	2	Total length of next three fields
zero$_2$	2	Always *0*
rinode	4	Unix's internal number for root of file system
rigener	4	Generation number for root (randomized for security)

Figure 24.1 The contents of the fields in an NFS file handle. This particular format comes from an NFS server that runs under the UNIX operating system; not all servers construct file handles the same way.

The chief danger in using a fixed format for file handles arises because NFS offers little protection against unauthorized access. A client wishing to access files can circumvent the mount protocol by manufacturing a handle for an arbitrary file. It can then obtain attribute information for the file, including the file ownership and protection bits. Thus, it will be able to access world-readable files even if the mount protocol does not authorize access. Furthermore, if the client has privilege on the local machine, it will be able to send requests to a server that contain arbitrary user identifiers. Thus, a client that has privilege can first find out who owns a particular file, and then send a request claiming to be that user.

To make it more difficult to guess file handles, many administrators often use a utility that randomizes file generation numbers. The utility goes through an entire disk and associates a random number with each file. The mount protocol uses the file's random number when passing out a file handle, and NFS checks that the value in the handle matches the file's number.

Randomizing generation numbers increases security, but it does not increase the computational overhead required to form a handle because randomization is performed before the mount protocol runs. Randomization makes file handles difficult to guess. A client attempting to obtain unauthorized access must choose among 2^{32} possible values for the generation number. Because the probability of guessing a valid handle is low, the probability of obtaining unauthorized access to a file is also low.

24.11 Changes In NFS Version 3

Although there are many small differences between NFS versions *2* and *3†*, most of the changes can be grouped into three broad categories:

- Changes to improve NFS performance.
- Changes to permit NFS to match the functionality found in conventional file systems.
- Changes to improve security.

The performance changes focus on tuning. For example, the version *3* protocol does not specify either a maximum data transfer size or a preferred size. Instead, version *3* allows the parameter sizes to be specified separately for each file system. To implement the change, version *3* includes a new procedure, *FSINFO* that a client calls to obtain information about a file system.

Individual procedures have been tuned to eliminate unnecessary overhead. For example, some version *3* procedure calls return information that was previously available only from a separate procedure call. Doing so reduces the total number of remote procedure call operations.

Version *3* of the protocol also permits caching and asynchronous operations. Although version *3* does not require clients to cache information or data, the protocol now includes additional information that clients can use to manage a cache more effectively. More important, version *3* allows write operations to be *asynchronous* at the server. That is, a client can specify whether the *WRITE* procedure call is allowed to return before the server has stored the data on disk. If a client chooses to use asynchronous *WRITE*, version *3* provides an additional *COMMIT* procedure that the client calls to force the server to write all data to disk.

The changes to accommodate additional file system functionality focus primarily on UNIX. For example, version *3* includes a procedure *MKNOD* that allows a client to create a special file similar to the way the UNIX system procedure *mknod* allows a program to create a special file. Similarly, version *3* allows a client to request exclusive file creation similar to the way a program can request exclusive file creation under UNIX. Finally, procedure *FSSTAT* allows a client to obtain information about a file system, including the total size, number of files, and amount of space that remains free. Thus, a remote client can obtain the same information that is provided by UNIX's *df* command.

The changes to improve security involve making handles and magic cookies larger and hence, more difficult to guess. For example, file handle size has increased from a fixed-size array of 32 bytes to a variable-size array of up to 64 bytes. Of course, using a larger handle means that remote procedure calls that require or return a handle take more network bandwidth. By making the handle size variable, version *3* allows a server to choose between a large handle size (for improved security) or small handle size (for improved performance).

---

†Many computers still run version 2.

24.12 Summary

When using RPC to define a protocol, one must provide definitions for the constants and data types used in the specification, the definitions of the procedures that a server offers, the types of all procedure arguments and results, and the semantics of each procedure. Protocol definition differs from the use of RPC to form a distributed version of a program because it requires the designer to deal with abstract concepts instead of an existing program.

NFS has been defined using RPC. The protocol standard specifies *18* procedures that comprise a server. In addition to operations that allow a client to *read* or *write* a file, the protocol defines data structures and operations that permit a client to read entries from a directory, create a file, remove a file, rename a file, or obtain information about a file.

A companion to NFS, the mount protocol provides client authentication and allows a client to find the handle for the root of a hierarchy. The mount protocol permits a given server to export multiple hierarchies, and allows the client to specify a particular hierarchy using a full path name.

NFS relies on the mount protocol for security. It assumes that any client can send access requests once the client obtains the handle for a root directory. Most NFS implementations construct a handle for a file by encoding information about the file. Among other items, NFS servers include a file's generation number in the handle. To prevent clients from guessing a file handle and then using it to obtain unauthorized access, many implementations of NFS allow administrators to use a tool that randomizes file generation numbers. The randomization makes it difficult for clients to guess a valid file handle.

Version *3* of NFS contains many small changes to improve functionality, performance, and security. Many computer systems continue to use version *2*.

FOR FURTHER STUDY

Sun Microsystems, Incorporated [RFC 1094] defines both the NFS version *2* and mount protocols using RPC. It provides declarations for the constants, types, and procedures that comprise each protocol as well as a description of the intended semantics and implementation hints. Callahan *et al.* [RFC 1813] describes version *3* of the NFS protocol. Additional information can be found in the documentation that accompanies each vendor's software.

EXERCISES

24.1 Write a program that uses the mount protocol to obtain file handles. What authentication did you choose? Why?

24.2 Using the program described in the previous exercise, check several files on a given server to see if the administrator has randomized generation numbers on that server's file systems.

24.3 Consult the protocol standard to find out about the NFS *NFSPROC_WRITECACHE* operation. What is its purpose?

24.4 NFS uses UDP for transport. Several companies now market software that uses TCP instead. How can the protocol be optimized to take advantage of a reliable stream transport?

24.5 The NFS protocol specification mentions that several operations are potentially not idempotent. Find the operations and explain how each could be non-idempotent.

24.6 In version *1*, NFS semantics guarantee that a *write* request will not complete until the data has been stored on a stable storage device (e.g., a disk). Estimate how much faster a *write* operation would execute on your local server if the protocol permitted the server to copy the data into an output buffer and allowed the procedure call to return without waiting for the buffer to be written to the disk.

24.7 NFS is designed to permit clients and servers to operate in a heterogeneous environment. Explain how symbolic links cause problems. (Hint: consider the protocol carefully to determine whether the client or server interprets a symbolic link).

24.8 Read the protocol specification and find out which file attributes can be set by a client.

24.9 Because RPC uses UDP, a remote procedure call can be duplicated, delayed, or delivered out of order. Explain how a valid set of NFS calls can appear from the client's perspective to create a file and write data into it, and yet result in a zero-length file.

24.10 Suppose a client calls *NFSPROC_STATFS* to find the preferred data transfer size. What constraints may make transfers of that size suboptimal?

24.11 Read the protocol specification to find out about stale file handles. Why might a server declare that a handle has become stale? How can making a handle stale improve security?

24.12 Write a program that calls *MOUNTPROC_UMNTALL* on some server, *S*. Does the call have any effect on subsequent calls to *S*? Why or why not?

24.13 Write a program that calls *MOUNTPROC_EXPORT*. Run the program and print the list of exported file system names.

25

A TELNET Client (Program Structure)

25.1 Introduction

Previous chapters use simple examples to illustrate the concepts and techniques used in client-server software. This chapter and the next explore how the client-server paradigm applies to a complex application protocol. The example protocol is *TELNET*, one of the most widely used application protocols in the TCP/IP suite.

This chapter focuses on the overall program structure. It assumes the reader is familiar with the basics of the TELNET protocol, and concentrates on explaining an implementation. It discusses the design of the client software, the thread structure, and the use of finite state machines to control processing. It explains how TCP can be used for communication between two threads running on the same computer, and shows how to establish local connections. In addition, it shows how a client maps TELNET communication to a local keyboard and display.

The next chapter completes the description. It focuses on the details of routines invoked to perform semantic actions associated with transitions of the finite state machines. The example code throughout both chapters illustrates clearly how the programming details dominate the code and how they complicate the implementation.

25.2 Overview

25.2.1 The User's Terminal

The TELNET protocol defines an interactive communication facility that permits users to communicate with a service on a remote machine. In most cases, users use TELNET to communicate with a remote login service. As the example in Chapter *1* shows, a well-designed TELNET client also permits a user to contact other services.

The TELNET protocol defines interactive, character-oriented communication. It specifies a *network virtual terminal* (*NVT*) that consists of a keyboard and display screen. The protocol defines the character set for the virtual terminal. Several of the keys correspond to conceptual operations instead of data values. For example, one key causes an *interrupt* or *abort*. The chief advantage of using a network virtual terminal is that it permits clients from a variety of computers to connect to a service. Like the XDR standard described in Chapter *19*, TELNET uses a symmetric data representation. Each client maps from its local terminal's character representation to the NVT character representation when it sends data, and from the NVT representation to the local character set when it receives data. To summarize:

> *TELNET is a character-oriented protocol that uses a standard encoding when it transfers data.*

25.2.2 Command And Control Information

In addition to character data, TELNET permits the client and server to exchange *command* or *control* information. Because all communication between the client and server passes across a single TCP connection, the protocol arranges to encode command or control information so the receiver can distinguish it from normal data. Thus, much of the protocol focuses on the definition of how the sender encodes a command and how the receiver recognizes it.

25.2.3 Terminals, Windows, and Files

TELNET defines communication between a user's *terminal* and a remote service. The protocol specification assumes that the terminal consists of a keyboard on which the user can enter characters and a display screen that can display multiple lines of text.

In practice, a user can decide to invoke a client with an input file in place of a keyboard or an output file in place of a display. On modern computers, a user invokes the client from within a window on the display. Although such alternatives introduce small

additions to the code, it will be easiest to understand both the protocol and the implementation if we imagine that users who invoke the client each have a conventional terminal. To summarize:

> *TELNET client software is designed to handle interactive communica-*
> *tion with a user's terminal.*

25.2.4 The Need For Concurrency

Conceptually, a TELNET client transfers characters between the user's terminal
and a remote service. On one side, it uses the local operating system functions when it
interacts with the user's terminal. On the other side, it uses a TCP connection when it
communicates with the remote service. Figure 25.1 illustrates the concept:

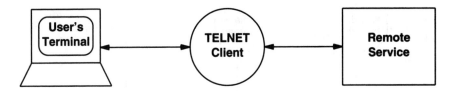

Figure 25.1 Conceptual role of a TELNET client. The client must transfer
characters from the user's keyboard to a remote service, and it
must transfer characters from the remote service to the user's
display.

To provide a full-duplex connection between the user's terminal and a remote service, a TELNET client must perform two tasks simultaneously:

- The client must read characters that the user types on the keyboard and send
  them across a TCP connection to the remote service.
- The client must read characters that arrive from the TCP connection and
  display them on the user's terminal screen.

Because the remote service can emit output at any time or the user can type at any
time, the client cannot know which source of data will become available first. Thus, it
cannot block indefinitely waiting for input from one of the two sources without also
checking for input from the other. In short, the client must transfer data in both directions concurrently.

25.2.5 A Thread Model For A TELNET Client

To accommodate concurrent data transfer, a client must either implement concurrent I/O in a single thread or it must use multiple threads that execute concurrently. Because the Windows *select* function restricts concurrent I/O to sockets, our example code uses a hybrid strategy. The client consists of two threads. The main thread handles concurrent I/O by blocking until input arrives from either the keyboard or the remote service. The other thread accommodates the restricted form of *select* by forwarding keystrokes from the user across a local TCP connection to the main thread (i.e., through a local socket). Figure 25.2 illustrates the thread structure we have chosen:

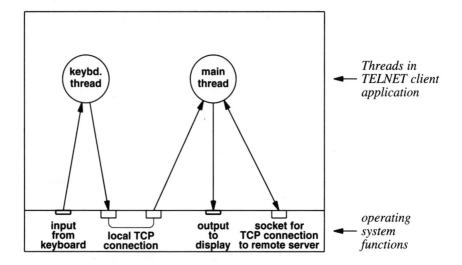

Figure 25.2 The thread structure of the example TELNET client. One thread forwards characters from the keyboard to a socket, and the other thread handles concurrent I/O on two sockets. The keyboard thread is needed because *select* only operates on sockets.

25.3 A TELNET Client Algorithm

Algorithm 25.1 specifies how the main thread of the TELNET client operates. The main thread is implemented like the singly-threaded, concurrent server design described in Chapter *12*. It uses the *select* function to implement Step *3* of Algorithm *25.1*. When the client calls *select*, it specifies that the thread should block until input arrives on either the local socket descriptor that corresponds to the user's keyboard or on the socket descriptor that corresponds to the TCP connection. When a descriptor becomes ready, the call to *select* returns and the client reads from whichever descriptor became ready.

Algorithm 25.1

1. Parse arguments and initialize data structures and threads.
2. Open a TCP connection to the specified port on the remote host.
3. Block until the user types on the keyboard or data arrives over the TCP connection.
4. If data arrives from the keyboard, read it, process it, translate it to NVT representation, and send it over the TCP connection. Otherwise, receive data from the TCP connection, process it, translate it to the local character representation, and send it to the user's display.
5. Return to step *3* above.

Algorithm 25.1 A TELNET client. The main thread relays characters in both
directions; it blocks until data is available from the keyboard
or the TCP connection.

25.4 Keyboard I/O In Windows

Algorithm 25.1 may seem extremely simple. Indeed, some aspects of the program are straightforward. For example, Windows provides functions that read characters from a keyboard. However, the details of the TELNET protocol and sending output to a display make parts of the code complex. This chapter focuses on the protocol and basic pieces of the program, leaving many details to the next chapter. We begin by considering the keyboard thread.

Windows offers two basic functions that handle a keyboard. Function *_getch* reads one character from the keyboard. Thus, the statement:

$$ch = \_getch();$$

reads one character from the keyboard and assigns the value to variable *ch*. A call to *_getch* is *blocking*. That is, the call waits until a user presses a key before it returns.

Interestingly, in most computer systems, the system function used to read input from a keyboard does not automatically display the character on the user's screen. The reason is simple: an application may not want characters displayed as a user enters them. For example, consider an application that asks the user to enter a password. To keep the password secure, the application can choose to hide the characters. Alternatively, a password application can choose to display a substitute character (e.g., an asterisk) that informs the user when a key has been pressed without showing which key.

As we will see, TELNET takes advantage of the ability to control whether keystrokes appear on the screen. When a TELNET program displays each keystroke as the user types, we say TELNET is using *character echo*. When it chooses not to display characters, we say that TELNET is suppressing character echo. Echo suppression is important because it allows the service on the remote computer to decide whether to display characters (e.g., a remote login service can choose not to display a password that the user types).

In addition to controlling character echo, an application can choose whether to assign special meanings to some keys or treat them as data. TELNET uses the functionality to allow a remote system to process keystrokes. For example, most applications choose to make the *backspace* or *delete* key erase the previous keystroke. However TELNET can choose to pass all characters, including *backspace* and *delete*, directly to the remote service.

Finally, software can choose to recognize a special character (or characters) that causes the system to *interrupt* or *abort* the current application. For example, some computer systems define *control-C* to mean *abort the running program*. When the user types the special character, it causes the application program to terminate.

25.5 Global Variables Used For Keyboard Control

File *local.h* contains the declaration of global variables *ttyflags*, *t_flushc*, *t_intrc*, *t_quitc*, *sg_erase*, and *sg_killc*. Variable *ttyflags* is used to control character echo, while the other variables are used to hold a character that has been assigned a special meaning. For example, *sg_erase* contains the character assigned to perform the backspace function.

```
/* local.h */

#define ECHO      0x0001

extern FILE      *scrfp;
extern char      scrname[];

extern unsigned int      ttyflags;
extern char                   t_flushc, t_intrc, t_quitc, sg_erase, sg_kill;

extern int       errno;

void     errexit(const char *, ...);
void     ttwrite(SOCKET, FILE *, unsigned char *, int);
void     sowrite(SOCKET, FILE *, unsigned char *, int);
void     fsmbuild(void);
int      sputc(const char, SOCKET);

#define SPUTS(s, sfd)     (send(sfd, s, strlen(s), 0))
```

25.6 Initializing The Keyboard Thread

In the example code, procedure *ttycon* performs two tasks: it initializes a socket which will be used to create the local TCP connection between the two program threads. It then creates the keyboard thread and establishes communication. File *ttycon.cpp* contains the code:

```
/* ttycon.cpp - ttycon, conreader */

#include <conio.h>
#include <process.h>
#include <stdio.h>
#include <string.h>
#include <winsock.h>

#include "local.h"

static void conreader(unsigned int);

unsigned int    ttyflags = ECHO;

/*------------------------------------------------------------------------
 * ttycon - set up console as SOCKET connection
 *------------------------------------------------------------------------
 */
SOCKET
ttycon(void)
{
        struct sockaddr_in      sin;
        SOCKET                  lsock, rsock;
        int                     len;

        /* initialize special characters */

        lsock = socket(PF_INET, SOCK_STREAM, IPPROTO_TCP);
        if (lsock == INVALID_SOCKET)
                errexit("ttycon: socket failed (%d)\n", GetLastError());
        memset(&sin, 0, sizeof sin);
        sin.sin_family = AF_INET;
        sin.sin_addr.s_addr = htonl(INADDR_LOOPBACK);
        sin.sin_port = 0;       /* let Windows pick a port */
        if (bind(lsock, (struct sockaddr *)&sin, sizeof sin) ==
            SOCKET_ERROR)
                errexit("ttycon: bind failed (%d)\n", GetLastError());
```

```
        len = sizeof sin;
        if (getsockname(lsock, (struct sockaddr *)&sin, &len) ==
            SOCKET_ERROR)
                errexit("ttycon: getsockname error %d\n", GetLastError());
        if (_beginthread((void (*)(void *))conreader, 0,
                        (void *)sin.sin_port) < 0)
                errexit("ttycon: beginthread failed (%s)\n",
                        strerror(errno));
        if (listen(lsock, 1) == SOCKET_ERROR)
                errexit("ttycon: listen failed (%d)\n", GetLastError());
        len = sizeof sin;
        rsock = accept(lsock, (struct sockaddr *)&sin, &len);
        if (rsock == INVALID_SOCKET)
                errexit("ttycon: accept failed (%d)\n", GetLastError());
        closesocket(lsock);
        return rsock;
}


/*
 * conreader - do blocking console I/O and relay it to a socket
 */
static void
conreader(unsigned int port)
{
        struct sockaddr_in      sin;
        SOCKET                  telsock;
        char                    ch;

        memset(&sin, 0, sizeof sin);
        sin.sin_family = AF_INET;
        sin.sin_addr.s_addr = ntohl(INADDR_LOOPBACK);
        sin.sin_port = port;
        telsock = socket(PF_INET, SOCK_STREAM, IPPROTO_TCP);
        if (telsock == INVALID_SOCKET)
                errexit("conreader: socket error %d\n", GetLastError());
        if (connect(telsock, (struct sockaddr *)&sin, sizeof sin) ==
            SOCKET_ERROR)
                errexit("conreader: connect error %d\n", GetLastError());

        while (1) {
                ch = _getch();
                if (ttyflags & ECHO)
                        putch(ch);
                if (send(telsock, &ch, 1, 0) == SOCKET_ERROR)
```

```
                    return;
        }
        return;
}
```


     Ttycon begins by creating a TCP connection between the keyboard thread and the main thread. To do so, it uses socket functions in much the same way that a client and server use them. For example, we will see that once the connection is in place, the two threads use *send* and *recv* to transfer data across the TCP connection: the keyboard thread calls *send* to transmit a character, and the main thread calls *recv* to receive the character.

     The threads also use conventional socket functions to establish the connection. *Ttycon* calls *socket* to create a local socket, and assigns the resulting descriptor to variable *lsock*. The threads do not use the local socket to communicate. Instead, the two threads use it to establish a connection. To do so, *ttycon* calls *bind* to assign the socket the address *INADDR_LOOPBACK*, a special Internet address reserved for use within a single computer system. *Ttycon* then calls *getsockname* to determine the TCP port number that has been assigned to the socket.

     Once it has created the local socket, *ttycon* calls *_beginthread* to create the keyboard thread. As the code shows, the keyboard thread executes procedure *conreader*. The procedure is invoked with the protocol port of the local socket as an argument.

     When it starts executing *conreader*, the keyboard thread creates a second socket, and assigns the descriptor to variable *telsock*. *Telsock* is the socket that the keyboard thread uses to send keystrokes to the main thread. Before it can do so, the socket must be connected. To establish the connection, the keyboard thread calls socket function, *connect*. How can the keyboard thread form a connection to the main thread? To do so, it specifies Internet address *INADDR_LOOPBACK*, which identifies the destination as the local machine, and the protocol port number that was passed as an argument, which identifies the port assigned to socket *lsock* in the main thread.

     Once the connection is in place, the keyboard thread executes the infinite loop in *conreader*. On each iteration it handles one character. First, it calls *_getch* to read the character. If global variable *ttyflags* specifies that the character should be echoed, the keyboard thread calls function *putch* to display the character. Finally, it calls *send* to transmit the character across the local TCP connection to the main thread.

     Before it can receive characters, the main thread must accept the TCP connection from the keyboard thread. To do so, the main thread calls *listen* and *accept* on socket *lsock*. The call to *accept* blocks until the connection has been made. When the connection arrives, *accept* creates a new socket for the connection and returns the descriptor, which is assigned to variable *rsock*.

     In essence, the main thread acts like a server, and the keyboard thread acts like a client. The main difference, of course, lies in the distance between the connection endpoints. In a typical client-server interaction, two separate programs communicate, usually on two separate computers. In this case, the connection between the two threads is local – the sockets used to access the connection are both on the same computer, and the threads are part of the same concurrent program. The use of sockets is also unusual because a conventional server usually accepts connections from multiple clients. In this case, the two threads only need to form a single connection. Once the connection is in place, the original socket, *lsock*, is not needed; the main thread calls *closesocket* to close it.

25.7 Finite State Machine Specification

The TELNET protocol specifies how a client passes characters to a remote service and how the client displays data that the remote service returns. Most of the traffic that passes across the connection consists of individual data characters. Data characters originate at the client when the user types on the keyboard; they originate from the server when the remote session generates output. In addition to data characters, TELNET also permits the client and server to exchange control information. In particular, the client can send a sequence of characters that comprise a *command* to the server that controls execution of the remote service. For example, a client can send a command sequence that *interrupts* the remote application program.

Most implementations of TELNET use a *finite state machine* (*FSM*) to specify the exact syntax and interpretation of command sequences. As a specification tool, a finite state machine provides a precise description of the protocol. It shows exactly how the sender embeds command sequences in the data stream, and specifies how the receiver interprets such sequences. More important, the finite state machine can be converted directly into a program that follows the protocol. Thus, it is possible to verify that the resulting program obeys the protocol specification. To summarize:

> *Because TELNET is a character-oriented protocol that embeds command sequences in the data stream between the client and server, most implementations use a finite state machine to define the correct behavior.*

25.8 Embedding Commands In A TELNET Data Stream

The idea underlying TELNET is simple: whenever a client or server wants to send a command sequence instead of normal data, it inserts a special, reserved character in the data stream. The reserved character is called an *Interpret As Command* character (*IAC*). When the receiver finds an IAC character in its incoming data stream, it processes succeeding octets as a command sequence. To send an IAC as data, the sender *character stuffs* an extra IAC in front of it.

An individual command sequence can contain an *option request* or an *option reply*. A request asks the receiving side to honor (or not honor) a particular *TELNET option*; a reply acknowledges the request and specifies whether the receiver will honor it.

The protocol defines two verbs that a sender can use to form a request: *DO* and *DONT*. Like most items that TELNET defines, the protocol standard specifies that each verb and each option must be encoded in a single character. Thus, a request usually consists of three characters when it appears in the data stream:

IAC verb option

where *verb* denotes an encoded character for either a *DO* or *DONT*, and *option* denotes an encoded character for one of the TELNET options.

The *TELNET echo option* provides a good example. Normally, the server echoes each character it receives (i.e., sends a copy back to the user's display). To turn off remote character echo, the client sends three encoded characters that correspond to:

IAC DONT ECHO

25.9 Option Negotiation

In general, the receiving side responds to a request using the verbs *WILL* or *WONT*. The receiver sends *WILL* to specify that it will honor the requested option and *WONT* to specify that it will not.

A response to a request provides an acknowledgement to the sender and tells the sender whether the receiver agrees to honor the request. For example, at startup, the client and server negotiate to decide which side will echo characters that the user types. Usually, the client sends characters to the server and the server echoes them to the user's terminal. However, if network delays become troublesome, a user may prefer to have the local system echo characters. Before a client enables character echo in the local system, it sends the server the sequence:

IAC DONT ECHO

When the server receives the request, it sends the 3-character response:

IAC WONT ECHO

Note that the verb *WONT* refers to the option; it does not necessarily mean that the server rejected the request. In this case, for example, the server has agreed to turn off echo as requested.

25.10 Request/Offer Symmetry

Interestingly, TELNET permits one side of a connection to offer a particular option before the other side requests it. To do so, the side offering to perform (or not perform) an option sends a message containing the verb *WILL* (or *WONT*). Thus, a *WILL* or *WONT* either acknowledges a previous request or offers to perform an option. For example, applications like text editors often send special control sequences to position the cursor. They cannot use the network virtual terminal encoding because it does not support all possible 8-bit characters. Thus, the TELNET server on most computers automatically sends *WILL* for the *transmit binary* option whenever a client connects to it, offering to use 8-bit binary (unencoded) character transmission instead of NVT encoding. A client must respond by sending a command sequence that specifies *DO transmit binary* or *DONT transmit binary*.

25.11 TELNET Character Definitions

File *telnet.h* contains the definitions of constants used in the protocol:

```
/* telnet.h */


/* TELNET Command Codes: */
#define TCSB            (u_char)250       /* Start Subnegotiation         */
#define TCSE            (u_char)240       /* End Of Subnegotiation        */
#define TCNOP           (u_char)241       /* No Operation                 */
#define TCDM            (u_char)242       /* Data Mark (for Sync)         */
#define TCBRK           (u_char)243       /* NVT Character BRK            */
#define TCIP            (u_char)244       /* Interrupt Process           */
#define TCAO            (u_char)245       /* Abort Output                 */
#define TCAYT           (u_char)246       /* "Are You There?" Function   */
#define TCEC            (u_char)247       /* Erase Character             */
#define TCEL            (u_char)248       /* Erase Line                   */
#define TCGA            (u_char)249       /* "Go Ahead" Function          */
#define TCWILL          (u_char)251       /* Desire/Confirm Will Do Option*/
#define TCWONT          (u_char)252       /* Refusal To Do Option         */
#define TCDO            (u_char)253       /* Request To Do Option         */
#define TCDONT          (u_char)254       /* Request NOT To Do Option     */
#define TCIAC           (u_char)255       /* Interpret As Command Escape  */

/* Telnet Option Codes: */
#define TOTXBINARY      (u_char)  0       /* TRANSMIT-BINARY option       */
#define TOECHO          (u_char)  1       /* ECHO Option                  */
#define TONOGA          (u_char)  3       /* Suppress Go-Ahead Option     */
#define TOTERMTYPE      (u_char) 24       /* Terminal-Type Option         */
```

```
/* Network Virtual Printer Special Characters: */
#define VPLF          '\n'      /* Line Feed                      */
#define VPCR          '\r'      /* Carriage Return                */
#define VPBEL         '\a'      /* Bell (attention signal)        */
#define VPBS          '\b'      /* Back Space                     */
#define VPHT          '\t'      /* Horizontal Tab                 */
#define VPVT          '\v'      /* Vertical Tab                   */
#define VPFF          '\f'      /* Form Feed                      */


/* Keyboard Command Characters: */
#define KCESCAPE      035       /* Local escape character ('^]')  */
#define KCDCON        '.'       /* Disconnect escape command      */
#define KCSCRIPT      's'       /* Begin scripting escape command */
#define KCUNSCRIPT    'u'       /* End scripting escape command   */
#define KCSTATUS      024       /* Print status escape command ('^T')  */
#define KCCR          '\r'      /* Newline character              */

#define KCANY         (NCHRS+1)


/* Option Subnegotiation Constants: */
#define TT_IS         0         /* TERMINAL_TYPE option "IS" command    */
#define TT_SEND       1         /* TERMINAL_TYPE option "SEND" command  */


/* Boolean Option and State variables */
extern unsigned char    synching, doecho, sndbinary, rcvbinary;
```

Note that the file defines symbolic names for each of the characters TELNET uses, including verbs like *WILL* and *WONT* as well as option codes.

25.12 A Finite State Machine For Data From The Server

Figure 25.3 shows the principle finite state machine that specifies the TELNET protocol, including states that correspond to the option negotiation described above. Think of the machine as specifying how a client handles the sequence of characters it receives from the server.

The FSM diagram uses conventional notation. Each transition from one state to another has a label of the form α/β, where α denotes a specific input character that causes the transition and β denotes an action to be taken when following the transition. A label α/β on a transition from state X to state Y means: *if character α arrives while in state X, execute action β and then change to state Y.* The names of states and characters in the figure have been taken from the software. For example, file *telnet.h* defines constant *TCIAC* to correspond to TELNET's IAC character. As shorthand, the name *TCANY* denotes any character other than the transitions listed explicitly.

To understand how the FSM works, imagine that the client uses it whenever data arrives over the TCP connection from the server. When a character arrives from the server, the client follows a transition in the finite state machine. Some transitions keep the machine in the same state; others cause a transfer to a new state.

25.13 Transitions Among States

The client starts its state machine in the state labeled *TSDATA* when it begins execution. State *TSDATA* corresponds to a situation where the client expects to receive normal characters and send them to the user's display (i.e., the client has not begun reading a command sequence). For example, if character *q* arrives, the client remains in state *TSDATA* and executes the action labeled *K* (i.e., the client calls procedure *ttputc* to display the character on the user's terminal screen, and then follows the loop back to the same state).

If character *TCIAC* arrives when the FSM is in state *TSDATA*, the client follows the transition to state *TSIAC* and executes action labeled *E* in the diagram. The legend specifies that action *E* corresponds to "no operation." Once it moves to state *TSIAC*, the client has begun interpreting a command sequence. If the character following the *TCIAC* is a verb (e.g., *TCDO*), the client will follow a transition to one of the option processing states.

The finite state machine for TELNET only needs six states because interpretation of the protocol only depends on a short history of the characters that have arrived. For example, following a *TCIAC* character, the server could send one of the option requests or responses: *TCDO*, *TCDONT*, *TCWILL*, or *TCWONT*, or it could send an *option subnegotiation request*. Option subnegotiation permits the sender to include a variable-length string in the option (e.g., the option a client uses to pass a terminal type to a server uses subnegotiation so it can send a string that encodes the name of the terminal). Although subnegotiation permits variable-length command sequences, the FSM needs only two states to handle it because a 2-character sequence terminates subnegotiation. The client enters state *TSSUBNEG* when it first encounters a subnegotiation request. It moves to state *TSSUBIAC* when it receives character *TCIAC*, and moves out of subnegotiation altogether if character *TCSE* follows immediately. If any other 2-character sequence occurs, the FSM remains in state *TSSUBNEG*.

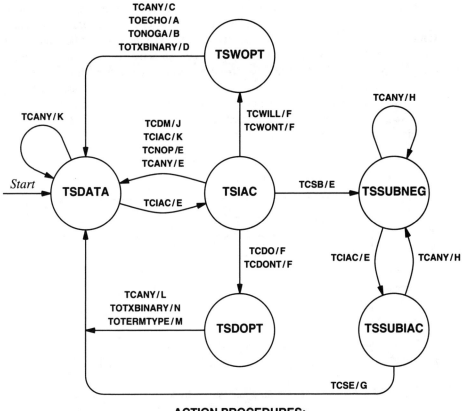

ACTION PROCEDURES:

A - do_echo   H - subopt
B - do_noga   J - tcdm
C - do_notsup   K - ttputc
D - do_txbinary L - will_notsup
E - no_op   M - will_termtype
F - recopt   N - will_txbinary
G - subend

Figure 25.3 The finite state machine that describes how TELNET encodes command sequences along with data. State and character names have been taken directly from the software. *TCANY* stands for "any character other than those shown explicitly."

25.14 A Finite State Machine Implementation

Because it is possible to construct an efficient implementation of a finite state machine and because such machines can describe character-oriented protocols easily, our example code uses three separate finite state machines. One controls how the client responds to characters from the keyboard, another controls how the client handles characters that arrive over the TCP connection from the server, and a third handles the details of option subnegotiation. All three FSMs use the same type of data structures, making it possible to share some of the procedures that manipulate the data structures.

To make processing efficient, our implementation encodes the transitions of a finite state machine into a *transition matrix* as Figure 25.4 shows.

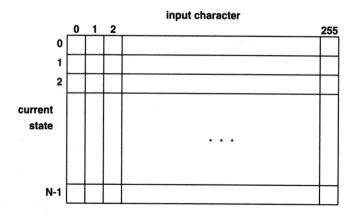

Figure 25.4 A finite state machine represented by a transition matrix. Each row corresponds to a state and each column corresponds to one possible input character.

At run-time, the client maintains an integer variable that records the current state. When a character arrives, the client uses the current state variable and the numeric value of the character to index the transition matrix.

25.15 A Compact FSM Representation

Writing C code to initialize a large matrix can be tedious. Furthermore, if each element of the transition matrix contains complete information about the action to take and the next state, the matrix can consume a large amount of memory. To keep the transition matrix small and to make initialization easy, our code uses a compact representation of a finite state machine.

In essence, the data structures chosen permit a programmer to create a compact data structure that represents a finite state machine and then arrange for the program to construct an associated transition matrix at run-time. File *tnfsm.h* contains the declaration of structure *fsm_trans* used in the compact representation:

```
/* tnfsm.h */


/* Telnet Socket-Input FSM States: */
#define TSDATA          0       /* normal data processing              */
#define TSIAC           1       /* have seen IAC                       */
#define TSWOPT          2       /* have seen IAC-{WILL/WONT}           */
#define TSDOPT          3       /* have seen IAC-{DO/DONT}             */
#define TSSUBNEG        4       /* have seen IAC-SB                    */
#define TSSUBIAC        5       /* have seen IAC-SB-...-IAC            */

#define NTSTATES        6       /* # of TS* states                     */


/* Telnet Keyboard-Input FSM States: */
#define KSREMOTE        0       /* input goes to the socket            */
#define KSLOCAL         1       /* input goes to a local func.         */
#define KSCOLLECT       2       /* input is scripting-file name        */

#define NKSTATES        3       /* # of KS* states                     */


/* Telnet Option Subnegotiation FSM States: */
#define SS_START        0       /* initial state                       */
#define SS_TERMTYPE     1       /* TERMINAL_TYPE option subnegotiation */
#define SS_END          2       /* state after all legal input         */

#define NSSTATES        3       /* # of SS_* states                    */

#define FSINVALID       0xff    /* an invalid state number             */

#define NCHRS           256             /* number of valid characters  */
#define TCANY           (NCHRS+1)       /* match any character         */

struct fsm_trans {
        u_char  ft_state;               /* current state               */
        short   ft_char;                /* input character             */
        u_char  ft_next;                /* next state                  */
        int     (*ft_action)(SOCKET sfd, FILE *tfp, int c);
                                        /* action to take              */
};
```

A compact FSM representation consists of a 1-dimensional array of *fsm_trans* structures. Each element specifies one transition. Field *ft_state* specifies the FSM state from which the transition begins. Field *ft_char* specifies the character that causes the transition (or *TC_ANY* to denote all characters other than those with explicit transitions). Field *ft_next* specifies the state in which the transition terminates, and field *ft_action* gives the address of the procedure to call that performs the action associated with the transition.

25.16 Keeping The Compact Representation At Run-Time

The example client does not copy all the information from the compact representation into the transition matrix. Instead, it leaves the compact representation unchanged and uses it to hold transition information. To do so, the software stores an integer in each element of the transition matrix. The integer gives the index of an entry in the compact representation that corresponds to the transition. Figure 25.5 illustrates the data structures:

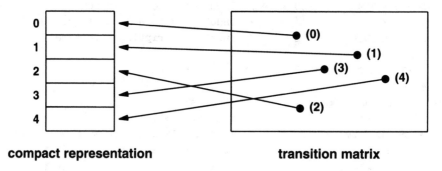

compact representation   **transition matrix**

Figure 25.5 The FSM data structures at run-time. Entries in the transition matrix contain an index that refers to an element of the compact representation.

25.17 Implementation Of A Compact Representation

File *ttfsm.cpp* contains an example compact FSM representation for the principle FSM shown in Figure 25.3:

```
/* ttfsm.cpp */

#include <stdio.h>
#include <winsock.h>

#include "telnet.h"
#include "tnfsm.h"
#include "local.h"

extern int do_echo(SOCKET,FILE *,int), do_noga(SOCKET,FILE *,int),
        do_notsup(SOCKET,FILE *,int), do_status(SOCKET,FILE *,int),
        no_op(SOCKET,FILE *,int), recopt(SOCKET,FILE *,int),
        subend(SOCKET,FILE *,int), subopt(SOCKET,FILE *,int),
        tcdm(SOCKET,FILE *,int), ttputc(SOCKET,FILE *,int),
        will_notsup(SOCKET,FILE *,int), will_termtype(SOCKET,FILE *,int),
        will_txbinary(SOCKET,FILE *,int), tnabort(SOCKET,FILE *,int),
        do_txbinary(SOCKET,FILE *,int);

struct fsm_trans ttstab[] = {
        /* State           Input          Next State      Action  */
        /* ------          ------         -----------     ------- */
        { TSDATA,          TCIAC,         TSIAC,          no_op        },
        { TSDATA,          TCANY,         TSDATA,         ttputc       },
        { TSIAC,           TCIAC,         TSDATA,         ttputc       },
        { TSIAC,           TCSB,          TSSUBNEG,       no_op        },
/* Telnet Commands */
        { TSIAC,           TCNOP,         TSDATA,         no_op        },
        { TSIAC,           TCDM,          TSDATA,         tcdm         },
/* Option Negotiation */
        { TSIAC,           TCWILL,        TSWOPT,         recopt       },
        { TSIAC,           TCWONT,        TSWOPT,         recopt       },
        { TSIAC,           TCDO,          TSDOPT,         recopt       },
        { TSIAC,           TCDONT,        TSDOPT,         recopt       },
        { TSIAC,           TCANY,         TSDATA,         no_op        },
/* Option Subnegotion */
        { TSSUBNEG,        TCIAC,         TSSUBIAC,       no_op        },
        { TSSUBNEG,        TCANY,         TSSUBNEG,       subopt       },
        { TSSUBIAC,        TCSE,          TSDATA,         subend       },
        { TSSUBIAC,        TCANY,         TSSUBNEG,       subopt       },

        { TSWOPT,          TOECHO,        TSDATA,         do_echo      },
        { TSWOPT,          TONOGA,        TSDATA,         do_noga      },
        { TSWOPT,          TOTXBINARY,    TSDATA,         do_txbinary  },
        { TSWOPT,          TCANY,         TSDATA,         do_notsup    },
```

```
      { TSDOPT,        TOTERMTYPE,      TSDATA,          will_termtype  },
      { TSDOPT,        TOTXBINARY,      TSDATA,          will_txbinary  },
      { TSDOPT,        TCANY,           TSDATA,          will_notsup    },

      { FSINVALID,     TCANY,           FSINVALID,       tnabort        },
};

#define NTRANS (sizeof(ttstab)/sizeof(ttstab[0]))

int     ttstate;
u_char  ttfsm[NTSTATES][NCHRS];
```

Array *ttstab* contains 22 valid entries that each correspond to one of the transitions shown in Figure 25.3 (plus an extra entry to mark the end of the array). Each entry in the array consists of an *fsm_trans* structure that specifies a single transition. Note that *ttstab* is both compact and easy to define. It is compact because it does not contain any empty entries; it is easy to define because each entry corresponds directly to one of the transitions in the FSM.

25.18 Building An FSM Transition Matrix

The utility of the compact representation will become clear once we see how it can be used to generate a transition matrix. File *fsminit.cpp* contains the code:

```
/* fsminit.cpp - fsminit */

#include <stdio.h>
#include <winsock.h>

#include "tnfsm.h"

#define TINVALID        0xff    /* an invalid transition index          */

/*------------------------------------------------------------------------
 * fsminit - Finite State Machine initializer
 *------------------------------------------------------------------------
 */
void
fsminit(u_char fsm[][NCHRS], struct fsm_trans ttab[], int nstates)
{
        struct fsm_trans        *pt;
```

```
int                         sn, ti, cn;

for (cn=0; cn<NCHRS; ++cn)
        for (ti=0; ti<nstates; ++ti)
                fsm[ti][cn] = TINVALID;

for (ti=0; ttab[ti].ft_state != FSINVALID; ++ti) {
        pt = &ttab[ti];
        sn = pt->ft_state;
        if (pt->ft_char == TCANY) {
                for (cn=0; cn<NCHRS; ++cn)
                        if (fsm[sn][cn] == TINVALID)
                                fsm[sn][cn] = ti;
        } else
                fsm[sn][pt->ft_char] = ti;
}
/* set all uninitialized indices to an invalid transition         */
for (cn=0; cn<NCHRS; ++cn)
        for (ti=0; ti<nstates; ++ti)
                if (fsm[ti][cn] == TINVALID)
                        fsm[ti][cn] = ti;
}
```

Procedure *fsminit* requires three arguments. Argument *fsm* specifies a transition matrix that must be initialized. Argument *ttab* gives the address of a compact FSM representation, and argument *nstates* specifies the number of states in the resulting FSM.

Fsminit first initializes the entire transition matrix to *TINVALID*. It then iterates through each element of the compact representation and adds the state transition specified by that element to the transition matrix. Finally, it iterates through the transition matrix again and changes any transitions that have not been filled in so they point to the invalid transition at the end of the compact representation.

Most of the code in *fsminit* is straightforward. When adding transitions, however, *fsminit* must distinguish between an explicit transition and an abbreviation. To understand the code, recall that the compact representation uses character *TCANY* to denote all characters that have not been specified explicitly. Thus, when *fsminit* examines an individual transition, it checks the character that causes the transition. If the entry specifies character *TCANY*, *fsminit* iterates through all possible characters and adds the transition to any character that has not been initialized. If the entry specifies any character other than *TCANY*, *fsminit* fills in the transition array for that single character.

25.19 The Socket Output Finite State Machine

The finite state machine shown in Figure 25.3 defines the actions the client takes for each character that arrives from the server. A separate, and simpler, finite state machine describes how the client handles characters that arrive from the keyboard. We call the FSM associated with keyboard input the *socket output FSM*. The name may seem unusual. Figure 25.6 shows how the client software organization supports such a name.

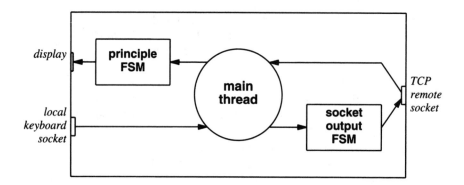

Figure 25.6 The client software organization. The main thread waits for either the TCP connection that leads to the remote server or the local connection that leads to the keyboard to become ready. It then reads a character from the ready socket, and calls an FSM procedure to process it. The socket output FSM that processes keyboard data is associated with the socket used to pass output to the remote server.

Unlike the principle finite state machine, the finite state machine used for socket output is straightforward. As Figure 25.7 shows, the machine contains three states. In essence, state *KSREMOTE* handles the normal case. While the machine remains in *KSREMOTE*, the client sends each character that a user types on the keyboard across the TCP connection to the server.

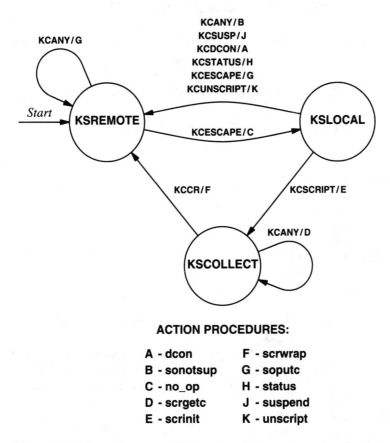

ACTION PROCEDURES:

A - dcon	F - scrwrap
B - sonotsup	G - soputc
C - no_op	H - status
D - scrgetc	J - suspend
E - scrinit	K - unscript

Figure 25.7 The socket output FSM used to define actions taken for each character the user types. The client sends most data characters to the remote server. However, the design permits the user to *escape* from the data connection and communicate with the local client program.

The socket output FSM begins in state *KSREMOTE*. Thus, when it first starts, the client merely sends each keystroke to the remote server. When the user types the *keyboard escape* key, the client enters state *KSLOCAL* where it waits for a keystroke. Most keystrokes that can follow the escape have no meaning, but a few cause the client to take action and return to state *KSREMOTE*. Only one, *KCSCRIPT*, causes the client to enter state *KSCOLLECT*, where it collects a file name to use for scripting.

25.20 Definitions For The Socket Output FSM

File *sofsm.cpp* defines the compact representation of the socket output FSM:

```
/* sofsm.cpp */

#include <stdio.h>
#include <winsock.h>

#include "telnet.h"
#include "tnfsm.h"

/* Special chars: */
char    t_flushc = '\017';      /* ^O */
char    t_intrc  = '\003';      /* ^C */
char    t_quitc  = '\034';      /* ^\ */
char    sg_erase = '\010';      /* ^H */
char    sg_kill  = '\030';      /* ^X */

extern int      soputc(SOCKET, FILE *, int), scrinit(SOCKET, FILE *, int),
                scrgetc(SOCKET, FILE *, int),scrwrap(SOCKET, FILE *, int),
                unscript(SOCKET, FILE *, int), dcon(SOCKET, FILE *, int),
                status(SOCKET, FILE *, int),sonotsup(SOCKET, FILE *, int),
                no_op(SOCKET, FILE *, int), tnabort(SOCKET, FILE *, int);

struct fsm_trans sostab[] = {
        /* State          Input           Next State      Action  */
        /* ------         ------          -----------     ------- */
/* Data Input */
        { KSREMOTE,       KCESCAPE,       KSLOCAL,        no_op       },
        { KSREMOTE,       KCANY,          KSREMOTE,       soputc      },
/* Local Escape Commands */
        { KSLOCAL,        KCSCRIPT,       KSCOLLECT,      scrinit     },
        { KSLOCAL,        KCUNSCRIPT,     KSREMOTE,       unscript    },
        { KSLOCAL,        KCESCAPE,       KSREMOTE,       soputc      },
        { KSLOCAL,        KCDCON,         KSREMOTE,       dcon        },
        { KSLOCAL,        KCSTATUS,       KSREMOTE,       status      },
        { KSLOCAL,        KCANY,          KSREMOTE,       sonotsup    },
/* Script Filename Gathering */
        { KSCOLLECT,      KCCR,           KSREMOTE,       scrwrap     },
        { KSCOLLECT,      KCANY,          KSCOLLECT,      scrgetc     },

        { FSINVALID,      KCANY,          FSINVALID,      tnabort     },
};
```

```
#define NTRANS   (sizeof(sostab)/sizeof(sostab[0]))

int     sostate;
u_char  sofsm[NKSTATES][NCHRS];
```

Array *sostab* contains the compact representation, and variable *sostate* contains an integer that gives the current state of the socket output FSM.

25.21 The Option Subnegotiation Finite State Machine

Figure 25.8 illustrates the third FSM used in the client. It handles the sequence of characters that arrive during *option subnegotiation*. Because it only recognizes one possible option subnegotiation (terminal type), the FSM only needs three states.

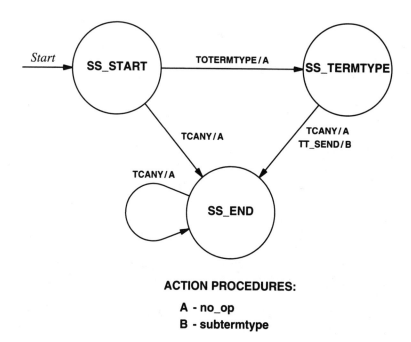

ACTION PROCEDURES:

A - no_op
B - subtermtype

Figure 25.8 The simple FSM used for option subnegotiation. The client reinitializes this machine each time it finishes an option subnegotiation.

The easiest way to think about subnegotiation is to imagine that it describes the interior structure of state *TSSUBNEG* in the principle FSM. While the main FSM operates in state *TSSUBNEG*, it calls procedure *subopt* to handle each incoming character. *Subopt* operates the subnegotiation FSM. As Figure 25.8 shows, the subnegotiation FSM makes an immediate decision that depends on the option. If it finds a terminal type subnegotiation, the machine moves to state *SS_TERMTYPE*. Otherwise, it moves directly to state *SS_END* and ignores the remainder of the subnegotiation string.

Once in state *SS_TERMTYPE*, the FSM checks the subnegotiation verb. It calls *subtermtype* if the verb is *TT_SEND*, and ignores the subnegotiation otherwise. The purpose and operation of the subnegotiation FSM will become clearer when we see how a client responds to the terminal type option.

25.22 Definitions For The Option Subnegotiation FSM

File *subfsm.cpp* contains the C declarations for the subnegotiation FSM:

```
/* subfsm.cpp */

#include <stdio.h>
#include <winsock.h>

#include "telnet.h"
#include "tnfsm.h"

extern int      no_op(SOCKET, FILE *, int),
                subtermtype(SOCKET, FILE *, int),
                tnabort(SOCKET, FILE *, int);

struct fsm_trans substab[] = {
        /* State          Input          Next State        Action   */
        /* ------         ------         ----------        -------   */
        { SS_START,       TOTERMTYPE,    SS_TERMTYPE,      no_op        },
        { SS_START,       TCANY,         SS_END,           no_op        },

        { SS_TERMTYPE,    TT_SEND,       SS_END,           subtermtype  },
        { SS_TERMTYPE,    TCANY,         SS_END,           no_op        },

        { SS_END,         TCANY,         SS_END,           no_op        },
        { FSINVALID,      TCANY,         FSINVALID,        tnabort      },
};

int     substate;
u_char  subfsm[NSSTATES][NCHRS];
```

25.23 FSM Initialization

At startup, the client calls procedure *fsmbuild* to initialize all finite state machines. As the code in file *fsmbuild.cpp* shows, *fsmbuild* calls *fsminit* to build the required data structure for each machine, and assigns each machine's state variable an initial state.

```
/* fsmbuild.cpp - fsmbuild */

#include <stdio.h>
#include <winsock.h>

#include "tnfsm.h"

extern struct fsm_trans ttstab[], sostab[], substab[];
extern u_char           ttfsm[][NCHRS], sofsm[][NCHRS], subfsm[][NCHRS];
extern int              ttstate, sostate, substate;

void fsminit(u_char fsm[][NCHRS], struct fsm_trans ttab[], int nstates);

/*------------------------------------------------------------------------
 * fsmbuild - build the Finite State Machine data structures
 *------------------------------------------------------------------------
 */
void
fsmbuild()
{
        fsminit(ttfsm, ttstab, NTSTATES);
        ttstate = TSDATA;

        fsminit(sofsm, sostab, NKSTATES);
        sostate = KSREMOTE;

        fsminit(subfsm, substab, NSSTATES);
        substate = SS_START;
}
```

25.24 Arguments For The TELNET Client

File *tclient.cpp* contains the code for the main program that executes when a user invokes the client:

```
/* tclient.cpp - main */

#include <stdlib.h>
#include <winsock.h>

#define WSVERS  MAKEWORD(2, 0)

char    *host = "localhost";     /* host to use if none supplied      */

void    errexit(const char *, ...);
void    telnet(const char *, const char *);

/*------------------------------------------------------------------------
 * main - TCP client for TELNET service
 *------------------------------------------------------------------------
 */
void
main(int argc, char *argv[])
{
        char    *service = "telnet";    /* default service name      */
        WSADATA wsdata;

        switch (argc) {
        case 1: break;
        case 3:
                service = argv[2];
                /* FALL THROUGH */
        case 2:
                host = argv[1];
                break;
        default:
                errexit("usage: telnet [host [port]]\n");
        }
        if (WSAStartup(WSVERS, &wsdata))
                errexit("WSAStartup failed.\n");
        telnet(host, service);
        exit(0);
}
```

The user can supply zero, one, or two command-line arguments that the program parses. With no arguments, (argc = 1), the client contacts a server on the local host and uses the *telnet* service. If one argument appears (argc = 2), the client takes the argument as the name of the remote host on which the server executes. Finally, if two arguments appear, the client takes the second to be the name of a service on the remote machine and takes the first to be the name of a remote host. After it has parsed its arguments, the main program calls function *telnet*.

25.25 The Heart Of The TELNET Client

File *telnet.cpp* contains the code that implements Algorithm *8.1*†:

```
/* telnet.cpp - telnet */

#include <io.h>
#include <stdlib.h>
#include <stdio.h>
#include <string.h>
#include <winsock.h>

#include "local.h"

extern unsigned char    synching;

#define BUFSIZE         2048    /* read buffer size    */


SOCKET  connectTCP(const char *host, const char *service);
SOCKET  ttycon(void);

/*------------------------------------------------------------------
 * telnet - do the TELNET protocol to the given host and port
 *------------------------------------------------------------------
 */
void
telnet(const char *host, const char *service)
{
        SOCKET  sock, con; /* remote and console socket descriptors */
        u_char  buf[BUFSIZE];
        int     cc;
        int     on = 1;
        fd_set  arfds, rfds;

        con = ttycon();

        sock = connectTCP(host, service);
```

---

†See page 107 for a description of Algorithm 8.1.

```
fsmbuild();        /* set up FSM's */


(void) setsockopt(sock, SOL_SOCKET, SO_OOBINLINE, (char *)&on,
                  sizeof(on));
FD_ZERO(&arfds);
FD_SET(sock, &arfds);     /* the socket                         */
FD_SET(con, &arfds);      /* standard input                     */


while (1) {
        memcpy(&rfds, &arfds, sizeof(rfds));

        if (select(FD_SETSIZE, &rfds, (fd_set *)0,
            (fd_set *)0, (struct timeval *)0) < 0) {
                if (GetLastError() == WSAEINTR)
                        continue;        /* just a signal*/
                errexit("select: %d\n", GetLastError());
        }
        if (FD_ISSET(sock, &rfds)) {
                unsigned long   no_urg;
                if (ioctlsocket(sock, SIOCATMARK, &no_urg) ==
                    SOCKET_ERROR)
                        errexit("socket ioctl error %d\n",
                                GetLastError());
                synching = !no_urg;

                cc = recv(sock, (char *)buf, sizeof(buf), 0);
                if (cc == SOCKET_ERROR)
                        errexit("socket recv: %d\n",
                                          GetLastError());
                else if (cc == 0)
                        errexit("\nconnection close.\n");
                else
                        ttwrite(sock, stdout, buf, cc);
        }
        if (FD_ISSET(con, &rfds)) {
                cc = recv(con, (char *)buf, sizeof(buf), 0);
                if (cc == SOCKET_ERROR)
                        errexit("tty read: %d\n",
                                          GetLastError());
                else if (cc == 0) {
                        FD_CLR(con, &arfds);
                        (void) shutdown(sock, 1);
                } else
                        sowrite(sock, stdout, buf, cc);
```

```
            }
        (void) fflush(stdout);
    }
}
```

Procedure *telnet* requires two arguments that specify the name of a remote machine and a service on that machine. The code begins by calling *connectTCP* to allocate a socket and form a TCP connection to the server. It then calls *fsmbuild* to initialize the three finite state machines.

Once it finishes initialization, the main thread of the client enters an infinite loop. At each iteration of the loop, it uses *select* to wait for I/O from the remote connection or from the keyboard. The *select* call will return value *WSAEINTR* if the program receives an interruption while the call to *select* is blocked. If that happens, the client continues with the next iteration of the loop.

If *select* returns normally, data can be available at the keyboard, at the remote connection, or at both. *Telnet* first checks the remote connection to see if data has arrived from the server. If so, it calls *recv* to extract the data and *ttwrite* to write the data to the user's display. We will see below that *ttwrite* implements the principle finite state machine that interprets the incoming data stream and handles escapes and embedded command sequences.

After *telnet* checks for incoming data at the socket leading to the remote server, it examines the keyboard socket. If data has arrived from the keyboard, *telnet* calls *recv* to extract the data and *sowrite* to write it to the socket. *Sowrite* contains the code that executes the finite state machine for local escape processing. As a special case, the client interprets an *end-of-file* entered on the keyboard to be a request to terminate the connection. If it receives an end-of-file (i.e., *recv* returns *0*), *telnet* calls *shutdown* to send an end-of-file condition to the server. In any case, *telnet* calls *fflush* at each iteration to ensure that the output routines do not buffer the data that has been written. *Fflush* forces the operating system to send all data immediately, even if the buffer is not full.

25.26 TELNET Synchronization

TELNET includes a mechanism that enables a client and server to bypass the effects of TCP buffering. Known as *synchronization*, the mechanism arranges for a server to use TCP *urgent data* to inform a client that synchronization is needed. The protocol specifies that when urgent data arrives, a client must *synchronize* with a server before processing more input. To synchronize, the client skips forward in the stream of data arriving from the server until it encounters the *DATA MARK* character.

To implement synchronization, the example code uses global variable *synching*. Procedure *telnet* tests for the presence of urgent data from the server when it finds the socket ready. If TCP reports that urgent data has arrived on the socket, *telnet* sets *synching* to nonzero. While *synching* is set, the FSM action procedure *ttputc* discards

incoming data without displaying it on the user's screen. When a *DATA MARK* character arrives, the FSM action procedure *tcdm* is called to turn off synchronization. The
code in file *sync.cpp* shows that *tcdm* resets *synching* to zero, which causes the client to
resume normal processing.

```
/* sync.cpp - tcdm */

#include <stdio.h>
#include <winsock.h>

unsigned char   synching;/* non-zero, if we are doing telnet SYNCH      */

/*------------------------------------------------------------------------
 * tcdm - handle the telnet "DATA MARK" command (marks end of SYNCH)
 *------------------------------------------------------------------------
 */
/*ARGSUSED*/
int
tcdm(SOCKET sfd, FILE *tfp, int c)
{
        if (synching > 0)
                synching--;
        return 0;
}
```

25.27 Handling A Severe Error

In some cases, when a socket function returns an error code, the error indicates a
minor unexpected event. In such cases a program can choose to ignore the error, print a
warning, or automatically correct the problem. In other cases, the error condition reported by a socket function is catastrophic – a problem is so severe that the application
cannot correct or ignore it. In such cases, an application cannot continue executing.

The *telnet* procedure contains code to handle both minor and severe errors. For example, if the call to *select* returns an error code (i.e., a value less than zero), *telnet* calls
GetLastError to determine the exact problem. If the error code specifies a minor error
– the operating system had to interrupt the *select* call before the operation could complete – *telnet* continues execution with the next iteration of the loop. If *GetLastError*
returns any other error code, the main thread calls procedure *errexit* to print a message
for the user and terminate execution. Similarly, if other socket functions indicate that
an error has occurred, *telnet* calls *errexit*. Thus, if the system runs out of resources
(e.g., sockets or memory), the application will print an error message and terminate.

Errexit takes an argument that is a string containing a message for the user. It displays the message and causes the entire process to exit. Note that if any thread in a multithreaded process calls *errexit*, all other threads in the process will be terminated. Thus, *errexit* should only be used for severe errors.

25.28 Implementation Of The Main FSM

Procedure *ttwrite* implements the FSM from Figure 25.3 that interprets data as it arrives from the server. The code appears in file *ttwrite.cpp*:

```
/* ttwrite.cpp - ttwrite */

#include <stdio.h>
#include <winsock.h>

#include "tnfsm.h"

extern struct fsm_trans ttstab[];
extern u_char           ttfsm[][NCHRS];
extern int              ttstate;

/*------------------------------------------------------------------------
 * ttwrite - do output processing for (local) network virtual printer
 *------------------------------------------------------------------------
 */
void
ttwrite(SOCKET sfd, FILE *tfp, u_char *buf, int cc)
{
        struct fsm_trans        *pt;
        int                     i, ti;

        for (i=0; i<cc; ++i) {
                int     c = buf[i];

                ti = ttfsm[ttstate][c];
                pt = &ttstab[ti];

                (pt->ft_action)(sfd, tfp, c);
                ttstate = pt->ft_next;
        }
}
```

Ttwrite extracts *cc* characters from the buffer, *buf*, one at a time. Each time it extracts a character, *ttwrite* uses the character and the current state (variable *ttstate*) to index the transition matrix. The transition matrix returns *ti*, the index of a transition in the compact representation (*ttstab*). *Ttwrite* calls the procedure associated with the transition (field *ft_action*), and sets the current state variable to the appropriate next state (field *ft_next*).

25.29 A Procedure For Immediate Disconnection

The socket output finite state machine† contains an entry that allows a user to *disconnect*. When the user specifies disconnection, the main thread calls procedure *dcon*, which can be found in file *dcon.cpp*:

```
/* dcon.cpp - dcon */

#include <stdlib.h>
#include <stdio.h>
#include <winsock.h>

#include "local.h"

/*------------------------------------------------------------------------
 * dcon - disconnect from remote
 *------------------------------------------------------------------------
 */
/*ARGSUSED*/
int
dcon(SOCKET sfd, FILE *tfp, int c)
{
        fprintf(tfp, "disconnecting.\n");
        WSACleanup();
        exit(0);
        return 0;        /* pro forma */
}
```

As the code shows, our client interprets disconnection as immediate and permanent; *dcon* calls the Windows function *exit*, which causes the entire process, including both the main and keyboard threads, to terminate. When a process exits, the system releases all resources that the process had allocated. Thus, both the local and remote TCP connections will be closed, and the sockets will be released.

---

†The socket output machine specification can be found on page 384.

25.30 Abort Procedure

In the socket output finite state machine, not all sequences of input move the machine to valid states. To prevent an illegal sequence of values from producing an error, invalid state transition are assigned procedure *tnabort*. If an invalid sequence should occur, *tnabort* calls *errexit* to print an error message and terminate the program. File *tnabort.cpp* contains the code:

```
/* tnabort.cpp - tnabort */

#include <stdio.h>
#include <winsock.h>

void     errexit(const char *, ...);

/*------------------------------------------------------------------------
 * tnabort - abort telnet due to invalid state
 *------------------------------------------------------------------------
 */
/*ARGSUSED*/
int
tnabort(SOCKET sfd, FILE *tfp, int c)
{
        errexit("invalid state reached (aborting)\n");
        return 0;        /* to keep picky compilers happy */
}
```

25.31 Summary

TELNET ranks among the most popular application protocols in the TCP/IP suite. The protocol provides for interactive character transport between a client and server. Usually, the client connects a user's terminal to a server across a TCP connection. Our example client software consists of two threads with a local TCP connection between them. The keyboard thread reads each character that the user types on the keyboard, and sends the character across the local TCP connection to the main thread. The main thread uses the socket function *select* to allow concurrent input. The thread waits until data arrives over the TCP connection from the remote server or over the local TCP connection from the keyboard. After receiving and processing the data, the main thread returns to *select*, which waits until additional input arrives.

TELNET uses escape sequences to embed commands and control information in the data stream. To simplify the code, our example client implementation uses three finite state machines to interpret character sequences. One handles data that arrives from the server, another handles data that arrives from the user's keyboard, and a third handles option subnegotiation.

The example code in this chapter illustrates the implementation of the two client threads as well as the data structures used to implement the finite state machines. The next chapter considers the details of the procedures that perform actions associated with transitions in the finite state machines.

FOR FURTHER STUDY

Postel [RFC 854] contains the standard for the basic TELNET protocol, including the network virtual terminal encoding. Postel and Reynolds [RFC 855] specifies the details of option negotiation and option subnegotiation. Details on individual options can be found in other RFCs. VanBokkelen [RFC 1091] specifies the terminal-type option. Postel and Reynolds [RFC 857] describes the echo option, while Postel and Reynolds [RFC 856] describes the binary transmission option. Information on the *rlogin* protocol, an alternative to TELNET, can be found in the documentation on most UNIX systems.

EXERCISES

25.1   Compare the design presented in this chapter to one in which one thread reads from the keyboard and sends to the remote server, and another thread reads from the remote connection and sends to the display. What are the advantages and disadvantages of each design?

25.2   Investigate the support for asynchronous I/O in Windows. How can asynchronous I/O be used in a TELNET client?

25.3   Compare a design that uses asynchronous I/O facilities described in the previous question to designs that use blocking I/O. What are the advantages and disadvantages of each?

25.4   To find out about I/O in other operating systems, read sections of the *UNIX Programmer's Manual* that describe terminal devices and device drivers. What are *cooked mode*, *cbreak mode*, and *raw mode*? How do they correspond to TELNET options?

25.5   Rewrite the principle FSM to include states for option subnegotiation.

25.6   The example FSM implementation uses a compact representation to save space. Estimate the space required for the principle FSM using a conventional representation, and compare the estimate to the space required for the compact representation.

25.7   Under what conditions will *recv* from the keyboard connection return the value *0*?

25.8   Read the TELNET protocol specification to find the exact rules for synchronization. When does the sender transmit *urgent data*? Why is *synching* necessary?

25.9   A server can choose to send more data after the client sends an end-of-file. How does the client know when to terminate the connection to the server?

25.10   Rewrite *ttwrite* so it does not use an FSM. What are the advantages and disadvantages of each implementation?

25.11   When an error occurs, the code prints a cryptic message and exits. Improve the code to print messages that make sense to a user.

25.12   In the previous exercise, examine the error codes that your local system can return. Will all errors make sense to a user? Why or why not?

25.13   The finite state machines do not have explicit states for synchronization. Revise the state diagrams to include synchronization. How many additional states are required?

25.14   Does it make sense to add states to the FSM for scripting? If so, which finite state machine(s) need to be modified? If not, explain why.

26

A TELNET Client
(Implementation Details)

26.1 Introduction

The previous chapter discusses the structure of a TELNET client and shows how it uses finite state machines to control processing. This chapter concludes the discussion by showing how semantic action procedures implement the details of character processing.

26.2 The FSM Action Procedures

Finite state machines implement most of the TELNET protocol details. They control processing, coordinate responses with requests, and map incoming command sequences to actions. Each time the client follows a transition in a finite state machine, it calls a procedure to perform the actions associated with the transition. Figure 25.3† shows the procedure names associated with transitions in the FSM that handles characters arriving from the server.

An action may be simple (e.g., discard the incoming character), or it may be complex (e.g., respond by sending a string that identifies the local terminal). Encapsulating each action in a procedure helps keep the machine specifications uniform and simplifies the code at the top level. However, dividing the software into a set of procedures for each action means that the relationship between procedures can only be understood by referring to the finite state machine that interconnects them.

---

†The figure appears on page 375.

399

The following sections each describe one of the action procedures associated with an FSM transition.

26.3 Recording The Type Of An Option Request

In state *TSIAC* (i.e., following the arrival of a *TCIAC* character), the arrival of *TCWILL* or *TCWONT* causes a transition to state *TSWOPT*. The FSM specifies that procedure *recopt* should be called. *Recopt* records the character that caused the transition so it can be used later. Similarly, the FSM uses *recopt* to record character *TCDO* or *TCDONT* during a transition to state *TSDOPT*. File *recopt.cpp* contains the code:

```
/* recopt.cpp - recopt, no_op */

#include <stdio.h>
#include <winsock.h>

u_char  option_cmd;      /* has value WILL, WONT, DO, or DONT            */

/*-------------------------------------------------------------------------
 * recopt - record option type
 *-------------------------------------------------------------------------
 */
/*ARGSUSED*/
int
recopt(SOCKET sfd, FILE *tfp, int c)
{
        option_cmd = c;
        return 0;
}


/*-------------------------------------------------------------------------
 * no_op - do nothing
 *-------------------------------------------------------------------------
 */
/*ARGSUSED*/
int
no_op(SOCKET sfd, FILE *tfp, int c)
{
        return 0;
}
```

26.4 Performing No Operation

File *recopt.cpp* also contains code for procedure *no_op*. Because the FSM must have an action for all possible combinations of a state and an input character, procedure *no_op* can be used for those transitions that do not require any action. For example, a transition from state *TSDATA* to *TSIAC* does not require any action. Therefore, the FSM specifies a call to *no_op*.

26.5 Responding To WILL/WONT For The Echo Option

The server sends *WILL* or *WONT* followed by the *ECHO* option to inform the client that it is willing to echo characters or is willing to stop echoing characters. The FSM specifies that procedure *do_echo* should be called when such a message arrives.

```
/* do_echo.cpp - do_echo */

#include <stdio.h>
#include <winsock.h>

#include "local.h"
#include "telnet.h"

unsigned char   doecho;              /* nonzero, if remote ECHO     */
extern u_char   option_cmd;

/*------------------------------------------------------------------------
 * do_echo - handle TELNET WILL/WON'T ECHO option
 *------------------------------------------------------------------------
 */
int
do_echo(SOCKET sfd, FILE *tfp, int c)
{
        if (doecho) {
                if (option_cmd == TCWILL)
                        return 0;        /* already doing ECHO         */
        } else if (option_cmd == TCWONT)
                return 0;                /* already NOT doing ECHO     */
        if (option_cmd == TCWILL)
                ttyflags &= ~ECHO;
        else
                ttyflags |= ECHO;
        doecho = !doecho;
```

```
        (void) sputc(TCIAC, sfd);
        if (doecho)
                (void) sputc(TCDO, sfd);
        else
                (void) sputc(TCDONT, sfd);
        (void) sputc((char)c, sfd);
        return 0;
}
```

The TELNET protocol specifies that the server can send a *WILL* or *WONT* to advertise its willingness to perform a given option or it can send such a message in
response to a client request. Therefore, if the client has sent a request containing a *DO*
or *DONT*, the message from the server constitutes a reply; otherwise, it constitutes an
advertisement.

The client uses its current condition to decide how to respond. Global variable
doecho contains a nonzero value if the client currently expects the server to perform
character echo. If the server sends *WILL* and the client already has remote echo enabled, the client does not reply. Similarly if the server sends *WONT* and the client has
remote echo disabled, the client does not reply. However, if the server sends *WILL* and
the client currently has remote echoing turned off, the client clears the *ECHO* bit in global variable *ttyflags* to disable local character echoing (recall that the keyboard thread
examines the bit to determine whether to echo keystrokes). If the client has local echo
disabled when a *WONT* arrives, the client assumes that the server has disabled the remote echo. Therefore, the client sets the *ECHO* bit in global variable *ttyflags* to enable
local echoing. The client only sends a *DO* or *DONT* response if it changes the echo
mode.

26.6 Sending A Response

When procedure *do_echo* needs to send a response back to the server, it calls function *sputc*. *Sputc* takes two arguments: a single character to be sent, and the descriptor
of a socket over which to send the character. Thus, a procedure such as *do_echo* that
needs to send a two-character response must call *sputc* twice (once for *IAC* and once for
DO or *DONT*). Because the response should be sent over the TCP connection that
leads to the server, the second argument in each call is *sfd*, the socket descriptor for the
connection.

The code for *sputc* is trivial; it can be found in file *sputc.cpp*:

```
/* sputc.cpp - sputc */

#include <winsock.h>

/*------------------------------------------------------------------
 * sputc - put one character on a socket
 *------------------------------------------------------------------
 */
int
sputc(const char c, SOCKET sfd)
{
        return send(sfd, &c, 1, 0);
}
```

26.7 Responding To WILL/WONT For Unsupported Options

When the client receives a *WILL* or *WONT* request for an option that it does not understand, it calls procedure *do_notsup* to reply *DONT*.

```
/* do_notsup.cpp - do_notsup */

#include <stdio.h>
#include <winsock.h>

#include "local.h"
#include "telnet.h"

extern u_char    option_cmd;

/*------------------------------------------------------------------
 * do_notsup - handle an unsupported telnet "will/won't" option
 *------------------------------------------------------------------
 */
/*ARGSUSED*/
int
do_notsup(SOCKET sfd, FILE *tfp, int c)
{
        (void) sputc(TCIAC, sfd);
        (void) sputc(TCDONT, sfd);
        (void) sputc((char)c, sfd);
        return 0;
}
```

26.8 Responding To WILL/WONT For The No Go-Ahead Option

The client uses procedure *do_noga* to respond when the server sends *WILL* or *WONT* requests for the *no go-ahead option*.

```
/* do_noga.cpp - do_noga */

#include <stdio.h>
#include <winsock.h>

#include "local.h"
#include "telnet.h"

extern u_char    option_cmd;

/*------------------------------------------------------------------------
 * do_noga - don't do telnet Go-Ahead's
 *------------------------------------------------------------------------
 */
/*ARGSUSED*/
int
do_noga(SOCKET sfd, FILE *tfp, int c)
{
        static  noga;

        if (noga) {
                if (option_cmd == TCWILL)
                        return 0;
        } else if (option_cmd == TCWONT)
                return 0;
        noga = !noga;
        (void) sputc(TCIAC, sfd);
        if (noga)
                (void) sputc(TCDO, sfd);
        else
                (void) sputc(TCDONT, sfd);
        (void) sputc((char)c, sfd);
        return 0;
}
```

As with other options, the client does not respond if the client's current setting for the option agrees with the server's request. If the server requests a change, the client reverses the current setting by negating global variable *noga*, and sends either a *DO* or *DONT* response.

26.9 Generating DO/DONT For Binary Transmission

The server can send characters to the client either encoded, using the network virtual terminal encoding, or unencoded, using 8-bit binary values. Global variable *rcvbinary* controls whether the client expects to receive data as binary characters or NVT encodings. The client calls procedure *do_txbinary* to respond when the server sends a *WILL* or *WONT* for the binary option. Like the other procedures that handle options, *do_txbinary* has been designed so it can be called to request that the server send binary or to respond to an advertisement from the server. It uses the global variable *option_cmd* to decide how to proceed, and assumes that it contains an incoming request. Procedure *do_txbinary* tests to see whether the client expects the server to send binary, sets *rcvbinary* according to the incoming request, and responds to the server if *rcvbinary* changes.

```
/* do_txbinary.cpp - do_txbinary */

#include <stdio.h>
#include <winsock.h>

#include "local.h"
#include "telnet.h"

unsigned char   rcvbinary;          /* non-zero if remote TRANSMIT-BINARY   */
extern u_char   option_cmd;

/*------------------------------------------------------------------------
 * do_txbinary - handle telnet "will/won't" TRANSMIT-BINARY option
 *------------------------------------------------------------------------
 */
/*ARGSUSED*/
int
do_txbinary(SOCKET sfd, FILE *tfp, int c)
{
        if (rcvbinary) {
                if (option_cmd == TCWILL)
                        return 0;
        } else if (option_cmd == TCWONT)
                return 0;
        rcvbinary = !rcvbinary;
        (void) sputc(TCIAC, sfd);
        if (rcvbinary)
                (void) sputc(TCDO, sfd);
        else
                (void) sputc(TCDONT, sfd);
```

```
        (void) sputc((char)c, sfd);
        return 0;
}
```

26.10 Responding To DO/DONT For Unsupported Options

The server sends *DO* or *DONT* messages to tell the client that it should enable or disable a specified option. The client responds by sending *WILL* if it agrees to honor the option, or *WONT* if it does not honor the option. As the FSM in Figure 25.3 shows, the client calls procedure *will_notsup* when it does not support a particular option. Procedure *will_notsup* sends *WONT* to tell the server it does not support the option.

```
/* will_notsup.cpp - will_notsup */

#include <stdio.h>
#include <winsock.h>

#include "local.h"
#include "telnet.h"

/*------------------------------------------------------------------------
 * will_notsup - handle an unsupported telnet "do/don't" option
 *------------------------------------------------------------------------
 */
/*ARGSUSED*/
int
will_notsup(SOCKET sfd, FILE *tfp, int c)
{
        (void) sputc(TCIAC, sfd);
        (void) sputc(TCWONT, sfd);
        (void) sputc((char)c, sfd);
        return 0;
}
```

26.11 Responding To DO/DONT For Transmit Binary Option

When the client starts, it uses the network virtual terminal encoding for all data it sends to the server. Although NVT encoding includes most printable characters, it does not provide an encoding for all control characters. Servers operating on systems that support screen-oriented applications usually need the ability to transfer arbitrary character data. Therefore, such servers usually advertise their willingness to transmit binary data and request that the client also transmit binary data.

A server sends *DO* for the *transmit binary option* to request that the client begin using 8-bit, unencoded transmission. The client calls procedure *will_txbinary* when such a request arrives.

```
/* will_txbinary.cpp - will_txbinary */

#include <stdio.h>
#include <winsock.h>

#include "local.h"
#include "telnet.h"

unsigned char   sndbinary;        /* non-zero if TRANSMIT-BINARY            */
extern u_char   option_cmd;

/*------------------------------------------------------------------------
 * will_txbinary - handle telnet "do/don't" TRANSMIT-BINARY option
 *------------------------------------------------------------------------
 */
/*ARGSUSED*/
int
will_txbinary(SOCKET sfd, FILE *tfp, int c)
{
        if (sndbinary) {
                if (option_cmd == TCDO)
                        return 0;
        } else if (option_cmd == TCDONT)
                return 0;
        sndbinary = !sndbinary;
        (void) sputc(TCIAC, sfd);
        if (sndbinary)
                (void) sputc(TCWILL, sfd);
        else
                (void) sputc(TCWONT, sfd);
        (void) sputc((char)c, sfd);
        return 0;
}
```

The client uses global variable *sndbinary* to control its transmission mode. If the request forces a change in the status, the client acknowledges the request by sending a *WILL* or *WONT*.

26.12 Responding To DO/DONT For The Terminal Type Option

Communicating the terminal type from client to server requires two steps. First, the server asks the client whether it honors the *termtype option*. Second, if the client agrees that it will honor the terminal type option, the server uses option subnegotiation to request a string that identifies the user's terminal type.

Unlike some systems, Windows does not have a standard mechanism that can be used to identify the type of a terminal. Our code examines the variable *TERM* in the program's *environment*. If the variable exists, the program assumes that it has been assigned a string that gives a valid terminal type.

When a request arrives for the terminal type option, the client calls procedure *will_termtype*. File *will_termtype.cpp* contains the code:

```
/* will_termtype.cpp - will_termtype */

#include <stdio.h>
#include <stdlib.h>
#include <winsock.h>

#include "local.h"
#include "telnet.h"

char            termtype;        /* non-zero if received "DO TERMTYPE"   */
char            *term;           /* terminal name                        */
extern u_char   option_cmd;

int     do_txbinary(SOCKET,FILE *,int), will_txbinary(SOCKET,FILE *,int);

/*------------------------------------------------------------------------
 * will_termtype - handle telnet "do/don't" TERMINAL-TYPE option
 *------------------------------------------------------------------------
 */
int
will_termtype(SOCKET sfd, FILE *tfp, int c)
{
        if (termtype) {
                if (option_cmd == TCDO)
                        return 0;
        } else if (option_cmd == TCDONT)
                return 0;
        termtype = !termtype;
        if (termtype)
                if (!term && !(term = getenv("TERM")))
                        termtype = !termtype;   /* can't do it... */
```

```
        (void) sputc(TCIAC, sfd);
        if (termtype)
                (void) sputc(TCWILL, sfd);
        else
                (void) sputc(TCWONT, sfd);
        (void) sputc((char)c, sfd);
        if (termtype) { /* set up binary data path; send WILL, DO */
                option_cmd = TCWILL;
                (void) do_txbinary(sfd, tfp, TOTXBINARY);
                option_cmd = TCDO;
                (void) will_txbinary(sfd, tfp, TOTXBINARY);
        }
        return 0;
}
```

Procedure *will_termtype* behaves much like other option handlers. It uses global variable *termtype* to record whether the server has requested the terminal type option previously, and checks to see if the current request changes the status. In addition, *will_termtype* checks to see whether the terminal type has been assigned to string *term* previously. If the terminal type is needed and has not been fetched before, *will_termtype* calls the library function *getenv* to obtain the value associated from environment variable *TERM*. If no such variable exists, *getenv* returns a *NULL* pointer, and the client responds that it will not honor the request.

A server requests terminal type information so applications can prepare output specifically for the user's terminal. For example, a text editor uses the terminal type when it generates the sequence of characters that clears the screen, moves the cursor, or highlights text. Thus, the client expects that once the remote application receives terminal type information it will send control sequences for the terminal. Because such sequences cannot be sent using the NVT encoding, *will_termtype* sends a *WILL* message that advertises the client's willingness to use binary transmission and a *DO* message that requests the server use binary transmission. Because functions *do_txbinary* and *will_txbinary* can be called from the FSM option processing code, they use global variable *option_cmd* to control processing. When calling the functions directly, other procedures must initialize *option_cmd* explicitly as if the client had received the appropriate *WILL* or *DO* message from the server before the call.

26.13 Option Subnegotiation

Once a client agrees to handle the terminal type option, a server uses option subnegotiation to request the terminal name. Unlike normal options which all have a fixed length, subnegotiation permits the sender to insert an arbitrary-length string in the data stream. To do so, the sender brackets the string by sending a subnegotiation header, the data for that particular option subnegotiation, and a trailer that identifies the end of the subnegotiation.

When the main FSM (Figure 25.3) encounters a subnegotiation command sequence, it enters state *TSSUBNEG*. Once in state *TSSUBNEG*, the client calls procedure *subopt* each time it receives a character. As the code in file *subopt.cpp* shows, *subopt* runs the option subnegotiation FSM to handle subnegotiation.

```
/* subopt.cpp - subopt */

#include <stdio.h>
#include <winsock.h>

#include "telnet.h"
#include "tnfsm.h"

extern struct fsm_trans substab[];
extern int              substate;
extern u_char           subfsm[][NCHRS];

/*------------------------------------------------------------------------
 * subopt - do option subnegotiation FSM transitions
 *------------------------------------------------------------------------
 */
int
subopt(SOCKET sfd, FILE *tfp, int c)
{
        struct  fsm_trans       *pt;
        int                     ti;

        ti = subfsm[substate][c];
        pt = &substab[ti];
        (pt->ft_action)(sfd, tfp, c);
        substate = pt->ft_next;
        return 0;
}
```

26.14 Sending Terminal Type Information

The option subnegotiation FSM† calls procedure *subtermtype* to reply to a request for a terminal type. The server sends the sequence:

         IAC SUBNEG TERMTYPE SEND IAC SUBEND

to request a terminal type. The client replies by sending:

         IAC SUBNEG TERMTYPE IS term_type_string IAC SUBEND

---

†See page 385 for a description of the option subnegotiation finite state machine.

File *subtermtype.cpp* contains the code:

```
/* subtermtype.cpp - subtermtype */

#include <stdio.h>
#include <winsock.h>

#include "local.h"
#include "telnet.h"

extern char     *term;              /* terminal name, from initialization   */

/*------------------------------------------------------------------------
 * subtermtype - do terminal type option subnegotation
 *------------------------------------------------------------------------
 */
/*ARGSUSED*/
int
subtermtype(SOCKET sfd, FILE *tfp, int c)
{
        /* have received IAC.SB.TERMTYPE.SEND */

        (void) sputc(TCIAC, sfd);
        (void) sputc(TCSB, sfd);
        (void) sputc(TOTERMTYPE, sfd);
        (void) sputc(TT_IS, sfd);
        SPUTS(term, sfd);
        (void) sputc(TCIAC, sfd);
        (void) sputc(TCSE, sfd);
        return 0;
}
```

The option subnegotiation FSM calls *subtermtype* after receiving the *SEND* request. Previously, the client must have replied positively to a request to honor the terminal type option, so global variable *term* must already point to a string that contains the terminal type. *Subtermtype* sends the reply by calling *sputc* to send the individual control characters and macro *SPUTS* to send the string that contains the terminal type information.

26.15 Terminating Subnegotiation

When the principle FSM shown in Figure 25.3 encounters the end of option subnegotiation, it moves back to state *TSDATA*. Whenever it does so, it calls procedure *subend*. *Subend* simply resets the option subnegotiation FSM to its start state so it is ready to handle the next subnegotiation. File *subend.cpp* contains the code:

```
/* subend.cpp - subend */

#include <stdio.h>
#include <winsock.h>

#include "tnfsm.h"

extern int              substate;

/*------------------------------------------------------------------------
 * subend - end of an option subnegotiation; reset FSM
 *------------------------------------------------------------------------
 */
/*ARGSUSED*/
int
subend(SOCKET sfd, FILE *tfp, int c)
{
        substate = SS_START;
        return 0;
}
```

26.16 Sending A Character To The Server

The client calls procedure *soputc* to convert an output character into the network virtual terminal encoding and send it through the TCP socket to the server. File *soputc.cpp* contains the code:

```
/* soputc.cpp - soputc */

#include <stdio.h>
#include <winsock.h>

#include "telnet.h"
#include "local.h"
```

```
/*-------------------------------------------------------------------------
 * soputc - move a character from the keyboard to the socket
 *-------------------------------------------------------------------------
 */
/*ARGSUSED*/
int
soputc(SOCKET sfd, FILE *tfp, int c)
{
        if (sndbinary) {
                if (c == TCIAC)
                        (void) sputc(TCIAC, sfd); /* byte-stuff IAC     */
                (void) sputc(c, sfd);
                return 0;
        }
        c &= 0x7f;      /* 7-bit ASCII only */
        if (c == t_intrc || c == t_quitc) {     /* Interrupt          */
                (void) sputc(TCIAC, sfd);
                (void) sputc(TCIP, sfd);
        } else if (c == sg_erase) {             /* Erase Char         */
                (void) sputc(TCIAC, sfd);
                (void) sputc(TCEC, sfd);
        } else if (c == sg_kill) {              /* Erase Line         */
                (void) sputc(TCIAC, sfd);
                (void) sputc(TCEL, sfd);
        } else if (c == t_flushc) {             /* Abort Output       */
                (void) sputc(TCIAC, sfd);
                (void) sputc(TCAO, sfd);
        } else
                (void) sputc(c, sfd);
        return 0;
}
```

When transmitting in binary mode, only the *IAC* character needs to be character stuffed. That is, *soputc* must replace each *IAC* character with two *IAC* characters. For any other character, *soputc* merely calls *sputc* to send it.

When transmitting in normal mode, *soputc* must convert from the local character set to the network virtual terminal character set. For example, if the character that arrives corresponds to the *interrupt* character, *soputc* sends the two characters:

IAC IP

It checks explicitly for each of the special characters that the NVT defines. *Soputc* must also handle characters for which no NVT encoding exists. However, the NVT protocol specifies that if the server does not request that the client use binary transmission, the server will discard most control characters that the user types.

26.17 Displaying Incoming Data On The User's Terminal

Data that arrives over the TCP connection from the server can either be unencoded (if the server has agreed to transmit binary) or it can consist of characters encoded according to the rules for an NVT. The client calls procedure *ttputc* to display an incoming character on the user's terminal.

```
/* ttputc.cpp - ttputc */

#include <stdio.h>
#include <winsock.h>

#include "telnet.h"

int     xputc(char, FILE *);

/*------------------------------------------------------------------------
 * ttputc - print a single character on a Network Virtual Terminal
 *------------------------------------------------------------------------
 */
/*ARGSUSED*/
int
ttputc(SOCKET sfd, FILE *tfp, int c)
{
        static  last_char;
        int     tc = 0;

        if (rcvbinary) {
                (void) xputc(c, tfp);    /* print uninterpretted */
                return 0;
        }
        if (synching)                    /* no data, if in SYNCH */
                return 0;

        if ((last_char == VPCR && c == VPLF) ||
            (last_char == VPLF && c == VPCR)) {
                (void) xputc(VPLF, tfp);
                last_char = 0;
                return 0;
        }
        if (last_char == VPCR)
                (void) xputc(VPCR, tfp);
        else if (last_char == VPLF)
                (void) xputc(VPLF, tfp);
```

```
    if (c >= ' ' && c < TCIAC)           /* printable ASCII      */
            (void) xputc(c, tfp);
    else {                                /* NVT special          */
            switch (c) {
            case VPLF:                    /* see if CR follows    */
            case VPCR:       tc = 1; /* see if LF follows    */
                             break;
            default:
                    break;   /* no action */
            }
            if (!tc)                      /* if no termcap, assume ASCII */
                    (void) xputc(c, tfp);
    }
    last_char = c;
    return 0;
}
```

If the server has agreed to send binary data, *ttputc* merely calls *xputc* to display each character. File *xput.cpp* contains the code:

```
/* xput.cpp - xputc, xfputs */

#include <stdio.h>

extern FILE      *scrfp;

/*-------------------------------------------------------------------
 * xputc - putc with optional file scripting
 *-------------------------------------------------------------------
 */
int
xputc(char ch, FILE *fp)
{
        if (scrfp)
                (void) putc(ch, scrfp);
        return putc(ch, fp);
}


/*-------------------------------------------------------------------
 * xfputs - fputs with optional file scripting
 *-------------------------------------------------------------------
 */
int
xfputs(char *str, FILE *fp)
{
        if (scrfp)
                return fputs(str, scrfp);
        return fputs(str, fp);
}
```

Xputc differs from the conventional *putc* function because the client provides a *scripting* facility. If scripting has been enabled, *xputc* writes a copy of the output character to the script file as well as sending a copy to the user's display. Otherwise, *xputc* only sends a copy to the display.

If the server is not sending binary data, *ttputc* must translate from the NVT encoding into an appropriate character sequence for the user's terminal. Two cases arise: the client can be in normal mode or in *synchronize mode*. The client enters synchronize mode when it receives a TELNET *SYNCH* command. While in synchronize mode, the client reads and discards all data. The client returns to normal mode when it encounters a TELNET *DATA MARK*.

When it receives a SYNCH command, procedure *telnet.cpp* sets global variable *synching*, which causes the client to enter synchronize mode and seek to the next *DATA MARK* character in the data stream. The client must discard all input in synchronize mode (i.e. not display it). To implement synchronization, *ttputc* checks variable *synch-*

ing on each call. If *synching* is nonzero, *ttputc* drops the character without displaying it on the user's screen.

Once it has checked for synchronize mode, *ttputc* must interpret the remaining characters using the NVT encoding. Because some NVT encodings consist of a 2-character sequence, *ttputc* keeps a copy of the previous character in global variable *last_char*.

First, *ttputc* handles *carriage return* (*CR*) and *linefeed* (*LF*). It recognizes either of the 2-character sequences *CR-LF* or *LF-CR* as an end-of-line, and translates them to the single character *LF* that Windows uses. Of course, if either a carriage return or line feed character occurs alone, *ttputc* sends the character to the screen.

Ttputc calls *xputc* to print any of the printable ASCII characters directly. Otherwise, it handles the special characters.

26.18 Writing A Block Of Data To The Server

Telnet calls procedure *sowrite* to write a block of data to the server.

```
/* sowrite.cpp - sowrite */

#include <stdio.h>
#include <winsock.h>

#include "tnfsm.h"

extern struct fsm_trans sostab[];
extern int              sostate;
extern u_char           sofsm[][NCHRS];

/*------------------------------------------------------------------------
 * sowrite - do output processing to the socket
 *------------------------------------------------------------------------
 */
void
sowrite(SOCKET sfd, FILE *tfp, u_char *buf, int cc)
{
        struct fsm_trans      *pt;
        int                   i, ki;

        for (i=0; i<cc; ++i) {
                int     c = buf[i];

                ki = sofsm[sostate][c];
                pt = &sostab[ki];
```

```
                  if ((pt->ft_action)(sfd, tfp, c) < 0)
                          sostate = KSREMOTE;       /* an error occurred    */
                  else
                          sostate = pt->ft_next;
          }
}
```

Sowrite iterates through each character in the specified block and runs finite state machine *sofsm* to process each character.

26.19 Interacting With The Local Client

Like most TELNET client programs, our implementation permits the user to interact with the local client program. To do so, a user types the *keyboard escape character* followed by a *command*. The table in Figure 26.1 lists the possible commands that can follow an escape character along with their meanings:

Symbolic Name	Character Typed	Meaning
KCDCON	.	**Terminate the session immediately.**
KCSTATUS	↑T	**Print status information about the current connection.**
KCESCAPE	↑]	**Send the escape character to the server as data.**
KCSCRIPT	s	**Begin scripting to a specified file.**
KCUNSCRIPT	u	**Terminate scripting.**

Figure 26.1 Keyboard input characters that the TELNET client interprets as commands when they follow *KCESCAPE*. The notation ↑*X* refers to the character generated by holding *CONTROL* and typing *X*.

File *telnet.h*† contains symbolic definitions for each of the keyboard command characters. For example, it defines the keyboard escape character, *KCESCAPE*, to be ↑] (i.e., the character with octal value 035).

When the client encounters the keyboard escape character, it changes the state of the socket output FSM from *KSREMOTE* to *KSLOCAL* and interprets the succeeding character as a command‡. Because most commands consist of a single character, the socket output FSM usually moves back to state *KSREMOTE* and executes an action procedure associated with the command. For example, if the FSM encounters character *KCDCON* following *KCESCAPE*, it calls procedure *dcon*.

---

†File *telnet.h* appears on page 372.

‡The socket output FSM is described in Figure 25.7 on page 383.

26.20 Responding To Illegal Commands

If the user types an unrecognized character following a keyboard escape, the socket output FSM calls action procedure *sonotsup* which prints an error message. File *sonotsup.cpp* contains the code:

```
/* sonotsup.cpp - sonotsup */

#include <stdio.h>
#include <winsock.h>

/*------------------------------------------------------------------------
 * sonotsup - an unsupported escape command
 *------------------------------------------------------------------------
 */
/*ARGSUSED*/
int
sonotsup(SOCKET sfd, FILE *tfp, int c)
{
        fprintf(tfp, "\nunsupported escape: %c.\n", c);
        fprintf(tfp, "s  - turn on scripting\t\t");
        fprintf(tfp, "u  - turn off scripting\n");
        fprintf(tfp, ".  - disconnect\t\t\t");
        fprintf(tfp, "^T - print status\n");
        return 0;
}
```

26.21 Scripting To A File

Our example TELNET client has one novel feature not found in most other clients: it permits the user to dynamically create a script file that contains a copy of all data being sent to the user's display. The idea underlying scripting is that a user may need to keep a record of all or part of a TELNET session.

Scripting is *dynamic* because the user can start or stop it at any time. Furthermore, the user can change the file into which the client writes the script. Thus, to capture the output of a single remote command, the user can log into the remote system with scripting disabled, then enable scripting and issue the command or commands for which the output must be kept, and finally, disable scripting. The script file will contain a copy of everything that the client displayed on the user's terminal while scripting was enabled.

26.22 Implementation Of Scripting

The socket output finite state machine illustrated in Figure 25.7 defines how the client handles scripting. If the user types ↑]s (i.e. character *KCESCAPE* followed by character *KCSCRIPT*), the socket output FSM calls action procedure *scrinit* and enters state *KSCOLLECT*. Until the user types an end-of-line character (i.e., *KCCR*), the FSM stays in state *KSCOLLECT* and calls procedure *scrgetc* to collect a string of characters that form the name of the script file. Once the user terminates the line of input, the FSM calls *scrwrap* to open the script file and move back to state *KSREMOTE*. The following sections each discuss one of the action procedures associated with scripting.

26.23 Initialization Of Scripting

When the socket output FSM first encounters a request to begin scripting, it calls action procedure *scrinit*.

```
/* scrinit.cpp - scrinit */

#include <stdio.h>
#include <string.h>
#include <winsock.h>

#include "telnet.h"
#include "local.h"

extern int            scrindex;
extern unsigned int   tnflags;


/*------------------------------------------------------------------------
 * scrinit - initialize tty modes for script file collection
 *------------------------------------------------------------------------
 */
/*ARGSUSED*/
int
scrinit(SOCKET sfd, FILE *tfp, int c)
{
        if (!doecho) {
                fprintf(tfp, "\nscripting requires remote ECHO.\n");
                return -1;
        }
        if (scrfp) {
                fprintf(tfp,"\nalready scripting to \"%s\".\n", scrname);
```

```
                    return -1;
        }
        scrindex = 0;
        tnflags = ttyflags;
        ttyflags = ECHO;
        fprintf(tfp, "\nscript file: ");
        (void) fflush(tfp);
        return 0;
}
```

Scrinit first verifies that the client is using remote echo (i.e., that all characters being displayed are coming from the server and not from keyboard input). It also verifies that the user does not already have scripting enabled. *Scrinit* sets global variable *scrindex* to zero. Another procedure will use *scrindex* to count characters as it reads the name of the script file. Finally, before it prints a prompt, *scrinit* saves the current control flags for the console in global variable *tnflags*, and changes the mode of the user's terminal so the local terminal driver will print the characters of the file name as the user types them.

26.24 Collecting Characters Of The Script File Name

The socket output FSM uses action procedure *scrgetc* to read a sequence of characters that will be used as the name of a script file. File *scrgetc.cpp* contains the code:

```
/* scrgetc.cpp - scrgetc */

#include <stdio.h>
#include <string.h>
#include <winsock.h>

#include "local.h"

#define SFBUFSZ          2048    /* script filename buffer size  */

unsigned int    tnflags;
FILE            *scrfp;
char            scrname[SFBUFSZ];
int             scrindex;

/*------------------------------------------------------------------
 * scrgetc - begin session scripting
 *------------------------------------------------------------------
 */
/*ARGSUSED*/
int
scrgetc(SOCKET sfd, FILE *tfp, int c)
{
        scrname[scrindex++] = c;
        if (scrindex >= SFBUFSZ) {      /* too far */
                fprintf(tfp, "\nname too long\n");
                ttyflags = tnflags;
                return -1;
        }
        return 0;
}
```

Each time a character arrives, the client calls *scrgetc*, which appends the character to string *scrname*.

26.25 Opening A Script File

When the client encounters an end-of-line, it calls procedure *scrwrap* to open the script file.

```
/* scrwrap.cpp - scrwrap */

#include <io.h>
#include <fcntl.h>
#include <stdio.h>
#include <string.h>
#include <errno.h>
#include <winsock.h>

#include "local.h"

extern char             scrname[];
extern int              scrindex;
extern unsigned int     tnflags;

/*-------------------------------------------------------------------
 * scrwrap - wrap-up script filename collection
 *-------------------------------------------------------------------
 */
/*ARGSUSED*/
int
scrwrap(SOCKET sfd, FILE *tfp, int c)
{
        int     fd;

        if (scrindex) {
                scrname[scrindex] = '\0';
                scrindex = 0;
                fd = open(scrname, O_WRONLY|O_CREAT|O_TRUNC, 0644);
                if (fd < 0)
                        fprintf(tfp, "\ncan't write \"%s\": %s\n",
                                scrname, strerror(errno));
                else
                        scrfp = fdopen(fd, "w");
        }
        putchar('\n');
        ttyflags = tnflags;
        return 0;
}
```

Scrwrap adds a null terminator to the string that has been collected, resets global variable *scrindex* so it can be used again, and calls *open* to open the script file. If it successfully obtains a new descriptor for the script file, *scrwrap* calls *fdopen* to create a standard I/O file pointer for the script file and places the pointer in global variable *scrfp*. Before it returns, *scrwrap* uses global variable *tnflags* to reset the terminal modes to the values they had before *scrinit* changed them.

26.26 Terminating Scripting

When the user decides to disable scripting, the socket output FSM calls action procedure *unscript*.

```
/* unscript.cpp - unscript */

#include <sys/types.h>
#include <sys/stat.h>

#include <stdio.h>
#include <winsock.h>

#include "local.h"

/*------------------------------------------------------------------------
 * unscript - end session scripting
 *------------------------------------------------------------------------
 */
/*ARGSUSED*/
int
unscript(SOCKET sfd, FILE *tfp, int c)
{
        struct stat      statb;

        if (scrfp == 0) {
                fprintf(tfp, "\nNot scripting.\n");
                return 0;
        }
        (void) fflush(scrfp);
        if (fstat(fileno(scrfp), &statb) == 0)
                fprintf(tfp, "\n\"%s\": %d bytes.\n", scrname,
                                statb.st_size);
        (void) fclose(scrfp);
        scrfp = 0;
        return 0;
}
```

Unscript prints an informational message to tell the user that the client has stopped scripting, uses the Windows function *fstat* to obtain information about the resulting script file, and prints a message that gives the size of the script file. Finally, *unscript* closes the script file and clears the global file pointer, *scrfp*.

26.27 Printing Status Information

The user can obtain status information about the current connection by using the *KCSTATUS* command following a keyboard escape. The socket output FSM calls action procedure *status* to print the connection status.

```
/* status.cpp - status */

#include <stdio.h>
#include <winsock.h>

#include "telnet.h"

extern  char    *host, scrname[];
extern  FILE    *scrfp;

/*------------------------------------------------------------------------
 * status - print connection status information
 *------------------------------------------------------------------------
 */
/*ARGSUSED*/
int
status(SOCKET sfd, FILE *tfp, int c)
{
        struct  sockaddr_in     sin;
        int                     sinlen;

        fprintf(tfp, "\nconnected to \"%s\" ", host);

        sinlen = sizeof(sin);
        if (getsockname(sfd, (struct sockaddr *)&sin,
                        &sinlen) == 0)
                fprintf(tfp, "local port %d ", ntohs(sin.sin_port));
        sinlen = sizeof(sin);
        if (getpeername(sfd, (struct sockaddr *)&sin,
                        &sinlen) == 0)
                fprintf(tfp, "remote port %d ", ntohs(sin.sin_port));
        (void) putc('\n', tfp);
```

```
        if (doecho || sndbinary || rcvbinary) {
                printf("options in effect: ");
                if (doecho)
                        fprintf(tfp, "remote_echo ");
                if (sndbinary)
                        fprintf(tfp, "send_binary ");
                if (rcvbinary)
                        fprintf(tfp, "receive_binary ");
                (void) putc('\n', tfp);
        }
        if (scrfp)
                fprintf(tfp, "scripting to file \"%s\"\n", scrname);
        return 0;
}
```

Procedure *status* prints information such as the name of the remote host, the local and remote TCP protocol ports used for the connection, and a list of the options in effect. To do so, it calls socket functions *getsockname* to obtain information about the local protocol port number, and *getpeername* to obtain information about the remote protocol port number. It uses library function *ntohs* to convert the port numbers from network byte order to the local host's byte order. Finally, *status* examines the options currently in effect. If either remote echo or binary transmission is enabled, *status* prints the status of the options.

26.28 Summary

Our example TELNET client uses three finite state machines to interpret sequences of characters that arrive from the server or from the user's keyboard. Each incoming character causes a transition in a finite state machine. When the client performs a transition, it calls a procedure that implements the action associated with the transition.

This chapter describes the action procedures for the three finite state machines that comprise the example client. Some actions are trivial while others are complex. The chief disadvantage of organizing the client software as action procedures for the finite state machine lies in readability. The resulting code can be difficult to understand because one cannot ascertain the relationships among the procedures without referring to the finite state machines.

FOR FURTHER STUDY

A series of RFCs documents the details of TELNET options, and contains protocol standards for each of the options handled by the example code. Postel and Reynolds [RFC 858] discusses the go-ahead option, while Postel and Reynolds [RFC 857] discusses character echo. Postel and Reynolds [RFC 856] describes the option that controls 8-bit binary transmission. Finally, VanBokkelen [RFC 1091] discusses the terminal-type option and the associated option subnegotiation.

EXERCISES

26.1   Some terminal types support multiple emulation modes, making it possible to have a set of terminal type names for a single terminal. Read RFC 1091. How can a client use a list of terminal names when it negotiates the terminal type with a server?

26.2   Read the protocol standard to find out exactly when a server must switch from sending data encoded using the network virtual terminal encoding to sending 8-bit binary data. In particular, how does the server handle transmission after it volunteers to transmit binary data, but has not received an acknowledgement?

26.3   Does a client send *WILL* or *DO* when it requests the server to perform a given option? What does the server send when it requests the client to perform an option?

26.4   What does the mode argument *O_WRONLY|O_CREAT|O_TRUNC* mean in the call to *open* found in procedure *scrwrap*?

26.5   Instrument the client to print a message when it receives an option request. Use the modified client to contact a variety of servers. What option requests do they send automatically?

26.6   What happens if the client sends *DO ECHO* and the server sends *WILL ECHO* simultaneously?

26.7   What happens if a client sends *DO ECHO* to a server that already has *ECHO* enabled?

27

Porting Servers From UNIX To Windows

27.1 Introduction

The example code throughout this text has been written to provide a tutorial illustration of the concepts for programmers who are building client-server software for a Windows environment from scratch. Many programmers face a more difficult challenge: porting software that was developed for another operating system to Windows. In particular, because many client-server applications are initially written for the UNIX operating system, programmers are often asked to port server code from UNIX.

This chapter facilitates porting efforts by describing conventions and practices that professional UNIX programmers follow when building production programs. Although some of the facilities and techniques described here have no direct Windows equivalent, understanding why they are used will help programmers understand how they affect the programs.

27.2 Operating In Background

UNIX allows a process to execute in *foreground* or in *background*. The easiest way to understand the difference is to imagine a user typing commands to a command interpreter. Normally, each command executes in foreground, meaning that the interpreter waits while the command executes. Once the command finishes, the command interpreter issues another prompt and allows the user to enter a new command. In contrast, a program that runs in background does not finish before the command interpreter issues another prompt. Instead all background programs continue to run at the same time as a single foreground program.

Most servers execute in background because they run forever. A server begins execution when the operating system starts, and executes in background waiting for requests to arrive. Usually, the operating system is configured to start each server when it runs the system startup script. (The startup script in UNIX, */etc/rc*, operates like *autoexec.bat* in a Windows system.)

Although it is possible to program the startup script to place each server process in background, most production servers put themselves in background quickly and automatically. In UNIX, the initial server program does not ''move itself to background.'' Instead, the initial server process exits after creating a new process that runs the server code in background. The technique used consists of calling *fork* to create the new process, and then calling *exit* to terminate the initial program. Thus, most servers execute code similar to the following almost immediately after they start execution:

```
i = fork();
if (i < 0) {          /* less than zero means error occurred*/
        fprintf(stderr, "error when forking: %s\n",
              strerror(errno);
        exit(1);
}
if (i) {              /* nonzero is parent                    */
        exit(0);      /* normal process exit                  */
}
/* child continues execution here and becomes the server   */
```

Unlike the *CreateProcess* function in Windows, *fork* makes a copy of the running program, and the *fork* call returns in both copies. There are three possible return values: a negative value means that an error occurred (e.g., the system had insufficient memory to create the new process), a positive result means that the call succeeded and the process is the parent, and a zero means that the call succeeded and the process is the newly created child.

If the call to *fork* fails, the example code prints an error message and calls *exit* with an argument of *1* to indicate abnormal termination. If the call to *fork* succeeds, the *if* statement uses the return value to distinguish between the parent and child processes. The parent process calls *exit* with an argument of *0* to indicate normal termination. The child continues execution and becomes the server. Note that in UNIX, a child is completely detached from the parent. Unlike a thread in Windows, the child process in UNIX can continue to operate after the parent exits.

27.3 Shared Descriptors And Inheritance

Like a newly created thread in Windows, a newly created process in UNIX inherits a copy of each socket descriptor that the parent had opened when the child was created. Unlike a Windows thread, however, UNIX makes a copy of descriptors for the child process. Furthermore, UNIX uses a reference count mechanism for each descriptor that counts the number of processes that have a copy. To understand reference counts, suppose a parent has a file open when it calls fork. Even if the parent closes its copy of the file descriptor, the child will still have a copy open, and the file will not be closed. As a result, the system will keep resources allocated for the file.

To avoid using resources, a production server closes the inherited file descriptors that it does not use. Usually, the server closes *all* descriptors before it creates any communication sockets. In UNIX, a single function, *close* can be used on either socket descriptors or file descriptors; calling *close* on an unopened descriptor has no effect. Thus, the code, usually executed immediately after the server moves to background, resembles this:

```
for (i=getdtablesize()-1; i>= 0; --i)
        (void) close(i);
```

Because the number of descriptors available to a process varies among UNIX systems, the example code does not contain a fixed constant. Instead, it calls function *getdtablesize* to find the size of the process descriptor table. The descriptor table is indexed starting at zero; the code iterates from the descriptor table size minus one down through zero, calling *close* on each descriptor.

There are two important differences in a Windows implementation. First, Windows does not use a reference count for each thread. Thus, a child thread should not close a descriptor that the parent needs. Second, Windows does not use a unified set of descriptors for both files and sockets, and consequently, does not have a single function that will close either one.

27.4 The Controlling TTY

Each process in UNIX inherits a connection to a terminal that has been designated as its *control terminal* or *controlling tty*. The association with a controlling tty permits a user who started a process to control it.

Unlike most processes, a server should not receive signals generated by the process that created it. To ensure that signals from a terminal do not affect a server running in background, a server usually detaches itself from the controlling tty. The code needed to detach from a controlling terminal consists of three lines:

```
fd = open("/dev/tty", O_RDWR);
(void) ioctl(fd, TIOCNOTTY, 0);
(void) close(fd);
```

The call to *open* obtains a descriptor for the controlling terminal, the call to *ioctl* detaches the process from the terminal, and the call to *close* releases the descriptor.

Windows does not have a concept of controlling terminal. Thus, there is no need for a Windows server to detach itself to avoid signals from the terminal. Consequently, code such as the above can be eliminated when porting a UNIX server to Windows.

27.5 Working Directories

Like DOS, UNIX uses the term *directory* for the file system abstraction that some systems and applications call a *folder*. In UNIX, each executing process is assigned a *current working directory*. A process can change its current directory at any time by calling the *chdir* function. For example, to change to directory */etc/server1*, a program executes the following:

```
(void) chdir("/etc/server1");
```

The current directory notion is most important for file names. A file name that does not begin with the slash character (*/*) is interpreted as a file in the program's current working directory. Thus, if a server that has current working directory */etc/server1* creates a file named *x*, the file will be located in disk file */etc/server1/x*. To translate to a Windows environment, the file names used with *chdir* must be valid, and each occurrence of backslash must be doubled in a string constant:

```
(void) chdir("C:\\server1");
```

27.6 File Creation And Umask

Similar to Windows, each file in UNIX has a protection mode that specifies the access that the owner and nonowners are permitted. The UNIX protection mode on a file is stored as nine bits, and each UNIX process has a *umask* that specifies the protection mode the system will assign to files that the process creates. The umask is an integer in which the low-order *9* bits are significant. Whenever a file is created, the system computes a mode for the file by performing a bit-wise *and* operation of the mode specified in the *open* call and the bit-wise complement of the process' umask. For example, suppose a process has umask *027* (octal). If the process tries to create a file with mode *0777* (readable, writable, and executable by everyone), the system arrives at the correct file mode by computing the bit-wise *and* of *0750* (the complement of umask *027*) and *0777* (the requested mode). As a result, the file mode will be *0750* (readable and executable by the owner and the file's group, writable only by the owner, and not accessible by others).

Servers often execute code that restricts file creation modes. The server usually calls function *umask* as in:

$$\text{(void) umask(027);}$$

The Windows *_umask* function works like the UNIX *umask* function. However, because Windows does not have provisions for groups or other users, only two modes are used: read-only or read-write. The corresponding constants are: *_S_IREAD* and *_S_IWRITE*.

27.7 Process Groups

UNIX has a *process group* abstraction that permits a set of processes to be treated as a single unit. Usually, each server operates independently from other processes, and calls function *setpgrp* to specify that it is not part of any process group:

$$\text{(void) setpgrp(0, getpid());}$$

The call can be eliminated when porting a server to Windows.

27.8 Descriptors For Standard I/O

In UNIX, many library routines expect three file descriptors to be open and available for I/O. Known as *standard input*, *standard output*, and *standard error*, the descriptors have values *0, 1,* and *2*. For example, the library routine *perror*, which prints error messages, writes to the standard error descriptor without checking to ensure it is open. To avoid problems, servers usually open the three descriptors, even if the server does not explicitly use them for I/O. The code resembles the following:

```
fd = open("/dev/null", O_RDWR);    /* stdin  */
(void) dup(fd);                    /* stdout */
(void) dup(fd);                    /* stderr */
```

The code assumes all descriptors have been closed; it does not need to specify descriptor numbers because UNIX assigns descriptors sequentially, starting at zero.

27.9 Mutual Exclusion For A Server

A server is *mutually exclusive* in the sense that only one copy of the master server should exist at any time. To avoid unintended errors, some servers invoke a mechanism that guarantees *mutual exclusion* when they begin execution. Most UNIX servers use a *lock file* mechanism to achieve mutually exclusive execution; a separate lock file is assigned to each server. When a copy of the server begins execution, it attempts to establish its designated lock file. If no other process is holding the lock, the attempt succeeds; if another copy of the server has already locked the file, the attempt fails.

The code to obtain a lock usually consists of:

```
/* Acquire an exclusive lock, or exit.  Assumes    */
/* symbolic constant LOCKF has been defined to be   */
/* the name of the server's lock file.  For example, */
/*        #define LOCKF /usr/spool/lpd.lock         */
/*                                                   */
lf = open(LOCKF, O_RDWR|O_CREAT, 0640);
if (lf < 0)              /* error occurred opening file */
        exit(1);
if (flock(lf, LOCK_EX|LOCK_NB))
        exit(0);         /* could not obtain a lock    */
```

In Windows, the *LockFile* function performs file locking that can be used for mutual exclusion.

27.10 Recording A Process ID

Because the UNIX signal mechanism requires the sender to know the ID of the process to which a signal is sent, many servers record their process ID in a file, enabling a system administrator to signal the server easily. Often, a server records its ID in its lock file, which contains no other information†. Thus, once a lock file has been created, one might find code such as:

```
char    pbuf[10];  /* an array to hold ASCII pid */

/* Write the ID of the current process in a     */
/* lock file, assuming the file has been opened  */
/* and its descriptor stored in variable lf      */

(void) sprintf(pbuf, "%d\n", getpid());
(void) write(lf, pbuf, strlen(pbuf));
```

---

†The locking system depends only on the presence of a file and not on its contents.

The Windows function *_getpid* operates like the UNIX *getpid*. Thus, a server running under Windows can call *_getpid* to find its process ID, and then record the ID in a file. The system administrator can use the information to terminate the server.

27.11 Waiting For A Child Process To Exit

When a UNIX process exits, two cases arise. Either the process is orphaned because the parent has already exited, or the parent still exists. If the parent has exited, the child will terminate. If not, the system cannot complete child termination until it informs the parent. The parent must call system function *wait* before the child's termination can complete. Meanwhile, the terminating child process exists in a *zombie state*, and is sometimes called a *defunct process*.

A concurrent UNIX server that creates a slave to handle each request must call *wait* when each slave completes. The system sends the server a signal, which the server must catch. The following code invokes procedure *cleanup* each time a child process terminates (*cleanup* calls *wait* or a variant such as *wait3*).

```
signal(SIGCHLD, cleanup);
```

A UNIX server may contain additional calls to the *signal* function to establish a handler for other signals. For example, a server that accepts connections over a dialup telephone line will contain a call to handle *SIGHUP*, the signal that is sent if the phone line is disconnected unexpectedly.

27.12 Using A System Log Facility

27.12.1 Generating Log Messages

We mentioned earlier that many servers, generate output for debugging and maintenance. In production servers, the output is usually restricted to error messages generated when the server finds unusual circumstances or unexpected events. However, some production servers are programmed to keep a log of each connection or transaction. UNIX servers often use a client-server mechanism known as *syslog*. When a running program needs to write a message to a log, it becomes a client of the *syslog* server, which can be located on another computer. The running program sends its message to the log server, and then continues execution. The log server handles the message by recording it (e.g., on disk).

As Figure 27.1 illustrates, the *syslog* system defines a set of facility types along with their meanings.

Facility Name	Subsystem that uses it
LOG_KERN	The operating system kernel
LOG_USER	Any application program
LOG_MAIL	The electronic mail system
LOG_DAEMON	System programs that operate in background
LOG_AUTH	The authorization and authentication system
LOG_LPR	The printer spooling system
LOG_RPC	The RPC and NFS subsystems
LOG_LOCAL0	Reserved for local use; names LOG_LOCAL1 through LOG_LOCAL7 are also reserved

Figure 27.1 The facility types defined by *syslog*. Each log message must originate from one of these facilities.

As the figure shows, *syslog* has a facility for each major subsystem. For example, programs associated with e-mail belong to the *LOG_MAIL* facility, while most servers that run in background belong to the *LOG_DAEMON* facility.

As Figure 27.2 shows, *Syslog* also defines eight priority levels that range from *LOG_EMERG*, which is intended for the most severe emergencies, to *LOG_DEBUG*, which programmers use to log debugging information.

Priority	Description
LOG_EMERG	An extreme emergency; the message should be broadcast to all users
LOG_ALERT	A condition that should be corrected immediately (e.g., a corrupted system database)
LOG_CRIT	A critical condition like a hardware error (e.g. disk failure)
LOG_ERR	An error that requires attention, but is not critical
LOG_WARNING	A warning that an error condition may exist
LOG_NOTICE	A condition that is not an error, but may need attention
LOG_INFO	An informational message (e.g., a message issued when a server starts execution)
LOG_DEBUG	A message used by a programmer for debugging

Figure 27.2 The eight priority levels defined by *syslog*. Each log message must have one of the priority levels specified.

Whenever a program uses *syslog* to handle a log message, the program must specify a facility and a priority level. To make *syslog* easier to use, the library routines permit a programmer to specify a facility when the program begins and to have *syslog* use the facility for successive messages. To specify an initial facility, a program calls procedure *openlog*. *Openlog* takes three arguments that specify an identification string, a set of handling options, and a facility specification. *Syslog* prepends the identification to all successive messages that the program writes to the log. Usually, a programmer chooses the name of the program as its identification string. *Openlog* initializes the facility, and stores the identification string and options for later use. For example, a programmer who is testing a private program can call:

```
openlog("myprog", LOG_PID, LOG_USER);
```

to specify identification string *myprog*, logging option *LOG_PID*, and facility *LOG_USER*. Option *LOG_PID* requests that *syslog* record the program's process ID with each log message.

When a program needs to send a log message, it calls procedure *syslog*, which sends the message to the server on the local machine. Procedure *syslog* takes a variable number of arguments. The first specifies a priority for the message, and the second specifies a *printf*-like format. As in *printf*, arguments following the format are variables to be printed according to the format. In the simplest case, a program calls *syslog* with a constant string as a format and no additional variables. For example, to record a debugging message on the system log, a program can call:

```
syslog(LOG_DEBUG, "server opened its input file");
```

Once a program finishes using *syslog*, it calls procedure *closelog* to close the log file (i.e., terminate contact with the server). *Closelog* terminates the connection, and releases the I/O descriptor allocated to it.

Although the *syslog* facility is not as widely used in Windows systems as in UNIX, versions of the client code are available. The local system administrator usually chooses a logging mechanism.

27.13 Miscellaneous Incompatibilities

Despite superficial similarities, substantial incompatibilities exist between UNIX and Windows. The differences make it difficult to port code because they often require changing the entire program structure. For example, although UNIX allows the I/O routines *read* and *write* to be used with sockets, Windows does not. Surprisingly, many programs call *read* and *write* indirectly – the programs contain calls to standard I/O functions which invoke *read* or *write* to transfer data. As a consequence, a program that uses any standard I/O function with a socket will not work under Windows.

Differences between the way UNIX and Windows handle descriptors also make porting difficult. In particular, UNIX programs can use functions like *select* with a set of descriptors that include both socket and file descriptors. For example, a UNIX version of the TELNET client described in Chapters 25 and 26 has a much different structure. Instead of a keyboard thread and a main thread, the UNIX version consists of a singly-threaded process. The process calls *select* to wait for input from the keyboard or the TCP socket connected to the server.

Another small incompatibility between UNIX and Windows arises from the way functions return error codes. Because UNIX socket functions return the value *-1* to indicate that an error occurred, most UNIX programs interpret a return value of less than zero as an error. In Windows, socket functions return an explicit value of *INVALID_SOCKET* or *SOCKET_ERROR* to indicate that an error occurred†. Thus, when porting a program, all error checking code must be changed.

A final difference between UNIX and Windows arises because UNIX systems restrict access to specific protocol ports. On a UNIX system, a server must have the highest privilege to use a TCP or UDP protocol port with a number less than *1024*. Client-server software that is created for a UNIX system often uses low port numbers as a form of security – each side knows that it must be communicating with a privileged program and not an average user. Under Windows, no such restrictions exist, so clients and servers cannot depend on low port numbers for security.

27.14 Summary

Windows programmers are often asked to port server code from the UNIX operating system or to design code that can be used on both Windows and UNIX. Because the facilities in UNIX differ from those in Windows, the code may differ significantly. This chapter discusses several techniques UNIX servers use, and shows examples of the code required for each. The particular techniques discussed include the following concepts:

- Operating in background
- Inheritance of descriptors
- Detaching the controlling terminal
- Changing directories
- File protection modes
- Process groups
- Standard I/O descriptors
- Mutual exclusion
- Recording process identifiers
- Child process termination signals
- Using *syslog* to record messages

FOR FURTHER STUDY

Beveridge and Weiner [1997] and Rector and Newcomer [1997] discuss programming under the Win32 interface, including multithreaded applications. Many of the rules UNIX programmers follow when implementing servers come from unwritten conventions and heuristics; often programmers learn techniques by reading existing pro-

---

†The value returned depends on the socket function and the error; consult Appendix *1* for examples.

grams. Stevens [1990] discusses how to write daemon programs and describes some of the techniques outlined in this chapter.

EXERCISES

27.1   Examine a UNIX server to see how many techniques from this chapter you can identify.

27.2   Consult the Windows literature and make a list of techniques described in this chapter for which analogous facilities exist in Windows.

27.3   What happens in Windows if a child thread closes all socket descriptors when it begins?

27.4   Can file creation be used to provide mutual exclusion in Windows? Explain.

27.5   Read about the functions available in Windows to open files. If your version allows *O_EXCL*, find out how it works. Can a server use it to provide mutual exclusion? Why or why not?

27.6   Examine the source code for a production server that runs under Windows. What techniques from this chapter does it use? What techniques does it use that are not covered in this chapter?

27.7   Read the vendor's literature for the *syslog* mechanism. How does a system administrator change the configuration after the server has begun? Suggest an alternative mechanism.

28

Deadlock And Starvation In Client-Server Systems

28.1 Introduction

Previous chapters focus on the design of client-server systems and the structure of individual client and server programs. They discuss ways that clients and servers support concurrent execution, consider tools like RPC that programmers use to construct client-server software, and show examples.

This chapter considers the dynamic behavior of distributed computation, focusing on some of the surprising ways that client-server systems can fail. It expands the discussions about potential problems found in previous chapters, and considers two conditions that can lead to delays or interruptions in service: deadlock and starvation. The conditions are especially important to programmers who work in a production environment, where disruptions in service cannot be tolerated.

In addition to examining how deadlock can result from ambiguous protocol specifications, the chapter discusses how programming errors and oversights can allow a misbehaving client to disrupt service for others. The chapter explains techniques that can be used to prevent deadlock in client-server systems, and explains consequences.

28.2 Definition Of Deadlock

In computer systems, the term *deadlock*† is used to characterize a situation in which computation cannot proceed because a set of two or more components in the system is blocked and each component is waiting on another component in the set. Typically, each component is a thread that is blocked waiting for a resource that is held by another thread in the set.

Deadlock is a permanent failure that should not be confused with temporary blocking. The test for whether a deadlock has occurred is simple: will an external input allow computation to proceed? For example, consider a set of three threads. Suppose two threads block while the third interacts with a user. Once the user responds, the third thread informs the other two, and processing continues. Although the three threads can remain blocked arbitrarily long while they wait for a user to respond, the set is not in a deadlock because input from the user will allow processing to continue.

In contrast, a set of threads is trapped in a deadlock when each thread in the set is waiting for input from another member of the set. Because each thread is blocked, no thread will ever emit output. Thus, none of the threads will ever receive input, and there is no way out of the deadlock. In terms of the test described above, the situation is a deadlock because none of the threads in the set is waiting for external input.

28.3 Difficulty Of Deadlock Detection

Detecting deadlock at run-time is difficult; doing so in a distributed system is usually impossible. There are two reasons. First, to distinguish deadlock from temporary blocking, a detection mechanism needs to know which resources each program holds and why the program is blocked. Obtaining such information in a client-server environment means consulting multiple operating systems, which may each use a unique set of operations. Second, because a programmer can invent abstract resources, it can be impossible for an operating system to determine which programs hold the resources – the state is known only to the programs that create and use the resources.

Surprisingly, even when source code is available for each component of a system, determining whether the system can deadlock is as difficult as proving a mathematical theorem. The potential for deadlock may not be apparent until the dynamic behavior of the system is considered. That is, deadlock can depend on the order of execution, and many different orders are possible when clients and servers operate on separate computers. More important, deadlocks can surface in a distributed system despite a reasonable design and implementation of each component. The consequence should be clear:

> *Because deadlock and starvation are extremely difficult or impossible to detect, the task of determining whether a set of clients and servers is trapped in a deadlock cannot be automated.*

---

†Synonyms for *deadlock* include *circular wait*, *deadly embrace*, and *synchronized lock*; this chapter makes no distinction among them.

28.4 Deadlock Avoidance

What can be done to guarantee that service will not be disrupted? In general, the answer lies in careful planning. Everyone who designs protocols, implements software, or installs and configures client-server systems must be aware of the potential for deadlock or starvation, and must take care to avoid creating a system that is susceptible.

To avoid deadlock and starvation, one must understand the ways they can occur. The next sections describe three ways the problems can appear in a client-server system: between a single client-server pair, among a set of clients and a server, and among a set of clients and servers.

28.5 Deadlock Between A Client And Server

The simplest form of client-server deadlock arises between a single client and a server. If the client blocks waiting for a message from the server, while the server blocks waiting for a message from the client, the pair will be trapped in a permanent deadlock.

To prevent such deadlocks, most application protocols are designed to use a *request-response* paradigm. That is, one side (usually the client) sends a request to which the other side responds. The protocol must specify which side creates requests and which side sends responses.

Deadlock errors can be introduced into a single client-server interaction in two ways. First, a protocol design that does not fully specify synchronization can lead to a client and server that fail to interoperate. Second, a protocol design that assumes reliable delivery can misbehave if used with an unreliable transport mechanism.

To understand how lack of a full synchronization specification can lead to problems, consider the following application protocol:

1. A client must first establish a connection to a server.
2. Immediately after the connection has been established, either the client or the server must send an initial message; the other end waits for the message and sends an initial message response.
3. After the initial message exchange, the client can send requests; the server sends a response to each request.
4. After receiving a response for its final request, the client closes the connection.

Such imprecise protocol specifications can arise when a designer attempts to give implementors freedom to choose details. In the example, the designer may have been unable to decide whether it would be best to have the client or the server send the first message. Thus, to permit maximum flexibility, the protocol has been worded to be purposefully ambiguous. Unfortunately, two implementations that each follow such a protocol can deadlock: a programmer who implements the client side might assume the initial message will come from the server, while the programmer who implements the server side might assume the initial message will come from the client. When the resulting client and server interact, they each block waiting for an initial message to arrive from the other.

To understand how unreliable transport introduces errors, consider a request-response protocol designed for a reliable transport (e.g., TCP). The protocol might specify that the client should send a request and then wait for a response. If such a protocol is used over an unreliable transport (e.g., UDP), a message can be lost. Unfortunately, a lost request or response produces a deadlock in which the client remains blocked waiting for a response, while the server remains blocked waiting for the next request.

28.6 Avoiding Deadlock In A Single Interaction

There are two ways to avoid deadlock between a single client and a server. First, the application protocol should be designed to specify synchronization. One side should be assigned responsibility for initiating the interaction (i.e., sending a request), and the order of interaction should be unambiguous. Second, the implementation must either use a reliable transport protocol or include a timer mechanism that places a maximum bound on the time that a sender will wait for a response before retransmitting a request.

Although deadlock among a client and a server is undesirable, the problem only affects the pair of programs involved. A shared server has an additional liability because any problem that causes the server to be unavailable prevents other clients from accessing the service. More important, a server that is susceptible to such problems is vulnerable to malicious clients that prevent service to others.

28.7 Starvation Among A Set Of Clients And A Server

The term *starvation* is used to describe a situation in which some clients cannot obtain access to a service, while other clients can. Starvation violates the principle of fairness, which states that a server must offer service to all clients equally.

An iterative server that permits arbitrarily long interaction is inherently unfair because it allows a single client to use the service while others are excluded. Thus, most interactive servers do not permit a single client to have exclusive, long-term use of the service. To guarantee fairness, an interactive server can limit the number of requests a given client is allowed to send. For example, an iterative, connection-oriented server might close the connection after handling a single client request. Alternatively, a server might close the connection after a fixed time elapses.

As an example of how a malicious client can prevent others from using a service, consider how a client can exploit an interactive, connection-oriented server. Suppose the protocol specifies that the client should send requests to which the server responds. To starve others, a malicious client can open a connection to the server, and then never send a request. The server will block waiting for a client request, which will never arrive. Meanwhile, no other client can use the server.

Of course, a server can prevent such problems by including a timer mechanism that automatically closes an idle connection after a fixed timeout. When a client first forms a connection, the server starts the timer at zero. When a request arrives, the server stops the timer, computes a response, and restarts the timer at zero. If the timer reaches value T, the server closes the connection.

28.8 Busy Connections And Starvation

Although the idle connection timer described in the previous section handles the case where a client does not send requests, starvation is still possible. To understand why, we need to observe two facts. First, the idle timer measures the time between the transmission of a response and the receipt of the next request. Second, a transport protocol uses buffers and implements flow control.

The details of buffering are important because a transport protocol places a buffer at each end of a connection. On the sending side, the sending application deposits outgoing data in the send buffer for TCP to transmit; on the receiving side, TCP deposits incoming data in the receive buffer, where the receiving application extracts it. As long as space remains in the receiver's buffer, TCP continues to transmit data from the buffer on the send side.

How can a client take an unfair portion of a server's time? The client can delay or prevent transmission. In particular, a client can:

- Specify a TCP receive buffer size that is small compared to the amount of data expected†.
- Send a request that requires the server to transmit data.
- Either allow the receive buffer to fill without reading the incoming data to prevent transmission or read incoming data slowly to delay transmission.

In such situations, the sending TCP will transmit data until the receiving TCP's buffer fills, at which time the receiver will advertise a zero window. The sender cannot transmit additional data until space becomes available in the receiver's buffer. Thus, transmission halts until the client reads data.

On the sending side, the server continues to write data into the outgoing buffer. Because transmission is delayed or stopped, the output buffer eventually fills. When the server attempts to write into a filled buffer, the server will be blocked. The situation is not solved by an idle connection timer because the server is not blocked waiting for a request. Instead, the server is blocked while sending a response.

---

†A socket option exists that allows an application to specify the size of the buffer TCP uses.

28.9 Avoiding Blocking Operations

How can a server avoid blocking during transmission? In general, there are two solutions: the server can be concurrent or the server can avoid making calls that block. In the former case, because a separate thread or process handles each client, a client that introduces delay will not affect other clients. In the latter case, a server can implement a timeout mechanism for a busy connection. Before each call to a blocking operation like *send*, the server must verify that the call will not block. If the system reports that a socket is not ready to accept data, the server sets a timer, and then tries again. If the socket does not become ready within the allotted timeout, the server can close the connection.

28.10 Threads, Connections, And Other Limits

Although concurrency helps solve many deadlock problems, concurrency has limits as well. Chapter 15 points out that concurrency must be managed because unbounded concurrency can cause problems. In particular, a server that creates a new thread for each client connection is vulnerable to clients that misbehave because operating systems do not permit arbitrary concurrency. Eventually, a concurrent server can exhaust system resources. For example, the operating system limits the number of threads, the number of active sockets, the total descriptors available, and the number of Transmission Control Blocks (TCBs) that TCP can allocate. In addition, each open TCP connection uses buffer space, so each additional connection requires memory.

To avoid making a server susceptible to problems of starvation, a programmer must plan all resource utilization, including memory utilization, open connections, and the degree of concurrency. Unfortunately, anticipating or controlling resource utilization can be difficult. Because a server is seldom built for a particular computer, the programmer usually does not know about system limits when writing code. Furthermore, servers often execute on sophisticated timesharing computer systems that share resources among all executing programs. Thus, the resources available to a server at any time depend on the resources currently being used by other applications.

In cases where concurrency and resource use cannot be anticipated or managed, programmers can at least arrange to have a server report problems. For example, a server can check the return value from each system call and use a log to report errors. A manager can examine the log periodically to determine whether the server has encountered difficulty. If errors occur, the manager can take further action to determine the cause. Although such reports do not prevent problems from occurring, they provide a mechanism that allows a manager to monitor server behavior.

28.11 Cycles Of Clients And Servers

Perhaps the most pernicious form of deadlock and starvation arises from inter-dependencies among multiple services. To understand the problem, recall that a server for one service can become the client of another. For example, imagine that a programmer is building a file server. If the file system records the time when a file is last changed, the server may need to obtain the time of day whenever it handles a *write* request.

In most operating systems, an application program calls a system function to obtain the current time. The system function extracts the current time from a hardware clock, and then returns the value to the application. In a client-server environment, however, the time can be obtained from a remote machine. In essence, the function that obtains the current time contains client code. The application that calls the function becomes a client of a time server. The client sends a request, waits for a response that contains the time, and then returns the value to the calling application.

In such environments, a deadlock can occur when clients and servers inadvertently form a cycle. In the above example, suppose a programmer is assigned to modify the time server. To help debug changes, the programmer might decide to emit a log of all calls to the time server. Unfortunately, if the log is written to a file, a circular dependency results: the file server calls the time server, which calls the file server to write a log message. If any of the servers is not concurrent, an immediate deadlock will result. If both servers are concurrent, the file server will again call the time server, which will call the file server, and the cycle will continue until resources are exhausted.

The above example illustrates a problem known as *livelock*. Like deadlock, a livelock results from circular dependencies. Unlike deadlock, however, participants in a livelock are busy using the CPU and sending messages. In the example, livelock occurs if the clients and servers are using a connectionless protocol to communicate. The file server sends a message to a time server, and waits for a reply. As the time server handles the message, it sends a request to the file server. When the request arrives, the file server generates a second message for the time server, causing the time server to generate a third request, and so on. Although both servers are busy sending and receiving messages, the cycle will never be broken. If either server is slow, its queue of incoming messages will become full, causing one or more messages to be lost. However, as soon as a server reads one message from the queue, another will arrive to take its place. The servers cannot perform useful work because they are locked in an endless cycle of messages.

28.12 Documenting Dependencies

To prevent cycles that lead to deadlock or livelock, programmers and managers must avoid introducing cyclic dependencies among servers. As computer systems move toward a client-server environment, understanding such dependencies becomes more difficult. For example, although a Windows system can be configured to use NFS to access remote files, file names do not inform users or programmers that a file is remote. Similarly, client software that is embedded in system commands (e.g., to retrieve the current time of day), may not be apparent.

To help avoid inadvertent dependencies, programmers who work with client-server software need to understand whether each library routine or operating system function accesses a remote server. To provide the necessary information, an organization should keep a detailed record of each server and the servers upon which it depends. Anyone who creates or installs software should update the list of dependencies.

There are two approaches to keeping dependency information: coarse-grained and fine-grained. Coarse-grained dependency avoidance treats each service as a separate entity, and ensures that no cycles exist among services. For example, if a remote file service depends on the time-of-day service, the time-of-day service cannot be programmed to use the remote file service. Fine-grained dependency avoidance treats each server as a separate entity, and ensures that no cycles exist among servers. For example, file server X can call time server Y, and time server Y can call file server Z (but not file server X).

The chief advantage of a coarse-grained approach is that it is easy to document – a typical environment contains only a dozen services, and there are few dependencies among them. The chief disadvantage of the coarse-grained approach is unnecessary constraint on interaction. In contrast, a fine-grained approach allows maximal dependencies – a cycle can exist among services as long as no cycle exists among individual servers. The chief disadvantage of the fine-grained approach arises from the additional level of detail that must be kept. The record of dependencies must be updated whenever a server is added to the set, or whenever a server configuration is changed.

28.13 Summary

Deadlock and starvation are fundamental problems in a client-server environment. Deadlock refers to a condition in which a set of two or more system components are blocked waiting for each other. Starvation is a more general concept that refers to any situation in which access to service is unfair: one group of clients obtains better access than another.

Deadlock can occur between a single client and a server. Such deadlocks usually result from an ambiguous protocol specification or from using an unreliable transport with a protocol that is designed for reliable transport.

When multiple clients access a single server, deadlock or livelock between one client and the server can cause starvation, meaning that other clients are prevented from accessing the service. Starvation can be caused by a client that opens a connection to an interactive server, but does not send requests, or by a client that generates requests, but does not consume responses. Idle connection timeout can prevent the former case, but not the latter.

Because a server can temporarily become a client, a set of two or more servers can deadlock if each server in the set attempts to become a client of another server in the set. To prevent such deadlocks, cyclic dependencies among servers must be prohibited.

FOR FURTHER STUDY

Most operating system texts, including Peterson and Silberschatz [1985], discuss the problems of deadlock and livelock among programs running on a single computer.

EXERCISES

28.1 Make a chart of dependencies among services at your organization.

28.2 Make a chart of dependencies among individual servers at your organization.

28.3 Can a file system on computer *A* use NFS to access files on computer *B* while the file system on computer *B* uses NFS to access files on computer *A*? Explain.

28.4 Can a deadlock occur among three servers on a single computer? Explain.

28.5 Experiment with servers at your organization to see how many simultaneous connections they permit.

28.6 Examine the configuration of your local operating system. Will the system run out of TCBs, buffers, or sockets first?

28.7 If you had a choice of debugging a deadlock problem or a livelock problem, which would you choose? Why? How would you proceed?

28.8 Can a client that uses TCP distinguish between a failure that occurs because the connection request queue for a server is full and a failure that occurs because the network is down?

28.9 In one implementation of NFS, the software that performed remote file system mounts was blocking – the NFS client software would block until the remote system responded. To avoid deadlock, a programmer used *ping* (ICMP echo) to determine whether another machine was available before attempting to mount its file system. Under what circumstances can a deadlock still occur?

28.10 Students in a networking course built network monitor devices that analyzed traffic on the network. Two of the students decided to use the X Window System to display their results on a color screen. Either group could run their project separately, but as soon as both started, the network became saturated. Explain.

Appendix 1

Functions And Library Routines Used With Sockets

Introduction

In the Windows Sockets API, network communication centers around the socket abstraction. Applications use a set of socket calls to communicate with TCP/IP software in the operating system. A client application creates a socket, connects it to a server on a remote machine, and uses it to transfer data and to receive data from the remote machine. Finally, when the client application finishes using the socket, it closes it. A server creates a socket, binds it to a well-known protocol port on the local machine, and waits for clients to contact it.

Each page of this appendix describes one of the system calls or library functions that programmers use when writing client or server applications. The functions are arranged in alphabetic order, with one page devoted to a given function. The functions listed include: *accept, bind, closesocket, connect, gethostbyaddr, gethostbyname, gethostname, getpeername, getprotobyname, getprotobynumber, getservbyname, getservbyport, getsockname, getsockopt, htonl, htons, inet_addr, inet_ntoa, ioctlsocket, listen, ntohl, ntohs, recv, recvfrom, select, send, sendto, setsockopt, shutdown, socket, WSACleanup, WSAGetLastError,* and *WSAStartup*

The Accept Function

Include File

#include <winsock.h>

Use

retvalue = accept (socket, addr, addrlen);

Description

Servers use the *accept* function to accept the next incoming connection on a passive socket after they have called *socket* to create a socket, *bind* to specify a local IP address and protocol port number, and *listen* to make the socket passive and to set the length of the connection request queue. *Accept* removes the next connection request from the queue (or waits until a connection request arrives), creates a new socket for the request, and returns the descriptor for the new socket. *Accept* only applies to stream sockets (e.g., those used with TCP).

Arguments

Arg	Type	Meaning
socket	SOCKET	A socket descriptor created by the *socket* function.
addr	struct sockaddr FAR*	A pointer to an address structure. *Accept* fills in the structure with the IP address and protocol port number of the remote machine.
addrlen	int FAR*	A pointer to an integer that initially specifies the size of the *sockaddr* argument and, when the call returns, specifies the number of bytes stored in argument *addr*.

Return value

If successful, *accept* returns a socket descriptor of type:

SOCKET

and the value *INVALID_SOCKET* to indicate that an error has occurred. When an error does occur, *WSAGetLastError()* can be called to retrieve a code that gives the specific cause of the error.

The Bind Function

Include File

```
#include <winsock.h>
```

Use

```
retvalue = bind ( socket, localaddr, addrlen );
```

Description

Bind specifies a local IP address and protocol port number for a socket. *Bind* is primarily used by servers, which need to specify a well-known protocol port.

Arguments

Arg	Type	Meaning
socket	SOCKET	A socket descriptor created by the *socket* function.
localaddr	const struct sockaddr FAR*	The address of a structure that specifies an IP address and protocol port number.
addrlen	int	The size of the address structure in the second argument in bytes.

Chapter 5 contains a description of the *sockaddr* structure.

Return value

Bind returns 0 if successful and *SOCKET_ERROR* to indicate that an error has occurred. When an error does occur, *WSAGetLastError()* can be called to retrieve a code that gives the specific cause of the error.

The Closesocket Function

Include File

#include <winsock.h>

Use

retvalue = closesocket (socket);

Description

An application calls *closesocket* after it finishes using a socket. *Closesocket* terminates communication gracefully and removes the socket. Any unread data waiting at the socket will be discarded.

In practice, Windows systems implement a reference count mechanism to allow multiple applications to share a socket. If *n* programs share a socket, the reference count will be *n*. *Closesocket* decrements the reference count on each call. Once the reference count reaches zero (i.e. all applications that were using the socket have called *closesocket*), the socket will be deallocated.

Arguments

Arg	Type	Meaning
socket	SOCKET	The descriptor of the socket to be closed.

Return value

Closesocket returns 0 if successful and *SOCKET_ERROR* to indicate that an error has occurred. When an error does occur, *WSAGetLastError()* can be called to retrieve a code that gives the specific cause of the error.

The Connect Function

Include File

```
#include <winsock.h>
```

Use

retvalue = connect (socket, addr, addrlen);

Description

Connect allows the caller to specify the remote endpoint address for a previously created socket. If the socket uses TCP, *connect* uses the 3-way handshake to establish a connection; if the socket uses UDP, *connect* specifies the remote endpoint but does not transfer any datagrams to it.

Arguments

Arg	Type	Meaning
socket	SOCKET	A socket descriptor created by the *socket* function.
addr	const struct sockaddr FAR*	The remote machine endpoint.
addrlen	int	The length of the second argument.

Chapter *5* contains a description of the *sockaddr* structure.

Return value

Connect returns *0* if successful and *SOCKET_ERROR* to indicate that an error has occurred. When an error does occur, *WSAGetLastError()* can be called to retrieve a code that gives the specific cause of the error.

The Gethostbyaddr Library Call

Include File

#include <winsock.h>

Use

retvalue = gethostbyaddr (addr, alen, atype);

Description

Gethostbyaddr searches for information about a host given its IP address.

Arguments

Arg	Type	Meaning
addr	const char FAR*	A pointer to an array that contains the address of a host (e.g., an IP address).
alen	int	An integer that gives the address length (*4* for IP).
atype	int	An integer that gives the address type (*PF_INET* for an IP address).

Return value

Gethostbyaddr returns a pointer to a *hostent* structure if successful and a *NULL* pointer to indicate that an error has occurred. When an error does occur, *WSAGet-LastError()* can be called to retrieve a code that gives the specific cause of the error. The *hostent* structure is declared to be:

```
struct hostent {                       /* entry for a host         */
     char FAR* h_name;                 /* official host name       */
     char FAR*  FAR* h_aliases[];/* list of other aliases         */
     short h_addrtype;                 /* host address type        */
     short h_length;                   /* length of host address   */
     char FAR* FAR* h_addr_list; /* list of addresses for host */
};
```

The Gethostbyname Library Call

Include File

```
#include <winsock.h>
```

Use

```
retvalue = gethostbyname ( name );
```

Description

Gethostbyname maps a host name to an IP address. On most systems, *gethostbyname* consults the Internet's Domain Name System (DNS) to perform the mapping.

Arguments

Arg	Type	Meaning
name	const char FAR*	The address of a character string that contains a host name. The name is null-terminated.

Return value

Gethostbyname returns a pointer to a *hostent* structure if successful and a *NULL* pointer to indicate that an error has occurred. When an error does occur, *WSAGetLastError()* can be called to retrieve a code that gives the specific cause of the error. The *hostent* structure is declared to be:

```
struct hostent {                      /* entry for a host          */
    char FAR* h_name;                 /* official host name        */
    char FAR*  FAR* h_aliases[];/* list of other aliases      */
    short h_addrtype;                 /* host address type         */
    short h_length;                   /* length of host address    */
    char FAR* FAR* h_addr_list; /* list of addresses for host */
};
```

The Gethostname Library Call

Include File

```
#include <winsock.h>
```

Use

retvalue = gethostname (name, namelen);

Description

    Gethostname returns the primary name of the computer on which it is invoked in the form of a text string.

Arguments

Arg	Type	Meaning
name	char FAR*	The address of the character array into which the name should be placed.
namelen	int	The length of the *name* array (it should be at least *65*).

Return value

    Gethostname places a null-terminated string in the array given by the first argument and returns *0* if successful. Otherwise, the call returns *SOCKET_ERROR*. When an error does occur, *WSAGetLastError()* can be called to retrieve a code that gives the specific cause of the error.

The Getpeername Function

Include File

```
#include <winsock.h>
```

Use

```
retvalue = getpeername ( socket, remaddr, addrlen );
```

Description

An application uses *getpeername* to obtain the address of the remote computer to which a socket is connected. Usually, a client knows the remote endpoint address because it calls *connect* to set it. However, a server that uses *accept* to obtain a connection may need to interrogate the socket to find out the remote address.

Note that although *getpeername* can be used on either a datagram or stream socket, the socket must be connected.

Arguments

Arg	Type	Meaning
socket	SOCKET	A socket descriptor created by the *socket* function.
remaddr	struct sockaddr FAR*	A pointer to a *sockaddr* structure that will contain the address of the remote endpoint to which the socket is connected.
addrlen	int FAR*	A pointer to an integer that contains the length of the second argument initially, and the actual length of the endpoint address upon return.

Chapter *5* contains a description of the *sockaddr* structure.

Return value

Getpeername returns 0 if successful and *SOCKET_ERROR* to indicate that an error has occurred. When an error does occur, *WSAGetLastError()* can be called to retrieve a code that gives the specific cause of the error.

The Getprotobyname Library Call

Include File

```
#include <winsock.h>
```

Use

```
retvalue = getprotobyname ( name );
```

Description

Applications call *getprotobyname* to obtain information about a protocol from its name. The information returned includes the official integer value.

Arguments

Arg	Type	Meaning
name	const char FAR*	The address of a string that contains the protocol name.

Return value

Getprotobyname returns a pointer to a structure of type *protoent* if successful and a *NULL* pointer to indicate that an error has occurred. When an error does occur, *WSAGetLastError()* can be called to retrieve a code that gives the specific cause of the error. Structure *protoent* is declared to be:

```
struct protoent {                  /* entry that describes a protocol  */
    char FAR* p_name;              /* official name of protocol        */
    char FAR* FAR* p_aliases;      /* list of aliases for the protocol */
    short p_proto;                 /* official protocol number         */
};
```

The Getprotobynumber Library Call

Include File

```
#include <winsock.h>
```

Use

```
retvalue = getprotobynumber ( number );
```

Description

Applications call *getprotobynumber* to obtain information about a protocol from its number. The information returned includes the official name.

Arguments

Arg	Type	Meaning
number	int	The number of a protocol (in the native byte order of the local host)

Return value

Getprotobynumber returns a pointer to a structure of type *protoent* if successful and a *NULL* pointer to indicate that an error has occurred. When an error does occur, *WSAGetLastError()* can be called to retrieve a code that gives the specific cause of the error. Structure *protoent* is declared to be:

```
struct protoent {               /* entry that describes a protocol  */
    char FAR* p_name;           /* official name of protocol        */
    char FAR* FAR* p_aliases;   /* list of aliases for the protocol */
    short p_proto;              /* official protocol number         */
};
```

The Getservbyname Library Call

Include File

```
#include <winsock.h>
```

Use

```
retvalue = getservbyname ( name, proto );
```

Description

Getservbyname obtains an entry from the network services database given a service name. Clients and servers both call *getservbyname* to map a service name to a protocol port number.

If the second argument is non-null, *getservbyname* matches both the service name and protocol. If the second argument is null, *getservbyname* ignores the argument and matches only the name.

Arguments

Arg	Type	Meaning
name	const char FAR*	A pointer to a string of characters that contains a service name.
proto	const char FAR*	A pointer to a string of characters that contains the name of the protocol to be used (e.g., *"tcp"*) or the value *NULL*.

Return value

Getservbyname returns a pointer to a *servent* structure if successful and a *NULL* pointer to indicate that an error has occurred. The *servent* structure is declared to be:

```
struct servent {              /* one service entry          */
    char FAR* s_name ;        /* official service name      */
    char FAR* FAR* s_aliases; /* list of other aliases      */
    short    s_port;          /* port used for this service */
    char FAR* s_proto;        /* protocol used for service  */
};
```

The Getservbyport Library Call

Include File

```
#include <winsock.h>
```

Use

```
retvalue = getservbyport ( port, proto );
```

Description

Getservbyport obtains an entry from the network services database given a port number. Although used infrequently, *getservbyport* can map a protocol port number to a service name.

If the second argument is non-null, *getservbyport* matches both the protocol port number and the protocol. If the second argument is null, *getservbyport* ignores the argument and matches only the port.

Arguments

Arg	Type	Meaning
port	int	A protocol port number in network byte order.
proto	const char FAR*	A pointer to a string of characters that contains the name of the protocol to be used (e.g., *tcp*) or the value *NULL*.

Return value

Getservbyport returns a pointer to a *servent* structure if successful and a *NULL* pointer to indicate that an error has occurred. The *servent* structure is declared to be:

```
struct servent {              /* one service entry          */
    char FAR* s_name ;        /* official service name      */
    char FAR* FAR* s_aliases; /* list of other aliases      */
    short     s_port;         /* port used for this service */
    char FAR* s_proto;        /* protocol used for service  */
};
```

The Getsockname Function

Include File

```
#include <winsock.h>
```

Use

retvalue = getsockname (socket, name, namelen);

Description

Getsockname obtains the local address and protocol port number of the specified socket.

Arguments

Arg	Type	Meaning
socket	SOCKET	A socket descriptor created by the *socket* function.
name	struct sockaddr FAR*	The address of a structure that will contain the IP address and protocol port number of the socket.
namelen	int FAR*	Initially, the number of positions in the *name* structure. On return, it contains the size of the structure in bytes.

Chapter *5* contains a description of the *sockaddr* structure.

Return value

Getsockname returns *0* if successful and *SOCKET_ERROR* to indicate that an error has occurred. When an error does occur, *WSAGetLastError()* can be called to retrieve a code that gives the specific cause of the error.

The Getsockopt Function

Include File

#include <winsock.h>

Use

retvalue = getsockopt (socket, level, opt, optval, optlen);

Description

Getsockopt permits an application to obtain the value of a parameter (option) for a socket or a protocol the socket uses.

Arguments

Arg	Type	Meaning
socket	SOCKET	A socket descriptor created by the *socket* function.
level	int	An integer that identifies a protocol level.
opt	int	An integer that identifies an option.
optval	char FAR*	The address of a buffer for the value returned.
optlen	int FAR*	Initially, the size of buffer *optval*; on return, it contains the length of the value found.

Examples of socket options include:

SO_BROADCAST	Permission to transmit broadcast messages?
SO_DONTROUTE	Bypass routing for outgoing messages?
SO_ERROR	Get and clear the last error for the socket
SO_LINGER	Linger on close if data present?
SO_OOBINLINE	Receive out-of-band data in band?
SO_RCVBUF	Buffer size for input?
SO_SNDBUF	Buffer size for output?

Return value

Getsockopt returns *0* if successful and *SOCKET_ERROR* to indicate that an error has occurred. When an error does occur, *WSAGetLastError()* can be called to retrieve a code that gives the specific cause of the error.

The Htonl Function

Include File

```
#include <winsock.h>
```

Use

```
retvalue = htonl ( hostlong );
```

Description

Htonl converts an unsigned long integer from the local host's native byte order to the network byte order.

Argument

Arg	Type	Meaning
hostlong	u_long	The 32-bit integer to convert.

Return value

Htonl returns the value in network byte order.

The Htons Function

Include File

```
#include <winsock.h>
```

Use

```
retvalue = htons ( hostshort );
```

Description

Htons converts an unsigned short integer from the local host's native byte order to the network byte order.

Argument

Arg	Type	Meaning
hostshort	u_short	The 16-bit integer to convert.

Return value

Htons returns the value in network byte order.

The Inet_addr Function

Include File

#include <winsock.h>

Use

retvalue = inet_addr (dotted);

Description

Both clients and servers use the *inet_addr* function to convert an IP address in dotted decimal form to the internal binary form that socket functions expect.

Argument

Arg	Type	Meaning
dotted	const char FAR*	A string that contains an IP address in dotted decimal notation.

Return value

If successful, *inet_addr* returns an unsigned long that contains the IP address in binary form. Otherwise, *inet_addr* returns *INADDR_NONE* to indicate that the argument does not contain a valid dotted decimal address (e.g., one of the values is larger than *255* or there are more than four numbers separated by dots).

The Inet_ntoa Function

Include File

#include <winsock.h>

Use

retvalue = inet_ntoa (ipaddr);

Description

Application software that must display IP addresses for humans calls *inet_ntoa* to convert an address from the internal binary form to a text string that contains the address in dotted decimal form.

Argument

Arg	Type	Meaning
ipaddr	struct in_addr	The IP address to be converted.

Return value

If successful, *inet_ntoa* returns a value of type

char FAR* PASCAL FAR

that is a pointer to a buffer containing a null-terminated string that gives the address in dotted decimal form. When an error occurs, *inet_ntoa* returns *NULL*.

The Ioctlsocket Function

Include File

```
#include <winsock.h>
```

Use

```
retvalue = ioctlsocket ( socket, cmd, argp );
```

Description

Ioctlsocket is used to retrieve or set information about a socket. For example, *ioctlsocket* can be used to determine whether the socket is blocking or whether all out-of-band data has been read.

The name of this function is derived from the Berkeley UNIX *ioctl* command, which can be used to control any I/O device. *Ioctlsocket* provides a subset of the *ioctl* functionality for sockets only.

Arguments

Arg	Type	Meaning
socket	SOCKET	A socket descriptor created by the *socket* function.
cmd	long	The specific command to perform on the socket.
argp	u_long FAR*	The address of parameters for *cmd*.

Return value

Ioctlsocket returns *0* if successful, and the value *SOCKET_ERROR* to indicate that an error has occurred. When an error does occur, *WSAGetLastError()* can be called to retrieve a code that gives the specific cause of the error.

The Listen Function

Include File

```
#include <winsock.h>
```

Use

retvalue = listen (socket, queuelen);

Description

Servers use *listen* to make a socket passive (i.e., ready to accept an incoming request). *Listen* also sets the number of incoming connection requests that the protocol software should enqueue for a given socket while the server handles another request. *Listen* only applies to sockets used with TCP.

Arguments

Arg	Type	Meaning
socket	SOCKET	A socket descriptor created by the *socket* function.
queuelen	int	The size of the incoming connection request queue (up to a maximum of *5*).

Return value

Listen returns 0 if successful and *SOCKET_ERROR* to indicate that an error has occurred. When an error does occur, *WSAGetLastError()* can be called to retrieve a code that gives the specific cause of the error.

The Ntohl Function

Include File

#include <winsock.h>

Use

retvalue = ntohl (netlong);

Description

Ntohl converts an unsigned long integer from the network byte order to the local host's native byte order.

Argument

Arg	Type	Meaning
netlong	u_long	The 32-bit integer to convert.

Return value

Ntohl returns the value in host byte order.

The Ntohs Function

Include File

#include <winsock.h>

Use

retvalue = ntohs (netshort);

Description

Ntohs converts an unsigned short integer from network byte order to the local host's native byte order.

Argument

Arg	Type	Meaning
netshort	u_short	The 16-bit integer to convert.

Return value

Ntohs returns the value in host byte order.

The Recv Function

Include File

```
#include <winsock.h>
```

Use

retvalue = recv (socket, buffer, length, flags);

Description

Recv obtains the next incoming message from a socket. For stream sockets, *recv* retrieves data up to the size of the buffer. For datagram sockets, *recv* obtains data up to the size of the buffer from one datagram (if the buffer is smaller than the datagram, the remaining data from that datagram is lost).

Arguments

Arg	Type	Meaning
socket	SOCKET	A socket descriptor created by the *socket* function.
buffer	char FAR*	The address of a buffer to hold the message.
length	int	The length of the buffer.
flags	int	Control bits that specify whether to receive out-of-band data and whether to look ahead for messages.

Return value

Recv returns the number of bytes in the message received if successful, *0* if the connection has been closed, and *SOCKET_ERROR* to indicate that an error has occurred. When an error does occur, *WSAGetLastError()* can be called to retrieve a code that gives the specific cause of the error.

The Recvfrom Function

Include File

#include <winsock.h>

Use

retvalue = recvfrom (socket, buffer, buflen, flags, from, fromlen);

Description

Recvfrom extracts the next message that arrives at a socket and records the sender's address (enabling the caller to send a reply). *Recvfrom* is especially useful for unconnected datagram sockets.

Arguments

Arg	Type	Meaning
socket	SOCKET	A socket descriptor created by the *socket* function.
buffer	char FAR*	The address of a buffer to hold the message.
buflen	int	The length of the buffer.
flags	int	Control bits that specify out-of-band data or message look-ahead.
from	struct sockaddr FAR*	The address of a structure to hold the sender's address.
fromlen	int FAR*	Initially, the size of the *from* buffer; returned as the size of the address in *from*.

Chapter 5 contains a description of the *sockaddr* structure.

Return value

Recvfrom returns the number of bytes in the message if successful, *0* if the connection has been closed, and *SOCKET_ERROR* to indicate that an error has occurred. When an error does occur, *WSAGetLastError()* can be called to retrieve a code that gives the specific cause of the error.

The Select Function

Include File

```
#include <winsock.h>
```

Use

retvalue = select (ignore, refds, wrfds, exfds, time);

Description

Select provides asynchronous I/O by permitting a single process to wait for the first of any socket descriptors in a specified set to become ready. The caller can also specify a maximum timeout for the wait.

Arguments

Arg	Type	Meaning
ignore	int	Not used (included to make *select* under Windows compatible with the UNIX version).
refds	fd_set FAR*	Address of file descriptors for input.
wrfds	fd_set FAR*	Address of file descriptors for output.
exfds	fd_set FAR*	Address of file descriptors for exceptions.
time	const struct timeval FAR*	Maximum time to wait or *NULL* to wait forever.

Arguments that refer to sets of descriptors can be manipulated with macros. Macros *FD_CLR* or *FD_SET* clear or set individual descriptors. Macro *FD_ISSET* tests whether a descriptor is set, and macro *FD_ZERO* initializes an entire set to empty. All macros use variable *FD_SETSIZE* to determine the maximum number of descriptors per set.

Return value

Select returns the number of ready file descriptors if successful, *0* if the time limit was reached, and *SOCKET_ERROR* to indicate that an error has occurred. When an error does occur, *WSAGetLastError()* can be called to retrieve a code that gives the specific cause of the error.

The Send Function

Include File

#include <winsock.h>

Use

retvalue = send (socket, msg, msglen, flags);

Description

Applications call *send* to transfer a message to another machine using a previously created socket.

Arguments

Arg	Type	Meaning
socket	SOCKET	Socket descriptor created by the *socket* function.
msg	const char FAR*	A pointer to the message.
msglen	int	The length of the message in bytes.
flags	int	Control bits that specify out-of-band data or message look-ahead.

Return value

Send returns the number of characters sent if successful and *SOCKET_ERROR* to indicate that an error has occurred. When an error does occur, *WSAGetLastError()* can be called to retrieve a code that gives the specific cause of the error.

The Sendto Function

Include File

#include <winsock.h>

Use

retvalue = sendto (socket, msg, msglen, flags, to, tolen);

Description

Sendto sends a message by taking the destination address from a structure. Servers using datagram sockets use *sendto* to return a message to a client.

Arguments

Arg	Type	Meaning
socket	SOCKET	Socket descriptor created by the *socket* function.
msg	const char FAR*	A pointer to the message.
msglen	int	The length of the message in bytes.
flags	int	Control bits that specify out-of-band data or message look-ahead.
to	const struct sockaddr FAR*	A pointer to the address structure.
tolen	int	The length of the address in bytes.

Chapter 5 contains a description of the *sockaddr* structure.

Return value

Sendto returns the number of bytes sent if successful and *SOCKET_ERROR* to indicate that an error has occurred. When an error does occur, *WSAGetLastError()* can be called to retrieve a code that gives the specific cause of the error.

The Setsockopt Function

Include File

```
#include <winsock.h>
```

Use

```
retvalue = setsockopt ( socket, level, opt, optval, optlen );
```

Description

Setsockopt permits an application to change an option associated with a socket or the protocols it uses.

Arguments

Arg	Type	Meaning
socket	SOCKET	A socket descriptor created by the *socket* function.
level	int	An integer that identifies a protocol (e.g., TCP).
opt	int	An integer that identifies an option.
optval	const char FAR*	The address of a buffer that contains a value (nonzero to enable an option or zero to disable it).
optlen	int	The length of *optval*.

The options supported by *setsockopt* include:

SO_BROADCAST	Permission to transmit broadcast messages
SO_DONTROUTE	Bypass routing for outgoing messages
SO_LINGER	Linger on close if data present
SO_OOBINLINE	Receive out-of-band data in band
SO_RCVBUF	Set buffer size for input
SO_SNDBUF	Set buffer size for output

Return value

Setsockopt returns *0* if successful and *SOCKET_ERROR* to indicate that an error has occurred. When an error does occur, *WSAGetLastError()* can be called to retrieve a code that gives the specific cause of the error.

The Shutdown Function

Include File

```
#include <winsock.h>
```

Use

retvalue = shutdown (socket, how);

Description

The *shutdown* function is used to terminate transmission, reception, or both. The function is often used with a connected TCP socket to close the connection in one direction (e.g., to close a data connection from a client to a server, but allow the server to send to the client).

Arguments

Arg	Type	Meaning
socket	SOCKET	A socket descriptor created by the *socket* function.
how	int	The direction in which shutdown is desired: *0* means to terminate further reception, *1* means to terminate further transmission, and *2* means to terminate both.

Return value

The *shutdown* call returns *0* if the operation succeeds or *SOCKET_ERROR* to indicate that an error has occurred. When an error does occur, *WSAGetLastError()* can be called to retrieve a code that gives the specific cause of the error.

The Socket Function

Include File

```
#include <winsock.h>
```

Use

retvalue = socket (afam, type, protocol);

Description

The *socket* function creates a socket used for network communication, and returns an integer descriptor for that socket.

Arguments

Arg	Type	Meaning
afam	int	Protocol or address family (*PF_INET* for TCP/IP).
type	int	Type of service (*SOCK_STREAM* for TCP or *SOCK_DGRAM* for UDP).
protocol	int	Protocol number to use with the socket or *0* to use the standard protocol that matches the specified *afam* and *type* values.

Return value

The *socket* call returns a descriptor for the newly created socket if successful, or *INVALID_SOCKET* to indicate that an error has occurred. When an error does occur, *WSAGetLastError()* can be called to retrieve a code that gives the specific cause of the error.

The WSACleanup Function

Include File

#include <winsock.h>

Use

retvalue = WSACleanup (void);

Description

An application uses the *WSACleanup* function to terminate all further use of sockets when it finishes executing. Open sockets should be closed with *Closesocket* before an application invokes *WSACleanup*. In normal operation, clients terminate but servers run forever.

Arguments

WSACleanup does not take any arguments.

Return value

WSACleanup returns *0* if successful, and the value *SOCKET_ERROR* to indicate that an error has occurred. When an error does occur, *WSAGetLastError()* can be called to retrieve a code that gives the specific cause of the error.

The WSAGetLastError Function

Include File

```
#include <winsock.h>
```

Use

retvalue = WSAGetLastError (void);

Description

An application calls the *WSAGetLastError* function to retrieve the specific error code following an unsuccessful socket function call. *WSAGetLastError* is the Windows Sockets replacement for the global variable *errno* that is used in earlier sockets implementations, but which cannot be used in a multithreaded environment.

Note: an application should call *WSAGetLastError* immediately after a socket function returns an error indication.

Arguments

WSAGetLastError does not take any arguments.

Return value

WSAGetLastError calls the underlying function *GetLastError*, which is used to retrieve error status for all Win32 API functions.

The WSAStartup Function

Include File

#include <winsock.h>

Use

retvalue = WSAStartup (rvers, wsimpl);

Description

An application Must call the *WSAStartup* function to initialize the socket software before using any of the socket functions. Both clients and servers use *WSAStartup*.

Arguments

Arg	Type	Meaning
rvers	WORD	A two-byte request for a version of the Windows Sockets API. The high-order byte specifies a minor version and the low-order byte specifies a major version.
wsimpl	WSADATA	A pointer to a structure into which the function will store information about the implementation of Windows Sockets being used.

Return value

WSAStartup returns *0* if successful. Otherwise, it returns one of the following error codes:

Value	Cause of the Error
WSASYSNOTREADY	The network subsystem is not ready for network communication.
WSAVERNOTSUPPORTED	The local Windows Sockets implementation does not support the version requested.
WSAEINVAL	The DLL being used does not support the version requested.

Appendix 2

Manipulation Of Windows Socket Descriptors

Introduction

In Windows, all network input and output operations use an abstraction known as the *socket descriptor*. A program calls the *socket* function to obtain a descriptor used for network communication. Chapters 4 and 5 describe the socket interface. Chapter 23 describes Windows descriptors and I/O in more detail; it points out that a newly created thread inherits access to all socket descriptors that the parent has open at the time of creation.

This appendix describes how programs can use I/O descriptors as arguments, and illustrates how a parent can inform a child which descriptor or descriptors the child must use. The technique is primarily used in concurrent servers that invoke a separate thread to handle each client.

Descriptors As Arguments

When the Windows *_beginthread* function creates a new thread, the newly created child inherits access to all the socket descriptors that the parent has open. Furthermore, the child shares the socket descriptor table, meaning that the descriptor for a given socket is exactly the same for both parent and child. Thus, if descriptor 5 in the parent corresponds to a TCP socket, the newly created child can also use 5 to access the same socket.

Conceptually, socket descriptors can form implicit or explicit arguments to newly created threads. In the explicit case, a parent passes an argument to the child for each descriptor that the child must use. For example, suppose a parent opens a TCP connection for the child to use. Further suppose that Windows Sockets allocates descriptor *4* to the connection. To inform the child about the connection, the parent passes the integer *4* as an argument when creating the child. When it begins execution, the child uses the argument to access the TCP connection.

Because Windows allows threads to share memory, concurrent programs can make descriptors implicit arguments. To pass an implicit argument, the parent places the value in shared memory. For example, a parent can open a socket, and then place the resulting descriptor in a shared variable. When the child begins execution, it extracts the value from the shared memory.

To summarize:

> *Network communication uses sockets, each of which is assigned an integer descriptor. A parent can use implicit or explicit arguments to pass descriptors to a newly created child thread.*

Implicit Arguments And Concurrency

Implicit arguments have several disadvantages. Most important, they make programs more difficult to understand and modify. Unlike explicit arguments, which specify the values being passed from parent to child, implicit arguments are hidden. In fact, the parent can assign a value to a shared memory variable at any time – the code that makes the assignment may not be located near the code that creates a thread that will use the variable. Thus, a programmer must read and understand the code thoroughly.

Programmers who are not accustomed to concurrent programming can make mistakes with implicit arguments. The resulting errors can be difficult to find and debug because they depend on the order in which the operating system chooses to run threads. To see how such errors occur, consider a concurrent program that uses the algorithm shown in Figure A2.1.

A program that follows the algorithm in the figure uses shared variable x to hold an implicit argument. The parent stores a value in x before creating a child, and the child extracts the value from x when it begins execution. The code for both the parent and child threads has been programmed to use variable x as an implicit argument; x does not appear in the call to *_beginthread*.

Parent:
do forever {
accept next TCP connection from client;
place descriptor for connection in shared variable *x*;
create child thread to handle connection;
}

Child:

extract descriptor for the client TCP connection from shared
variable *x* and place in local variable *d*;
handle connection using descriptor *d*;
close descriptor *d*;
exit;

Figure A2.1 An example of an algorithm using implicit arguments that contains a flaw. The program may work correctly or incorrectly, depending on how the operating system schedules threads.

Unfortunately, such a program is incorrect. To understand why, remember that an operating system does not guarantee the order of execution among threads. Consider what happens if the operating system chooses to run the parent for a long time before running a child. The parent might run long enough to accept two connections and create two children. However, the program only uses a single, shared variable for implicit arguments. Suppose the first client connection arrives on descriptor *5*. The parent will place *5* in variable *x* and create a thread. Because the parent continues to run, it accepts the second client connection. If the second connection arrives on descriptor *6*, the parent will overwrite *x* with the value *6* and create a second thread. When the operating system finally runs one of the two new threads, the thread will find the value *6* in *x*. When the operating system runs the other new thread, that thread will also find the value *6* in *x*. Thus, both children will attempt to communicate with the same client. The point is:

Implicit argument passing requires coordination; a parent cannot use the same shared variable to pass implicit arguments to multiple children.

How can one avoid the problem illustrated above? The program must be written to avoid any possible reuse of a shared variable before the first use is complete. There are three possible approaches. The simplest and usually the most efficient way to avoid reuse is to eliminate sharing (i.e., use only explicit arguments). Another approach allocates a separate area in shared memory for the implicit arguments that are passed to a given thread. The parent passes an explicit argument to the child that contains the location in shared memory of the child's implicit arguments. Of course, if the only implicit argument consists of an integer, passing the value of the argument to the child is as easy as placing the value in shared memory and passing the location. Thus, the second approach is used only when a parent is passing many implicit arguments. The third approach uses coordination primitives supplied by the operating system to allow the parent and child to coordinate use of shared memory. After a parent creates a child, the parent waits for the child to read implicit arguments. Once it finishes extracting values, the child informs the operating system that the parent can continue execution. Such coordination is seldom used for implicit arguments because it is difficult to program and introduces run-time overhead.

Summary

Concurrent programs that communicate over networks often pass socket descriptors as arguments when creating a new thread. The arguments to a child thread can be explicit or implicit. Explicit arguments are included in the call to *_beginthread*; implicit arguments are placed in shared memory.

When using implicit arguments, threads must coordinate to ensure that only one child thread uses a given shared variable at a time. Absence of coordination can result in a program that fails under some circumstances. Coordination errors are especially hard to debug because they depend on the operating system and the timing of network connections, making them difficult to reproduce.

Bibliography

ABRAMSON, N. and F. KUO (EDS.) [1973], *Computer Communication Networks,* Prentice Hall, Upper Saddle River, New Jersey.

ADLER, R., [April 1995], Distributed Coordination Models for Client/Server Computing, *IEEE Computer,* 14-22.

ANDREWS, G. [March 1991], Paradigms for Interprocess Interactions in Distributed Programs, *ACM Computing Surveys,* 49-90.

AT&T [1989], *UNIX System V Release 3.2 – Programmer's Reference Manual,* Prentice Hall, Upper Saddle River, New Jersey.

ATM FORUM [1993], *ATM User-Network Interface Specification Version 3.0* Prentice Hall, Upper Saddle River, New Jersey.

BACH, M. [1986], *The Design Of The UNIX Operating System,* Prentice Hall, Upper Saddle River, New Jersey.

BALL, J. E., E. J. BURKE, I. GERTNER, K. A. LANTZ, and R. F. RASHID [1979], Perspectives on Message-Based Distributed Computing, *IEEE Computing Networking Symposium,* 46-51.

BARRET, J. and E. WUNDERLICH [September 1991], LAN interconnection Using X.25 Network Services, *IEEE Network,* 12-17.

BBN [1981], A History of the ARPANET: The First Decade, *Technical Report,* Bolt, Beranek, and Newman, Inc.

BBN [December 1981], Specification for the Interconnection of a Host and an IMP (revised), *Technical Report 1822,* Bolt, Beranek, and Newman, Inc.

BERSON, A. [1993], *Client/Server Architectures,* McGraw-Hill, New York, New York.

BERNSTEIN, P. [February 1996], Middleware: A Model for Distributed Systems Services, *ACM,* 86-98.

BERTSEKAS D. and R. GALLAGER [1987], *Data Networks,* Prentice Hall, Upper Saddle River, New Jersey.

BEVERIDGE, J. and R. WIENER [1997], *Multithreading Applications In Win32: The Complete Guide To Threads,* Addison Wesley, Reading, Massachusetts.

BIRRELL, A. and B. NELSON [February 1984], Implementing Remote Procedure Calls, *ACM Transactions on Computer Systems*, 2(1), 39-59.

BJORN, M. [1995], *A WWW Gateway for Interactive Relational Database Management*, Doctoral Program of Socio-Economic Planning, 1-1-1 Tennodai, Tsukuba, Ibaraki, 305, Japan.

BLACK, U. [1994], *Emerging Communication Technologies*, Prentice Hall, Upper Saddle River, New Jersey.

BOGGS, D., J. SHOCH, E. TAFT, and R. METCALFE [April 1980], Pup: An Internetwork Architecture, *IEEE Transactions on Communications*.

BOLSKY, M. I. and D. G. KORN [1989], *The Kornshell Command And Programming Language*, Prentice Hall, Upper Saddle River, New Jersey.

BONNER, P. [1996], *Network Programming with Windows Sockets*, Prentice Hall, Upper Saddle River, New Jersey.

BORMAN, D. [April 1989], Implementing TCP/IP on a Cray Computer, *Computer Communication Review*, 19(2), 11-15.

BRADNER, S. and A. MANKIN [1996], *IPng, Internet Protocol Next Generation*, Addison-Wesley, Reading, Massachusetts.

BROWN, M., K. KOLLING, and E. TAFT [November 1985], The Alpine File System, *Transactions on Computer Systems*, 3(4), 261-293.

BROWNBRIDGE, D., L. MARSHALL, and B. RANDELL [December 1982], The Newcastle Connections or UNIXes of the World Unite!, *Software – Practice and Experience*, 12(12), 1147-1162.

CERF, V. and E. CAIN [October 1983], The DOD Internet Architecture Model, *Computer Networks*.

CERF, V. and R. KAHN [May 1974], A Protocol for Packet Network Interconnection, *IEEE Transactions of Communications*, Com-22(5).

CERF, V. [October 1989], A History of the ARPANET, *ConneXions, The Interoperability Report*, Foster City, California.

CHERITON, D. R. [1983], Local Networking and Internetworking in the V-System, *Proceedings of the Eighth Data Communications Symposium*.

CHERITON, D. R. [April 1984], The V Kernel: A Software Base for Distributed Systems, *IEEE Software*, 1(2), 19-42.

CHERITON, D. [August 1986], VMTP: A Transport Protocol for the Next Generation of Communication Systems, *Proceedings of ACM SIGCOMM '86*, 406-415.

CHERITON, D. and T. MANN [May 1984], Uniform Access to Distributed Name Interpretation in the V-System, *Proceedings IEEE Fourth International Conference on Distributed Computing Systems*, 290-297.

CHESSON, G. [June 1987], Protocol Engine Design, *Proceedings of the 1987 Summer USENIX Conference*, Phoenix, Arizona.

CHESWICK, W. and S. BELLOVIN [1996], *Firewalls and Internet Security*, Addison Wesley Longman, Reading, Massachusetts.

CLARK, D. [December 1985], The Structure of Systems Using Upcalls, *Proceedings of the Tenth ACM Symposium on Operating Systems Principles,* 171-180.

CLARK, D., M. LAMBERT, and L. ZHANG [August 1987], NETBLT: A High Throughput Transport Protocol, *Proceedings of ACM SIGCOMM '87.*

COHEN, D. [1981], On Holy Wars and a Plea for Peace, *IEEE Computer,* 48-54.

COMER, D. E. and J. T. KORB [1983], CSNET Protocol Software: The IP-to-X25 Interface, *Computer Communications Review,* 13(2).

COMER, D. E. [1984], *Operating System Design – The XINU Approach,* Prentice Hall, Upper Saddle River, New Jersey.

COMER, D. E. [1987], *Operating System Design Vol II. – Internetworking With XINU,* Prentice Hall, Upper Saddle River, New Jersey.

COMER, D. E. [1995], *Internetworking With TCP/IP Vol 1: Principles, Protocols, and Architecture,* 3rd edition, Prentice Hall, Upper Saddle River, New Jersey.

COMER, D. E. and D. L. STEVENS [1994], *Internetworking With TCP/IP Vol 2: Design, Implementation, and Internals,* 2nd edition, Prentice Hall, Upper Saddle River, New Jersey.

COMER, D. E. and D. L. STEVENS [1996], *Internetworking With TCP/IP Vol 3: Client Server Programming and Applications (BSD socket version),* 2nd edition, Prentice Hall, Upper Saddle River, New Jersey.

COMER, D. E. and D. L. STEVENS [1994], *Internetworking With TCP/IP Vol 3: Client Server Programming and Applications (AT&T TLI version),* Prentice Hall, Upper Saddle River, New Jersey.

COTTON, I. [1979], Technologies for Local Area Computer Networks, *Proceedings of the Local Area Communications Network Symposium.*

CROWLEY, T., H. FORSDICK, M. LANDAU, and V. TRAVERS [June 1987], The Diamond Multimedia Editor, *Proceedings of the 1987 Summer USENIX Conference,* Phoenix, Arizona.

DALAL, Y. K. and R. S. PRINTIS [1981], 48-Bit Absolute Internet and Ethernet Host Numbers, *Proceedings of the Seventh Data Communications Symposium.*

DAVIS, R. [1994], *Windows NT Network Programming,* Addison-Wesley, Reading, Massachusetts.

DEERING, S. E. and D. R. CHERITON [May 1990], Multicast Routing in Datagram Internetworks and Extended LANs, *ACM Transactions on Computer Systems,* 8(2), 85-110.

DENNING, P. J. [September-October 1989], The Science of Computing: Worldnet, *American Scientist,* 432-434.

DENNING, P. J. [November-December 1989], The Science of Computing: The ARPANET After Twenty Years, *American Scientist,* 530-534.

DIGITAL EQUIPMENT CORPORATION., INTEL CORPORATION, and XEROX CORPORATION [September 1980], *The Ethernet: A Local Area Network Data Link Layer and Physical Layer Specification.*

DION, J. [Oct. 1980], The Cambridge File Server, *Operating Systems Review,* 14(4), 26-35.

DRIVER, H., H. HOPEWELL, and J. IAQUINTO [September 1979], How the Gateway Regulates Information Control, *Data Communications.*

DUTTON, H. and P. LENHARD [1995], *High-Speed Networking Technology: An Introductory Survey*, 3rd edition, Prentice Hall, Upper Saddle River, New Jersey.

EDGE, S. W. [1979], Comparison of the Hop-by-Hop and Endpoint Approaches to Network Interconnection, in *Flow Control in Computer Networks*, J. L. GRANGE and M. GIEN (EDS.), North-Holland, Amsterdam, 359-373.

EDGE, S. [1983], An Adaptive Timeout Algorithm for Retransmission Across a Packet Switching Network, *Proceedings of ACM SIGCOMM '83*.

ENSLOW, P. [January 1978], What is a 'Distributed' Data Processing System? *Computer,* 13-21.

FALK, G. [1983], The Structure and Function of Network Protocols, in *Computer Communications, Volume I: Principles,* W. CHOU (ED.), Prentice Hall, Upper Saddle River, New Jersey.

FARMER, W. D. and E. E. NEWHALL [1969], An Experimental Distributed Switching System to Handle Bursty Computer Traffic, *Proceedings of the ACM Symposium on Probabilistic Optimization of Data Communication Systems,* 1-33.

FCCSET [November 1987], A Research and Development Strategy for High Performance Computing, *Report from the Executive Office of the President and Office of Science and Technology Policy.*

FEDOR, M. [June 1988], GATED: A Multi-Routing Protocol Daemon for UNIX, *Proceedings of the 1988 Summer USENIX Conference*, San Francisco, California.

FEINLER, J., O. J. JACOBSEN, and M. STAHL [December 1985], *DDN Protocol Handbook Volume Two, DARPA Internet Protocols,* DDN Network Information Center, SRI International, Menlo Park, California.

FRANK, H. and W. CHOU [1971], Routing in Computer Networks, *Networks,* 1(1), 99-112.

FRANK, H. and J. FRISCH [1971], *Communication, Transmission, and Transportation Networks,* Addison-Wesley, Reading, Massachusetts.

FRANTA, W. R. and I. CHLAMTAC [1981], *Local Networks,* Lexington Books, Lexington, Massachusetts.

FRICC [May 1989], *Program Plan for the National Research and Education Network*, Federal Research Internet Coordinating Committee, US Department of Energy, Office of Scientific Computing Report ER-7.

FRIDRICH, M. and W. OLDER [December 1981], The Felix File Server, *Proceedings of the Eighth Symposium on Operating Systems Principles,* 37-46.

FULTZ, G. L. and L. KLEINROCK, [June 14-16, 1971], Adaptive Routing Techniques for Store-and-Forward Computer Communication Networks, presented at *IEEE International Conference on Communications,* Montreal, Canada.

GERLA, M. and L. KLEINROCK [April 1980], Flow Control: A Comparative Survey, *IEEE Transactions on Communications.*

GOSIP [April 1989], *U.S. Government Open Systems Interconnection Profile (GOSIP) Version 2.0,* GOSIP Advanced Requirements Group, National Institute of Standards and Technology (NIST).

GRANGE, J. L. and M. GIEN (EDS.) [1979], *Flow Control in Computer Networks,* North-Holland, Amsterdam.

GREEN, P. E. (ED.) [1982], *Computer Network Architectures and Protocols,* Plenum Press, New York, New York.

HALL, M., M. TOWFIG, G. ARNOLD, D. TREADWELL, and H. SANDERS [1993], *Windows Sockets: An Open Interface For Programming Under Microsoft Windows,* Microdyne Corporation (reachable via e-mail winsock@microdyne.com).

HALL, M., M. TOWFIG, and D. TREADWELL (MODERATORS) [1996], *Windows Sockets 2: A Service Provider Interface,* Microdyne Corporation.

HINDEN, R., J. HAVERTY, and A. SHELTZER [September 1983], The DARPA Internet: Interconnecting Heterogeneous Computer Networks with Gateways, *Computer.*

INTERNATIONAL ORGANIZATION FOR STANDARDIZATION [June 1986a], Information processing systems — Open Systems Interconnection — *Transport Service Definition,* International Standard 8072, ISO, Switzerland.

INTERNATIONAL ORGANIZATION FOR STANDARDIZATION [July 1986b], Information processing systems — Open Systems Interconnection — *Connection Oriented Transport Protocol Specification,* International Standard 8073, ISO, Switzerland.

INTERNATIONAL ORGANIZATION FOR STANDARDIZATION [May 1987a], Information processing systems — Open Systems Interconnection — *Specification of Basic Specification of Abstract Syntax Notation One (ASN.1),* International Standard 8824, ISO, Switzerland.

INTERNATIONAL ORGANIZATION FOR STANDARDIZATION [May 1987b], Information processing systems — Open Systems Interconnection — *Specification of Basic Encoding Rules for Abstract Syntax Notation One (ASN.1),* International Standard 8825, ISO, Switzerland.

INTERNATIONAL ORGANIZATION FOR STANDARDIZATION [May 1988a], Information processing systems — Open Systems Interconnection — *Management Information Service Definition, Part 2: Common Management Information Service,* Draft International Standard 9595-2, ISO, Switzerland.

INTERNATIONAL ORGANIZATION FOR STANDARDIZATION [May 1988a], Information processing systems — Open Systems Interconnection — *Management Information Protocol Definition, Part 2: Common Management Information Protocol,* Draft International Standard 9596-2, ISO, Switzerland.

JAIN, R. [January 1985], On Caching Out-of-Order Packets in Window Flow Controlled Networks, *Technical Report,* DEC-TR-342, Digital Equipment Corporation.

JAIN, R. [March 1986], Divergence of Timeout Algorithms for Packet Retransmissions, *Proceedings Fifth Annual International Phoenix Conference on Computers and Communications,* Scottsdale, Arizona.

JAIN, R. [October 1986], A Timeout-Based Congestion Control Scheme for Window Flow-Controlled Networks, *IEEE Journal on Selected Areas in Communications,* Vol. SAC-4, no. 7.

JAIN, R., K. RAMAKRISHNAN, and D. M. CHIU [August 1987], Congestion Avoidance in Computer Networks With a Connectionless Network Layer. *Technical Report,* DEC-TR-506, Digital Equipment Corporation.

JENNINGS, D. M., L. H. LANDWEBER, and I. H. FUCHS [February 28, 1986], Computer Networking for Scientists and Engineers, *Science* vol 231, 941-950.

JOHNSON and REICHARD [1990], *Advanced XWindow Applications Programming*, MIT Press, Cambridge, Massachusetts.

JUBIN, J. and J. TORNOW [January 1987], The DARPA Packet Radio Network Protocols, *IEEE Proceedings*.

KAHN, R. [November 1972], Resource-Sharing Computer Communications Networks, *Proceedings of the IEEE*, 60(11), 1397-1407.

KARN, P., H. PRICE, and R. DIERSING [May 1985], Packet Radio in the Amateur Service, *IEEE Journal on Selected Areas in Communications*,

KARN, P. and C. PARTRIDGE [August 1987], Improving Round-Trip Time Estimates in Reliable Transport Protocols, *Proceedings of ACM SIGCOMM '87*.

KAUFMAN, C., R. PERLMAN, and M. SPECINER [1995], *Network Security, Private Communication in a Public World*, Prentice Hall, Upper Saddle River, New Jersey.

KENT, C. and J. MOGUL [August 1987], Fragmentation Considered Harmful, *Proceedings of ACM SIGCOMM '87*.

KERNIGHAN, B. and D. RITCHIE [1988], *The C Programming Language*, 2nd edition, Prentice Hall, Upper Saddle River, New Jersey.

KLINE, C. [August 1987], Supercomputers on the Internet: A Case Study, *Proceedings of ACM SIGCOMM '87*.

KOCHAN, S. G. and P. H. WOODS [1989], *UNIX Networking*, Hayden Books, Indianapolis, Indiana.

LAMPSON, B. W., M. PAUL, and H. J. SIEGERT (EDS.) [1981], *Distributed Systems - Architecture and Implementation (An Advanced Course)*, Springer-Verlag, Berlin.

LANZILLO, A. L. and C. PARTRIDGE [January 1989], Implementation of Dial-up IP for UNIX Systems, *Proceedings 1989 Winter USENIX Technical Conference*, San Diego, California.

LAQUEY, T. L. [July 1989], *User's Directory of Computer Networks*, Digital Press, Bedford, Massachusetts.

LAZAR, A. [November 1983], Optimal Flow Control of a Class of Queuing Networks in Equilibrium, *IEEE Transactions on Automatic Control*, Vol. AC-28:11.

LEFFLER, S., M. MCKUSICK, M. KARELS, and J. QUARTERMAN [1989], *The Design and Implementation of the 4.3BSD UNIX Operating System*, Addison-Wesley, Reading, Massachusetts.

LEWIS, T. [April 1995], Where is Client/Server Software Headed?, *IEEE Computer*, 49-55.

LYNCH, D. C. (CHAIRMAN AND FOUNDER) [1987-1995], *The NETWORLD+INTEROP Conference*, Softbank Forums, Foster City, California.

MARTIN, J. and J. LEBEN [1995], *Client/Server Databases*, Prentice Hall, Upper Saddle River, New Jersey.

MARZULLO, K. and S. OWICKI [July 1985], Maintaining The Time In A Distributed System, *Operating Systems Review*, 19(3), 44-54.

MCKUSICK, M., W. JOY, S. LEFFLER, and R. FABRY [August 1984], A Fast File System For UNIX, *ACM Transactions On Computer Systems*, 2, 181-197.

MCNAMARA, J. [1982], *Technical Aspects of Data Communications,* Digital Press, Digital Equipment Corporation, Bedford, Massachusetts.

MCQUILLAN, J. M., I. RICHER, and E. ROSEN [May 1980], The New Routing Algorithm for the ARPANET, *IEEE Transactions on Communications,* (COM-28), 711-719.

MERIT [November 1987], *Management and Operation of the NSFNET Backbone Network: A Proposal Funded by the National Science Foundation and the State of Michigan,* MERIT Incorporated, Ann Arbor, Michigan.

METCALFE, R. M. and D. R. BOGGS [July 1976], Ethernet: Distributed Packet Switching for Local Computer Networks, *Communications of the ACM,* 19(7), 395-404.

MICROSOFT [1996], *Windows NT Resource Kit,* Microsoft Press, Redmond, Washington.

MILLER, C. K. and D. M. THOMPSON [March 1982], Making a Case for Token Passing in Local Networks, *Data Communications.*

MILLS, D. [September 1991], On the Chronometry and Metrology of Computer Network Timescales and Their Application to the Network Time Protocol, *Proceedings of ACM SIGCOMM '91,* 8-17.

MILLS, D. and H. W. BRAUN [August 1987], The NSFNET Backbone Network, *Proceedings of ACM SIGCOMM '87.*

MITCHELL, J. and J. DION [April 1982], A Comparison of Two Network-Based File Servers, *Communications of the ACM,* 25(4), 233-245.

MORRIS, R. [1979], Fixing Timeout Intervals for Lost Packet Detection in Computer Communication Networks, *Proceedings AFIPS National Computer Conference*, AFIPS Press, Montvale, New Jersey.

NAGLE, J. [April 1987], On Packet Switches With Infinite Storage, *IEEE Transactions on Communications*, (COM-35:4).

NARTEN, T. [Sept. 1989], Internet Routing, *Proceedings ACM SIGCOMM '89.*

NEEDHAM, R. M. [1979], System Aspects of the Cambridge Ring, *Proceedings of the ACM Seventh Symposium on Operating System Principles,* 82-85.

NEHMER, J. and F. MATTERN [May 1992], Framework for the Organization of Cooperative Services in Distributed Client/Server Systems, *Computer Communications,* 15(4), 261-269.

NELSON, J. [September 1983], 802: A Progress Report, *Datamation.*

NESSET, D. and G. LEE [1990], Terminal Services in Heterogeneous Distributed Systems, *Journal of Computer Networks and ISDN Systems,* 19, 105-128.

NEUMAN, B. and T. TS'O [1994], Kerberos: An Authentication Service for Computer Networks, *IEEE Communications,* 33-37.

NUTT, G. [1992], *Centralized and Distributed Operating Systems*, Prentice Hall, New York. Upper Saddle River, New Jersey.

ONEY, W. [1996], *Systems Programming for Windows 95,* Microsoft Press, Redmond, Washington.

OPPEN, D. and Y. DALAL [October 1981], The Clearinghouse: A Decentralized Agent for Locating Named Objects, Office Products Division, XEROX Corporation.

ORFALI, R., D. HARKEY, and J. EDWARDS [1994], *Client/Server Survival Guide*, Van Nostrand Reinholt, New York, New York.

OTTE, R., P. PATRICK and M. ROY [1996], *Understanding CORBA*, Prentice Hall, Upper Saddle River, New Jersey.

PADLIPSKY, M. [1983], A Perspective On The ARPANET Reference Model, *Proceedings of the IEEE INFOCOM Conference*, San Diego, California.

PARTRIDGE, C. [June 1986], Mail Routing Using Domain Names: An Informal Tour, *Proceedings of the 1986 Summer USENIX Conference*, Atlanta, Georgia.

PARTRIDGE, C. [June 1987], Implementing the Reliable Data Protocol (RDP), *Proceedings of the 1987 Summer USENIX Conference*, Phoenix, Arizona.

PARTRIDGE, C. [1994], *Gigabit Networking*, Addison-Wesley, Reading, Massachusetts.

PARTRIDGE, C. and M. ROSE [June 1989], A Comparison of External Data Formats, in *Message Handling Systems and Distributed Applications*, E. STEFFERUD and O. JACOBSEN (EDS.) Elsevier-North Holland.

PERLMAN, R. [1992], *Interconnections*, Addison-Wesley, Reading, Massachusetts.

PETERSON, J. and A. SILBERSCHATZ [1985], *Operating System Concepts*, 2nd edition, Addison-Wesley, Reading, Massachusetts.

PETERSON, L. [1985], *Defining and Naming the Fundamental Objects in a Distributed Message System*, Ph.D. Dissertation, Purdue University, West Lafayette, Indiana.

PETERSON, L. and B. DAVIE [1996], *Computer Networks: A Systems Approach*, Morgan Kaufmann.

PETERSON, M. [1995], *DCE: A Guide to Developing Portable Applications*, McGraw-Hill, New York, New York.

PETZOLD, C. [1996], *Programming Windows 95*, Microsoft Press, Redmond, Washington.

PIERCE, J. R. [1972], Networks for Block Switching of Data, *Bell System Technical Journal,* 51.

PLATT, D. [1996], *Windows 95 and NT: Win32 API from Scratch: A Programmer's Workbook*, Prentice Hall, Upper Saddle River, New Jersey.

POSTEL, J. B. [April 1980], Internetwork Protocol Approaches, *IEEE Transactions on Communications,* (COM-28), 604-611.

POSTEL, J. B., C. A. SUNSHINE, and D. CHEN [1981], The ARPA Internet Protocol, *Computer Networks.*

PRESOTTO, D. L. and D. M. RITCHIE [June 1990], Interprocess Communication in the Ninth Edition Unix System, *Software – Practice And Experience*, 20(S1), S1/3-S1/17.

QUARTERMAN, J. S. [1990], *The Matrix: Computer Networks and Conferencing Systems Worldwide*, Digital Press, Digital Equipment Corporation, Maynard, Massachusetts.

QUARTERMAN, J. S. and J. C. HOSKINS [October 1986], Notable Computer Networks, *Communications of the ACM*, 29(10).

QUIN, B. and D. SHUTE [1996], *Windows Sockets Network Programming*, Addison Wesley Longman, Reading, Massachusetts.

RECTOR, B.E. and J.M. NEWCOMER [1997], *Win32 Programming*, Addison-Wesley Developers Press, Reading, Massachusetts.

REYNOLDS, J., J. POSTEL, A. R. KATZ, G. G. FINN, and A. L. DESCHON [October 1985], The DARPA Experimental Multimedia Mail System, *IEEE Computer*.

RITCHIE, D. M. and K. THOMPSON [July 1974], The UNIX Time-Sharing System, *Communications of the ACM*, 17(7), 365-375; revised and reprinted in *Bell System Technical Journal*, 57(6), [July-August 1978], 1905-1929.

ROSENBERRY, W., D. KENNEY, and G. FISHER [1993], *Understanding DCE*, O'Reilly and Associates, Sebastopol, California.

ROSENTHAL, R. (ED.) [November 1982], *The Selection of Local Area Computer Networks*, National Bureau of Standards Special Publication 500-96.

RYAN. T. [1996], *Distributed Object Technology*, Prentice Hall, Upper Saddle River, New Jersey.

SALTZER, J. [1978], Naming and Binding of Objects, *Operating Systems, An Advanced Course*, Springer-Verlag, 99-208.

SALTZER, J. [April 1982], Naming and Binding of Network Destinations, *International Symposium on Local Computer Networks*, IFIP/T.C.6, 311-317.

SALTZER, J., D. REED, and D. CLARK [November 1984], End-to-End Arguments in System Design, *ACM Transactions on Computer Systems*, 2(4), 277-288.

SCHILLER, J. [November 1994], *Secure Distributed Computing*, Scientific American, 72-76.

SCHEIFE, R. [1990], *Protocol Reference Manual*, O'Reilly and Associates, Sebastopol, California.

SCHWARTZ, M. and T. STERN [April 1980], *IEEE Transactions on Communications*, COM-28(4), 539-552.

SHOCH, J. F. [1978], Internetwork Naming, Addressing, and Routing, *Proceedings of COMPCON*.

SHOCH, J. F., Y. DALAL, and D. REDELL [August 1982], Evolution of the Ethernet Local Computer Network, *Computer*.

SINHA, A. [July 1992], Client/Server Computing: Current Technology Review, *Communications of ACM*, 7, 77-96.

SINHA, A. [1996], *Network Programming in Windows NT*, Addison Wesley Longman, Reading, Massachusetts.

SNA [1975], *IBM System Network Architecture – General Information*, IBM System Development Division, Publications Center, Department E01, Research Triangle Park, North Carolina.

SOLOMON, M., L. LANDWEBER, and D. NEUHEGEN [1982], The CSNET Name Server, *Computer Networks* (6), 161-172.

STALLINGS, W. [1984], *Local Networks: An Introduction*, Macmillan Publishing Company, New York.

STALLINGS, W. [1985], *Data and Computer Communications*, Macmillan Publishing Company, New York.

STEVENS, W. R. [1990], *UNIX Network Programming,* Prentice Hall, Upper Saddle River, New Jersey.

STEVENS, W. R. [1994], *TCP/IP Illustrated, Volume 1: The Protocols,* Addison-Wesley, Reading, Massachusetts.

STEVENS, W. R. and G. R. WRIGHT [1994], *TCP/IP Illustrated, Volume 2,* Addison-Wesley, Reading, Massachusetts.

SWINEHART, D., G. MCDANIEL, and D. R. BOGGS [December 1979], WFS: A Simple Shared File System for a Distributed Environment, *Proceedings of the Seventh Symposium on Operating System Principles,* 9-17.

TANENBAUM, A. [1981], *Computer Networks: Toward Distributed Processing Systems,* Prentice Hall, Upper Saddle River, New Jersey.

TICHY, W. and Z. RUAN [June 1984], Towards a Distributed File System, *Proceedings of Summer 84 USENIX Conference,* Salt Lake City, Utah, 87-97.

TOMLINSON. R. S. [1975], Selecting Sequence Numbers, *Proceedings ACM SIGOPS/SIGCOMM Interprocess Communication Workshop,* 11-23.

UMAR, A. [1997a], *Application Engineering/Reengineering Building Web-based Object-Oriented Applications and Dealing with Legacies,* Prentice Hall, Upper Saddle River, New Jersey.

UMAR, A. [1993], *Distributed Computing and Client/Server Systems,* Prentice Hall, Upper Saddle River, New Jersey.

UMAR, A. [1997b], *Object-Oriented Client/Server Internet Environments,* Prentice Hall, Upper Saddle River, New Jersey.

WARD, A. A. [1980], TRIX: A Network-Oriented Operating System, *Proceedings of COMPCON,* 344-349.

WATSON, R. [1981], Timer-Based Mechanisms in Reliable Transport Protocol Connection Management, *Computer Networks,* North-Holland Publishing Company.

WEINBERGER, P. J. [1985], The UNIX Eighth Edition Network File System, *Proceedings 1985 ACM Computer Science Conference,* 299-301.

WELCH, B. and J. OSTERHAUT [May 1986], Prefix Tables: A Simple Mechanism for Locating Files in a Distributed System, *Proceedings IEEE Sixth International Conference on Distributed Computing Systems,* 184-189.

WILKES, M. V. and D. J. WHEELER [May 1979], The Cambridge Digital Communication Ring, *Proceedings Local Area Computer Network Symposium.*

WOOD, A. [April 1995], Predicting Client/Server Availability, *IEEE Computer,* 41-48.

XEROX [1981], Internet Transport Protocols, *Report XSIS 028112,* Xerox Corporation, Office Products Division, Palo Alto, California.

ZHANG, L. [August 1986], Why TCP Timers Don't Work Well, *Proceedings of ACM SIGCOMM '86.*

Index

Index